GoodFood

500 triple-tested recipes
from Britain's bestselling cookery magazine

GoodFood

500 triple-tested recipes

from Britain's bestselling cookery magazine

Compiled by Helena Caldon

Contents

Introduction

At *Good Food* magazine we love food, and we like making it simple, healthy, special and delicious!

In this new bumper collection we've compiled over 500 of our favourite recipes from seven of our bestselling 101 titles. Whether you're looking for a recipe for tonight's supper, a family get-together or afternoon tea, there's something here for you.

Packed with tempting full-colour photographs and simple step-by-step instructions, you can cook with confidence, knowing that each recipe is triple-tested by the *Good Food* cookery team, so that it works first time for you.

On a budget or short of time? You'll find plenty of thrifty, easy-to-make recipes using seasonal or storecupboard ingredients. Mouthwatering meals don't have to be expensive or time-consuming to prepare, and this collection is packed with budget dishes, simple suppers and easy one-pots.

Want to keep things simple? Nothing beats pasta and noodles for versatility – they are the ultimate convenience food – and we've come up with plenty of new ideas to ring the changes.

If you're health conscious when it comes to food, you'll be pleased to see that every recipe includes a full nutritional breakdown, focusing on the fat, salt, sugar, protein, fibre,

carbohydrate and calorie content of the dish. With many low–fat dishes in here, you'll see how easy it is to enjoy good-for-you food that tastes great, too. Simply changing your cooking methods to include grilling, griddling and steaming means you can get maximum flavour from your ingredients, but with minimum calories. And if you're feeling deprived of the sweet stuff, our low-fat treats will hit the spot every time.

Anxious about entertaining? With a little *Good Food* know-how you'll be able to prepare a delicious meal ahead of time, leaving it to cook while you get ready for your guests. Whatever the occasion, there are loads of easy one-pots and smart suppers to pick from.

While we encourage sensible eating and a good, balanced diet, every now and again we're all entitled to a treat. So when you think you deserve something a bit wicked, choose from our indulgent desserts, simple puds, cakes and bakes. Whether they're teatime favourites, after-school snacks or dinner-party desserts you don't need to be an expert baker to achieve great results with these recipes.

Whether simple or showstopping, you'll find the perfect dish in this book, whatever the occasion. So relax, get into your kitchen and start cooking, knowing that the team at *Good Food* has made it oh–so-simple.

Conversion tables

Notes on the recipes
- Eggs are large in the UK and Australia unless stated otherwise.
- Wash all fresh produce before preparation.
- Recipes contain nutritional analyses for 'sugar', which means the total sugar content including all natural sugars in the ingredients unless otherwise stated.

Oven temperatures

Gas	C	Fan C	F	Oven temp.
¼	110	90	225	Very cool
½	120	100	250	Very cool
1	140	120	275	Cool or slow
2	150	130	300	Cool or slow
3	160	140	325	Warm
4	180	160	350	Moderate
5	190	170	375	Moderately hot
6	200	180	400	Fairly hot
7	220	200	425	Hot
8	230	210	450	Very hot
9	240	220	475	Very hot

Approximate weight conversions
- All the recipes in this book list both metric and imperial measurements. Conversions are approximate and have been rounded up or down. Follow one set of measurements only; do not mix the two.
- Cup measurements, which are used by cooks in Australia and America, have not been listed here as they vary from ingredient to ingredient. Kitchen scales should be used to measure dry/solid ingredients.

Spoon measures
- Spoon measurements are level unless otherwise specified.
- 1 teaspoon (tsp) = 5ml
- 1 tablespoon (tbsp) = 15ml
- 1 Australian tablespoon = 20ml (cooks in Australia should measure 3 teaspoons where 1 tablespoon is specified in a recipe)

Approximate liquid conversions

metric	imperial	AUS	US
50ml	2fl oz	¼ cup	¼ cup
125ml	4fl oz	½ cup	½ cup
175ml	6fl oz	¾ cup	¾ cup
225ml	8fl oz	1 cup	1 cup
300ml	10fl oz/½ pint	½ pint	1¼ cups
450ml	16fl oz	2 cups	2 cups/1 pint
600ml	20fl oz/1 pint	1 pint	2½ cups
1 litre	35fl oz/1¾ pints	1¾ pints	1 quart

Easy everyday meals

Vegetable and cheese soup

To make the croûtons, toss bread cubes in oil and bake in a hot oven for 10–12 minutes until crisp, topping with cheese halfway through.

■ **Takes 50 minutes** ■ **Serves 4**

25g/1oz butter
1 tbsp olive oil
1 onion, chopped
1 potato, about 200g/8oz, chopped
2 sticks celery, chopped
550g/1lb 4oz mixed root vegetables, such as potato, swedes, parsnips and carrots, chopped
1 litre/1¾ pints vegetable stock
140g/5oz mature Cheddar
1 tbsp wholegrain mustard
cheesy croûtons, to serve

1 Heat the butter and oil in a large pan. Add the onion and cook until golden. Add the other vegetables and stir. Season, cover, reduce the heat and cook for 10 minutes, stirring occasionally, until just tender.
2 Pour the stock into the pan, bring to the boil, then cover and simmer for 20 minutes until the vegetables are softened. Whizz in a food processor until smooth. Meanwhile, grate half the cheese and cut the rest into small cubes.
3 Reheat the soup in the pan and stir in most of the grated cheese and all the cubes, until the cheese begins to melt. Stir in the mustard and season. Sprinkle with cheesy croûtons and the remaining cheese.

■ Per serving 320 kcalories, protein 13g, carbohydrate 21g, fat 21g, saturated fat 11g, fibre 4g, added sugar none, salt 1.78g

Vegetable satay soup

Use a jar of satay (peanut) sauce as a base to make this simple soup.

■ **Takes 20 minutes** ■ **Serves 4**

450g/1lb new potatoes
1 carrot
175g/6oz green beans
1 vegetable stock cube
100g/4oz podded broad beans (or frozen or canned)
330ml jar satay sauce
175g/6oz cherry tomatoes, halved
pitta bread, to serve

1 Cut the potatoes into 2.5cm chunks (no need to peel). Quarter the carrot lengthways, then cut across into small pieces. Trim the green beans, then cut into short sticks.
2 Put the potatoes and carrot in a medium pan with 850ml/1½ pints water and the stock cube. Bring to the boil, stir to dissolve the cube, then simmer, covered, for 10–12 minutes until the vegetables are almost tender. Tip in the green and broad beans and simmer for 2 minutes.
3 Pour in the satay sauce and simmer for 3–4 minutes. Stir in the tomatoes. Serve hot with warm pitta bread.

■ Per serving 596 kcalories, protein 19g, carbohydrate 40g, fat 42g, saturated fat 9g, fibre 10g, added sugar 6g, salt 3.27g

Hot–sour coconut soup

This is a really light, subtle soup with fresh, vibrant flavours. Serve it without the rice as a starter.

■ **Takes 30 minutes** ■ **Serves 4**

100g/4oz Thai fragrant rice
1.2 litres/2 pints chicken or vegetable stock
1 stalk lemongrass, thinly sliced
1 tbsp finely chopped galangal or ginger
4 fresh or freeze-dried kaffir lime leaves, chopped or crumbled
2 red chillies, seeded and finely chopped
250g/9oz boneless skinless chicken breast, thinly sliced
175g/6oz chestnut mushrooms, sliced
200g/8oz cherry tomatoes, halved
1 tbsp lime juice
2 tbsp fish sauce (nam pla)
200ml carton coconut cream
a handful of fresh coriander, chopped

1 Cook the rice in salted boiling water for about 10 minutes, until tender, then drain and set aside.
2 Meanwhile, heat the stock in a large pan, add the lemongrass, galangal or ginger, lime leaves and chillies and simmer for 5 minutes. Add the chicken and mushrooms and simmer for a further 5 minutes.
3 Stir in the tomatoes, lime juice, fish sauce and coconut cream and simmer for 5 minutes more. Scatter over the coriander and serve each portion with a little cooked rice spooned in.

■ Per serving 356 kcalories, protein 22g, carbohydrate 26g, fat 19g, saturated fat 15g, fibre 1g, added sugar none, salt 2.47g

TOP: Vegetable and cheese soup

BOTTOM LEFT: Vegetable satay soup

BOTTOM RIGHT: Hot–sour coconut soup

TOP: Tricolore salad with lemon dressing

BOTTOM LEFT: Mediterranean couscous salad

BOTTOM RIGHT: Cannellini bean salad

Tricolore salad with lemon dressing

It's worth buying mozzarella made from buffalo milk, not cow's milk, for this salad.

■ **Takes 20 minutes** ■ **Serves 4**

200g/8oz buffalo mozzarella
2 large firm ripe tomatoes
40g bag rocket

FOR THE DRESSING
½ lemon
good pinch of sea salt
½ tsp freshly ground black pepper
4 tbsp extra-virgin olive oil

1 Cut the mozzarella and tomatoes into slices of an equal thickness. Arrange alternate slices of mozzarella and tomato on four side plates. Put a pile of rocket leaves beside each.
2 Pare the lemon using a lemon zester to make small, thin strips of peel. (If you don't have a zester, use a sharp knife to pare off strips of the rind, taking care not to include any white pith, then cut the strips into minute strands.) Squeeze the juice from the lemon into a bowl and add the sea salt and black pepper. Whisk, gradually mixing in the olive oil until the dressing is thickened.
3 Drizzle the lemon dressing over the rocket, mozzarella and tomato on the plates, then scatter over the lemon strips and serve.

■ Per serving 260 kcalories, protein 14g, carbohydrate 3g, fat 22g, saturated fat 8g, fibre 1g, added sugar none, salt 1.04g

Mediterranean couscous salad

There's no need to cook the couscous – just soak it and mix in the tasty bits.

■ **Takes 20 minutes** ■ **Serves 4 (easily halved)**

200g/8oz couscous
400ml/14fl oz vegetable stock
10 sun-dried or SunBlush tomatoes, quartered
2 medium avocados, peeled, stoned and cut into large chunks
100g/4oz black olives
a good handful of nuts, such as pine nuts, cashew nuts or almonds
200g/8oz feta, roughly crumbled
130g bag green salad leaves

FOR THE DRESSING
5 tbsp olive oil
2 tbsp fresh lemon juice

1 Tip the couscous into a large bowl, stir in the stock, cover and leave to soak for 5 minutes.
2 Make the dressing by whisking together the olive oil, lemon juice and seasoning. Stir 2 tablespoons into the couscous, then gently mix in the tomatoes, avocados, olives, nuts and feta. Taste for seasoning.
3 Toss the salad leaves with the remaining dressing, divide among four plates and spoon the couscous on top.

■ Per serving 636 kcalories, protein 14g, carbohydrate 29g, fat 52g, saturated fat 11g, fibre 4g, added sugar none, salt 3.82g

Cannellini bean salad

This colourful salad travels well in a lunchbox. Try other beans and cheeses in combination too.

■ **Takes 10 minutes** ■ **Serves 4**

1 small red onion
1 red or yellow pepper
400g can cannellini beans
4 tbsp ready-made vinaigrette
½ iceberg or 1 cos lettuce
250g pack feta
warm Italian bread, to serve

1 Halve and finely slice the onion and pepper. Drain and rinse the beans. Put the ingredients in a salad bowl.
2 Add the vinaigrette and mix well. Tear the lettuce leaves straight into the bowl.
3 Break the feta into chunks, throw into the salad and season with black pepper. Serve with warm Italian bread.

■ Per serving 348 kcalories, protein 16g, carbohydrate 17g, fat 25g, saturated fat 10g, fibre 4g, added sugar none, salt 2.57g

Warm Caesar-style salad

A simple salad but one with plenty of contrasting textures. You'll find Caesar dressing in most supermarkets.

■ **Takes 30 minutes** ■ **Serves 4**

6 medium eggs
140g/5oz green beans, trimmed
1 ciabatta loaf
2 tbsp extra-virgin olive oil
50g/2oz Parmesan, finely grated, plus extra
    shavings to garnish
1 cos lettuce, roughly chopped
ready-made Caesar dressing

1 Heat the grill. Bring a pan of water to the boil, carefully drop in the eggs and cook for 4 minutes. Place in cold water to cool. Cook the green beans in lightly salted boiling water for 4 minutes until tender. Drain well and place in a large salad bowl.
2 Cut the ciabatta loaf into large cubes and toss in the oil and the Parmesan. Tip the bread on to a baking tray and grill, turning, until golden.
3 Peel the eggs and cut into four lengthways. Add the croûtons and lettuce to the beans. Season and mix well. Pile on to serving plates and top with the eggs. Drizzle over the dressing and finish with the Parmesan shavings.

■ Per serving 684 kcalories, protein 27g, carbohydrate 67g, fat 36g, saturated fat 8g, fibre 4g, added sugar none, salt 2.68g

Cheddar and chicory salad

Crisp and tangy, chicory adds a soft tang to salads. Just pull off the leaves and discard the core.

■ **Takes 20 minutes** ■ **Serves 4**

FOR THE DRESSING
5 tbsp olive oil
2 tsp clear honey
1 tbsp wholegrain mustard
2 tbsp lemon juice

FOR THE SALAD
200g/8oz chicory
1 red-skinned apple
85g/3oz walnut pieces
100g/4oz mature Cheddar

1 To make the dressing, put all the ingredients into a small bowl and blend thoroughly with a small whisk or fork. Season to taste and set aside.
2 Separate the chicory leaves and divide among four plates. Cut the apple into quarters, core and thinly slice. Scatter the apple slices over the chicory and sprinkle with the walnuts.
3 Using a vegetable peeler, make Cheddar shavings and scatter over each serving. Drizzle the dressing over the salad and finish with a grating of black pepper.

■ Per serving 441 kcalories, protein 10g, carbohydrate 9g, fat 38g, saturated fat 9g, fibre 2g, added sugar 2g, salt 0.59g

Chickpea and feta salad

A jar of marinated feta cubes from the supermarket cheese counter provides the protein and the dressing.

■ **Takes 15 minutes, plus draining** ■ **Serves 4**

1 cucumber, thickly sliced
1 small red onion, thinly sliced
300g jar marinated feta cubes in oil
4 large tomatoes, cut into wedges
420g can chickpeas, drained and rinsed
few black olives
juice of ½ lemon
2 Little Gem lettuces

TO SERVE
4 pitta breads
1 spring onion, chopped

1 Put the cucumber and onion in a sieve over a bowl, sprinkle with salt and leave to drain for 20 minutes. Drain the cheese cubes, reserving the oil.
2 Heat the grill. Toss the cucumber and onion with the tomatoes, chickpeas, olives, cheese, 3 tablespoons of the oil and the lemon juice. Season. Line salad bowls with the lettuce leaves and pile the salad on top.
3 Grill the pitta on one side, turn over and brush with a little oil from the cheese. Sprinkle the spring onion over and grill until crisp. Serve with the salad.

■ Per serving 637 kcalories, protein 28g, carbohydrate 67g, fat 31g, saturated fat 11g, fibre 8g, added sugar none, salt 4.37g

TOP: Warm Caesar-style salad

BOTTOM LEFT: Cheddar and chicory salad

BOTTOM RIGHT: Chickpea and feta salad

TOP: Oriental prawn and pasta salad

BOTTOM LEFT: Runner bean and bacon salad

BOTTOM RIGHT: Warm mackerel and beetroot salad

Oriental prawn and pasta salad

This recipe is easily multiplied to feed a crowd as part of a buffet.

■ **Takes 30 minutes** ■ **Serves 4**

100g/4oz fresh beansprouts
250g/9oz fresh tagliatelle
2 carrots, cut into thin sticks
1 bunch spring onions, cut into shreds
¼ cucumber, cut into thin ribbons with
    a potato peeler
200g/8oz cooked peeled prawns
sesame oil, to serve

FOR THE DRESSING
5 tbsp sunflower oil
2 tbsp light soy sauce
2 tbsp rice vinegar or white wine vinegar
1 tbsp finely chopped ginger
1 large garlic clove, crushed
1 tsp clear honey

1 Put the beansprouts in a bowl, cover with cold water and leave for 10 minutes, then drain (this crisps them up). Meanwhile cook the pasta in a pan of salted boiling water according to the packet instructions.
2 Tip the pasta into a colander and run under the cold tap, then drain thoroughly. Toss with the carrots, spring onions, cucumber, prawns and beansprouts.
3 For the dressing, whisk together the sunflower oil, soy sauce, vinegar, ginger, garlic and honey. Pour over the pasta and lightly toss. Drizzle with a little sesame oil to serve.

■ Per serving 439 kcalories, protein 21g, carbohydrate 54g, fat 17g, saturated fat 2g, fibre 4g, added sugar 1g, salt 3.42g

Runner bean and bacon salad

The runner-bean season is a precious time so make the most of it. Buy the beans on the day you intend to eat them, if possible.

■ **Takes 20 minutes** ■ **Serves 4**

450g/1lb runner beans, cut into fine slivers
100g/4oz good-quality streaky bacon, cut
    into strips
2 tbsp sherry vinegar or white wine vinegar
4 tbsp extra-virgin olive oil
1 tbsp wholegrain mustard
140g/5oz cherry tomatoes, halved,
    or small tomatoes, cut into wedges

1 Blanch the runner beans in a large pan of salted boiling water for 3 minutes, then drain and cool under cold running water. Drain well and transfer to a serving bowl.
2 Heat a frying pan, then add the bacon and let it sizzle until crisp. Remove from the pan and set aside. Stir the vinegar and oil into the hot pan and warm through, then whisk in the mustard. Pour the warm dressing over the beans.
3 Toss in the tomatoes, then season well. Garnish with the crispy bacon and serve warm.

■ Per serving 204 kcalories, protein 6g, carbohydrate 5g, fat 18g, saturated fat 4g, fibre 3g, added sugar none, salt 1.22g

Warm mackerel and beetroot salad

With the main ingredients bought ready-cooked, you've only got the potatoes to do.

■ **Takes 20 minutes** ■ **Serves 4 (easily halved)**

450g/1lb new potatoes, cut into bite-size
    pieces
3 smoked mackerel fillets, skinned
250g pack cooked beetroot
120g bag mixed salad leaves
2 celery sticks, finely sliced
50g/2oz walnut pieces

FOR THE DRESSING
3 tbsp walnut oil
2 tbsp sunflower oil
2 tbsp fresh lemon juice
2 tsp creamed horseradish sauce

1 Cook the potatoes in salted boiling water for 12–15 minutes until just tender. Meanwhile, flake the mackerel fillets into large pieces. Cut the beetroot into bite-sized chunks.
2 Drain the potatoes and cool slightly. Mix together all the dressing ingredients and season.
3 Tip the potatoes into a bowl and add the salad leaves, mackerel, beetroot, celery and walnuts. Pour over the dressing and toss well. Serve warm.

■ Per serving 634 kcalories, protein 22g, carbohydrate 26g, fat 50g, saturated fat 2g, fibre 4g, added sugar none, salt 1.91g

Bacon and Camembert salad

Choose a soft, ripe Camembert and let it rest at room temperature before using.

■ **Takes 15 minutes** ■ **Serves 4**

8 rashers smoked streaky bacon
125g pack Camembert
2 thick slices bread (about 85g/3oz), crusts removed
7 tbsp olive oil
140g bag crisp green salad
2 tbsp white wine vinegar
1 tbsp wholegrain mustard
1 garlic clove, finely chopped

1 Heat the grill and cook the bacon for 5–8 minutes until crisp, turning halfway through. Set aside to cool. Cut the Camembert into bite-size wedges.
2 Grate the bread into coarse crumbs. Heat 2 tablespoons of the oil in a frying pan and cook the crumbs, stirring, until crisp and golden. Season and set aside.
3 Tip the salad into a bowl. Break the bacon into bite-sized pieces and mix into the salad with the cheese. Mix together the vinegar, mustard, garlic and remaining olive oil. Pour over the salad and toss well. Sprinkle with the crisp crumbs and serve.

■ Per serving 465 kcalories, protein 17g, carbohydrate 12g, fat 39g, saturated fat 12g, fibre 1g, added sugar none, salt 2.56g

Chicken salad with honey dressing

Buy a bottle of honey and mustard dressing or mix up your own version.

■ **Takes 40 minutes** ■ **Serves 4**

450g/1lb new potatoes, scrubbed and quartered lengthways
175g/6oz fine green beans, trimmed
6 rashers rindless streaky bacon
120g bag mixed salad leaves
4 roasted chicken breasts, skinned and cut into chunks, or about 700g/1lb 9oz cooked chicken
ready-made honey and mustard dressing

1 Cook the potatoes in salted boiling water for 8–10 minutes. Add the beans to the water and cook for a further 3 minutes until just tender. Drain, cool quickly under running cold water, then cool completely.
2 Meanwhile, fry or grill the bacon for 3–4 minutes until crispy. Allow to cool, then break into small pieces.
3 Scatter the salad leaves, potatoes and beans over a large serving plate. Toss the chicken with the dressing to taste, then spoon over the salad leaves. Scatter the crispy bacon over the salad and serve.

■ Per serving 505 kcalories, protein 42g, carbohydrate 26g, fat 27g, saturated fat 5g, fibre 3g, added sugar 6g, salt 2.02g

Leaf salad with griddled chicken

Choose a bag with radicchio, frisée, watercress or rocket – the bitter flavours are great with sweet red peppers.

■ **Takes 25 minutes** ■ **Serves 4**

4 boneless skinless chicken breasts, each cut into 7–8 slices
2 red peppers, seeded and cut into strips
3 tbsp olive oil, plus extra for tossing
juice of 1 lemon
142ml pot soured cream
200g bag mixed salad leaves

1 Heat a large griddle or frying pan. In a bowl, toss together the chicken, peppers, a little oil, some seasoning and a little of the lemon juice.
2 Cook the chicken and peppers in batches, in one layer in the hot pan for 5–8 minutes. Turn them halfway through until the chicken is cooked and the peppers are slightly charred. Allow to cool.
3 Mix together the remaining lemon juice and the soured cream. Whisk in the 3 tablespoons of oil and season. Tip the salad leaves into a bowl. Add the chicken and peppers, pour over the dressing, toss lightly and serve.

■ Per serving 331 kcalories, protein 36g, carbohydrate 7g, fat 18g, saturated fat 6g, fibre 2g, added sugar none, salt 0.26g

TOP: Bacon and Camembert salad

BOTTOM LEFT: Chicken salad with honey dressing

BOTTOM RIGHT: Leaf salad with griddled chicken

TOP: Croque monsieur

BOTTOM LEFT: Pizza jackets

BOTTOM RIGHT: Mackerel and horseradish pâté

Croque monsieur

A French speciality – a toasted ham and cheese sandwich that's perfect as a snack.

■ **Takes 10 minutes** ■ **Serves 1**

2 thick slices crusty bread
butter, for spreading
2–3 slices wafer-thin ham
25g/1oz Gruyère or Cheddar, grated
4 tsp freshly grated Parmesan
green salad, to serve

1 Heat the grill. Butter the bread and make a sandwich with the ham and Gruyère or Cheddar. Press down firmly.
2 Spread butter over the top of the sandwich and sprinkle with half the Parmesan, then toast under the grill until the bread is crisp and the cheese browned.
3 Repeat on the other side. Cut in half and serve hot with a green salad.

■ Per serving 533 kcalories, protein 25g, carbohydrate 51g, fat 27g, saturated fat 16g, fibre 2g, added sugar none, salt 2.97g

Pizza jackets

These potatoes are cooked in the microwave for speed. Vary the filling according to what's in the fridge.

■ **Takes 25 minutes** ■ **Serves 4**

4 baking potatoes
2 tomatoes
2 × 150g balls mozzarella
4 small ham slices
4 fresh rosemary sprigs
olive oil, for drizzling

1 Wash the potatoes and prick them all over with a fork. Cook in the microwave on High for 10–12 minutes, turning halfway through, until cooked.
2 Heat the grill. Slice each tomato and each mozzarella ball into six. Tear each ham slice into three strips. Cut three vertical slits in each potato and stuff each with a slice of cheese, ham and tomato. Tuck a rosemary sprig in the central slit.
3 Drizzle over a little oil and season. Grill for about 5 minutes until the cheese has melted.

■ Per serving 421 kcalories, protein 28g, carbohydrate 32g, fat 21g, saturated fat 11g, fibre 3g, added sugar none, salt 2.36g

Mackerel and horseradish pâté

If you can't find fresh horseradish, add creamed horseradish to taste. Serve with toast.

■ **Takes 25 minutes, plus chilling** ■ **Serves 4**

200g/8oz smoked mackerel fillets, skinned and boned
3 tbsp freshly grated horseradish
100g/4oz ricotta
4 tsp fresh lemon juice
1 tsp fennel seeds, crushed
2 tbsp melted butter
bay leaves and pink or green peppercorns, to garnish
toast or rye bread, to serve

1 In a food processor, blend the fish, horseradish, ricotta, lemon juice, fennel and pepper to a smooth paste.
2 Taste and add more lemon juice, if necessary. Spoon into a serving bowl and drizzle over the butter.
3 Garnish with bay leaves and peppercorns, and chill for 1 hour before serving with the toast or rye bread.

■ Per serving 283 kcalories, protein 13g, carbohydrate 3g, fat 25g, saturated fat 9g, fibre 1g, added sugar none, salt 1.17g

Tortilla chips with cheese and salsa

If you prefer, heat the beans in a pan and grill the cheese-topped chips.

■ **Takes 10 minutes** ■ **Serves 2 (easily doubled)**

2 tomatoes, quartered
½ small red onion, quartered
juice of ½ lime or lemon
4–5 drops Tabasco sauce, plus extra to serve
2 tbsp tomato purée
150g bag tortilla chips
220g can refried beans
85g/3oz mature Cheddar, grated
142ml pot soured cream, to serve

1 Put the tomatoes, onion, lime or lemon juice and Tabasco in a food processor and whizz briefly until finely chopped. Stir in the tomato purée and season.
2 Divide the tortilla chips between two microwave-proof plates. Spoon the beans into the centre, then top with the salsa.
3 Sprinkle the cheese over everything, then microwave on High, one plate at a time, for 2½ minutes. Serve with soured cream and extra Tabasco, if you like.

■ Per serving 784 kcalories, protein 26g, carbohydrate 72g, fat 46g, saturated fat 17g, fibre 6g, added sugar none, salt 3.8g

Cheese and onion potato wedges

A cheap and easy family supper. Make a veggie version by omitting the ham.

■ **Takes 30 minutes** ■ **Serves 4**

4 baking potatoes, cut into thick wedges
1 red pepper
bunch spring onions
100g/4oz Cheddar
100g/4oz wafer-thin ham
1 tsp paprika
200ml pot crème fraîche

1 Heat the grill to high. Cook the potato wedges in a large pan of salted boiling water for 15 minutes until tender.
2 Meanwhile, seed and thinly slice the pepper, chop the spring onions and grate the cheese. Drain the potatoes well, then mix with the red pepper, spring onions and ham. Transfer to a heatproof dish. Season well and sprinkle with paprika. Grill for 3 minutes until golden brown.
3 Spoon over the crème fraîche, sprinkle with the cheese and grill for 2–3 minutes more, until the cheese has melted and the crème fraîche has made a sauce.

■ Per serving 456 kcalories, protein 18g, carbohydrate 41g, fat 26g, saturated fat 14g, fibre 4g, added sugar none, salt 1.36g

Cheese-stuffed mushrooms

Choose large, flat mushrooms for stuffing with cheesy mashed potato.

■ **Takes 25 minutes** ■ **Serves 4**

4 large or 8 medium flat mushrooms
3 tbsp olive oil
2 large floury potatoes
4 or 8 rashers rindless smoked streaky bacon
125g pack soft cheese with garlic and herbs

1 Heat the oven to 200C/180C fan/gas 6. Wipe the mushrooms clean. Put them in an ovenproof dish, drizzle with the oil and bake for 15–20 minutes.
2 Meanwhile, cut the potatoes into small cubes, then cook in a pan of salted boiling water for 8–10 minutes until just tender.
3 Heat a frying pan and dry-fry the bacon until crisp. Drain the potatoes, return to the pan and spoon in the cheese. Mix together lightly, then season. Pile the mixture on top of the mushrooms and top with the bacon.

■ Per serving 392 kcalories, protein 14g, carbohydrate 22g, fat 28g, saturated fat 5g, fibre 3g, added sugar none, salt 1.58g

TOP: Tortilla chips with cheese and salsa

BOTTOM LEFT: Cheese and onion potato wedges

BOTTOM RIGHT: Cheese-stuffed mushrooms

TOP: Stilton cauliflower cheese

BOTTOM LEFT: Pasta and spinach tortilla

BOTTOM RIGHT: Smoked salmon frittata

Stilton cauliflower cheese

A rich alternative to everyday cauliflower cheese, with a crisp almond topping.

■ **Takes 25 minutes** ■ **Serves 4**

1 large cauliflower
50g/2oz blanched almonds

FOR THE SAUCE
25g/1oz butter
2 tbsp plain flour
300ml/½ pint milk
1 tsp dry mustard
85g/3oz Stilton, plus 25g/1oz extra for sprinkling

1 Divide the cauliflower into florets and discard all inedible parts. Steam for 10 minutes until just tender. Meanwhile, heat the grill. Halve the almonds lengthways and toast for 4–5 minutes, turning halfway through, until browned.
2 To make the sauce, put all the ingredients (including the cheese) in a wide pan and season. Heat gently and bring to the boil, whisking all the time, then simmer for 2 minutes, stirring constantly. Season carefully (go easy on the salt).
3 Put the cauliflower in a wide, heatproof serving dish and sprinkle with half the toasted almonds. Top with the sauce, remaining almonds and the extra cheese. Grill for 5–10 minutes until the cheese is brown and bubbling.

■ Per serving 366 kcalories, protein 17g, carbohydrate 17g, fat 26g, saturated fat 11g, fibre 4g, added sugar none, salt 1.1g

Pasta and spinach tortilla

You could use leftover cooked pasta in this recipe. Be sure to drain the spinach well.

■ **Takes 25 minutes** ■ **Serves 4**

85g/3oz pasta shells
450g/1lb fresh spinach leaves
8 eggs
100g/4oz mature Cheddar, coarsely grated
200g/8oz cherry tomatoes, halved
1 tbsp olive oil

1 Cook the pasta in salted boiling water according to the packet instructions. Wash the spinach well, then put in the pan with just the water that clings to it and a little salt. Put over a medium heat. When the spinach starts to steam, cover and cook for 3–4 minutes until just wilted. Drain the spinach well, then roughly chop. Mix into the drained pasta.
2 Lightly beat the eggs and mix into the pasta with three-quarters of the cheese and the tomatoes. Season. Heat the grill. Heat the tablespoon of olive oil in a large frying pan and cook the pasta-and-egg mixture for 8–10 minutes, until almost set.
3 Sprinkle the omelette with the remaining cheese, then grill to brown the top. Serve warm or cold cut into wedges.

■ Per serving 361 kcalories, protein 25g, carbohydrate 19g, fat 21g, saturated fat 9g, fibre 4g, added sugar none, salt 1.2g

Smoked salmon frittata

Frittata is an Italian omelette. Use cheaper smoked-salmon trimmings for this light supper.

■ **Takes 40 minutes** ■ **Serves 4**

500g/1lb 2oz new potatoes, thickly sliced
200g pack smoked salmon
8 eggs
2 tbsp chopped fresh dill
100g/4oz frozen petits pois
3 tbsp olive oil

1 Cook the potatoes in salted boiling water until just tender, about 10 minutes. Drain and leave to cool slightly. Cut the salmon into wide strips. Crack the eggs into a bowl, beat with a fork until foamy, then stir in the smoked salmon, dill and peas, and season. Finally, stir in the potatoes.
2 Heat the olive oil in a large non-stick frying pan and carefully pour in the egg mixture. Cook over a fairly low heat for 10–15 minutes, until the egg is starting to set just under the surface.
3 Put a plate over the pan and invert the frittata on to it. Slide it back into the pan and cook for a further 5 minutes to brown the underside. Slide on to a plate and cool for 5 minutes before cutting into wedges.

■ Per serving 423 kcalories, protein 31g, carbohydrate 22g, fat 24g, saturated fat 5g, fibre 3g, added sugar none, salt 3.15g

Nasi goreng

This spicy rice mix is a favourite snack in Indonesia.

■ **Takes 35 minutes** ■ **Serves 4**

350g/12oz long grain rice
2 tbsp sunflower oil, plus 1 tsp
2 garlic cloves, roughly chopped
450g/1lb boneless skinless chicken breasts
    or thighs, cut into chunks
1 red pepper, seeded and diced
1 tbsp curry paste or powder
bunch spring onions, thinly sliced
2 tbsp soy sauce, plus extra to serve
2 eggs
50g/2oz roasted peanuts, roughly chopped
4 tbsp roughly chopped fresh coriander

1 Cook the rice in salted boiling water for
12–15 minutes. Drain well. Meanwhile, heat the
2 tablespoons of oil in a wok or large frying pan.
2 Fry the garlic, chicken and pepper for 10
minutes, stirring, until golden. Add the curry paste
or powder and cook for 1 minute. Stir in the rice
and spring onions and cook for 5 minutes until
piping hot. Stir in the soy sauce.
3 Push the rice to one side of the pan. Pour the
remaining teaspoon of oil in to the space, crack in
the eggs and lightly scramble them. Mix into the
rice. Sprinkle over the peanuts, coriander and a
little extra soy sauce. Serve immediately.

■ Per serving 625 kcalories, protein 34g, carbohydrate
73g, fat 24g, saturated fat 2g, fibre 4g, added sugar none,
salt 2.23g

Steak and noodle stir fry

Look for stir-fry sauces and no-need-to-cook noodles in the supermarket.

■ **Takes 10 minutes** ■ **Serves 2**

200g/8oz rump steak
200g/8oz pak choi (Chinese greens)
1 red pepper, seeded
2 tbsp sunflower oil
100–120g sachet stir fry sauce
2 × 150g packs no-cook noodles

1 Trim any visible fat from the steak, then
slice into thin strips. Cut each head of pak
choi into four lengthways. Dice the pepper into
small squares.
2 Heat the sunflower oil in a pan. Add the
pepper and fry quickly for 1 minute. Add the beef
and fry until browned all over. Add the pak choi
and cook briefly until starting to wilt.
3 Tip in the stir-fry sauce and 2 tablespoons
water and stir. Bring to the boil, then add the
noodles and warm through, loosening them until
they are all coated in sauce. Serve immediately.

■ Per serving 499 kcalories, protein 32g, carbohydrate
53.8g, fat 18.9g, saturated fat 3.1g, fibre 3.8g, added
sugar 1.6g, salt 2.52g

Asparagus carbonara

A delicious combination of tender asparagus, creamy sauce and crispy crumbs.

■ **Takes 30 minutes** ■ **Serves 4**

knob of butter
1 small onion, chopped
2 garlic cloves, finely chopped
200g/8oz ham, cut into chunks
600g/1lb 5oz asparagus spears
2 eggs
142ml pot single cream
4 tbsp freshly grated Parmesan
85g/3oz fresh white breadcrumbs
2 tbsp olive oil
2 tbsp finely chopped fresh parsley

1 Melt the butter in a small frying pan, then cook
the onion, garlic and ham for 5–10 minutes until
golden. Meanwhile, cook the asparagus in a pan
of salted boiling water for 3–4 minutes until just
tender. Drain and set aside.
2 Whisk together the eggs, cream and 3
tablespoons of the Parmesan. Stir in the onion
mixture and season. In a separate bowl, mix
together the breadcrumbs, olive oil, parsley and
remaining Parmesan.
3 Heat the grill. Toss the asparagus with the
cream mixture. Tip into a gratin dish and sprinkle
over the breadcrumb mixture. Grill for 2–3
minutes, until the breadcrumbs are golden and
the carbonara sauce is hot.

■ Per serving 381 kcalories, protein 25g, carbohydrate
21g, fat 22g, saturated fat 9g, fibre 4g, added sugar none,
salt 2.07g

TOP: Nasi goreng

BOTTOM LEFT: Steak and noodle stir fry

BOTTOM RIGHT: Asparagus carbonara

TOP: Cheese and mustard bake

BOTTOM LEFT: Spicy lamb burgers

BOTTOM RIGHT: Florentine egg grill

Cheese and mustard bake

Cut the slices from a nice loaf, a few days old, for the best texture.

■ **Takes 50 minutes** ■ **Serves 4**

175g/6oz mature Cheddar, finely grated
2 tsp Dijon or English mustard
850ml/1½ pints semi-skimmed milk
25g/1oz butter, at room temperature
5 thick slices white bread
3 eggs
4 rashers rindless streaky bacon
Worcestershire sauce, to serve

1 Heat the oven to 180C/160C fan/gas 4. Mix together most of the cheese, the mustard and 3 tablespoons of the milk. Season. Butter the bread. Spread each slice with the cheese mixture. Cut each slice into four triangles. Butter a 2.25 litre ovenproof dish and arrange the bread in the dish with the points uppermost.
2 Beat together the remaining milk and the eggs, and season. Pour the liquid over the bread. Sprinkle with the remaining cheese. Bake for 35 minutes until risen and golden.
3 Meanwhile, heat the grill. Grill the bacon for 8–10 minutes until crispy, turning halfway through. Break into pieces and scatter over the bake. Sprinkle with a little Worcestershire sauce and serve immediately.

■ Per serving 569 kcalories, protein 31g, carbohydrate 36g, fat 35g, saturated fat 12g, fibre 1g, added sugar none, salt 2.94g

Spicy lamb burgers

Make these ahead and store in the fridge, covered with cling film.

■ **Takes 30 minutes** ■ **Serves 6**

1 onion, roughly chopped
2.5cm/1in ginger, peeled and chopped
2 garlic cloves, roughly chopped
bunch fresh coriander or parsley
2 tsp each ground cumin and ground
    coriander
1 tsp ground cinnamon
100g/4oz ready-to-eat dried apricots, finely
    chopped
700g/1lb 9oz lean minced lamb
oil, for brushing

TO SERVE
6 large buns, such as ciabatta rolls
2 tsp harissa paste (available from large
    supermarkets) or chilli paste
8 tbsp mayonnaise
a few lettuce leaves, tomato and
    cucumber slices

1 Whizz the onion, ginger, garlic and coriander or parsley (stems too) in a food processor until finely chopped. Add the spices, apricots, lamb, and plenty of seasoning, then pulse until just mixed.
2 Shape into six burgers, brush lightly with oil and cook on a hot griddle, or under the grill, for 4–5 minutes on each side.
3 Split and toast the buns. Swirl the harissa or chilli paste into the mayonnaise. Serve the burgers, lettuce, tomato and cucumber in the buns, with the mayonnaise on the side.

■ Per serving 497 kcalories, protein 30g, carbohydrate 34g, fat 28g, saturated fat 8g, fibre 2g, added sugar none, salt 1.21g

Florentine egg grill

You could use cooked bacon instead of ham and Gruyère in place of Cheddar.

■ **Takes 25 minutes** ■ **Serves 2**

200g/8oz frozen leaf spinach, thawed
freshly grated nutmeg
knob of butter
2 ham slices, cut into thin strips
2 eggs
2 tbsp single or double cream
85g/3oz Cheddar, grated

1 Drain the thawed spinach well. Tip into a bowl and stir in a little nutmeg, a knob of butter and the ham. Season. Form into two mounds on the base of a shallow, buttered ovenproof dish.
2 Heat the grill to high. Poach the eggs in a pan half full of lightly salted water until just set.
3 Lift out with a slotted spoon, drain well and place on the spinach cakes. Drizzle with the cream and sprinkle with the cheese. Grill until golden brown.

■ Per serving 368 kcalories, protein 26g, carbohydrate 3g, fat 28g, saturated fat 15g, fibre 2g, added sugar none, salt 2.12g

Spaghetti with cherry tomatoes

These tiny tomatoes taste extra sweet when roasted and are a contrast to the salty cheese.

■ **Takes 25 minutes** ■ **Serves 4**

500g/1lb 2oz cherry tomatoes
3 tbsp olive oil
400g/14oz spaghetti
250g/9oz feta
generous handful fresh flatleaf parsley
a handful of black olives
freshly grated Parmesan, to serve

1 Heat the oven to 200C/180C fan/gas 6. Tip the tomatoes into a shallow ovenproof dish, drizzle over the olive oil, and season. Roast for 15 minutes until slightly scorched.
2 Cook the spaghetti in plenty of salted boiling water for 10–12 minutes, until just tender. Meanwhile, cut the feta into cubes and roughly chop the parsley.
3 Drain the pasta, then return to the pan. Add the roasted tomatoes, along with their pan juices, the feta, olives and parsley. Toss together until well mixed, then serve with freshly grated Parmesan for sprinkling.

■ Per serving 530 kcalories, protein 23g, carbohydrate 79g, fat 16g, saturated fat 8g, fibre 5g, added sugar none, salt 3.02g

Penne with blue cheese

A creamy vegetarian pasta that's perfect when you fancy some comfort food.

■ **Takes 20 minutes** ■ **Serves 4**

350g/12oz penne
200g/8oz frozen leaf spinach
85g/3oz Danish blue, crumbled
pinch of chilli flakes
250g tub mascarpone
25g/1oz freshly grated Parmesan
green salad, to serve

1 Bring a large pan of salted water to the boil. Add the pasta and cook for 10–12 minutes until tender, adding the spinach to the pan for the last 3 minutes of cooking time. Drain.
2 Tip the pasta and spinach into a shallow heatproof dish along with the Danish blue, chilli flakes and plenty of black pepper.
3 Dot spoonfuls of the mascarpone over the top of the pasta mixture. Sprinkle with the Parmesan and grill for 5 minutes, until the mascarpone melts into a sauce and the Parmesan turns golden. Serve with a green salad.

■ Per serving 698 kcalories, protein 21g, carbohydrate 70g, fat 39g, saturated fat 24g, fibre 4g, added sugar none, salt 1.06g

Stilton and broccoli pasta

Tube-shaped pasta shapes work best in this recipe, as the sauce gets trapped inside and clings to their ridged surfaces.

■ **Takes 25 minutes** ■ **Serves 4**

350g/12oz penne or rigatoni
350g/12oz broccoli, cut into florets
140g/5oz Stilton
6 rashers rindless streaky bacon
200ml pot crème fraîche

1 Cook the pasta in a large pan of salted boiling water for 5 minutes. Add the broccoli, return the water to the boil and cook for a further 5–7 minutes, until the pasta and broccoli are just tender.
2 While the pasta is cooking, crumble the Stilton into a small bowl. Grill the bacon until crispy, then cut into pieces. Drain the pasta, reserving a few tablespoons of the cooking water. Return the pasta and reserved water to the pan.
3 Stir in the crumbled Stilton, crème fraîche and plenty of freshly ground black pepper. Stir gently until the cheese starts to melt into the sauce. Serve sprinkled with the bacon pieces and an extra grinding of ground black pepper.

■ Per serving 736 kcalories, protein 30g, carbohydrate 70g, fat 39g, saturated fat 20g, fibre 5g, added sugar none, salt 2.2g

TOP: Spaghetti with cherry tomatoes

BOTTOM LEFT: Penne with blue cheese

BOTTOM RIGHT: Stilton and broccoli pasta

TOP: Creamy salmon pasta

BOTTOM LEFT: Tagliatelle with crab and salsa

BOTTOM RIGHT: Pasta and haddock gratin

Creamy salmon pasta

Reduce the calories by using a low-fat soft cheese with garlic and herbs.

■ **Takes 20 minutes** ■ **Serves 4**

300g/10oz penne or rigatoni
350g/12oz broccoli, cut into small florets
300g/10oz boneless skinless salmon
fillet (about 2 fillets)
150g pack soft cheese with garlic and herbs
142ml pot single cream
2 tbsp sun-dried tomato paste

1 Cook the pasta according to the packet instructions, adding the broccoli for the last 3 minutes of cooking. Meanwhile, put the salmon in a frying pan, season and just cover with water. Bring to the boil, then simmer, covered, for 6 minutes until the flesh flakes easily with a fork. Using a slotted spoon, transfer to a plate and keep warm.
2 Mix the soft cheese with the cream and sun-dried tomato paste to make a smooth sauce. Season to taste.
3 Drain the pasta and broccoli, then tip back into the pan. Pour in the sauce and stir well. Flake the salmon into large chunks and gently mix into the pasta. Transfer to a warm serving bowl, season with black pepper and serve.

■ Per serving 586 kcalories, protein 33g, carbohydrate 61g, fat 25g, saturated fat 6g, fibre 5g, added sugar none, salt 0.53g

Tagliatelle with crab and salsa

Try this easy, no-cook sauce when you see dressed crab on the fish counter.

■ **Takes 20 minutes** ■ **Serves 2**

200g/8oz tagliatelle
4 tbsp olive oil
1 tbsp fresh lemon juice
3 tbsp chopped fresh parsley
1 small red onion, finely chopped
3 ripe tomatoes, seeded and chopped
170g can white crabmeat, drained, or
    175g/6oz fresh or frozen crabmeat
green salad, to serve

1 Cook the tagliatelle in a large pan of salted boiling water according to the pack instructions.
2 Whisk together the olive oil and lemon juice, season and stir in the parsley.
3 Drain the pasta and toss with the olive-oil mixture, red onion, tomatoes and crabmeat. Serve straight away with a green salad.

■ Per serving 634 kcalories, protein 26g, carbohydrate 82g, fat 25g, saturated fat 3g, fibre 5g, added sugar none, salt 1.02g

Pasta and haddock gratin

This all-in-one sauce gives perfect results. Whisk until the mixture boils, then simmer for 5 minutes.

■ **Takes 30 minutes** ■ **Serves 4**

350g/12oz penne or rigatoni
175g/6oz frozen leaf spinach
25g/1oz butter
25g/1oz plain flour
600ml/1 pint milk
450g/1lb skinless haddock or cod fillet,
    cut into chunks
175g/6oz mature Cheddar, grated
2 tomatoes, sliced

1 Cook the pasta in salted boiling water for about 12 minutes. Add the spinach for the last 3 minutes of cooking time.
2 Meanwhile, whisk the butter, flour and milk in a large pan and heat until the mixture comes to the boil. Reduce the heat, add the fish and simmer for 5 minutes or until the fish is just cooked. Remove from the heat and stir in three-quarters of the cheese. Season to taste.
3 Heat the grill. Drain the pasta and stir into the sauce. Pour into a 1.2–1.4 litre shallow ovenproof dish. Put the tomatoes on top and sprinkle with the remaining cheese. Grill for 5–7 minutes until golden.

■ Per serving 751 kcalories, protein 48g, carbohydrate 80g, fat 29g, saturated fat 17g, fibre 4g, added sugar none, salt 1.61g

Broccoli and spaghetti bake

You'll find most of these ingredients in your storecupboard. Vary the green vegetables as you like.

■ **Takes 45 minutes** ■ **Serves 4**

1 tbsp olive oil
1 onion, chopped
400g can chopped tomatoes
25g/1oz butter
25g/1oz plain flour
600ml/1 pint semi-skimmed milk
freshly grated nutmeg, to taste
300g/10oz broken-up spaghetti
300g/10oz broccoli, cut into florets
100g/4oz mature Cheddar, grated

1 Heat the oil in a small pan and fry the onion until soft. Stir in the tomatoes and season. Boil for 10 minutes, stirring until thickened. Meanwhile, put the butter, flour and milk into a pan. Bring to the boil, whisking until thick and smooth.
2 Cook the spaghetti in salted boiling water for 8 minutes, then add the broccoli and cook for 4 more minutes. Heat the grill. Stir most of the cheese into the white sauce.
3 Drain the pasta and broccoli, mix with the cheese sauce and spoon half into a 1.7 litre heatproof dish. Spoon the tomato sauce over. Cover with the rest of the pasta and broccoli and sprinkle with the remaining cheese. Grill for 5–8 minutes until golden.

■ Per serving 574 kcalories, protein 26g, carbohydrate 75g, fat 21g, saturated fat 11g, fibre 6g, added sugar none, salt 0.98g

Prawn tagliatelle with lemon

Use raw prawns for special occasions, but frozen ones will do for a midweek supper.

■ **Takes 15 minutes** ■ **Serves 4**

350g/12oz tagliatelle
200g/8oz fine green beans, trimmed and halved
85g/3oz butter
2 tbsp olive oil
finely grated zest and juice of 1 small lemon
300g/10oz raw peeled king prawns
2 tbsp chopped fresh dill, to serve

1 Cook the pasta according to the packet instructions. Three minutes before the end of the cooking time, throw in the green beans.
2 While the pasta is cooking, melt the butter in a small pan and stir in the olive oil, lemon zest and juice, and the prawns. Cook over a low heat for 3–4 minutes, stirring occasionally, until the prawns turn pink. Season to taste.
3 Drain the pasta and beans, reserving about 4 tablespoons of the cooking liquid. Toss with the prawns and add enough cooking liquid to make a sauce. Serve sprinkled with the fresh dill.

■ Per serving 581 kcalories, protein 25g, carbohydrate 68g, fat 25g, saturated fat 12g, fibre 4g, added sugar none, salt 0.79g

Fusilli with turkey and mushrooms

Using cartons of ready-made sauce saves time and effort. Look for them in supermarket chiller cabinets.

■ **Takes 25 minutes** ■ **Serves 6**

1 tbsp olive oil
1 onion, sliced
1 red pepper, seeded and chopped
450g/1lb turkey fillet, cut into chunks
350g/12oz fusilli
300g–350g carton wild mushroom sauce, made up to 600ml/1 pint with milk
200g/8oz sliced ham, cut into chunks
200g/8oz frozen leaf spinach
freshly grated nutmeg, to taste
100g/4oz mature Cheddar, grated

1 Heat the oil in a large pan, then cook the onion and pepper for 5 minutes. Add the turkey and cook for another 5 minutes, stirring occasionally. Cook the pasta in salted boiling water for about 8–10 minutes until just tender. Drain well.
2 Heat the grill to hot. Add the wild mushroom sauce mix to the turkey in the pan and bring to the boil, then stir in the pasta, ham and spinach.
3 Season and add nutmeg to taste. Simmer for 5 minutes until piping hot. Spoon into a shallow heatproof dish, sprinkle with the cheese and grill until brown.

■ Per serving 501 kcalories, protein 40g, carbohydrate 51g, fat 17g, saturated fat 7g, fibre 3g, added sugar none, salt 2.54g

TOP: Broccoli and spaghetti bake

BOTTOM LEFT: Prawn tagliatelle with lemon

BOTTOM RIGHT: Fusilli with turkey and mushrooms

TOP: Summer garden spaghetti

BOTTOM LEFT: Pasta with bacon and peas

BOTTOM RIGHT: Ham and courgette tagliatelle

Summer garden spaghetti

Tzatziki, a cucumber and mint dip from Greece, adds a refreshing kick to this dish.

■ **Takes 25 minutes** ■ **Serves 4 (easily halved)**

1 tbsp olive oil
200g/8oz smoked streaky bacon, chopped
350g/12oz spaghetti
250g/9oz runner beans, sliced diagonally
250g/9oz cherry tomatoes, halved
170g carton tzatziki

1 Heat the oil in a frying pan, add the bacon and fry for about 10 minutes, stirring occasionally, until crisp.
2 Meanwhile, bring a large pan of salted water to the boil, add the spaghetti, stir once and cook at a rolling boil for 6 minutes. Stir in the beans and cook for 6 minutes more until tender.
3 Drain the pasta and beans and return to the pan with the bacon and cooking juices, the tomatoes and tzatziki. Toss together well, and season with plenty of freshly ground black pepper. Serve warm.

■ Per serving 515 kcalories, protein 22g, carbohydrate 70g, fat 19g, saturated fat 7g, fibre 5g, added sugar 5g, salt 2.02g

Pasta with bacon and peas

If you can't find orecchiette (literally, 'little ears') pasta, so-called because of their curved shape, substitute another shape.

■ **Takes 20 minutes** ■ **Serves 4**

300g/10oz pasta shapes, such as orecchiette
200g/8oz frozen peas
1 tbsp olive oil
1 onion, chopped
4 rashers back bacon, cut into strips
100ml/3½fl oz crème fraîche
fresh country bread and green salad,
    to serve

1 Cook the pasta in salted boiling water for 12 minutes, adding the frozen peas for the last 3 minutes of cooking.
2 Meanwhile, heat the oil in a frying pan, then cook the onion for 2–3 minutes until starting to brown. Add the bacon and cook over a high heat, stirring, until both the bacon and onion are golden and crisp.
3 Drain the pasta and toss with the onion and bacon. Stir in the crème fraîche. Season. Serve piping hot with fresh country bread and a simple green salad.

■ Per serving 461 kcalories, protein 17g, carbohydrate 65g, fat 17g, saturated fat 7g, fibre 5g, added sugar none, salt 1.07g

Ham and courgette tagliatelle

Instead of courgettes, you could use a 200g pack of prepared stir-fry vegetables instead.

■ **Takes 25 minutes** ■ **Serves 4**

400g/14oz tagliatelle
3 tbsp olive oil
1 plump garlic clove, halved and thinly sliced
4 courgettes, very thinly sliced
175g/6oz wafer-thin ham, cut into thin strips
3 tbsp pesto

1 Cook the tagliatelle in salted boiling water according to the packet instructions.
2 Meanwhile, heat the oil in a large pan or wok. Add the garlic slices and the courgettes, and fry over a high heat for about 3 minutes until soft and lightly browned. (You may need to do this in two batches.) Add the ham and toss together until heated through.
3 Drain the pasta well, add to the courgettes with the pesto, and season to taste. Toss well and serve.

■ Per serving 555 kcalories, protein 24g, carbohydrate 77g, fat 19g, saturated fat 5g, fibre 4g, added sugar none, salt 1.31g

Pasta with asparagus and mustard

Instead of a sauce this light, summery pasta has a mustardy vinaigrette dressing.

■ Takes 25 minutes ■ Serves 4

250g/9oz spaghetti
300g/10oz unsmoked back bacon, rind removed
1 tbsp olive oil
250g/9oz asparagus, cut into 2.5cm/1in pieces
250g/9oz cherry tomatoes, halved
50g/2oz Parmesan shavings (use a potato peeler)

FOR THE DRESSING
5 tbsp olive oil
1½ tbsp white wine vinegar
2 tsp Dijon mustard

1 To make the dressing, put all the ingredients in a bowl and whisk until creamy. Season to taste, then set aside. Break the spaghetti into 7.5cm pieces and cook in salted boiling water for 10–12 minutes, until just tender.
2 Cut the bacon into strips. Heat the oil in a large frying pan and fry the bacon for 5–6 minutes. Drain all but 1 tablespoon of the fat. Add the asparagus and fry for 3–4 minutes. Add the tomatoes and cook for 2 minutes.
3 Drain the pasta and tip into a serving bowl. Mix in the bacon and asparagus mixture and the mustard dressing. Top with Parmesan shavings. Serve warm or cold with extra black pepper.

■ Per serving 610 kcalories, protein 27g, carbohydrate 50g, fat 35g, saturated fat 10g, fibre 4g, added sugar none, salt 3.5g

Stir-fried tuna rice

Tuna and bacon may seem an odd combination but they taste good together.

■ Takes 30 minutes ■ Serves 4

350g/12oz long grain rice
8 rashers rindless streaky bacon, roughly chopped
2 tbsp vegetable oil
200g/8oz frozen peas, thawed
200g can tuna, drained
2–3 tbsp soy sauce, plus extra to serve

1 Cook the rice, according to the packet instructions, then set aside to cool slightly.
2 Heat a wok until hot. Add the bacon and stir fry for 2 minutes until crispy and browned. Remove from the wok and set aside.
3 Heat the oil in the wok and stir fry the rice for 2 minutes. Add the peas and tuna and stir fry over a high heat for 2–3 minutes. Add the soy sauce and crispy bacon and cook for a further minute. Serve immediately, with extra soy sauce, if liked.

■ Per serving 552 kcalories, protein 25g, carbohydrate 81g, fat 17g, saturated fat 5g, fibre 3g, added sugar none, salt 2.98g

Linguine with watercress sauce

Salty anchovies and capers add a piquant flavour to this peppery watercress sauce.

■ Takes 20 minutes ■ Serves 4

300g/10oz linguine or spaghetti
1 garlic clove, peeled
6 anchovies in oil, drained
1 tbsp capers, drained and well rinsed
50g/2oz watercress
6 tbsp olive oil

1 Cook the pasta in a large pan of salted boiling water according to the packet instructions, until the pasta is tender.
2 Meanwhile, put the garlic, anchovies and capers in a food processor and whizz until well blended. Add the watercress and whizz again until the mixture is finely chopped. With the motor running, drizzle in the olive oil to make a soft paste.
3 Mix 4 tablespoons of the pasta cooking water into the watercress sauce, then season to taste. Drain the pasta and return to the pan. Stir in the sauce and divide among four bowls. Grind over plenty of black pepper and serve immediately.

■ Per serving 422 kcalories, protein 11g, carbohydrate 56g, fat 19g, saturated fat 3g, fibre 3g, added sugar none, salt 0.53g

TOP: Pasta with asparagus and mustard

BOTTOM LEFT: Stir-fried tuna rice

BOTTOM RIGHT: Linguine with watercress sauce

TOP: Parmesan chicken

BOTTOM LEFT: Chicken rare-
bits

BOTTOM RIGHT: Easy chicken
and spinach pie

Parmesan chicken

No crackers? Crush a good handful of cornflakes to make an equally quick and simple coating.

■ **Takes 30 minutes** ■ **Serves 4**

4 boneless skinless chicken breasts
juice of 1 small lemon
1 egg
4 cream crackers
50g/2oz Parmesan, finely grated
2 tbsp oil
4 heaped tbsp crème fraîche
4 tsp sweet chilli dipping sauce
crisp salad and new potatoes, to serve

1 Separate the chicken into breast and fillet pieces. Season all the pieces with lemon juice, salt and pepper. Beat the egg on a plate. Put the crackers in a bag and crush into crumbs, then mix with the Parmesan on another plate.
2 Dip the chicken in the egg, then the cracker mixture, pressing it on evenly. Heat the oil in a large pan and fry the chicken on each side for 4–5 minutes, until well browned and crisp.
3 Transfer the chicken to serving plates, spoon some crème fraîche on to each plate and drizzle over the chilli sauce. Serve with a crisp salad and steamed new potatoes.

■ Per serving 345 kcalories, protein 32g, carbohydrate 7g, fat 21g, saturated fat 9g, fibre trace, added sugar none, salt 0.78g

Chicken rarebits

Made from just five ingredients, but smart enough for midweek entertaining.

■ **Takes 35 minutes** ■ **Serves 4**

4 skinless boneless chicken breasts
olive oil, for greasing
140g/5oz Cheddar, coarsely grated
1 rounded tbsp wholegrain mustard
3 tbsp milk, preferably full fat
150g cherry tomatoes, on the vine
broccoli and new potatoes, to serve

1 Heat the oven to 200C/180C fan/gas 6. Slice the breasts in half horizontally so you have thinner pieces that will cook quicker. Lightly oil a shallow baking dish and arrange the chicken in it in a single layer. Mix the cheese, mustard and milk, then pile the mixture on top of each piece of chicken.
2 Throw the tomatoes, still on the vine, all round the chicken, then cook for 20–30 minutes, until the chicken is golden and the tomatoes squashy.
3 Serve with steamed broccoli and new potatoes. Suggest to everyone that they squash the tomatoes on their plates to blend into the cheesy sauce.

■ Per serving 316 kcalories, protein 44g, carbohydrate 2g, fat 15g, saturated fat 8g, fibre 1g, added sugar none, salt 1.09g

Easy chicken and spinach pie

Use ready-made sauce and pastry to save time on the preparation of this tasty pie.

■ **Takes 50 minutes** ■ **Serves 4**

2 tbsp olive oil
4 boneless skinless chicken thighs, cut into 2.5cm/1in chunks
200g/8oz button mushrooms, halved
250g/9oz frozen spinach leaves
225g jar porcini mushroom sauce
375g pack ready-rolled puff pastry
beaten egg, for glazing

1 Heat the oven to 220C/200C fan/gas 7. Heat the oil in a frying pan and fry the chicken, stirring occasionally, for 10 minutes until browned. Add the mushrooms and cook for a further 2 minutes. Stir in the spinach and the mushroom sauce and season.
2 Spoon into a 1.7 litre pie dish. Brush the rim of the dish with water and lay the sheet of pastry over the filling. Press on to the rim to seal, then trim the pastry edges.
3 Brush with beaten egg and make a small air vent in the middle of the pastry lid with the tip of a knife. Bake for 30–35 minutes until the pastry is crisp, puffed up and golden brown.

■ Per serving 603 kcalories, protein 30g, carbohydrate 41g, fat 36g, saturated fat 3g, fibre 2g, added sugar none, salt 1.36g

Chickpeas with bacon and cabbage

There are lots of interesting textures in this tasty one-pot meal. Serve it with couscous.

■ **Takes 50 minutes** ■ **Serves 4**

1 tbsp oil
1 onion, roughly chopped
100g/4oz smoked streaky bacon, roughly chopped
1 small butternut squash, about 400g/14oz, peeled, seeded and cubed
300ml/½ pint vegetable or chicken stock
1 tbsp wholegrain mustard
2 × 400g cans chickpeas, drained and rinsed
½ green cabbage, shredded
couscous, to serve

1 Heat the oil in a large pan. Add the onion and cook until golden. Tip in the bacon and cook, stirring for 5 minutes until beginning to turn crisp.
2 Stir in the squash and stock. Bring to the boil, then lower the heat and simmer for 15 minutes, stirring occasionally, until the squash is almost soft.
3 Stir in the mustard, chickpeas and cabbage. Cover and cook for a further 5 minutes until the cabbage is just cooked. Season with plenty of black pepper and serve with couscous.

■ Per serving 297 kcalories, protein 16g, carbohydrate 31g, fat 13g, saturated fat 3g, fibre 9g, added sugar none, salt 1.89g

Chilli lamb skewers

Use leg of lamb or fillet to be sure the meat is tender. Marinate the pieces the day before cooking.

■ **Takes 30 minutes** ■ **Serves 4**

700g/1lb 9oz lean boneless lamb
a small bunch mint, stalks removed
1 fresh red chilli, seeded
3 tbsp olive oil
2 small red onions
150g pot low-fat natural yogurt
leafy salad and new potatoes, to serve

1 Cut the lamb into bite-sized chunks. Chop the mint and put half in a large bowl and half in a small bowl. Finely chop the chilli and add half to each bowl.
2 Stir the olive oil into the large bowl, season, then add the lamb and turn until glistening and well coated. Finely chop half an onion and add to the small bowl with the yogurt. Season, stir well, then chill until ready to eat (it will keep for a day in the fridge). Cut the rest of the onion into wedges and separate the layers.
3 Thread the lamb on to four large skewers (if wooden, soak them in water first to prevent them burning), with onion in between. Heat the barbecue or grill and cook the skewers for 6–8 minutes, turning until evenly browned. Serve with the yogurt, a salad and potatoes.

■ Per serving 307 kcalories, protein 38g, carbohydrate 6g, fat 15g, saturated fat 7g, fibre none, added sugar none, salt 0.39g

Lamb with root veg crush

Roughly mashed root vegetables make a colourful accompaniment to roast meat, sausages or chops.

■ **Takes 40 minutes** ■ **Serves 4**

2 parsnips, peeled and cubed
1 small swede or 3 carrots, peeled and cubed
600g/1lb 5oz floury potatoes
4 lamb leg steaks (or 8 lamb chops)
olive oil, for brushing
2 tsp dried rosemary
142ml pot soured cream
2 tsp wholegrain mustard

1 Cook all the vegetables in a large pan of salted boiling water for 15–18 minutes, until tender. Heat the grill.
2 Brush the lamb with a little oil, sprinkle with rosemary and season. Grill the steaks for 4–5 minutes on each side.
3 Drain the vegetables and crush with a fork, then stir in the soured cream and mustard and season well. Serve with the lamb.

■ Per serving 541 kcalories, protein 47g, carbohydrate 41g, fat 22g, saturated fat 11g, fibre 7g, added sugar none, salt 0.46g

Lamb's liver with mixed mushrooms

Buy a pack of assorted mushrooms in the supermarket, or mix ordinary and wild mushrooms together.

■ **Takes 15 minutes** ■ **Serves 2**

300g/10oz lamb's liver, sliced
2 tbsp seasoned flour
2 tbsp oil
150g pack wild and exotic mushrooms, or an equivalent mix
2 garlic cloves, finely chopped
300ml/½ pint chicken stock
good handful of chopped fresh parsley
mashed potatoes, to serve

1 Coat the slices of liver in the seasoned flour. Heat 1 tablespoon of the oil in a frying pan. Add the liver and fry for 30 seconds on each side until just browned. Remove from the pan and set aside.
2 Pour the remaining tablespoon of oil into the pan and fry the mushrooms and garlic for 2–3 minutes. Pour in the stock and return the liver to the pan. Simmer for 1–2 minutes.
3 Stir in the parsley and season. Serve with mashed potatoes.

■ Per serving 390 kcalories, protein 35g, carbohydrate 17g, fat 21g, saturated fat 4g, fibre 1g, added sugar none, salt 1.17g

Smoked sausage with leeks

Use any boiling sausage, such as German knackwurst or Polish kielbasa. You'll find them with the deli meats.

■ **Takes 55 minutes** ■ **Serves 2**

1 tbsp oil
500g/1lb 2oz leeks, trimmed and thickly sliced
1 onion, chopped
6 tbsp dry white wine
6 tbsp chicken stock
2 large firm waxy potatoes, peeled and roughly diced
300g/10oz uncooked smoked boiling sausage
3–4 tbsp crème fraîche
chopped fresh parsley, to garnish

1 Heat the oil in a large pan, add the leeks and onion, and cook for 3–4 minutes until just softened. Season, pour in the wine and stock, cover and simmer for 10 minutes.
2 Tip in the diced potatoes, cover the pan again and simmer for 10 minutes or until the potatoes are just tender.
3 Prick the sausage and put it on top of the vegetables. Lower the heat, cover the pan and cook gently for 20 minutes. Lift out the sausage and cut into thick diagonal slices. Stir the crème fraîche into the vegetables and spoon on to plates. Top with the sausage slices and serve garnished with parsley.

■ Per serving 727 kcalories, protein 29g, carbohydrate 53g, fat 43g, saturated fat 15g, fibre 9g, added sugar none, salt 2.91g

Greek lamb with potatoes

A one-pot meal – all you need to serve with it is a green vegetable, such as buttered cabbage.

■ **Takes 1¼ hours** ■ **Serves 4**

4 lamb leg steaks or 8 chump chops, about 750g/1lb 10oz total
2 tsp dried oregano
1kg/2lb 4oz floury potatoes, such as King Edward, sliced
2 onions, sliced
3 tbsp olive oil
4 fat garlic cloves
300ml/½ pint lamb or chicken stock or water

1 Heat the oven to 190C/170C fan/gas 5. Wipe the steaks or chops and sprinkle with salt, pepper and half the oregano.
2 Tip the potatoes and onions into a roasting tin and drizzle over the olive oil and the rest of the oregano. Season. Mix until the potatoes and onions are well coated. Tuck the unpeeled garlic cloves among the potatoes.
3 Roast the potatoes for 20 minutes until they are just starting to soften, then put the chops on top. Pour in the lamb or chicken stock or water and return to the oven for 30–35 minutes, until the lamb is tender and the potatoes tinged brown. Make sure everyone gets a garlic clove to squeeze out and mix with the other ingredients.

■ Per serving 545 kcalories, protein 44g, carbohydrate 50g, fat 20g, saturated fat 9g, fibre 4g, added sugar none, salt 0.61g

Lemon and oregano pork

Liven up a simple pork escalope by dipping it in lemon juice then coating with a breadcrumb and herb mixture.

■ **Takes 20 minutes** ■ **Serves 4**

finely grated zest and juice of 1 lemon
100g/4oz ready-made natural coloured
　breadcrumbs
2 tsp dried oregano
4 pork escalopes
2 tbsp sunflower oil
lemon mayonnaise, potatoes and green
　beans, to serve

1 On a plate, mix together the lemon zest, breadcrumbs and oregano. Pour the lemon juice on to another plate. Dip each pork escalope first in the lemon juice and then into the breadcrumb mixture until well coated.
2 Heat the oil in a large frying pan over a high heat and fry the pork for 3–4 minutes on each side, until the crumbs are crisp and the pork is cooked through.
3 Serve each escalope with a spoonful of lemon mayonnaise, some potatoes and green beans.

■ Per serving 291 kcalories, protein 29g, carbohydrate 20g, fat 11g, saturated fat 2g, fibre 1g, added sugar none, salt 0.68g

Speedy pork pan-fry

Make a more sophisticated sauce for the pork by replacing half the stock with red or white wine.

■ **Takes 20 minutes** ■ **Serves 4**

500g/1lb 2oz pork tenderloin fillet
1 tbsp plain flour
2 tsp dried rosemary
3 tbsp olive oil
250g/9oz chestnut mushrooms, sliced
1 fat garlic clove, finely chopped
300ml/½ pint vegetable stock
rice or mashed potatoes, and vegetables,
　to serve

1 Cut the pork diagonally into finger-thick slices. Tip the flour and rosemary into a plastic bag, season and add the pork. Toss until the meat is well coated.
2 Heat 2 tablespoons of the oil in a large frying pan. Add the pork and fry for about 3–4 minutes, turning once, until browned on both sides. Remove from the pan.
3 Heat the remaining oil in the pan and fry the mushrooms until they soften, about 2 minutes. Add the garlic and return the pork to the pan with any flour left in the bag. Gradually stir in the stock and bring to the boil. Simmer for 5 minutes or until the pork is cooked. Serve with rice or mashed potatoes and vegetables.

■ Per serving 288 kcalories, protein 30g, carbohydrate 5g, fat 17g, saturated fat 4g, fibre 1g, added sugar none, salt 0.42g

Creamy pork escalopes

If you can't get these thin meat slices, buy pork steaks. Put between cling film and flatten by bashing with a rolling pin.

■ **Takes 30 minutes** ■ **Serves 4 (easily halved)**

4 tsp plain flour
1 tsp dried sage
4 pork escalopes
2 tbsp oil
knob of butter
1 small onion, finely chopped
200g/8oz chestnut mushrooms, sliced
3 tbsp sherry
200ml pot crème fraîche
noodles, to serve

1 Mix the flour with the sage, season, and use to coat the escalopes. Heat 1 tablespoon of the oil and the butter in a frying pan, and fry the pork quickly on each side until nicely browned. Remove from the pan and keep warm.
2 Heat the remaining oil and fry the onion for 1 minute. Add the mushrooms and fry for 2–3 minutes. Add the sherry and let it bubble, scraping up any bits with a wooden spoon.
3 Stir in the crème fraîche. Add the pork and heat through gently for 5 minutes. Serve with noodles.

■ Per serving 437 kcalories, protein 28g, carbohydrate 9g, fat 31g, saturated fat 13g, fibre 1g, added sugar none, salt 0.34g

TOP: Lemon and oregano pork

BOTTOM LEFT: Speedy pork pan-fry

BOTTOM RIGHT: Creamy pork escalopes

TOP: Meatball kebabs

BOTTOM LEFT: Paprika pork

BOTTOM RIGHT: Thai red pork curry

Meatball kebabs

Use good-quality ready-made meatballs for these quick and colourful kebabs.

■ **Takes 25 minutes** ■ **Serves 4**

350g pack Swedish meatballs
2 courgettes, cut into chunks
2 peppers (1 red and 1 yellow), seeded and cut into chunks
6 tbsp ready-made honey and mustard dressing
green salad, to serve

1 Soak eight wooden kebab sticks in water for 15–20 minutes. Put a griddle pan on the hob over a medium heat. While it's heating up, thread the meatballs onto the kebab sticks with the courgette and pepper chunks.
2 Brush them with some of the honey and mustard dressing. Put the skewers on the hot griddle and cook for 4–5 minutes on each side – you may need to do this in batches. Brush them occasionally with the remaining dressing.
3 Remove the skewers from the pan and serve with a dressed green salad.

■ Per serving 343 kcalories, protein 16g, carbohydrate 12g, fat 26g, saturated fat 8g, fibre 4g, added sugar none, salt 1.46g

Paprika pork

A simple pan-fry enriched with caramelised onions and crème fraîche.

■ **Takes 55 minutes** ■ **Serves 4**

2 tbsp olive oil
3 onions, thinly sliced
600g/1lb 5oz pork fillet
2 tbsp paprika
300ml/½ pint chicken or vegetable stock
100ml/3½fl oz crème fraîche (about ½ carton)
freshly chopped parsley, to garnish
rice and a green vegetable, to serve

1 Heat 2 tablespoons oil in a pan, add the onions and fry for 10–15 minutes, stirring occasionally, until softened and lightly coloured.
2 Cut the pork into bite-sized pieces, then add to the pan and stir over a fairly high heat to seal and brown all over. Stir in the paprika, cook briefly, then add the stock and bring to the boil.
3 Cover and cook for 30–35 minutes, until the pork is tender. Stir in the crème fraîche and simmer for a further 2 minutes. Sprinkle the parsley over the pork, before serving with rice and a green vegetable.

■ Per serving 357 kcalories, protein 36.5g, carbohydrate 11.3g, fat 18.7g, saturated fat 7.6g, fibre 1.3g, added sugar none, salt 0.52g

Thai red pork curry

Thai red curry paste is a concentrated mixture of herbs and spices, flavoured with dried red chillies.

■ **Takes 35 minutes** ■ **Serves 4**

250g/9oz green beans, trimmed
1 tbsp vegetable oil
4 tsp Thai red curry paste
1 tbsp finely chopped ginger
500g/1lb 2oz pork fillet, thinly sliced
300ml/½ pint vegetable stock
2 tbsp fish sauce (nam pla)
1 tsp light muscovado sugar
400ml can coconut milk
400g can palm hearts, drained, rinsed and sliced
grated zest and juice of 1 large lime
a handful each of basil and coriander leaves
rice noodles, to serve

1 Cook the beans in salted boiling water for 5 minutes, then drain and refresh under cold running water. Set aside.
2 Heat the oil in a pan, add the curry paste and ginger, and fry gently until the oil separates out. Tip in the pork and stock, bring to the boil, then simmer for 5 minutes.
3 Add the fish sauce, sugar, coconut milk, palm hearts, lime zest and juice, and simmer for a further 5 minutes, adding the beans halfway through. Throw in the basil and coriander, and serve with rice noodles.

■ Per serving 396 kcalories, protein 32g, carbohydrate 10g, fat 26g, saturated fat 16g, fibre 2g, added sugar 1g, salt 2.29g

Tartiflette

A tasty combination of potatoes, bacon and melted cheese, much enjoyed by French skiers.

■ **Takes 45 minutes** ■ **Serves 4**

750g/1lb 10oz potatoes, peeled
1 onion, finely chopped
25g/1oz butter
drizzle of olive oil
6 rashers smoked back bacon
250g/9oz reblochon or Pont l'Evêque
142ml pot single cream
salad, to serve

1 Heat the oven to 220C/200C fan/gas 7. Thickly slice the potatoes, then boil in salted water for 8–10 minutes, until just tender. Drain.
2 Fry the onion in the butter and olive oil for 5 minutes. Snip the bacon into pieces with scissors and add to the pan. Cook for a further 5 minutes, until the onion and bacon are lightly coloured.
3 Chop the cheese into chunks, rind and all. Layer half the potatoes in a 1.5 litre pint buttered ovenproof dish and scatter over half the onion, bacon and cheese. Lightly season. Repeat the layers, pour the cream evenly over the top and bake for 10–12 minutes until golden. Leave it to rest for 5 minutes and then serve with a salad.

■ Per serving 500 kcalories, protein 23g, carbohydrate 30g, fat 32g, saturated fat 19g, fibre 2g, added sugar none, salt 2g

Ham and cheese pancakes

You can buy ready-made pancakes from most supermarkets – you'll find them in the bread section.

■ **Takes 35 minutes** ■ **Serves 4**

250g/9oz broccoli, cut into small florets
6 smoked ham slices
6 ready-made pancakes
250g whole Camembert, chilled
25g/1oz Cheddar, grated
4 tomatoes, roughly chopped
salad, to serve

1 Heat the oven to 200C/180C fan/gas 6. Cook the broccoli in boiling water for 3 minutes until just tender. Drain and set aside.
2 Lay a slice of ham over each pancake. Top with the broccoli. Cut the Camembert into thin slices and lay over the broccoli. Season with black pepper. Roll each pancake up like a cigar and put in a single layer in a shallow ovenproof dish.
3 Sprinkle the grated Cheddar over the pancakes, then spoon over the chopped tomatoes. Season and bake for 20 minutes until the cheese has melted. Serve with a salad.

■ Per serving 379 kcalories, protein 28g, carbohydrate 11g, fat 25g, saturated fat 14g, fibre 3g, added sugar none, salt 2.3g

Ham-stuffed marrow

You could use the same stuffing for other squash too. Cook in the microwave to save time.

■ **Takes 25 minutes** ■ **Serves 4**

1 marrow, about 1.5kg/3lb 5oz
25g/1oz butter, cut into cubes
6 tbsp ready-made tomato pasta sauce
about 10 slices wafer-thin ham
4 eggs
85g/3oz Double Gloucester or Cheddar, grated

1 Heat the oven to 190C/170C fan/gas 5. Peel and halve the marrow and scoop out the seeds. Put in a shallow microwave-proof dish, dot with butter and season. Cover with cling film, pierce several times and cook on High for 7 minutes, until tender.
2 Spoon the tomato sauce into each marrow half, then arrange the ham on top. Break 2 eggs into each half and sprinkle with the cheese.
3 Bake for 12–15 minutes, until the eggs are softly set and the cheese has melted and turned golden.

■ Per serving 281 kcalories, protein 20g, carbohydrate 6g, fat 20g, saturated fat 10g, fibre 1g, added sugar none, salt 2g

TOP: Tartiflette

BOTTOM LEFT: Ham and cheese pancakes

BOTTOM RIGHT: Ham-stuffed marrow

TOP: Trout with warm potato salad

BOTTOM LEFT: Prawn and spring onion omelette

BOTTOM RIGHT: Smoked salmon muffins

Trout with warm potato salad

Don't miss out on trout because you don't like bones. Fillets are easy to eat with salad.

■ Takes 20 minutes ■ Serves 4

600g/1lb 5oz new potatoes
200g/8oz broccoli, cut into small florets
4 trout fillets about 100g/4oz each
3 tbsp olive oil, plus extra for brushing
1 tbsp white wine vinegar
12 cherry tomatoes, halved
2 tbsp toasted flaked almonds

1 Wash the potatoes and cut each in half or quarters if large. Cook in salted boiling water for 12 minutes, adding the broccoli for the last 3 minutes of cooking time.
2 Heat the grill to high. Put the trout fillets on the grill pan. Brush each with a little oil and season. Grill for 3–4 minutes.
3 Drain the potatoes and broccoli well. Tip into a bowl. Whisk together the oil and the vinegar. Add to the hot vegetables along with the tomatoes, almonds and a little seasoning. Toss well and serve with the grilled trout.

■ Per serving 378 kcalories, protein 26g, carbohydrate 26g, fat 19g, saturated fat 2g, fibre 4g, added sugar none, salt 0.43g

Prawn and spring onion omelette

Prawns and eggs are a surprisingly successful combination. Try this for a late supper for two.

■ Takes 10 minutes ■ Serves 2 (easily doubled)

1 tbsp olive oil
4 eggs
100g/4oz peeled cooked prawns
4 spring onions, trimmed and thinly sliced
tomato salad and crusty bread, to serve

1 Heat the grill. Heat the oil in a frying pan. Lightly beat the eggs and season. Pour into the frying pan and cook over a medium heat for 30 seconds until the egg mixture starts to set.
2 Using a fork, gently draw some of the egg mixture from the edge into the middle. Sprinkle over the prawns and spring onions, and cook for 2 minutes.
3 Transfer the pan to the grill and cook for a further 1–2 minutes until golden brown. Fold the omelette over. Cut in half and serve with a tomato salad and crusty bread.

■ Per serving 250 kcalories, protein 24g, carbohydrate none, fat 17g, saturated fat 4g, fibre none, added sugar none, salt 1.36g

Smoked salmon muffins

The perfect late-night snack for one. Or multiply the recipe for a weekend family brunch.

■ Takes 10 minutes ■ Serves 1

1 English muffin
knob of unsalted butter, plus extra for spreading
2 eggs
1 tbsp milk
25g/1oz smoked salmon trimmings
1 tsp freshly snipped chives

1 Heat the grill to hot. Split and toast the muffin until golden. Spread with butter and keep warm. Meanwhile, lightly beat the eggs and milk together in a bowl and season with freshly ground black pepper.
2 Melt the butter in a pan and when foaming pour in the eggs. Cook over a low heat, pulling the cooked egg from the edges of the pan into the centre until the egg begins to set.
3 Stir in the smoked salmon and chives and cook for a further 1–2 minutes. Pile on top of the toasted, buttered muffin halves and serve.

■ Per serving 502 kcalories, protein 26g, carbohydrate 34g, fat 30g, saturated fat 13g, fibre 1g, added sugar none, salt 2.39g

Lemon cod with chickpeas

Chickpeas, cooked Indian-style with spinach and chilli, accompany simply grilled fish.

■ **Takes 20 minutes** ■ **Serves 4**

zest and juice of 1 lemon
3 tbsp light olive oil, plus extra to grease and drizzle
4 × 140g/5oz cod fillets, skinned
1 onion, sliced into thin wedges
250g/9oz fresh spinach, stems trimmed
½ –1 tsp dried chilli flakes
420g can chickpeas, rinsed and drained

1 Heat the grill. Mix the lemon zest with 1 tablespoon of oil. Line a roasting tin with foil, oil lightly and arrange the fillets on it. Brush with the lemon oil. Season and grill for 8–10 minutes until cooked (no need to turn).
2 Meanwhile, heat the rest of the oil and fry the onion until golden. Add the spinach and cook until wilted. Stir in the chilli flakes. Tip in the chickpeas and 1 tablespoon of the lemon juice, and heat through. Season to taste.
3 Spoon the chickpea mixture on to hot plates and serve the fish on top. Drizzle with a little extra oil and the remaining lemon juice.

■ Per serving 306 kcalories, protein 32g, carbohydrate 14g, fat 13g, saturated fat 2g, fibre 4g, added sugar none, salt 1.03g

Plaice with bacon topping

The fish will continue cooking once it's out of the oven, so if you intend to keep it waiting, slightly undercook it.

■ **Takes 30 minutes** ■ **Serves 4**

2 tbsp olive oil
4 rashers streaky bacon, chopped
100g/4oz fresh white breadcrumbs
grated zest of 1 lemon
2 tbsp chopped fresh parsley
4 plaice fillets, about 200g/8oz each
new potatoes and green beans, to serve

1 Heat the oven to 230C/210C fan/gas 8. Heat the oil in a frying pan and fry the bacon until crisp. Remove from the heat and stir in the breadcrumbs, lemon zest and parsley. Season with pepper.
2 Line a baking sheet with buttered foil and lay the plaice fillets on top. Sprinkle the crispy-bacon topping over the plaice and press down gently.
3 Bake for 7 minutes or until the plaice is cooked and the topping is golden. Serve with new potatoes and green beans.

■ Per serving 305 kcalories, protein 30g, carbohydrate 19g, fat 13g, saturated fat 3g, fibre 1g, added sugar none, salt 1.55g

Gently spiced prawn curry

Use raw king prawns to make this simple but extra-special supper.

■ **Takes 30 minutes** ■ **Serves 2**

10 raw king prawns, shells on
4 tsp vegetable oil
1 tsp mustard seeds
1 small onion, finely chopped
1 tbsp finely chopped ginger
1 plump garlic clove, finely chopped
¼ tsp ground turmeric
¼ tsp hot chilli powder
½ tsp ground coriander
2 fresh bay leaves
1 small green chilli, seeded and thinly sliced
200ml carton coconut cream
1 lime, halved
basmati rice, to serve

1 Peel the prawns and set aside. Heat the oil in a medium frying pan. Fry the mustard seeds until they crackle and pop. Add the onion. Fry, stirring, until golden. Add the ginger and garlic. Stir-fry for 1 minute.
2 Add the turmeric, chilli powder and coriander, and stir fry for 30 seconds. Add the bay leaves and chilli. Stir over a medium heat for 1 minute. Pour in 150ml/¼ pint water and bubble for 1 minute.
3 Add the prawns and spoon over the sauce. Lower the heat and simmer for 3–4 minutes, until the prawns are cooked. Pour in the coconut cream, warm through and squeeze in the juice of half the lime. Season with salt. Serve with basmati rice and the other half of the lime as wedges to squeeze over.

■ Per serving 519 kcalories, protein 23g, carbohydrate 12g, fat 42g, saturated fat 31g, fibre 1g, added sugar none, salt 3.08g

TOP: Lemon cod with chick-peas

BOTTOM LEFT: Plaice with bacon topping

BOTTOM RIGHT: Gently spiced prawn curry

TOP: Honey and soy salmon

BOTTOM LEFT: Salmon water-cress puffs

BOTTOM RIGHT: Salmon and salad stir fry

Honey and soy salmon

A simple, savoury finish for plain salmon fillets, cooked in just one pan.

■ **Takes 20 minutes** ■ **Serves 4**

1 tbsp wholegrain mustard
2 tsp clear honey
1 tbsp soy sauce
1 tsp olive oil
4 boneless skinless salmon fillets, about 140g/5oz each
100ml/3½fl oz vegetable stock
1 bunch spring onions, halved lengthways, then cut into strips
boiled rice, to serve

1 Mix together the mustard, honey and soy sauce in a small bowl. Heat the oil in a frying pan. Add the salmon fillets and fry for 5 minutes, turning halfway through, until almost cooked.
2 Pour the soy mixture over the salmon and bring just to the boil. Add the stock and mix lightly with the pan juices.
3 Sprinkle over the spring onion strips and let the liquid bubble for 1–2 minutes, until the onions are heated through. Serve with boiled rice.

■ Per serving 281 kcalories, protein 29g, carbohydrate 4g, fat 17g, saturated fat 3g, fibre 1g, added sugar 2g, salt 1.08g

Salmon watercress puffs

As a variation, instead of the garlic and herb soft cheese, try using the black-pepper variety.

■ **Takes 30 minutes** ■ **Serves 4**

75g bag watercress
375g pack ready-rolled puff pastry, thawed
4 skinless salmon fillets, about 140g/5oz each
grated zest of 1 lemon
150g pack soft cheese with garlic and herbs
milk or beaten egg, for brushing
new potatoes, to serve

1 Heat the oven to 200C/180C fan/gas 6. Put half the watercress in a pan with a tablespoon of water and cook for a few minutes until wilted. Drain and chop.
2 Roll out the pastry to a 38x30cm rectangle. Cut in quarters to make four smaller rectangles. Put a salmon fillet on one half of each rectangle. Scatter over a little lemon zest and season. Divide the cheese and cooked watercress among the fillets. Damp the pastry edges with a little milk or egg, fold over the pastry and seal to enclose the filling.
3 Put the pastry parcels on a baking sheet and brush with the rest of the milk or egg. Bake for 20 minutes until the pastry is puffed and golden. Serve with the remaining watercress and new potatoes.

■ Per serving 675 kcalories, protein 38g, carbohydrate 36g, fat 43g, saturated fat 3g, fibre trace, added sugar none, salt 1.21g

Salmon and salad stir fry

Choose a salad that contains radicchio and a mixture of white and red cabbage to give this dish a lovely crunch.

■ **Takes 25 minutes** ■ **Serves 4**

1 tbsp oil
5cm/2in ginger, grated
450g/1lb salmon fillet, skinned and cut into 2.5cm/1in cubes
1 bunch spring onions, cut into 4cm/1½in lengths
150ml/¼ pint vegetable stock
200g bag mixed salad leaves
2 tbsp light soy sauce
steamed or boiled rice, to serve

1 Heat the oil in a frying pan, add the ginger and cook for 30 seconds, stirring. Season the salmon, add to the pan and cook for 5 minutes, turning once until just cooked through and beginning to brown.
2 Remove the salmon from the pan and keep warm. Add the spring onions and stir fry for 3–4 minutes until just soft.
3 Pour over the stock and bring to the boil. Tip in the salad and cook for 1 minute to wilt. Return the salmon to the pan, tip in the soy sauce and serve hot from the pan with rice.

■ Per serving 248 kcalories, protein 24g, carbohydrate 3g, fat 16g, saturated fat 3g, fibre 1g, added sugar none, salt 0.26g

Herby grilled plaice

If you prefer to use cod fillets, add 3–4 minutes to the cooking time, depending on the thickness of the fillets.

■ **Takes 25 minutes** ■ **Serves 2 (easily doubled)**

2 tbsp olive oil, plus extra
1 small shallot, finely chopped
finely grated zest of 1 lemon, plus 2 tsp juice
2 tsp chopped fresh dill
2 tsp chopped fresh parsley
2 plaice fillets
steamed new potatoes and peas, to serve

1 Heat the grill. Put the oil and the shallot in a small pan and cook for 2–3 minutes, until the shallot has softened slightly. Stir in the lemon zest and juice and the chopped herbs, and season.
2 Season the plaice fillets, then lay them skin-side down on a grill pan lined with a little oiled foil. Spoon over the shallot and herby oil and grill the fish for 5 minutes (there's no need to turn them).
3 Slide the fish on to warm serving plates and pour over the pan juices. Serve with steamed new potatoes and peas.

■ Per serving 230 kcalories, protein 27g, carbohydrate 1g, fat 13g, saturated fat 2g, fibre trace, added sugar none, salt 0.5g

Salmon with tarragon cream

Whipping cream is rich enough to heat without separating, but has less fat than double cream (35% instead of 42%), making it a slightly lighter option.

■ **Takes 25 minutes** ■ **Serves 2 (easily doubled)**

2 salmon fillets
1 tbsp vegetable oil
1 finely chopped shallot or ½ small onion
2 tbsp chopped fresh tarragon
6 tbsp whipping cream
2 tbsp chopped fresh parsley
lemon wedges, to garnish
new potatoes and green beans,
    to serve

1 Heat the oven to 180C/160C fan/gas 4. Season the salmon steaks on both sides. Heat one tablespoon of oil in a frying pan (preferably non-stick) until fairly hot. Add the salmon, flesh-side down, and fry quickly for about 3 minutes until lightly browned. Turn over and fry the skin side for 2 minutes.
2 Transfer to a shallow ovenproof dish and sprinkle over the shallot or onion and the tarragon. Spoon over the cream and season.
3 Cook in the oven for 12–15 minutes until the salmon is cooked. Sprinkle with chopped parsley, transfer to warm plates and garnish with lemon wedges. Serve with new potatoes and green beans.

■ Per serving 448 kcalories, protein 32g, carbohydrate 3g, fat 34g, saturated fat 14g, fibre 1g, added sugar none, salt 0.23g

Seafood pancakes

This is a breeze to make – ready-made pancakes and a sauce from a carton of soup is simplicity itself.

■ **Takes 40 minutes** ■ **Serves 6**

25g/1oz butter
1 onion, chopped
2 celery sticks, chopped
1 tbsp plain flour
500g carton fresh watercress soup
142ml pot double cream
700g/1lb 9oz mixed fresh fish, such as cod
    fillet and salmon, cut into chunks, and
    seafood such as prawns or mussels
2 packs (12) ready-made pancakes
50g/2oz mature Cheddar, grated

1 Heat the oven to 200C/180C fan/gas 6 from cold. Heat the butter in a pan and fry the onion and celery for 5 minutes until softened. Stir in the flour and cook for 1 minute more. Add half the soup and half the cream. Bring to the boil.
2 Add the fish and simmer for 5 minutes, stirring gently, until the fish is just cooked. Season with black pepper. Spoon the mixture into the centre of the pancakes and fold into square parcels. Arrange in a shallow ovenproof dish.
3 Heat the remaining soup and cream, spoon over the pancakes and sprinkle with the cheese. Bake for 20–25 minutes until the cheese is golden.

■ Per serving 571 kcalories, protein 28g, carbohydrate 28g, fat 39g, saturated fat 20g, fibre 2g, added sugar none, salt 1.99g

TOP: Herby grilled plaice

BOTTOM LEFT: Salmon with tarragon cream

BOTTOM RIGHT: Seafood pancakes

TOP: Chocolate cream pots

BOTTOM LEFT: Black forest trifle

BOTTOM RIGHT: Summer fruits ice yogurt

Chocolate cream pots

Use a potato peeler to make shavings from a chocolate bar. Or use a chocolate flake instead.

■ **Takes 20 minutes** ■ **Serves 4**

140g/5oz dark chocolate
142ml pot whipping cream
5 tbsp Irish cream liqueur
250g tub mascarpone
chocolate shavings, to decorate (optional)

1 Break the chocolate into a bowl and microwave on High for about 2 minutes or until melted. Alternatively, melt in a bowl set over simmering water, making sure the bottom of the bowl doesn't touch the water. Stir and set aside to cool.
2 Whisk the cream to soft peaks and whisk in the Irish cream liqueur. Beat the mascarpone until smooth, then beat in the Irish cream liqueur mixture. Pour in the cooled chocolate and stir lightly together to make a swirly pattern.
3 Spoon the mixture into 150ml pots or ramekins. Cover generously with chocolate shavings, if liked, and serve.

■ Per serving 703 kcalories, protein 5g, carbohydrate 37g, fat 59g, saturated fat 34g, fibre 1g, added sugar 32g, salt 0.24g

Black forest trifle

An easily assembled dessert. Make it boozy by adding a little kirsch or brandy to the cherry syrup.

■ **Takes 20 minutes, plus chilling** ■ **Serves 4 generously**

200g ready-made Madeira cake
425g can pitted black cherries in syrup
1 chocolate flake
100g pack dark chocolate drops
400g tub fresh custard
200ml pot crème fraîche

1 Cut the cake into thick slices and use to line the base of a 2.5 litre serving bowl. Cut three cherries in half and reserve, and spoon the rest over the cake along with the syrup. Crumble half the flake over the cherries and scatter over half the chocolate drops.
2 Heat the remaining chocolate drops in a microwave-proof bowl on Medium for 2 minutes, stirring halfway through, until melted. Cool for 5 minutes, then in a small bowl, whisk into the custard gradually, until you have a smooth chocolate custard. Pour over the cherries.
3 Spoon the crème fraîche over the custard. Sprinkle with the reserved cherries and crumble over the remaining flake. Chill until ready to serve.

■ Per serving 478 kcalories, protein 7g, carbohydrate 59g, fat 25g, saturated fat 14g, fibre 1g, added sugar 16g, salt 0.57g

Summer fruits ice yogurt

An instant iced dessert, guaranteed to make a refreshing finale to a meal.

■ **Takes 10 minutes** ■ **Serves 4**

500g bag frozen mixed summer fruits
2 × 200g pot Greek yogurt
100ml/3½fl oz (about 7 tbsp) fresh orange juice
1 tbsp icing sugar
biscuits, shortbread or almond thins, to serve (optional)

1 Put the frozen fruits, yogurt, orange juice and icing sugar in a food processor. Whizz until blended.
2 Scrape the mixture from the sides of the processor and whizz again. Repeat until the mixture looks like frozen yogurt.
3 Spoon into chunky glasses and serve immediately, with biscuits, if liked.

■ Per serving 184 kcalories, protein 8g, carbohydrate 18g, fat 9g, saturated fat 6g, fibre 3g, added sugar 7g, salt 0.2g

Fried rum bananas

Keep the heat quite high during the cooking so the sugar melts to produce a sticky sauce.

■ **Takes 10 minutes** ■ **Serves 4**

knob of butter
4 bananas, sliced diagonally into 4 pieces
4 tbsp rum or brandy
4 tbsp double cream or crème fraîche
2 tbsp light muscovado sugar

1 Melt the butter in a large frying pan. When the butter is foaming, fry the bananas for 2 minutes, then turn them and pour in the rum or brandy. Fry for 1–2 minutes more until browned.
2 Stir the cream or crème fraîche and sugar into the pan, and warm through for 1 minute.
3 Divide the bananas among four plates and spoon over the sauce. Serve immediately.

■ Per serving 237 kcalories, protein 2g, carbohydrate 32g, fat 9g, saturated fat 5g, fibre 1g, added sugar 8g, salt 0.11g

Roasted stuffed nectarines

Try nectarines (or peaches) served warm for a change. You'll love this combination of fruit and soft cheese.

■ **Takes 25 minutes** ■ **Serves 4**

4 nectarines
8 ginger nut biscuits
25g/1oz butter
2 tsp clear honey
finely grated zest and juice of 1 orange
200g/8oz soft cheese
2 tbsp caster sugar

1 Heat the oven to 180C/160C fan/gas 4. Halve the nectarines, and remove and discard the stones. Put the nectarines flesh-side up in a shallow ovenproof dish.
2 Put the biscuits in a plastic bag and roughly crush with a rolling pin. Melt the butter in a small pan over a low heat. Stir the crushed biscuits into the melted butter along with the honey. Spoon a little of the mixture on top of each nectarine.
3 Pour the orange juice over the nectarines and bake for 20 minutes. Meanwhile, put the soft cheese in a bowl, and beat in the sugar and orange zest. Serve with the warm nectarines and juices.

■ Per serving 416 kcalories, protein 8g, carbohydrate 43g, fat 25g, saturated fat 4g, fibre 3g, added sugar 14g, salt 1g

Apricot cookies 'n' cream

A really quick dessert combining no-cook ingredients. Try it with other fruits too.

■ **Takes 10 minutes** ■ **Serves 4**

411g can apricots in natural juice
284ml pot extra-thick double cream
200g pot Greek yogurt
10 chocolate biscuits, such as chocolate-covered oat biscuits or chocolate digestives
1 tsp ground cinnamon
2 tbsp demerara sugar

1 Drain the apricots, reserving half of the juice. Roughly chop the apricots and divide among four glasses. Spoon over the reserved juice.
2 In a bowl, mix together the cream and the yogurt. Roughly chop the biscuits and stir into the cream mixture, then spoon over the apricots.
3 Mix together the cinnamon and the sugar. Sprinkle over the cream mixture and serve straight away.

■ Per serving 649 kcalories, protein 8g, carbohydrate 47g, fat 49g, saturated fat 29g, fibre 2g, added sugar 19g, salt 0.66g

TOP: Fried rum bananas

BOTTOM LEFT: Roasted stuffed nectarines

BOTTOM RIGHT: Apricot cookies 'n' cream

TOP: Raspberry syllabub
Eton mess

BOTTOM LEFT: Baked Jamaica

BOTTOM RIGHT: Oaty red fruit
crumble

Raspberry syllabub Eton mess

If using an electric hand whisk, don't over whip the cream or it will be too stiff to mix easily with the meringue and fruit.

■ **Takes 10 minutes** ■ **Serves 4**

3 ready-made meringue nests
350g/12oz fresh raspberries
4 tbsp dry white wine
85g/3oz caster sugar
finely grated zest and juice of 1 lemon
284ml pot double cream
icing sugar, for dusting

1 Break the meringues into pieces in a bowl. Add 250g/9oz of the raspberries.
2 In a large bowl, stir together the wine, sugar, lemon zest and juice, until the sugar has dissolved. Using a wire whisk, gradually whisk in the cream, until it just holds its shape.
3 Spoon the syllabub over the meringue and raspberries, and gently stir together. Do not overmix or the cream will turn pink. Spoon into a serving bowl, scatter with the remaining raspberries and chill. Dust with icing sugar just before serving.

■ Per serving 502 kcalories, protein 3g, carbohydrate 46g, fat 34g, saturated fat 21g, fibre 2g, added sugar 39g, salt 0.12g

Baked Jamaica

Based on the Baked Alaska idea – baked ice cream and meringue – but using a moist ginger cake.

■ **Takes 20 minutes** ■ **Serves 4**

227g can pineapple chunks in natural juice
1 ready-made Jamaica ginger cake, sliced horizontally
3 egg whites
175g/6oz light muscovado sugar
500ml tub vanilla ice cream

1 Heat the oven to 220C/200C fan/gas 7. Drain the pineapple, reserving 3 tablespoons of juice. Put the ginger cake slices side by side in a rectangular shallow ovenproof dish. Drizzle over the pineapple juice and pineapple chunks.
2 Whisk the egg whites until stiff. Whisk in the sugar, a tablespoon at a time, whisking well between each addition until the meringue is thick and glossy.
3 Slice the ice cream and cover the fruit and sponge with it, pressing down to level. Completely cover with the meringue, swirling the top with a fork. Bake for 5 minutes until golden. Serve at once.

■ Per serving 484 kcalories, protein 9g, carbohydrate 85g, fat 14g, saturated fat 7g, fibre 1g, added sugar 59g, salt 0.53g

Oaty red fruit crumble

Try this easy-mix crumble topping with other fruits too. A microwave speeds cooking but is not essential.

■ **Takes 40 minutes** ■ **Serves 4**

4 dessert apples, peeled, cored and chopped
300g can summer fruits in syrup
100g/4oz butter
50g/2oz light muscovado sugar
140g/5oz porridge oats
ready-made custard, ice cream or cream, to serve

1 Heat the oven to 190C/170C fan/gas 5. Mix together the apples, summer fruits and their syrup in a 850ml microwave-proof pie dish. Microwave on High for 5–8 minutes (depending on the wattage), stirring halfway through, until the apples are cooked. Alternatively, cook in a pan on the hob, stirring for 12–15 minutes.
2 Melt the butter in a bowl on Medium in the microwave for 1–2 minutes (or in a small pan), until just melted. Stir in the sugar and oats. Spoon over the fruit.
3 Bake for 20 minutes until the topping is golden and the filling is just bubbling. Serve with custard, ice cream or cream.

■ Per serving 478 kcalories, protein 5g, carbohydrate 65g, fat 24g, saturated fat 14g, fibre 5g, added sugar 19g, salt 0.56g

One-pot recipes

Mexican soup with chicken

The fun of this fresh spicy soup is that everyone can add whatever they like to their own bowl. Don't hold back, as it's low in fat, too.

■ **Takes 30 minutes** ■ **Serves 4**

2 tbsp olive oil
1 onion, chopped
4 garlic cloves, crushed
a pinch of dried chilli flakes
½ tsp ground cumin
400g can plum tomatoes
1.5 litres/2¾ pints chicken stock
2 skinless chicken breasts, sliced (or use leftover cooked chicken)
juice of 2 limes

FOR THE TOPPINGS
tortilla chips, chopped avocado, lime wedges, red onion and coriander leaves

1 Heat the oil in a large pan. Add the onion and garlic, soften for 5 minutes, then stir in the chilli, cumin, tomatoes and chicken stock. Blitz in a food processor in batches, or use a hand blender to purée until smooth.
2 Return to the pan, then bring to the boil. If using raw chicken, add then reduce the heat and simmer for 10 minutes until cooked through. If using cooked, simply warm through. Stir in the lime juice and some seasoning, then ladle into bowls. Put the toppings in the middle of the table for everyone to help themselves.

■ Per serving (soup only) 257kcalories, protein 34g, carbohydrate 10g, ffat 10g, saturated fat 1g, fibre 2g, sugar 6g, salt 2.12g

Sweet potato and rosemary soup

This rustic soup is super quick and cheap to make, but full of flavour. Leave it chunky or whizz it until silky smooth – the choice is yours.

■ **Takes 30 minutes** ■ **Serves 4**

2 tsp olive oil, plus extra for brushing
1 onion, chopped
2 garlic cloves, crushed
750g/1lb 10oz sweet potatoes, peeled and cubed
1 litre/1¾ pints vegetable or chicken stock, plus extra (if needed)
1 fresh rosemary sprig, plus extra to garnish
toasted bread, to serve

1 Heat the oil in a large pan, then fry the onion for 5 minutes until soft. Add the garlic, then fry for 1 minute more. Stir in the sweet potatoes, then cover with the stock and bring to the boil. Strip the leaves from the rosemary sprig, and add them to the pan. Simmer for 10 minutes until the potato is soft.
2 Use a hand blender to purée the soup, adding a splash more hot water or stock if it seems too thick. Season well, then pour into warmed bowls and serve with toasted bread and a few extra leaves of rosemary, if you like.

■ Per serving 253 kcalories, protein 13g, carbohydrate 45g, fat 4g, saturated fat 0.4g, fibre 6g, sugar 13g, salt 1.46g

Roast chicken soup

Turn your leftover chicken into a hearty soup, finished with a delicious fresh swirl of creamy lemon and garlic Greek yogurt.

■ **Takes 40 minutes** ■ **Serves 4**

1 tbsp olive oil
2 onions, chopped
3 medium carrots, chopped
1 tbsp fresh thyme leaves, roughly chopped
1.4 litres/2½ pints chicken stock
300g/10oz leftover roast chicken, meat shredded and skin removed
200g/8oz frozen peas
3 tbsp Greek yogurt
1 garlic clove, crushed
squeeze of fresh lemon juice
crusty bread, to serve

1 Heat the oil in a large heavy-based pan. Add the onions, carrots and thyme, then gently fry for 15 minutes. Stir in the stock, bring to a boil, cover, then simmer for 10 minutes.
2 Add the chicken. Remove half the soup mixture and purée it with a stick blender. Tip back into the pan with the rest of the soup, the peas and some seasoning, then simmer for 5 minutes until hot through.
3 Mix together the yogurt, garlic and lemon juice. Swirl into the soup once spooned into bowls, then serve with crusty bread.

■ Per serving 339 kcalories, protein 39g, carbohydrate 18g, fat 13g, saturated fat 3g, fibre 6g, sugar 11g, salt 2g

TOP: Sticky green stir-fry with beef

BOTTOM LEFT: 10-minute pad Thai

BOTTOM RIGHT: Pork and peanut noodles

Sticky green stir-fry with beef

Low in fat, high in iron and vitamin C, and including three of your 5-a-day, this is just about the perfect healthy stir-fry.

■ **Takes 20 minutes** ■ **Serves 4**

1 tbsp sunflower oil
2 × 200g/8oz sirloin steaks, trimmed of fat
    and thinly sliced
1 broccoli head, cut into small florets
2 garlic cloves, sliced
300g/10oz sugar snap peas
4 spring onions, thickly sliced
3 pak choi, leaves separated and cut into
    quarters
4 tbsp hoisin sauce

1 Heat the oil in a large wok or deep frying pan, then sizzle the beef strips for 3–4 minutes until browned. Remove and set aside. Toss the broccoli and garlic into the wok with a splash of water, then fry over a high heat for 4–5 minutes until starting to soften.
2 Add the peas, spring onions and pak choi, then stir-fry for another 2–3 minutes, then stir in the hoisin sauce and beef. Heat through quickly, adding a splash of water if it seems a little dry. Great with noodles or rice.

■ Per serving 245 kcalories, protein 31g, carbohydrate 12g, fat 9g, saturated fat 2g, fibre 4g, sugar 10g, salt 0.8g

10-minute pad Thai

It's easy to make your own version of this classic Thai street food. Better still, this version is low in fat. Use raw prawns if you can as they'll add masses more flavour than ready-cooked ones.

■ **Takes 10 minutes** ■ **Serves 2 (easily doubled)**

200g/8oz raw peeled prawns
1 small pack fresh coriander, stalks finely
    chopped, leaves roughly chopped
2 × 200g packs straight-to-wok pad Thai
    noodles
85g/3oz beansprouts
1 egg, beaten
juice of 1 lime, plus extra wedges to serve
1 tbsp fish sauce
2 tsp sugar
1 tbsp roasted peanuts, roughly chopped,
    to garnish

1 Dry-fry the prawns and coriander stalks in a non-stick frying pan for 1–2 minutes until the prawns are just pink. Add the noodles, beansprouts, egg, lime juice, fish sauce and sugar. Quickly toss together for 1 minute more until the egg is just cooked and everything is well mixed (you might want to use a pair of tongs to make this easier).
2 Remove from the heat, mix in most of the coriander leaves, then divide between two bowls. Scatter with the remaining coriander and the peanuts, and serve with lime wedges for squeezing over.

■ Per serving 494 kcalories, protein 37g, carbohydrate 69g, fat 10g, saturated fat 2g, fibre 4g, sugar 9g, salt 2.91g

Pork and peanut noodles

All the flavours of pork satay come together in this delicious stir-fry. If your noodles look like they're sticking once drained, just add a few drops of vegetable or sesame oil to the bowl and toss to coat.

■ **Takes 20 minutes** ■ **Serves 4**

300g/10oz thin rice noodles
500g pack minced pork
1 garlic clove, crushed
250g pack mangetout
3 tbsp crunchy peanut butter
1 red chilli, seeded and finely chopped
2 tsp light muscovado sugar
1 tbsp light soy sauce
1 small bunch fresh coriander, chopped,
    to garnish

1 Place the noodles in a large bowl and cover with boiling water. Leave to soak for 5 minutes, then drain and set aside.
2 Meanwhile, heat a wok or large frying pan and cook the pork mince over a high heat for 10 minutes, or until the juices have evaporated and the pork is starting to look crisp. Throw in the garlic and mangetout, and fry together for 2 minutes.
3 Whisk together the peanut butter, chilli, sugar and soy sauce in a bowl, then loosen with 2 tablespoons warm water. Add the noodles and peanut sauce to the pan, toss everything well, then fry for 1 minute, stirring until warmed through. Sprinkle over the coriander and serve in bowls.

■ Per serving 551 kcalories, protein 33g, carbohydrate 68g, fat 18g, saturated fat 6g, fibre 2g, sugar 6g, salt 1.02g

Spicy tomato chicken

All this quick-and-easy chicken dish needs is a big hunk of crusty bread on the side. It's versatile too: try it stirred through pasta or as a topping for a baked potato.

■ **Takes 30 minutes** ■ **Serves 4**

2 tbsp seasoned plain flour
1 tsp chilli powder
8 boneless chicken thighs
1 tbsp vegetable oil
1 onion, chopped
600ml/1 pint chicken stock
2 garlic cloves, chopped
2 tbsp tomato purée
2 courgettes, cut into chunks
450g/1lb tomatoes, quartered
small handful of fresh basil leaves, to garnish

1 Mix together the seasoned flour and chilli powder. Add the chicken and toss to coat. Set aside the remaining seasoned flour. Heat the oil in a large frying pan with a lid, add the chicken and fry for 8 minutes, until well browned, turning once. Transfer to a plate.
2 Add the onion to the pan and fry for around 5 minutes. Sprinkle over the reserved seasoned flour and cook for 1 minute, stirring all the time. Stir in the stock, garlic and tomato purée. Return the chicken to the pan and bring to the boil. Add the courgettes and tomatoes, cover and simmer for 15 minutes. Scatter with fresh basil leaves and serve.

■ Per serving 424 kcalories, protein 33g, carbohydrate 19g, fat 25g, saturated fat 7g, fibre 3g, added sugar none, salt 1.2g

Speedy meatball stew

Like many stews, the flavour of this meal in a bowl will actually improve if you make it ahead then reheat it.

■ **Takes 20 minutes** ■ **Serves 4**

2 medium potatoes, peeled and cut into bite-sized cubes
1 tbsp olive oil
250g pack small lean beef meatballs
1 onion, chopped
2 garlic cloves, chopped
1 tbsp chopped fresh rosemary
560g jar passata
200g/8oz frozen peas
a few Parmesan shavings, to garnish (optional)
good crusty bread, to serve

1 Boil the potatoes for 10 minutes until they are tender. Set aside.
2 Meanwhile, heat the oil in a large pan. Season the meatballs, then brown them all over for about 5 minutes. Remove from the pan, drain off any excess fat, then add the onion, garlic and rosemary. Fry gently for 5 minutes.
3 Add the passata to the pan, bring to a simmer, then add the meatballs. Simmer for 5 minutes or until everything is cooked through. Add the potatoes and peas, then simmer for 1 minute. Top with the Parmesan, if using, and eat with good crusty bread.

■ Per serving 286 kcalories, protein 20g, carbohydrate 28g, fat 11g, saturated fat 4g, fibre 4g, sugar 9g, salt 1.68g

Beans and bangers

If your family goes mad for sausages, put this in the middle of the table and watch them dive in. The beans make a healthy and convenient change to potatoes.

■ **Takes 40 minutes** ■ **Serves 4**

1 tbsp olive oil
8 good-quality pork sausages (Toulouse or Sicilian varieties work well)
2 carrots, halved then sliced
2 onions, finely chopped
2 tbsp red wine vinegar
2 × 410g cans mixed beans in water, drained and rinsed
400ml/14fl oz chicken stock
100g/4oz frozen peas
2 tbsp Dijon mustard

1 Heat the oil in a large pan. Sizzle the sausages for about 6 minutes, turning occasionally, until brown on all sides. Remove to a plate. Tip the carrots and onions into the pan, and cook for 8 minutes, stirring occasionally, until the onions are soft. Add the vinegar to the pan, then stir in the drained beans. Pour over the stock, nestle the sausages in with the beans, then simmer everything for 10 minutes.
2 Scatter in the frozen peas, cook for 2 minutes more until heated through, then take off the heat and stir in the mustard. Season to taste. Serve scooped straight from the pan.

■ Per serving 569 kcalories, protein 35g, carbohydrate 41g, fat 31g, saturated fat 9g, fibre 11g, sugar 13g, salt 2.81g

TOP: Spicy tomato chicken

BOTTOM LEFT: Speedy meatball stew

BOTTOM RIGHT: Beans and bangers

TOP: Aubergine and mushroom curry

BOTTOM LEFT: Bean and dill pilaf with garlicky yogurt

BOTTOM RIGHT: Leek, butter bean and chorizo gratin

Aubergine and mushroom curry

Here's a one-pan curry that both meat eaters and vegetarians will love. The texture of the aubergine plus the almonds in the creamy sauce makes it a really satisfying meat-free meal.

■ **Takes 30 minutes** ■ **Serves 4**

3 tbsp olive oil
2 aubergines, each cut into about 8 chunks
250g/9oz chestnut mushrooms, halved
20g pack fresh coriander, stalks and leaves separated
2 large onions, quartered
a thumb-sized piece of ginger
3 garlic cloves, coarsely chopped
1 fat red chilli, seeded and half roughly chopped
1 tbsp each ground cumin and ground coriander
1 tbsp tomato purée
450ml/16fl oz vegetable stock
5 tbsp ground almonds
200g/8oz full-fat natural yogurt

1 Heat 2 tablespoons of the oil in a large frying pan, then fry the aubergines for 10 minutes until golden and soft. (The chunks will absorb all the oil at first, but keep cooking and it will be released again.) Add the mushrooms after 5 minutes; once golden, tip the veg out of the pan.
2 Meanwhile, whizz the coriander stalks, onions, ginger, garlic and chopped chilli to a paste in a food processor. Add the remaining 1 tablespoon of oil to the pan, then fry the paste for 2 minutes.
3 Tip in the spices and tomato purée. Stir for 2 minutes, then return the aubergines and mushrooms. Tip in the stock, ground almonds and most of the yogurt. Simmer for 5 minutes until the sauce has thickened. Garnish with slices of the remaining chilli, coriander leaves and a drizzle of the remaining yogurt to serve.

■ Per serving 307 kcalories, protein 11g, carbohydrate 20g, fat 21g, saturated fat 3g, fibre 7g, sugar 14g, salt 0.32g

Bean and dill pilaf with garlicky yogurt

Make the most of what's in your storecupboard and freezer with this easy throw-together rice dish.

■ **Takes 25 minutes** ■ **Serves 2 (easily doubled)**

2 onions, halved and thinly sliced
25g/1oz butter
175g/6oz basmati rice
20g pack fresh dill, stalks and fronds chopped but kept separate
450ml/16fl oz vegetable stock mixed with a good pinch of saffron strands or ground turmeric
300g/10oz frozen mixed broad beans, peas and green beans
100g/4oz Greek yogurt
1 tbsp milk
1 small garlic clove, crushed

1 Fry the onions in the butter for 5 minutes until golden. Add the rice and dill stalks then stir them around the pan.
2 Pour in the saffron or turmeric stock, bring to the boil, then cover and simmer for 5 minutes. Add the beans and half the dill fronds. Cook for 5 minutes more until the liquid has been absorbed into the rice.
3 Meanwhile, stir the yogurt, milk and garlic together with some seasoning. Spoon the yogurt on top of the rice, then sprinkle with the remaining dill.

■ Per serving 609 kcalories, protein 20g, carbohydrate 99g, fat 18g, saturated fat 10g, fibre 10g, sugar 13g, salt 0.63g

Leek, butter bean and chorizo gratin

Use up slightly stale bread to make the crunchy topping for this easy bake. Just a little chorizo goes a long way, keeping the dish low in fat but with a big, gutsy flavour.

■ **Takes 35 minutes** ■ **Serves 4**

1 tbsp olive oil
75g pack chorizo, roughly chopped
4 large leeks, thinly sliced
3 garlic cloves, sliced
100ml/3½fl oz dry sherry
2 × 400g cans butter beans, drained and rinsed
450ml/16fl oz hot vegetable stock
85g/3oz bread, torn into pieces

1 Heat the oven to 200C/180C fan/gas 6. Pour the oil into a baking dish, toss with the chorizo, leeks and half the garlic then bake uncovered for 10 minutes. Stir in the sherry, beans and stock, and return to the oven for 5 minutes. Season to taste.
2 Meanwhile, blitz the bread to coarse crumbs with the remaining garlic. Scatter this over the chorizo, leek and bean mix, and bake for 10 minutes more until golden.

■ Per serving 275 kcalories, protein 15g, carbohydrate 32g, fat 9g, saturated fat 2g, fibre 9g, sugar 7g, salt 2.41g

Fragrant pork and rice

Mild spices and a rich tomato sauce make so much more of sausages. The rice is cooked in the sauce and absorbs the tasty juices.

■ **Takes 40 minutes** ■ **Serves 4**

4–6 good-quality sausages
1 tbsp olive oil
½ onion, finely chopped
2 garlic cloves, crushed
2 tsp each ground cumin and coriander
140g/5oz long grain rice
850ml/1½ pints vegetable stock
400g can chopped tomatoes
½ small bunch fresh coriander, leaves
    picked, to garnish
crusty bread, to serve

1 Split the sausage skins, squeeze out the meat, then roll it into small meatballs, each about the size of a large olive. Heat the oil in a large non-stick pan, then brown the meatballs well on all sides until cooked – you might need to do this in batches. Set the meatballs aside.
2 Add the onion and garlic to the pan. Soften for 5 minutes, stir in the spices and rice, then cook for another minute. Pour in the stock and tomatoes. Bring to a simmer, scraping up any sausagey bits from the bottom of the pan. Simmer for 10 minutes until the rice is just cooked, then stir in the meatballs with some seasoning. Ladle into bowls, scatter with coriander and serve with crusty bread.

■ Per serving 408 kcalories, protein 17g, carbohydrate 43g, fat 20g, saturated fat 5g, fibre 2g, sugar 6g, salt 1.56g

Pepper-crusted salmon with garlic chickpeas

Add a mildly spicy twist to salmon with this satisfying and smart one-pot.

■ **Takes 25 minutes** ■ **Serves 4**

4 tbsp olive oil
2 garlic cloves, finely chopped
2 × 400g cans chickpeas, drained and rinsed
150ml/¼ pint vegetable or fish stock
4 skinless salmon fillets, about 150g/5oz
    each
2 tsp black peppercorns, roughly crushed
1 tsp paprika
zest and juice of 2 limes, plus extra wedges
    to garnish
130g bag baby leaf spinach

1 Heat the oven to 190C/170C fan/gas 5. Heat 3 tablespoons of the oil in an ovenproof pan, add the garlic, then gently cook for around 5 minutes without browning. Add the chickpeas and stock. Sit the salmon fillets on top of the chickpeas, then scatter the fillets with the pepper, paprika, lime zest and some salt. Drizzle with the remaining oil. Bake for 12–15 minutes until the salmon is just cooked and the chickpeas are warmed right through.
2 Lift off the salmon and keep warm. Put the pan over a medium heat and lightly mash the chickpeas using a potato masher. Fold in the spinach leaves – they will quickly wilt. Season with lime juice and salt and pepper. Serve with the salmon, garnished with lime wedges.

■ Per serving 531 kcalories, protein 41g, carbohydrate 23g, fat 32g, saturated fat 5g, fibre 6g, sugar 2g, salt 1.01g

Cheese, bacon and onion puff

Bake a basic batter mixture with a few added ingredients for a simple family supper from the storecupboard.

■ **Takes 50 minutes** ■ **Serves 4**

140g/5oz plain flour
4 eggs
200ml/7fl oz milk
butter, for greasing
2 tbsp finely grated Parmesan
8 rashers ready-cooked streaky bacon or
    3 slices ham, chopped
4 spring onions, thinly sliced
140g/5oz Cheddar, grated

1 Heat the oven to 230C/210C fan/gas 8. To make the batter, tip the flour into a bowl and beat in the eggs until smooth. Gradually add the milk and carry on beating until the mix is completely lump free. Grease a large, round ceramic dish, about 22cm wide, and dust it with the grated Parmesan.
2 Tip the bacon or ham, onions and Cheddar into the batter, and stir until completely combined. Tip the batter into the prepared dish so it comes almost to the top, then bake for 30–35 minutes until puffed up and golden. Bring it to the table and serve piping hot, straight from the dish.

■ Per serving 680 kcalories, protein 27g, carbohydrate 30g, fat 51g, saturated fat 18g, fibre 1g, sugar 3g, salt 2.15g

TOP: Fragrant pork and rice

BOTTOM LEFT: Pepper-crusted salmon with garlic chickpeas

BOTTOM RIGHT: Cheese, bacon and onion puff

TOP: Fully-loaded Cajun chicken burgers

BOTTOM LEFT: Smoky maple duck salad

BOTTOM RIGHT: Chicken with harissa and tomatoes

Fully-loaded Cajun chicken burgers

Stack up the flavours in these big and bold chicken burgers.

■ **Takes 35 minutes** ■ **Serves 4**

1 tbsp ground cumin
1 tbsp ground coriander
1 tbsp paprika
2 tbsp olive oil
4 skinless chicken breasts, flattened a little
4 ciabatta rolls, split
4 rashers smoked bacon
2 avocados
mayonnaise, to spread (optional)
4 small handfuls of baby leaf spinach

1 Mix together the spices in a large dish with some salt and pepper and 1 tablespoon of the oil. Coat the chicken in the mix.
2 Heat a large frying pan, then toast the cut sides of the buns in the pan. Set aside. Heat the remaining oil in the pan then sizzle the chicken for 5 minutes on each side. Push to one side of the pan, then fry the bacon for a few minutes until cooked.
3 While the chicken is cooking, slice the avocados. To assemble the burgers, spread the buns with mayonnaise, if using, top with a handful of spinach. To keep the avocado in place, slice the chicken and place the avocado between the chicken slices. Top with a rasher of bacon and lastly the bun lid; press down lightly and serve.

■ Per serving 721 kcalories, protein 51g, carbohydrate 51g, fat 36g, saturated fat 10g, fibre 5g, sugar 2g, salt 2.84g

Smoky maple duck salad

The smoky chipotle chilli paste in this recipe can easily be swapped for harissa. Either way, it's a one-pan winner.

■ **Takes 30 minutes** ■ **Serves 2 (easily doubled)**

2 duck breasts, skin on and slashed
3 tbsp maple syrup
1 garlic clove, crushed
1 tbsp chipotle chilli paste
160g bag bistro salad
1 bunch radishes, about 200g/8oz, thinly
    sliced or grated
1 tbsp sherry vinegar

1 Heat the oven to 220C/200C fan/gas 7. Place a roasting tin in the oven for 5 minutes. Season the duck well, then carefully put into the hot tin, skin-side down. Roast for 10 minutes until the skin is golden and crisp, and the fat has run out. (Or leave for 15 minutes if you prefer well done.)
2 Meanwhile, mix 2 tablespoons of the maple syrup with the garlic and chilli paste. Tip the fat out of the pan, turn the duck over, then roast for 5 minutes, basting with the maple mix once or twice until glazed and sticky. Remove and let the duck rest for 5 minutes.
3 Pile the salad and the radishes on to plates. Slice the duck; nestle it into the salad. Stir the rest of the maple syrup and the sherry vinegar into the pan juices, then drizzle over the salad to serve.

■ Per serving 527 kcalories, protein 32g, carbohydrate 20g, fat 36g, saturated fat 10g, fibre 2g, sugar 18g, salt 0.54g

Chicken with harissa and tomatoes

Big on flavour, easy on effort, this spicy chicken is just the thing for a busy weeknight supper.

■ **Takes about 20 minutes** ■ **Serves 4**

4 skinless chicken breasts
2 tsp harissa paste
1 tsp olive oil
1 tsp dried oregano
250g pack cherry tomatoes
a handful of pitted olives (we used Kalamata)

1 Heat the oven to 200C/180C fan/gas 6. Put the chicken into a medium roasting tin, then rub with the harissa, oil and oregano. Cover with foil and roast for 5 minutes.
2 Remove the foil and add the cherry tomatoes and olives to the tin. Roast for 10 minutes more until the tomato skins start to split and the chicken is cooked through.

■ Per serving 184 kcalories, protein 34g, carbohydrate 2g, fat 4g, saturated fat 1g, fibre 1g, sugar 2g, salt 0.41g

Honey-mustard chicken pot with parsnips

If you've got time, this casserole will gently bubble away for up to 90 minutes; the meat becomes tender and falls away from the bones.

■ **Takes 45 minutes** ■ **Serves 4**

1 tbsp olive oil
8 skinless chicken thighs, bone in
2 onions, finely chopped
350g/12oz parsnips, cut into sticks
300ml/½ pint vegetable stock
2 tbsp wholegrain mustard
2 tbsp clear honey
a few fresh thyme sprigs
flatleaf parsley, to garnish (optional)
steamed greens, to serve

1 Heat half the oil in a large frying pan or shallow casserole with a lid. Brown the chicken until golden, then set aside. Heat the remaining oil, then cook the onions for 5 minutes until softened.
2 Nestle the thighs back among the onions and add the parsnips. Mix the stock with the mustard and honey, then pour in. Scatter over the thyme, then bring to a simmer. Cover, then cook for 30 minutes (or longer) until the chicken is tender. Season and scatter with parsley, if using, and serve with steamed greens.

■ Per serving 326 kcalories, protein 39g, carbohydrate 23g, fat 10g, saturated fat 2g, fibre 6g, sugar 15g, salt 0.82g

Italian chicken and butternut pie

This one-pot recipe has an Italian theme running through it with the wine, pancetta and plum tomatoes. But although this is a pie, you don't have to make any pastry – there's not a rolling pin in sight.

■ **Takes 1¼–1½ hours** ■ **Serves 6**

3 tbsp olive oil
8 large skinless chicken thigh fillets, quartered
130g pack cubed pancetta
1 large butternut squash, flesh cut into 2.5cm/1in cubes
1 large onion, thinly sliced
2 garlic cloves, thinly sliced
1 tsp dried marjoram
200ml/7fl oz Italian red wine
1 level tbsp plain flour
2 × 400g cans Italian plum tomatoes
2 tbsp redcurrant or cranberry jelly
1 garlic and herb or plain ciabatta, very thinly sliced
3 tbsp freshly grated Parmesan

1 Heat 2 tablespoons of the oil in a large casserole and lightly brown the chicken all over. Lift out of the pan, tip in the pancetta, squash and onion, and soften for 8 minutes, stirring occasionally. Return the chicken to the pan, add the garlic and marjoram and cook for 1 minute. Pour all but 2 tablespoons of the wine into the pan and bubble for 5 minutes.
2 Blend the flour with the reserved wine until smooth. Stir into the pan with the tomatoes, jelly and seasoning. Lower the heat, half-cover, then simmer for 30–40 minutes until the squash is tender.
3 Heat the oven to 220C/200C fan/gas 7. Lay the slices of ciabatta on top of the casserole, drizzle with the remaining olive oil, sprinkle with the Parmesan and some black pepper. Bake for 15 minutes or until golden.

■ Per serving 491 kcalories, protein 41g, carbohydrate 42g, fat 16g, saturated fat 5g, fibre 4g, added sugar 2g, salt 2.17g

Spring chicken in a pot

Chicken thighs cook to melting softness and inject plenty of flavour into the stock in this vibrant and healthy herby casserole. They are also easier on the purse than breast meat.

■ **Takes about 1 hour** ■ **Serves 4**

1 tbsp olive oil
1 onion, chopped
500g/1lb 2oz boneless skinless chicken thighs
300g/10oz small new potatoes
425ml/¾ pint low-salt vegetable stock
350g/12oz broccoli, cut into small florets
350g/12oz spring greens, shredded
140g/5oz petits pois
1 bunch spring onions, sliced
2 tbsp pesto

1 Heat the oil in a large, heavy pan. Add the onion, gently fry for 5 minutes until softened, add the chicken, then fry until lightly coloured. Add the potatoes, stock and plenty of freshly ground black pepper, then bring to the boil. Cover, then simmer for 30 minutes until the potatoes are tender and the chicken is cooked through.
2 Add the broccoli, spring greens, petits pois and spring onions, stir well, then return to the boil. Cover, then cook for 5 minutes more, stir in the pesto and serve.

■ Per serving 339 kcalories, protein 36g, carbohydrate 27g, fat 10g, saturated fat 3g, fibre 8g, sugar 12g, salt 0.5g

TOP: Honey-mustard chicken pot with parsnips

BOTTOM LEFT: Italian chicken and butternut pie

BOTTOM RIGHT: Spring chicken in a pot

TOP: One-pan duck with Savoy cabbage

BOTTOM LEFT: Flambéed chicken with asparagus

BOTTOM RIGHT: Creamy pesto chicken with roasted tomatoes

One-pan duck with Savoy cabbage

Create a smart plated dinner from just one pan with this clever recipe.

■ **Takes 40 minutes** ■ **Serves 4**

2 duck breasts, skin on and scored
1 tsp black peppercorns, crushed
600g/1lb 5oz cooked new potatoes, thickly sliced
1 bunch flatleaf parsley, roughly chopped
1 garlic clove, finely chopped
6 rashers smoked streaky bacon, chopped
1 Savoy cabbage, trimmed, quartered, cored and finely sliced
1 tbsp balsamic vinegar
2 tbsp olive oil

1 Generously season the duck skin with the peppercorns and a sprinkling of salt. Lay the duck skin-side down in a non-stick sauté pan, then place over a low heat. Leave for 15 minutes to brown and release its fat, then flip over on to the flesh side for 5 minutes.
2 Remove the duck from the pan, then turn up the heat. Add the potatoes to the pan, fry until brown and crisp, then scatter over the parsley and garlic. Scoop out with a slotted spoon on to a plate, then season with salt.
3 Keep the pan on the heat. Fry the bacon until crisp, then add the cabbage. Cook for 1 minute, add a splash of water, then fry for 2 minutes, just until the cabbage is wilted.
4 Meanwhile, mix any duck juices with the vinegar and oil. Slice the duck, serve with the cabbage and potatoes, and top with a drizzle of dressing.

■ Per serving 504 kcalories, protein 25g, carbohydrate 33g, fat 31g, saturated fat 8g, fibre 6g, sugar 7g, salt 1.16g

Flambéed chicken with asparagus

An elegant one-pan spring dish that looks and tastes very special.

■ **Takes 45 minutes** ■ **Serves 4**

4 skinless chicken breasts
1 tbsp seasoned plain flour
2 tbsp olive oil
a knob of butter
4 shallots, finely chopped
4 tbsp brandy or Cognac
300ml/½ pint chicken stock
16 asparagus spears, halved
4 rounded tbsp crème fraîche
1 tbsp chopped fresh tarragon
boiled new potatoes, to serve

1 Dust the chicken with the flour. Heat the oil and butter in a large, wide pan with a lid, add the chicken, then fry on all sides until nicely browned. Add the shallots, then fry for about 2 minutes until they start to soften, but not colour. Pour in the brandy or Cognac, carefully ignite, then stand well back until the flames have died down. Stir in the stock and bring to the boil. Reduce the heat, cover, then cook for 15 minutes until the chicken is just tender.
2 Add the asparagus to the sauce. Cover, then cook for 5 minutes more until tender. Stir in the crème fraîche and tarragon, and warm through. Season to taste and serve with boiled new potatoes.

■ Per serving 395 kcalories, protein 42g, carbohydrate 7g, fat 19g, saturated fat 8g, fibre 3g, sugar 4g, salt 0.9g

Creamy pesto chicken with roasted tomatoes

This is pure summer in a pan; simple to make and bursting with fresh Italian flavours.

■ **Takes 35 minutes** ■ **Serves 4**

4 skinless chicken breasts
3 tbsp pesto
85g/3oz mascarpone
4 tbsp olive oil
100g/4oz fresh breadcrumbs (preferably from day-old bread)
175g/6oz cherry tomatoes on the vine
a handful of pine nuts
a handful of fresh basil leaves, to garnish
crusty bread, to serve

1 Heat the oven to 200C/180C fan/gas 6. Use a small sharp knife to make a slit along the side of each chicken breast to form a pocket. Mix together the pesto and mascarpone, then carefully spoon a quarter of the mixture into each chicken breast and smooth over the opening to seal.
2 Brush a little oil, about 1 teaspoon, all over each chicken breast and season well. Tip the breadcrumbs on to a plate and season. Press each breast into the crumbs to coat. Place in a lightly oiled, shallow baking dish along with the tomatoes. Drizzle over the remaining oil.
3 Roast for 20–25 minutes until the chicken is golden and cooked through. Scatter over the pine nuts and cook for 2 minutes more. Sprinkle with basil leaves and serve with crusty bread.

■ Per serving 545 kcalories, protein 40g, carbohydrate 22g, fat 33g, saturated fat 10g, fibre 1g, sugar 3g, salt 0.82g

Spiced chicken balti

If you haven't yet tried quinoa, give this a go. It's a filling grain that's super-good for you and cooks in the sauce just like rice would in a pilaf.

■ Takes 35 minutes ■ Serves 4

1 tbsp sunflower oil
2 large onions, thickly sliced
4 skinless chicken breasts
4 tbsp balti paste
200g/8oz quinoa
400g can chopped tomatoes
1 litre/1¾ pints chicken stock
50g/2oz roasted salted cashews
1 small bunch fresh coriander, leaves chopped

1 Heat the oil in a large pan, fry the onions for 5 minutes until golden and softened, then tip out on to a plate. Add the chicken breasts to the pan, browning them for a few minutes on each side, then stir in the balti paste, quinoa and onions. Sizzle for a few minutes, then pour in the tomatoes and stock, and give everything a good mix. Bubble for 25 minutes until the quinoa is tender and saucy.
2 Stir in the cashews and most of the coriander with some seasoning, then scatter over the rest of the coriander to serve.

■ Per serving 527 kcalories, protein 47g, carbohydrate 45g, fat 19g, saturated fat 3g, fibre 5g, sugar 14g, salt 1.83g

Massaman curry roast chicken

This full-flavoured chicken would make a great one-pan alternative to your usual weekend roast. Massaman curry paste is mild, so it's ideal for all the family.

■ Takes 1 hour 40 minutes ■ Serves 4

1 whole chicken, about 1.8kg/4lb
2 thumb-sized pieces of ginger, 1 roughly chopped, 1 grated
1 lemongrass stick, bashed with a rolling pin
1 lime, cut into quarters
70g pack Massaman curry paste
1 tsp olive oil
450g/1lb baby new potatoes, any larger ones halved
400ml can coconut milk
1 tsp brown sugar (any type)
200g/8oz green beans, trimmed
1 tsp fish sauce
2 tbsp unsalted peanuts, crushed, to scatter

1 Heat the oven to 200C/180C fan/gas 6. Put the chicken in a medium roasting tin. Stuff the chopped ginger, lemongrass and half the lime into the cavity. Tie the legs together with string. Mix 1 teaspoon of curry paste with the oil, rub all over the chicken, then season.
2 Cover the chicken loosely with foil, then roast for 35 minutes. Uncover, add the potatoes and stir them around in any juices. Roast for 40 minutes more or until the chicken is cooked through and golden and the potatoes tender. Rest the chicken, loosely covered.
3 Meanwhile, add the remaining curry paste and the grated ginger to a pan and fry for 2 minutes. Stir in the coconut milk and sugar, and boil for 5 minutes until slightly thickened.
4 Tip in the beans. Simmer for 4 minutes, splash in the fish sauce, resting juices and a squeeze of the remaining lime and scatter with peanuts, to serve.

■ Per serving 895 kcalories, protein 61g, carbohydrate 25g, fat 62g, saturated fat 27g, fibre 2g, sugar 7g, salt 1.75g

Chicken and couscous one-pot

If you like the zesty, spicy flavours of Moroccan food, you'll enjoy this simple-to-make chicken dish. The couscous absorbs all the cooking juices, keeping in every bit of flavour.

■ Takes 1 hour 10 minutes ■ Serves 4

8 chicken thighs, skin on and bone in
2 tsp ground turmeric
1 tbsp garam masala
2 tbsp sunflower oil
2 onions, finely sliced
3 garlic cloves, sliced
450ml/16fl oz chicken stock
a large handful of whole green olives
zest and juice of 1 lemon
250g/9oz couscous
1 small bunch flatleaf parsley, chopped

1 Toss the chicken thighs in half the spices and a pinch of salt. Heat 1 tablespoon of the oil in a large pan. Fry the chicken, skin-side down, for 10 minutes, then turn and cook for 2 minutes more. Remove from the pan. Add the remaining oil then gently fry the onions and garlic for 8 minutes until golden. Stir in remaining spices for 1 minute. Add the stock, olives and chicken to the pan, skin-side up.
2 Cover, then simmer for 40 minutes. Lift the chicken on to a plate and keep warm. Off the heat, stir the lemon juice and couscous into the pan – add boiling water just to cover the couscous, if needed. Re-cover then let stand for 5 minutes until the couscous is soft. Fork half the parsley and lemon zest through the couscous, then sit the chicken on top. Scatter with the remaining parsley and zest, to serve.

■ Per serving 900 kcalories, protein 60g, carbohydrate 42g, fat 56g, saturated fat 15g, fibre 2g, sugar 5g, salt 1.75g

TOP: Spiced chicken balti

BOTTOM LEFT: Massaman curry roast chicken

BOTTOM RIGHT: Chicken and couscous one-pot

TOP: Rosemary and balsamic chicken with roast onions

BOTTOM LEFT: Rosemary chicken with tomato sauce

BOTTOM RIGHT: French bean and duck Thai curry

Rosemary and balsamic chicken with roast onions

A honey glaze adds a lovely sweetness to a classic roast chicken, perfect against the tangy sweetness of roasted red onions.

■ Takes about 2 hours ■ Serves 4

1 whole chicken, about 1.5kg/3lb 5oz
1 bunch fresh rosemary
4 red onions, peeled and trimmed but left whole
3 tbsp olive oil
3 tbsp balsamic vinegar
1 tbsp clear honey

1 Heat the oven to 190C/170C fan/gas 5. Starting at the neck, carefully loosen the breast skin away from the flesh. Place a sprig of rosemary down each side; put the rest in the cavity. Season the chicken, place in a roasting tin, then sit an onion in each corner of the tin. Drizzle the olive oil over everything then roast for 1 hour 20 minutes.
2 Meanwhile, stir the vinegar and honey together. After 40 minutes, take the chicken from the oven, drizzle the vinegar mix over the chicken and onions, then continue to roast.
3 At the end of the cooking time, remove the chicken from the tin, cover loosely with foil and set aside to rest for 20 minutes. Meanwhile, turn the onions over and continue to roast them until soft. Serve everything up with some of the sticky pan juices.

■ Per serving 629 kcalories, protein 48g, carbohydrate 15g, fat 42g, saturated fat 11g, fibre 2g, sugar 12g, salt 0.44g

Rosemary chicken with tomato sauce

Anchovies are often used in Italian cooking to add a deeply savoury edge to a recipe. This is a great dish for the freezer.

■ Takes 35 minutes ■ Serves 4

1 tbsp olive oil
8 boneless skinless chicken thighs
1 fresh rosemary sprig, leaves finely chopped
1 red onion, finely sliced
3 garlic cloves, sliced
2 anchovy fillets, chopped
400g can chopped tomatoes
1 tbsp capers, drained
75ml/2½fl oz red wine, water or stock
crusty bread, to serve

1 Heat half the oil in a non-stick pan, then brown the chicken all over. Add half the chopped rosemary, stir to coat, then set aside on a plate.
2 In the same pan, heat the rest of the oil, then gently fry the onion for roughly 5 minutes until soft. Add the garlic, anchovies and remaining rosemary, then fry for a few minutes more until fragrant. Pour in the tomatoes and capers with the wine, water or stock.
3 Bring to the boil, then return the chicken pieces to the pan. Cover, then cook for 20 minutes until the chicken is tender. Season and serve with crusty bread.

■ Per serving 275 kcalories, protein 44g, carbohydrate 5g, fat 9g, saturated fat 3g, fibre 2g, sugar 4g, salt 1.09g

French bean and duck Thai curry

It's really worth making your own Thai curries for their lively freshness of flavour. Duck makes an unusual and luxurious alternative to chicken.

■ Takes 2 hours ■ Serves 4

3–4 duck breasts, about 700g/1lb 9oz total
6 tbsp Thai green curry paste
1 tbsp light brown sugar, plus extra to taste
400ml can coconut milk
2 tbsp fish sauce, plus extra to taste
juice of 2 limes
6 kaffir lime leaves, 3 left whole and 3 finely shredded
200g/8oz French beans, trimmed
2 handfuls of beansprouts
a handful of coriander leaves
1 red chilli, seeded and sliced

1 Place a deep frying pan over a low heat and add the duck breasts, skin-side down. Slowly fry until golden and there's a pool of fat in the bottom; about 20 minutes. Flip on to the other side for 1 minute, then remove.
2 Pour all but 2 tablespoons of the fat from the pan. Fry the curry paste and sugar for around 1–2 minutes then tip in the coconut milk, a can of water, the fish sauce, half the lime juice and the whole lime leaves. Simmer, then slice the duck breasts and add to the curry. Cover, then cook very gently for 1 hour.
3 Add the beans, then simmer, covered, for 10 minutes. Add the remaining lime juice and a little more fish sauce and sugar to season. Stir in the beansprouts, cook for 1 minute more, then serve topped with coriander, the shredded lime leaves and sliced chilli.

■ Per serving 638 kcalories, protein 28g, carbohydrate 11g, fat 57g, saturated fat 26g, fibre 2g, sugar 9g, salt 2.32g

Shallot tarte Tatin

This special dish can be relished by everyone, whether vegetarian or not. If you want to make it ahead, it will sit in the fridge, ready to bake, for a day or two.

■ **Takes 1 hour** ■ **Serves 4**

2 tbsp olive oil
25g/1oz butter
500g/1lb 2oz shallots, peeled and halved
2 tbsp balsamic vinegar
1 tbsp fresh thyme leaves or 2 tsp dried
300g/10oz puff pastry, defrosted if frozen and cut into two
100g/4oz grated Cheddar or Emmental

1 Heat the oil and butter in a frying pan, add the shallots and fry gently for 10 minutes until softened and lightly browned. Stir in the vinegar, thyme and 1 tablespoon water; cook for 5 minutes, stirring occasionally. Tip into a shallow non-stick cake or pie tin, roughly 20cm across. Leave to cool.
2 Heat the oven to 200C/180C fan/gas 6. Roll out each piece of pastry to about 5cm larger than the top of the cake tin. Put one piece over the shallots. Sprinkle evenly with cheese then cover with the second piece. Tuck the edges down between the shallots and the side of the tin.
3 Bake for 25–30 minutes until the pastry is crisp and golden. Cool in the tin for around 5 minutes, turn out on to a flat plate, cut into wedges and serve warm.

■ Per serving 510 kcalories, protein 13g, carbohydrate 33g, fat 37g, saturated fat 17g, fibre 2g, sugar 6g, salt 1.18g

Deep-dish cheese, onion and potato pie

Food doesn't get much heartier, or fun to make, than this big, comforting cheese pie. Great with a simple salad.

■ **Takes 2 hours, plus resting time** ■ **Serves 6**

200g/8oz strong hard cheese, ½ coarsely grated, ½ cut into small chunks
200ml pot crème fraîche
500g/1lb 2oz shortcrust pastry
1kg/2lb 4oz floury potatoes, thinly sliced
2 onions, finely sliced
1 bunch spring onions, roughly chopped
a small pinch of grated nutmeg
a large pinch of paprika
1 egg, beaten

1 Heat the oven to 200C/180C fan/gas 6. Mix the grated cheese with the crème fraîche. Grease and lightly flour a pie dish or shallow cake tin about 23cm wide. Roll out two-thirds of the pastry on a floured surface until large enough to line the tin.
2 Layer the potatoes, onions, spring onions and chunks of cheese with splodges of the crème fraîche mix, seasoning with some black pepper and the nutmeg and paprika as you go. The filling will come up way above the pastry.
3 Roll the remaining pastry so it fits over the filling. Brush the edges with egg, lay the pastry over, then trim with a knife. Crimp the edges, brush all over with egg then bake on a baking sheet for 30 minutes. Reduce the oven to 180C/160C fan/gas 4, then bake for 1 hour more. Rest the pie for 10 minutes, then slice.

■ Per serving 820 kcalories, protein 20g, carbohydrate 73g, fat 52g, saturated fat 26g, fibre 5g, sugar 5g, salt 1.53g

Fennel with tomatoes and white wine

Try something different and tuck into a plateful of beautifully simple fennel and tomatoes. Serve with some goat's cheese, if you like, and scoop the whole lot up with crusty bread.

■ **Takes 1 hour 20 minutes** ■ **Serves 2 as a main or 4 as a starter**

4 fennel bulbs
2 tbsp fruity olive oil
2 garlic cloves, crushed
a generous pinch of crushed dried chilli
1 tbsp chopped fresh thyme leaves
4 ripe tomatoes, peeled and roughly chopped
150ml/¼ pint dry white wine
100ml/3½fl oz vegetable stock (a cube is fine)
a pinch of caster sugar (optional)
1 tbsp chopped flatleaf parsley, to garnish

1 Heat the oven to 180C/160C fan/gas 4. Trim the fennel and cut into quarters through the root. (You may need to cut larger ones in half, then into thirds so they all cook evenly.) Heat the oil in a roasting tin on the hob, add the fennel and cook until golden brown on all sides. Remove from the pan.
2 Fry the garlic, chilli and thyme for around 30 seconds, add the tomatoes and cook for a further 3 minutes. Add the wine and bring to the boil. Simmer for 1 minute, add the stock, bring back to the boil and simmer for 2–3 minutes.
3 Season the tomato mix, adding a pinch of sugar, if needed, then add the fennel and spoon the sauce over it. Cover with foil and cook in the oven for 1 hour or until the fennel is tender. Scatter with the parsley and serve.

■ Per serving 110 kcalories, protein 2g, carbohydrate 6g, fat 6g, saturated fat 1g, fibre 4g, added sugar none, salt 0.2g

TOP: Shallot tarte Tatin

BOTTOM LEFT: Deep-dish cheese, onion and potato pie

BOTTOM RIGHT: Fennel with tomatoes and white wine

TOP: More-ish mushroom and rice

BOTTOM LEFT: Risotto with squash and sage

BOTTOM RIGHT: Broccoli, walnut and blue cheese pasta

More-ish mushroom and rice

Take a handful of simple storecupboard ingredients and turn them into this hearty, comforting family supper. Little will they know that it's low in fat and includes three of their 5-a-day!

■ **Takes 50 minutes** ■ **Serves 4**

200g/8oz basmati rice
1 tbsp olive oil
1 large onion, chopped
2 tsp chopped fresh rosemary or 1 tsp dried
250g/9oz chestnut mushrooms, quartered
2 red peppers, seeded and sliced
400g can chopped tomatoes
425ml/¾ pint vegetable stock
chopped fresh parsley, to garnish

1 Heat the oven to 190C/170C fan/gas 5. Tip the rice into a sieve, rinse under cold running water, then leave to drain. Heat the oil in a flameproof casserole, add the onion, then fry until softened, which will take around 5 minutes.
2 Stir in the rosemary and mushrooms, then fry briefly. Add the rice, stir to coat in the oil, then tip in the peppers, tomatoes, stock and seasoning. Bring to the boil, stir, cover tightly with a lid, then bake for 20–25 minutes until the rice is tender. Scatter over the parsley and serve.

■ Per serving 282 kcalories, protein 9g, carbohydrate 55g, fat 5g, saturated fat 1g, fibre 4g, sugar 7g, salt 0.36g

Risotto with squash and sage

Our butternut risotto is so satisfying – bags of flavour, two of your 5-a-day and just one pan to deal with.

■ **Takes 1 hour** ■ **Serves 4**

2½ tbsp olive oil
a handful of fresh sage leaves, 6 finely chopped, the rest left whole
4 slices dried porcini mushrooms
2 litres/3½ pints hot low-salt vegetable stock
1 onion, finely chopped
2 garlic cloves, finely chopped
2 fresh thyme sprigs
700g/1lb 9oz butternut squash, peeled and cubed
350g/12oz carnaroli (or arborio) rice
100ml/3½fl oz dry white wine
a handful of flatleaf parsley, chopped
50g/2oz Parmesan, grated
2 tbsp light mascarpone

1 Heat ½ tablespoon oil in a pan, fry the whole sage leaves for a few seconds until starting to colour. Drain on kitchen paper. Soak the mushrooms in the hot stock.
2 Heat 2 tablespoons oil in the cooled pan. Add the onion, garlic, chopped sage, thyme and squash; gently fry for 10 minutes. On a medium heat, tip in the rice. Stir for 3 minutes then add the wine and stir for 1 minute.
3 Stir in a ladleful of hot stock (leaving the porcini behind). Continue gradually adding and stirring until the rice is soft with a little bite and almost all the stock is used. Season to taste.
4 Off the heat, add a splash more stock to the pan then scatter over the parsley, half the Parmesan and the mascarpone. Cover for 3–4 minutes then stir. Scatter with remaining Parmesan and the crisp sage leaves to serve.

■ Per serving 517 kcalories, protein 15g, carbohydrate 85g, fat 15g, saturated fat 5g, fibre 5g, sugar 10g, salt 0.37g

Broccoli, walnut and blue cheese pasta

Add colour, crunch and a dollop of cheesy indulgence to your weeknight pasta with this simple recipe.

■ **Takes 15 minutes** ■ **Serves 2**

200g/8oz penne pasta
250g/9oz broccoli florets
2 tbsp olive oil
4 tbsp walnut pieces
100g/4oz creamy blue cheese, such as dolcelatte, cubed
squeeze of fresh lemon juice, to taste

1 Cook the pasta according to the packet instructions and, 4 minutes before the end of cooking, throw in the broccoli. Drain, keeping a cup of the cooking water, then set aside.
2 Heat the oil in the pan, then add the walnuts and fry gently for 1 minute. Add 4 tablespoons of the reserved cooking water to the walnuts. Stir in the cheese until it melts, season, then stir in the lemon juice to taste. Tip the drained pasta and broccoli into the sauce, toss well, then serve.

■ Per serving 758 kcalories, protein 28g, carbohydrate 80g, fat 38g, saturated fat 12g, fibre 7g, sugar 6g, salt 0.82g

Easy ratatouille with poached eggs

This punchy dish can be prepared in advance. Cook until the end of step 2, then gently re-heat and crack in the eggs.

■ **Takes 1 hour 20 minutes** ■ **Serves 4**

1 tbsp olive oil
1 large onion, chopped
1 red or orange pepper, seeded and thinly sliced
2 garlic cloves, finely chopped
1 tbsp chopped fresh rosemary
1 aubergine, diced
2 courgettes, diced
400g can chopped tomatoes
1 tsp balsamic vinegar
4 large eggs
a handful of fresh basil leaves, to garnish
crusty bread, to serve

1 Heat the oil in a large frying pan. Add the onion, pepper, garlic and rosemary, then cook for 5 minutes, stirring frequently, until the onion has softened. Add the aubergine and courgettes, then cook for 2 minutes more.
2 Add the tomatoes, then fill the can with water, swirl it around and tip into the pan. Bring to the boil, cover, then simmer for 40 minutes, uncovering after 20 minutes, until reduced and pulpy.
3 Stir the vinegar into the ratatouille, then make four spaces for the eggs. Crack an egg into each hole and season with black pepper. Cover, then cook for 2–5 minutes until the eggs are set as softly or firmly as you like. Scatter over the basil and serve with some crusty bread to mop up the juices.

■ Per serving 190 kcalories, protein 12g, carbohydrate 13g, fat 11g, saturated fat 2g, fibre 5g, sugar 10g, salt 0.36g

Springtime pasta

Filled pasta such as tortellini freezes really well and only takes 1–2 minutes more to cook than it would unfrozen. Use all frozen veg, or vary the recipe by using asparagus or broccoli instead.

■ **Takes 10 minutes** ■ **Serves 2**

250g pack frozen ricotta and spinach tortellini
50g/2oz frozen peas
50g/2oz frozen broad beans
1 tbsp olive oil
zest of 1 lemon
50g/2oz ricotta

1 Bring a pan of salted water to the boil. Tip in the pasta and cook for 3–4 minutes, then lift it out with a slotted spoon into a large bowl. Add the peas and broad beans to the pan, bring back to boil, then boil for 1 minute or until tender.
2 Drain well, then add to the pasta and toss through the olive oil and lemon zest. Place on plates, dollop over the ricotta and serve.

■ Per serving 472 kcalories, protein 18g, carbohydrate 62g, fat 19g, saturated fat 8g, fibre 5g, sugar 5g, salt 1.34g

Singapore noodles with tofu

You'll love the combination of fresh tastes and textures in this dish – the crunch from the veg, the smooth noodles and the soft tofu, combined with a sweet and spicy sauce.

■ **Takes 25 minutes** ■ **Serves 2 (easily doubled)**

140g/5oz firm tofu
2 tbsp sunflower oil
3 spring onions, shredded
1 small piece of ginger, finely chopped
1 red pepper, seeded and thinly sliced
100g/4oz mangetout
300g pack straight-to-wok thin rice noodles
100g/4oz beansprouts
1 tsp tikka masala curry paste
2 tsp reduced-salt soy sauce
1 tbsp sweet chilli sauce
roughly chopped fresh coriander and lime wedges, to garnish

1 Rinse the tofu in cold water, then cut into small chunks. Pat dry with kitchen paper. Heat 1 tablespoon of the oil in a wok or large frying pan, add the tofu, then stir-fry for around 2–3 minutes until lightly browned. Drain on kitchen paper.
2 Add the remaining oil to the wok and let it heat up. Tip in the spring onions, ginger, pepper and mangetout, then stir-fry for 1 minute. Add the noodles and beansprouts, then stir to mix. Blend together the curry paste, soy, chilli sauce and 1 tablespoon water, then add to the wok, stirring until everything is well coated in the sauce. Serve sprinkled with coriander, with lime wedges for squeezing over on the side.

■ Per serving 392 kcalories, protein 12g, carbohydrate 57g, fat 15g, saturated fat 2g, fibre 4g, sugar 12g, salt 3.2g

TOP: Easy ratatouille with poached eggs

BOTTOM LEFT: Springtime pasta

BOTTOM RIGHT: Singapore noodles with tofu

TOP: Vietnamese veggie hotpot

BOTTOM LEFT: Roast summer vegetables and chickpeas

BOTTOM RIGHT: Cheesy baked onions

Vietnamese veggie hotpot

Vietnamese food is known for its hot, sour, sweet and fresh herby flavours. You'll find all of them in this reviving bowlful to be enjoyed by itself or with rice.

■ **Takes 25 minutes** ■ **Serves 4**

2 tsp vegetable oil
a thumb-sized piece of ginger, shredded
2 garlic cloves, chopped
½ large butternut squash, peeled, seeded
    and cut into chunks
2 tsp soy sauce
2 tsp light muscovado sugar
200ml/7fl oz vegetable stock
100g/4oz green beans, trimmed and sliced
4 spring onions, sliced
chopped fresh coriander, to garnish

1 Heat the oil in a medium-sized lidded pan. Add the ginger and garlic, then stir-fry for about 5 minutes. Add the squash, soy sauce, sugar and stock. Cover, then simmer for 10 minutes.
2 Remove the lid, add the green beans, then cook for 3 minutes more until the squash and beans are tender. Stir the spring onions through at the last minute, then sprinkle with coriander.

■ Per serving 75 kcalories, protein 2g, carbohydrate 13g, fat 2g, saturated fat none, fibre 3g, sugar 9g, salt 0.53g

Roast summer vegetables and chickpeas

Summery tomato-based stews like this one are perfect to make ahead. You could switch the chickpeas for butter or cannellini beans.

■ **Takes 1 hour 10 minutes** ■ **Serves 4**

3 courgettes, thickly sliced
1 aubergine, cut into thick fingers
3 garlic cloves, chopped
2 red peppers, seeded and chopped into
    chunks
2 large baking potatoes, peeled and cut into
    bite-sized chunks
1 onion, chopped
1 tbsp coriander seeds
4 tbsp olive oil
400g can chopped tomatoes
400g can chickpeas, drained and rinsed
a small bunch of coriander, roughly chopped
hunks of bread, to serve

1 Heat the oven to 220C/200C fan/gas 7. Tip all the vegetables into a large roasting tin or flameproof dish and toss with the coriander seeds, most of the olive oil and some salt and pepper. Spread everything out in a single layer and roast for 45 minutes, tossing once or twice until the vegetables are roasted and brown round the edges.
2 Place the tin over a low heat and add the tomatoes and chickpeas. Bring to a simmer and stir gently. Season to taste, drizzle with the remaining olive oil and scatter over the coriander. Serve from the tin or dish, or pile into a serving dish. Eat with hunks of bread.

■ Per serving 327 kcalories, protein 11g, carbohydrate 40g, fat 15g, saturated fat 2g, fibre 9g, sugar 13g, salt 0.51g

Cheesy baked onions

Make onions into a meal with a simple cheesy stuffing and a salad on the side.

■ **Takes 35 minutes** ■ **Serves 4**

4 large onions, peeled
½ × 150g ball reduced-fat mozzarella,
    roughly chopped
85g/3oz Cheddar, grated
2 tbsp pitted black olives, halved
50g/2oz roasted red peppers from a jar,
    drained and roughly chopped
1 garlic clove, crushed
50g/2oz fresh breadcrumbs
leaves from a few fresh thyme sprigs

1 Heat the oven to 220C/200C fan/gas 7. Halve each onion through the middle. Microwave in a baking dish in pairs for around 4 minutes on High until soft. Remove the middles of the onions, leaving about three outer layers in place, like little bowls.
2 Whizz the onion middles in a food processor until pulpy. Mix with the mozzarella, half of the Cheddar, the olives, peppers, garlic, breadcrumbs and most of the thyme, then season well. Spoon the filling into the onion cases and return to the baking dish. Sprinkle with the remaining Cheddar and thyme, then roast for 15 minutes until hot through and lightly golden.

■ Per serving 255 kcalories, protein 13g, carbohydrate 27g, fat 11g, saturated fat 6g, fibre 4g, sugar 12g, salt 1.16g

Spicy beef stew with beans and peppers

A warming winter twist on chilli con carne; perfect for Bonfire Night. It's made with chunks of braising steak instead of mince for a meltingly tender result.

■ **Takes 3 hours** ■ **Serves 6–8**

3½ tbsp vegetable oil
1kg/2lb 4oz stewing beef, cut into chunks
1 onion, sliced
2 garlic cloves, sliced
1 tbsp plain flour
1 tbsp black treacle
1 tsp ground cumin
400g can chopped tomatoes
600ml/1 pint beef stock
2 red peppers, seeded and sliced
400g can cannellini beans, drained and
    rinsed
soured cream and fresh coriander, to garnish
crusty bread, to serve

1 Heat 1 tablespoon of the oil in a large pan with a lid. Season the meat, then cook about one-third of it over a high heat for 10 minutes until browned. Tip on to a plate and repeat with 2 tablespoons of the oil and rest of the meat.
2 Add a splash of water and scrape the bottom of the pan. Add the remaining ½ tablespoon of oil. Turn down the heat; fry the onion and garlic until softened. Return the meat to the pan, add the flour and stir for 1 minute. Add the treacle, cumin, tomatoes and stock. Bring to the boil, reduce the heat, cover, then simmer for 1¾ hours. Stir occasionally and check that the meat is covered with liquid.
3 Add the peppers and beans, and cook for a further 15 minutes. Serve in bowls, with a dollop of soured cream and sprinkling of coriander, and bread to serve.

■ Per serving 400 kcalories, protein 43g, carbohydrate 18g, fat 18g, saturated fat 5g, fibre 4g, sugar 8g, salt 1.2g

Irish stew

The trick with this classic one-pot is to use a cheap cut of meat, which means you'll skimp on price but not quality. Middle neck or scrag end are both really flavoursome and perfect for braising.

■ **Takes 2½ hours** ■ **Serves 6**

1 tbsp sunflower oil
200g/8oz smoked streaky bacon,
    preferably in one piece, skinned and cut
    into chunks
900g/2lb stewing lamb, cut into large chunks
5 medium onions, sliced
5 carrots, cut into chunks
3 bay leaves
1 small bunch fresh thyme
100g/4oz pearl barley
850ml/1½ pints lamb stock
6 medium potatoes, cut into chunks
a small knob of butter
3 spring onions, finely sliced, to garnish

1 Heat the oven to 160C/140C fan/gas 3. Heat the oil in a flameproof casserole. Sizzle the bacon for 4 minutes until crisp. Turn up the heat, add the lamb and brown for 6 minutes. Remove with a slotted spoon. Add the onions, carrots and herbs to the pan, then soften for 5 minutes. Return the meat to the pan, stir in the pearl barley and stock, then bring to a simmer.
2 Sit the chunks of potato on top of the stew, cover, then braise in the oven, undisturbed, for about 1½ hours until the potatoes are soft and the meat is tender. Remove from the oven, dot the potatoes with butter, scatter with the spring onions and serve scooped straight from the dish.

■ Per serving 627 kcalories, protein 49g, carbohydrate 44g, fat 30g, saturated fat 14g, fibre 5g, sugar 11g, salt 2.13g

Greek lamb with orzo

All this needs is some crusty bread and perhaps a salad, and you're looking at a real feast. Orzo looks like large grains of rice, but is actually pasta. If you can't find it, use another small pasta, like trofie.

■ **Takes about 3 hours** ■ **Serves 6**

1kg/2lb 4oz boned shoulder of lamb
2 onions, sliced
1 tbsp chopped fresh oregano or 1 tsp dried
2 cinnamon sticks, broken in half
½ tsp ground cinnamon
2 tbsp olive oil
400g can chopped tomatoes
1.2 litres/2 pints hot vegetable or chicken
    stock
400g/14oz orzo
freshly grated Parmesan, to garnish

1 Heat the oven to 180C/160C fan/gas 4. Cut the lamb into 4cm chunks, then spread over the base of a large, wide casserole dish. Add the onions, oregano, cinnamon sticks, ground cinnamon and olive oil, then stir well. Bake, uncovered, for around 45 minutes, stirring halfway.
2 Pour over the chopped tomatoes and stock, cover tightly, then return to the oven for 1½ hours, until the lamb is very tender.
3 Remove the cinnamon sticks, then stir in the orzo. Cover again, then cook for a further 20 minutes, stirring halfway through. The orzo should be cooked and the sauce thickened. Sprinkle with grated Parmesan and serve.

■ Per serving 696 kcalories, protein 40g, carbohydrate 58g, fat 36g, saturated fat 16g, fibre 4g, sugar 7g, salt 0.68g

TOP: Spicy beef stew with beans and peppers

BOTTOM LEFT: Irish stew

BOTTOM RIGHT: Greek lamb with orzo

TOP: Coddled pork with cider

BOTTOM LEFT: One-pan rogan josh

BOTTOM RIGHT: Spiced pineapple pork

Coddled pork with cider

You could use lamb chops for this recipe, if you prefer. Simply trim the excess fat off the chops before browning.

■ **Takes 35 minutes** ■ **Serves 2 (easily doubled)**

a small knob of butter
2 pork loin chops
4 rashers smoked bacon, cut into pieces
1 carrot, cut into large chunks
2 potatoes, cut into chunks
½ small swede, cut into chunks
¼ large cabbage, cut into smaller wedges
1 bay leaf
100ml/3½fl oz cider
100ml/3½fl oz chicken stock

1 Heat the butter in a casserole dish until sizzling, then fry the pork for 2–3 minutes on each side until browned. Remove from the pan. Tip the bacon, carrot, potatoes and swede into the pan, then gently fry until slightly coloured.
2 Stir in the cabbage, sit the chops back on top, add the bay leaf, then pour over the cider and stock. Cover the pan, then leave everything to simmer gently for 20 minutes until the pork is cooked through and the vegetables are tender. Serve at the table spooned straight from the dish.

■ Per serving 717 kcalories, protein 44g, carbohydrate 37g, fat 44g, saturated fat 17g, fibre 12g, sugar 20g, salt 2.59g

One-pan rogan josh

Rich, tomatoey and better than anything you can buy – a homemade rojan josh is just three simple steps away. For a rich beef curry, use chunks of braising steak instead.

■ **Takes 1 hour 40 minutes** ■ **Serves 6**

2 onions, quartered
4 tbsp sunflower oil
4 garlic cloves, finely crushed
a thumb-sized piece of ginger, peeled and very finely grated
2 tbsp Madras curry paste
2 tsp paprika
1 cinnamon stick
6 green cardamoms, bashed to break the shells
4 cloves
2 bay leaves
1 tbsp tomato purée
1kg/2lb 4oz lean leg of lamb, cut into generous cubes
150g/5oz Greek yogurt
chopped fresh coriander leaves, to garnish

1 Put the onions in a food processor and whizz until very finely chopped. Heat the oil in a large heavy-based pan, then gently fry the onion with the lid on, stirring every now and then, until it is really golden and soft. Add the garlic and ginger, then fry for 5 minutes more.
2 Tip the curry paste, all the spices, bay leaves and tomato purée into the pan. Stir well over the heat for about 30 seconds, then add the meat and 300ml/½ pint water. Stir to mix, turn down the heat, then add the yogurt.
3 Cover the pan, then gently simmer for 40 minutes–1 hour until the meat is tender and the sauce nice and thick. Serve scattered with coriander.

■ Per serving 386 kcalories, protein 37g, carbohydrate 6g, fat 24g, saturated fat 9g, fibre 1g, sugar 3g, salt 0.54g

Spiced pineapple pork

The classic combination of pork and pineapple lives on in this slightly retro and irresistible sweet-and-sour one-pan dish.

■ **Takes 20 minutes** ■ **Serves 4**

2 tsp vegetable oil
4 pork steaks, trimmed of excess fat
2 tbsp light muscovado sugar
1 tbsp dark soy sauce
1 tsp tomato purée
432g can pineapple rings in juice, drained but juice reserved
½ tsp chilli powder
1 tsp Chinese five-spice powder
coriander leaves, to garnish

1 Add the oil to a large non-stick pan, season the steaks well, then fry for 5 minutes on each side until golden and almost cooked through. Mix together the sugar, soy sauce, tomato purée and most of the pineapple juice in a bowl.
2 Add the pineapple rings to the pan and let them caramelize a little alongside the pork. Add the chilli and five-spice to the pan, then fry for 1 minute until aromatic. Tip in the soy mix and let it bubble around the pork and pineapple for a few minutes until slightly reduced and sticky. Sprinkle with coriander before serving.

■ Per serving 315 kcalories, protein 39g, carbohydrate 22g, fat 9g, saturated fat 3g, fibre 1g, sugar 21g, salt 1.25g

Lincolnshire sausage and lentil simmer

You can offer this one-pot to just about anyone – kids and adults alike. The Puy lentils and pancetta make it a bit special, and everyone loves sausages.

■ **Takes 1½ hours** ■ **Serves 6**

1 tbsp vegetable oil
130g pack cubed pancetta or diced bacon
2 pack Lincolnshire pork or other good-
   quality sausages
2 onions, roughly chopped
1 large carrot, chopped
4 garlic cloves, roughly chopped
3 fresh rosemary sprigs
300g/10oz Puy lentils
850ml/1½ pints hot chicken stock
1 tbsp white wine vinegar
400g can chopped tomatoes
2 tbsp chopped flatleaf parsley, to garnish

1 Heat the oil in a large casserole or very large sauté pan with a lid. Add the pancetta or bacon and the sausages, and sizzle for 10 minutes, turning the sausages occasionally until nicely browned and sticky. Scoop the sausages out on to a plate.
2 Add the onions, carrot and garlic to the pancetta and continue to cook for 3–4 minutes until the onions soften.Return the sausages to the pan and add the rosemary, lentils, stock, vinegar and tomatoes, then season with salt and pepper. Bring to the boil and simmer rapidly for 5 minutes, then lower the heat, cover and simmer for 45 minutes, stirring every so often until the lentils are tender. Check the seasoning, scatter over the parsley and serve from the pan.

■ Per serving 640 kcalories, protein 39g, carbohydrate 37g, fat 37g, saturated fat 13g, fibre 6g, added sugar none, salt 4.24g

Lighter lamb burgers with smoky oven chips

The combination of lean lamb, couscous and carrot makes these burgers both nutritionally balanced and so satisfying.

■ **Takes 50 minutes** ■ **Serves 4**

100g/4oz couscous
2 carrots, finely grated
250g pack extra-lean minced lamb
1 bunch spring onions, finely chopped
1 bunch fresh mint, finely chopped
1 egg, beaten
rocket leaves and raita or natural yogurt,
   to garnish

FOR THE SMOKY OVEN CHIPS
1 tbsp olive oil
750g/1lb 10oz sweet potatoes, peeled and
   cut into chips
1–2 tsp smoked paprika

1 Heat the oven to 200C/180C fan/gas 6. Place the couscous in a heatproof bowl and pour over 100ml/3½fl oz boiling water. Leave for a couple of minutes until all the liquid has been absorbed. Squeeze any liquid out of the carrots, then stir into the couscous along with the mince, spring onions, mint and egg. Season well and shape into four large burgers. Set aside.
2 Pour the oil for the chips into a large, shallow non-stick baking sheet and heat in the oven. Add the sweet potato chips, stir around until coated with oil, then roast for 35 minutes.
3 After 15 minutes, add the burgers to the sheet. Ten minutes after this, sprinkle the paprika over the chips, shake to coat, then roast for 10 minutes more until the chips and the burgers are cooked through. Serve with the rocket and a dollop of the raita or yogurt.

■ Per serving 400 kcalories, protein 19g, carbohydrate 58g, fat 12g, saturated fat 4g, fibre 6g, sugar 15g, salt 0.28g

Corned beef hash

This is a basic, economical but still completely delicious one-pan supper. Serve with plenty of ketchup, Worcestershire or brown sauce.

■ **Takes 50 minutes** ■ **Serves 4**

4 tbsp vegetable oil
900g–1kg/2–2lb 4oz large potatoes, cut
   into small chunks
a knob of butter
1 large onion, roughly chopped
340g can corned beef, cut into chunks

1 Heat 2 tablespoons of the oil in a large non-stick frying pan, then fry the potatoes for 5 minutes, stirring often. Add a cup of water to the pan and let it boil and bubble off for 5 minutes more until the potatoes are just tender. Tip out on to a plate.
2 Put the butter and 1 tablespoon more oil into the pan over a high heat. Once foaming, tip in the onion and cook for 5 minutes until golden. Pour in the remaining oil, turn up the heat then tip in the potatoes and corned beef. Season to taste.
3 Cook for 15 minutes, folding and turning the hash every 2–3 minutes until you get lots of golden, crispy bits. Reduce the heat halfway to medium–low; cook for 5 minutes more, folding and turning the hash every so often. Season, then serve from the pan.

■ Per serving 487 kcalories, protein 28g, carbohydrate 42g, fat 24g, saturated fat 7g, fibre 4g, added sugar none, salt 2.14g

Hearty lamb and barley soup

Come home to a bowl of this hearty soup on a cold winter's day. Pearl barley plumps up as it cooks and thickens the soup beautifully.

■ **Takes 35 minutes** ■ **Serves 4**

1 tsp olive oil
200g/8oz lamb neck fillet, trimmed of fat and cut into small pieces
½ large onion, finely chopped
50g/2oz pearl barley
600g/1lb 5oz mixed root vegetables (we used potato, parsnip and swede, peeled and cubed)
2 tsp Worcestershire sauce
1 litre/1¾ pints lamb or beef stock
1 fresh thyme sprig
100g/4oz green beans (frozen are fine), halved
granary bread, to serve

1 Heat the oil in a large pan. Season the lamb, then fry for a few minutes until browned. Add the onion and barley, then gently fry for 1 minute. Add the veg, cook for 2 more minutes, then add the Worcestershire sauce, stock and thyme. Cover, then simmer for 20 minutes.
2 When everything is cooked, spoon about a quarter of the soup into a blender or processor and whizz, then stir it back into the rest of the soup. Add the green beans, simmer for 3 minutes, then ladle the soup into bowls and serve with granary bread.

■ Per serving 258 kcalories, protein 17g, carbohydrate 26g, fat 11g, saturated fat 4g, fibre 4g, sugar 12g, salt 1.48g

Classic Swedish meatballs

All these need is some crusty bread – though they're especially delicious with a spoonful of cranberry jelly or sauce.

■ **Takes 35 minutes** ■ **Serves 4**

400g/14oz lean minced pork
1 egg, beaten
1 small onion, finely chopped or grated
85g/3oz fresh white breadcrumbs
1 tbsp finely chopped fresh dill, plus extra to garnish
1 tbsp each olive oil and butter
2 tbsp plain flour
400ml/14fl oz hot beef stock

1 In a bowl, mix the mince with the egg, onion, breadcrumbs, dill and seasoning. Form into small meatballs about the size of walnuts – you should get about 20.
2 Heat the olive oil in a large non-stick frying pan and brown the meatballs. You may have to do this in two batches. Remove from the pan, melt the butter, then sprinkle over the flour and stir well. Cook for 2 minutes, then slowly whisk in the stock. Keep whisking until it is a thick gravy, then return the meatballs to the pan and heat through. Sprinkle with dill and serve.

■ Per serving 301 kcalories, protein 26g, carbohydrate 22g, fat 13g, saturated fat 4g, fibre 1g, sugar 2g, salt 1.73g

Quick and creamy steak with onion

This great little treat is easy to rustle up when you fancy something a bit special that won't take an age to put together.

■ **Takes 30 minutes** ■ **Serves 2 (easily doubled)**

300g/10oz rump steak
1 tsp seasoned plain flour
a generous knob of butter
a drizzle of olive oil
1 red onion, finely chopped
175g/6oz chestnut mushrooms, sliced
2 tsp wholegrain mustard
142ml pot soured cream

1 Thinly slice the steak into long strips across the grain, trimming off any fat. Toss the strips in a the teaspoon of seasoned flour.
2 Heat the butter and olive oil in a frying pan, then add the onion and fry for about 8 minutes, until softened and lightly coloured. Add the meat and quickly stir-fry until browned all over. Add the mushrooms and cook for 3 minutes, or until softened.
3 Season well with salt and freshly ground black pepper, then stir in the mustard and soured cream, and bring to a gentle simmer, stirring, to make a smooth, creamy sauce.

■ Per serving 502 kcalories, protein 38g, carbohydrate 9g, fat 35g, saturated fat 17g, fibre 2g, sugar 6g, salt 0.93g

Steak and sticky red-wine shallots

To turn this recipe into a quick coq au vin, make it with chicken breasts, leaving them in the pan as the wine reduces.

■ **Takes 25 minutes** ■ **Serves 2**

8 shallots, peeled and quartered
2 sirloin steaks, about 175g/6oz each
crushed black peppercorns, to taste
25g/1oz butter
4 tbsp balsamic vinegar
1 large glass red wine, about 175ml/6fl oz
150ml/¼ pint beef stock

1 Half fill a frying pan with water. Bring to the boil then add the shallots and simmer for 2–3 minutes, then drain and set aside.
2 Season the steaks with a little salt and plenty of crushed peppercorns. Heat half the butter in the pan until sizzling, then cook the steaks for 3 minutes on each side for medium or until done to your liking.
3 Remove the steaks and keep warm. While they rest, add the remaining butter to the pan, throw in the shallots, then sizzle in the sticky pan until starting to brown. Add the balsamic vinegar and bubble for a few minutes. Add the wine and boil down until sticky, then add the beef stock and simmer until everything comes together. Spoon the shallots over the steaks and serve.

■ Per serving 524 kcalories, protein 40g, carbohydrate 10g, fat 33g, saturated fat 16g, fibre 1g, sugar 10g, salt 1.87g

Pork ragout with carrots and cumin

A super-healthy stew for all the family. The kids will enjoy the sweet flavours from the carrots and raisins, and everyone will love the warm, mild spices.

■ **Takes 55 minutes** ■ **Serves 4**

1 tbsp olive oil
450g/1lb pork fillet, trimmed of all visible fat and cut into cubes
2 large onions, sliced
450g/1lb carrots, sliced thickly and diagonally
2 tsp ground cumin
½ tsp ground cinnamon
2 tbsp tomato purée
100g/4oz raisins
1 tbsp each toasted sesame seeds and chopped fresh coriander, to garnish
bread or rice, to serve

1 Heat the oil in a large pan, add the pork, then fry until the meat is sealed. Lift on to a plate. Add the onions, fry until lightly coloured, then stir in the carrots, spices, tomato purée and raisins. Add 450ml/16fl oz water, then bring to the boil.
2 Cover, gently cook for 25 minutes until the carrots are tender, add the pork to the pan, then simmer for 5 minutes until cooked through. Scatter over the sesame seeds and coriander, then serve with bread or rice.

■ Per serving 328 kcalories, protein 28g, carbohydrate 34g, fat 10g, saturated fat 2g, fibre 5g, sugar 30g, salt 0.35g

Rosemary roast chops and potatoes

A quick one-pan family roast that won't leave you arguing about the washing up!

■ **Takes 40 minutes** ■ **Serves 4**

3 tbsp olive oil
8 lamb chops
1kg/2lb 4oz potatoes, chopped into small chunks
4 fresh rosemary sprigs
4 garlic cloves, left whole
250g/9oz cherry tomatoes
1 tbsp balsamic vinegar

1 Heat the oven to 220C/200C fan/gas 7. Heat half the oil in a flameproof roasting tin or a shallow ovenproof casserole. Brown the lamb for 2 minutes on each side, then lift out of the pan. Add the rest of the oil, throw in the potatoes and fry for 4–5 minutes until starting to brown. Toss in the rosemary and garlic, then nestle the lamb in along with the potatoes.
2 Roast everything together for 20 minutes, then scatter over the tomatoes and drizzle with the vinegar. Place back in the oven for 5 minutes until the tomatoes just begin to split. Remove from the oven and serve straight from the dish.

■ Per serving 754 kcalories, protein 36g, carbohydrate 46g, fat 48g, saturated fat 21g, fibre 4g, sugar 4g, salt 0.34g

TOP: Steak and sticky red-wine shallots

BOTTOM LEFT: Pork ragout with carrots and cumin

BOTTOM RIGHT: Rosemary roast chops and potatoes

Tilapia in Thai sauce

This is a popular way to serve fish in Thailand. The only difference is they deep-fry the fish; here we've kept everything in one pan.

■ **Takes 30 minutes** ■ **Serves 2**

4 tilapia fillets (or choose any sustainably caught white fish)
2 tbsp cornflour
2 tbsp sunflower oil
4 spring onions, sliced
2 garlic cloves, crushed
a piece of ginger, finely chopped
2 tbsp soy sauce
1 tbsp brown sugar
juice of 1 lime, plus 1 lime chopped into wedges, to serve
1 red chilli, seeded and sliced, and a handful of Thai basil or coriander leaves, to garnish

1 Coat the fish fillets in the cornflour. Heat the oil in a large non-stick frying pan, sizzle the fillets for 2–3 minutes on each side until crisp, then remove and keep warm.
2 In the same pan, briefly fry the spring onions, garlic and ginger, then add the soy sauce, brown sugar and lime juice, and simmer until slightly syrupy. Spoon the sauce over the fish, scatter with the chilli and Thai basil or coriander, then serve with the lime wedges on the side.

■ Per serving 328 kcalories, protein 28g, carbohydrate 25g, fat 14g, saturated fat 2g, fibre 1g, sugar 10g, salt 2.94g

Savoy cabbage and beans with white fish

This cabbage stew is based on a peasant dish from south-west France and is served with everything from duck to fish.

■ **Takes 50 minutes** ■ **Serves 4**

a small knob of butter
5 rashers smoked streaky bacon, chopped
1 onion, finely chopped
2 celery sticks, diced
2 carrots, diced
1 small bunch fresh thyme
1 Savoy cabbage, shredded
4 tbsp white wine
300ml/½ pint chicken stock
410g can flageolet beans in water, drained and rinsed

FOR THE FISH
2 tbsp olive oil
4 sustainably caught white fish fillets, about 140g/5oz each, skin on
2 tbsp plain flour

1 Heat the butter in a large non-stick frying pan until starting to sizzle, add the bacon, then fry for a few minutes. Add the onion, celery and carrots and cook for 8–10 minutes until softening, but not brown. Stir in the thyme and cabbage, then cook for a few minutes until the cabbage starts to wilt. Pour in the wine, simmer until evaporated, then add the stock and beans. Season, cover the pan, then simmer gently for 10 minutes until the cabbage is soft but still vibrant. Spoon the cabbage into serving bowls and keep warm.
2 Wipe out the pan and heat the oil for the fish in it. Season each fillet, then dust the skin with flour. Fry the fish, skin-side down, for 4 minutes until crisp, then flip over and finish on the flesh side until cooked through. Serve each fish fillet on top of the cabbage and beans.

■ Per serving 423 kcalories, protein 42g, carbohydrate 29g, fat 16g, saturated fat 4g, fibre 10g, sugar 13g, salt 1.45g

One-pan Spanish fish stew

Use any sustainably caught white fish or salmon fillets in this recipe – perfect mopped up with crusty bread.

■ **Takes 50 minutes** ■ **Serves 4**

a handful of flatleaf parsley leaves, chopped
zest and juice of 1 lemon
2 garlic cloves, finely chopped
3 tbsp olive oil, plus extra to drizzle
1 medium onion, finely sliced
500g/1lb 2oz floury potatoes, cut into small cubes
1 tsp paprika
a pinch of cayenne pepper
400g can chopped tomatoes
1 fish stock cube, crumbled
200g/8oz raw peeled king prawns
½ × 410g can chickpeas, drained and rinsed
500g/1lb 2oz skinless fish fillets, cut into very large chunks

1 In a small bowl, mix the parsley with the lemon zest and half the garlic, then set aside. Heat 2 tablespoons oil in a large sauté pan. Add the onion and potatoes, cover and cook for 5 minutes until the onion has softened. Add the remaining oil and garlic and the spices, then cook for 2 minutes more.
2 Pour over the lemon juice, sizzle for a few seconds, then add the tomatoes, half a can of water and the stock cube. Season, cover, and simmer for 15–20 minutes until the potatoes are just cooked.
3 Stir through the prawns and chickpeas, then nestle the fish into the top of the stew. Reduce the heat, re-cover, then cook for about 8 minutes, stirring very gently once or twice. Scatter with the parsley mix and drizzle with a little extra olive oil to serve.

■ Per serving 382 kcalories, protein 39g, carbohydrate 33g, fat 11g, saturated fat 2g, fibre 5g, sugar 5g, salt 1.92g

TOP: Tilapia in Thai sauce

BOTTOM LEFT: Savoy cabbage and beans with white fish

BOTTOM RIGHT: One-pan Spanish fish stew

Tomato and thyme cod

So few ingredients, yet this dish really performs. The soy sauce adds a deep, savoury flavour to the tomatoes.

■ **Takes 20 minutes** ■ **Serves 4**

1 tbsp olive oil
1 onion, chopped
400g can chopped tomatoes
1 heaped tsp light brown soft sugar
a few fresh thyme sprigs, leaves stripped
1 tbsp soy sauce
4 sustainably caught white fish fillets

1 Heat the oil in a frying pan, add the onion, then fry for 5–8 minutes until lightly browned. Stir in the tomatoes, sugar, thyme and soy sauce, then bring to the boil. Simmer for 5 minutes, then slip the fish into the sauce.
2 Cover and gently cook for 8–10 minutes until the cod flakes easily.

■ Per serving 172 kcalories, protein 27g, carbohydrate 7g, fat 4g, saturated fat 1g, fibre 1g, sugar 6g, salt 1.1g

Trout with almonds and red peppers

Trout is quick and easy to cook, and makes a great heart-healthy meal. Swap for salmon, if you like; the cooking times will be the same.

■ **Takes 40 minutes** ■ **Serves 2**

1 large red pepper, seeded and chopped
2 large tomatoes, roughly chopped, or a
    handful of cherry tomatoes, halved
1 garlic clove, chopped
1 tbsp olive oil
1 tbsp balsamic vinegar
2 trout fillets, about 140g/5oz each
2 tbsp flaked almonds
lemon wedges and rocket leaves, to serve

1 Heat the oven to 190C/170C fan/gas 5. Tip the pepper, tomatoes, garlic, oil and vinegar into a roasting tin, then toss them together. Roast for 20 minutes, then make a space in the roasting tin for the trout fillets, scattering with the almonds and a little salt and pepper.
2 Return the tin to the oven for a further 10–15 minutes, until the fish is cooked and the almonds lightly toasted. Serve with lemon wedges for squeezing over and rocket on the side.

■ Per serving 326 kcalories, protein 31g, carbohydrate 11g, fat 18g, saturated fat 3g, fibre 3g, sugar 11g, salt 0.24g

Steamed mussels with leeks, thyme and bacon

For this dish, try to buy the smallest mussels you can find; they will always be the sweetest.

■ **Takes 35 minutes** ■ **Serves 2**

750g/1lb 10oz mussels
25g/1oz butter
6 rashers smoked streaky bacon, chopped
    into small pieces
2 small leeks, sliced on the diagonal
a handful of fresh thyme sprigs
1 small glass cider or white wine
crusty bread, to serve

1 Scrub and de-beard the mussels. Heat half the butter in a pan, then sizzle the bacon for 3–4 minutes until starting to brown. Add the leeks and thyme, then gently fry everything together for 4–5 minutes until soft.
2 Turn the heat up high, add the mussels and cider or wine, then cover and cook for 4–5 minutes, shaking the pan occasionally, until the mussels have opened. Discard any that don't open.
3 Scoop the mussels and the other solid bits into a dish, then place the pan back on the heat. Boil the juices for 1 minute with the rest of the butter, then pour over the mussels and serve with crusty bread.

■ Per serving 377 kcalories, protein 24g, carbohydrate 9g, fat 26g, saturated fat 12g, fibre 2g, sugar 5g, salt 2.76g

TOP: Tomato and thyme cod

BOTTOM LEFT: Trout with almonds and red peppers

BOTTOM RIGHT: Steamed mussels with leeks, thyme and bacon

TOP: Lemon and rosemary crusted fish fillets

BOTTOM LEFT: Smoked haddock with colcannon and mustard

BOTTOM RIGHT: Zesty roast salmon and cod

Lemon and rosemary crusted fish fillets

Pressing a layer of breadcrumbs on to fish not only adds crunch but also helps to cook it to perfection, protecting it from the direct heat of the grill. The crumbs can be made using any green herbs.

■ **Takes 20 minutes** ■ **Serves 4**

4 sustainably caught white fish fillets
2 fresh rosemary sprigs,
    leaves chopped, or 1 tsp dried
50g/2oz bread (about 2 slices), torn into
    pieces
zest of 2 lemons, plus extra wedges to serve
1 tbsp olive oil

1 Heat the grill to medium. Place the fish fillets, skin-side up, on a baking sheet, then grill for 4 minutes.
2 Meanwhile, place the rosemary, bread, lemon zest and some seasoning in a food processor, then blitz to make fine crumbs.
3 Turn the fish over, then press the crumbs over the top of each fillet. Drizzle with the olive oil, then grill for 4 minutes until the crust is golden and the fish is cooked through and just flaking. Serve with lemon wedges for squeezing over.

■ Per serving 184 kcalories, protein 26g, carbohydrate 6g, fat 6g, saturated fat 1g, fibre none, sugar none, salt 0.51g

Smoked haddock with colcannon and mustard

Take the time to cook yourself something special with this full-flavoured meal for one.

■ **Takes 30–40 minutes** ■ **Serves 1 (easily doubled)**

200ml/7fl oz vegetable stock
1 medium potato, peeled and chopped into
    small chunks
a large handful of kale, spring greens or
    cabbage, finely shredded
a small knob of butter
140g/5oz piece smoked skinned haddock
    (undyed is best)
1 heaped tbsp Dijon mustard
25g/1oz melted butter

1 Put the stock and potato in a small pan. Cover and boil for 6 minutes until the potato starts to fluff round the edges and the stock has reduced slightly. Throw in the greens and butter, stir, then cover the pan again, lower the heat and simmer for 4 minutes to soften the greens.
2 Lay the haddock fillet on top of the greens and potatoes, cover the pan and leave to steam gently for 5 minutes. Meanwhile, whisk the mustard, a splash of water and seasoning into the melted butter.
3 Prod a corner of the haddock fillet – it's ready when it flakes easily. Lift out the cooked haddock and put it to one side. Mash the potato and greens together in the pan with the pan juices. Scoop the mash on to a warmed plate, sit the haddock on top and spoon the sauce over.

■ Per serving 459 kcalories, protein 34g, carbohydrate 21g, fat 27g, saturated fat 15g, fibre 3g, added sugar none, salt 6.21g

Zesty roast salmon and cod

Roasting is a foolproof way of cooking fish. In this recipe the fish stays moist and the peppers become soft and sweet.

■ **Takes about 1 hour, plus marinating**
■ **Serves 8**

800g/1lb 12oz thick skinless salmon fillet,
    cut into 8
800g/1lb 12oz thick skinless sustainably
    caught cod loin, cut into 8
85g/3oz raisins
3 tbsp olive oil
zest and juice of 2 oranges
3 red peppers, halved, seeded and cut into 6
3 orange peppers, halved, seeded and cut
    into 6
50g/2oz toasted pine nuts
a large handful of flatleaf parsley,
    roughly chopped, to garnish

1 Place the fish and raisins in a large bowl, add 2 tablespoons of the olive oil and the orange zest and juice, and season well. Carefully toss the fish to coat, cover, and leave to marinate for 30 minutes or up to 2 hours. Heat the oven to 200C/180C fan/gas 6.
2 Meanwhile, place the peppers in a large, shallow roasting tin and drizzle with the remaining olive oil. Season, toss together and roast in the oven for 30 minutes.
3 Arrange the fish and raisins on top of the peppers and pour over the juices. Scatter the pine nuts over and season with a good pinch of salt. Cook in the oven for 12–15 minutes until the fish is just cooked through. Scatter with parsley and bring to the table.

■ Per serving 407 kcalories, protein 41g, carbohydrate 15g, fat 21g, saturated fat 3g, fibre 2g, added sugar none, salt 0.3g

Italian chicken with ham, basil and beans

Fresh tomatoes and garlic cook down to sweet, saucy pan juices in this sophisticated but so easy recipe.

■ **Takes about 1½ hours** ■ **Serves 4**

8 skinless chicken thighs, bone in
1 large bunch fresh basil
8 slices prosciutto or other dry-cured ham
2 tbsp olive oil
2 garlic bulbs, halved across the middle
800g/1lb 12oz mix yellow and red tomatoes, halved or quartered if large
175ml/6fl oz dry white wine
400g can cannellini or other white beans, drained and rinsed

1 Season the chicken thighs. Pinch off eight basil sprigs and lay one on top of each chicken thigh. Wrap each thigh in a piece of ham, with the ends tucked underneath.
2 Heat the oven to 160C/140C fan/gas 3. Heat the oil over a medium heat in a large roasting tin. Add the chicken and fry for 4 minutes each side or until the ham is just crisped and the chicken lightly golden.
3 Add the garlic, tomato, half the remaining basil leaves and the wine. Season, cover with foil, then cook in the oven for 40 minutes.
4 Take out of the oven; turn the temperature up to 220C/200C fan/gas 7. Remove the foil then stir the beans into the tomatoey juices. Return to the oven, uncovered, and cook for 30 minutes until the tomatoes, chicken and garlic are starting to crisp and chicken is very tender. Scatter over the remaining basil.

■ Per serving 455 kcalories, protein 55g, carbohydrate 22g, fat 16g, saturated fat 4g, fibre 6g, sugar 10g, salt 1.79g

Red-wine braised lamb shanks

Lamb shanks are great value and will transform into a fantastic meal with very little effort. Make them the day before for a really full flavour.

■ **Takes 2½ hours** ■ **Serves 4**

2 tbsp olive oil
4 lamb shanks
2 large onions, sliced
1 carrot, peeled and sliced
1 celery stick, sliced
2 garlic cloves, sliced
250ml/9fl oz full-bodied red wine
250ml/9fl oz beef or lamb stock
175ml/6fl oz tomato passata
1 tsp golden caster sugar
1 bay leaf
1 fresh thyme sprig
chopped flatleaf parsley, to garnish

1 Heat the oven to 160C/140C fan/gas 3. Put a large casserole dish over a high heat with 1 tablespoon olive oil. Add the lamb shanks and brown really well on all sides. Remove and set aside.
2 Reduce the heat, add the remaining olive oil and the sliced onions, carrot and celery. Cook for 5 minutes until the vegetables are mostly tender. Add the garlic and continue to cook for a further minute.
3 Pour the red wine into the pan, boil, then simmer for 3 minutes. Add the stock, passata, sugar, bay leaf, thyme and seasoning, and bring back to the boil. Add the lamb shanks, coating them in the braising liquid. Cover with a tight-fitting lid and braise for about 2 hours or until the meat is really tender, turning the meat in the liquid every 30 minutes. Check the seasoning, scatter with parsley and serve.

■ Per serving 460 kcalories, protein 37g, carbohydrate 15g, fat 24g, saturated fat 10g, fibre 3g, added sugar 2g, salt 1g

All-in-one leek and pork pot roast

Leeks are at their loveliest when slow cooked – they virtually melt into this stunning pot roast, perfect for friends to share.

■ **Takes 2¼ hours** ■ **Serves 6**

1kg/2lb 4oz boned and rolled shoulder joint of pork
6 bay leaves
2 garlic cloves, sliced
1 bunch fresh thyme sprigs
25g/1oz butter
1 tbsp sunflower oil
2 onions, peeled and cut into wedges
5 juniper berries, crushed
1 tsp golden caster sugar
1 tbsp white wine vinegar
4 whole leeks, trimmed then each cut into 3
250ml/9fl oz white wine

1 Heat the oven to 180C/160C fan/gas 4. Untie and unroll the joint then lay four bay leaves, the sliced garlic and half the thyme sprigs along the centre of the meat. Retie with string.
2 Heat the butter and oil in a casserole, then brown the pork on all sides; about 10 minutes. Add the onions, then cook for 5 minutes. Add the juniper berries, sugar and vinegar. Simmer, then tuck the leeks, remaining bay and thyme around the pork. Add the wine, cover, then cook in the oven for 1½–1¾ hours until the meat is tender.
3 To serve, remove the meat to a board. Season the veg, then use a slotted spoon to lift it into a bowl. Serve generous slices of meat with the bowl of vegetables and the sauce on the side.

■ Per serving 470 kcalories, protein 32g, carbohydrate 9g, fat 33g, saturated fat 13g, fibre 3g, sugar 7g, salt 0.36g

TOP: Italian chicken with ham, basil and beans

BOTTOM LEFT: Red-wine braised lamb shanks

BOTTOM RIGHT: All-in-one leek and pork pot roast

TOP: Roast chicken with butternut squash, chorizo and chilli

BOTTOM LEFT: Herby baked lamb in tomato sauce

BOTTOM RIGHT: Whole roast bream with potatoes and olives

Roast chicken with butternut squash, chorizo and chilli

Swap the usual spuds and gravy for warmly spiced veg and tasty nuggets of chorizo in this aromatic autumnal roast.

■ **Takes 2½ hours** ■ **Serves 6**

4 medium red onions, 1 halved, the rest cut into wedges
12 fresh sage leaves, 8 shredded, 4 left whole, plus to garnish
1 large whole chicken, about 2.25kg/5lb
1 tbsp olive oil, plus extra for greasing
1 butternut squash, peeled and cut into large chunky wedges
500g bag Charlotte potatoes, halved
2 red chillies, seeds left in and sliced
110g pack chorizo sausage, sliced
1 garlic bulb, separated into cloves

1 Heat the oven to 190C/170C fan/gas 5. Tuck two onion halves and four sage leaves inside the chicken cavity, rub the skin with a little oil, then season. Cook in the oven in a large roasting tin, breast-side down for 45 minutes. Turn over then roast for around 30 minutes more.
2 Toss the onion wedges with the shredded sage, squash, potatoes, chillies, chorizo, garlic cloves, 1 tablespoon oil and seasoning. Scatter round the chicken, toss in the pan juices; roast for 45 minutes.
3 Set the chicken aside to rest, turn the oven up to 220C/200C fan/gas 7. Toss the vegetables in the pan juices, spread over the tin to give them a bit of space, then return to the oven for 15 minutes to brown. Garnish the chicken with fresh sage leaves and serve.

■ Per serving 501 kcalories, protein 42g, carbohydrate 30g, fat 25g, saturated fat 8g, fibre 4g, sugar 11g, salt 0.57g

Herby baked lamb in tomato sauce

This is so easy to prepare and the dish almost looks after itself – the end result is packed with flavour.

■ **Takes 4¼ hours** ■ **Serves 4 (with leftovers)**

1.8kg/4lb–2kg/4lb 8oz shoulder of lamb
2 tbsp olive oil
3 fresh oregano sprigs, leaves stripped from 2
3 fresh rosemary sprigs, leaves stripped from 2
3 garlic cloves, roughly chopped
600ml/1 pint red wine
2 × 400g cans chopped tomatoes
1 tbsp caster sugar

1 Heat the oven to 220C/200C fan/gas 7. Put the lamb into a large ovenproof dish. Whizz the oil, oregano and rosemary leaves, garlic and seasoning in a food processor. Rub all over the lamb; roast for 20 minutes. Cover, lower the oven to 150C/130C fan/gas 2, then roast for 3 hours more.
2 Remove from the oven, spoon off the fat, leaving any meat juices in the pan. Add the wine, tomatoes and remaining herb sprigs, then return to the oven, uncovered, for 40 minutes more. The lamb should now be meltingly tender. Carefully transfer the lamb to a plate; cover and leave to rest.
3 Meanwhile, simmer the sauce for around 10–15 minutes until thickened. Season with the sugar, and a little salt and pepper, then return the lamb to the pan to serve.

■ Per serving 595 kcalories, protein 42g, carbohydrate 11g, fat 40g, saturated fat 19g, fibre 1g, sugar 10g, salt 0.51g

Whole roast bream with potatoes and olives

Don't be daunted by cooking whole fish – this special main course is easy to make and sure to impress.

■ **Takes 50 minutes** ■ **Serves 2 (easily doubled)**

400g/14oz new or small potatoes, thickly sliced
2 tbsp olive oil
a large handful of pitted small black olives
1 garlic clove, chopped
1 large bunch flatleaf parsley, leaves roughly chopped, stalks reserved
zest of ½ lemon
1 whole sea bream, about 450g/1lb, gutted, head on (ask your fishmonger to do this for you)
1 small glass white wine

1 Heat the oven to 220C/200C fan/gas 7. Put the potatoes in a gratin dish, toss with 1 tablespoon of the oil then roast for 20 minutes until just starting to soften. Toss the olives, garlic, half the chopped parsley, the lemon zest and some salt and pepper with the potatoes then spread over the dish.
2 Season the fish and place the parsley stalks in the cavity. Lay the fish on top of the potatoes and drizzle with the rest of the olive oil. Bake for 15 minutes. Pour the wine over, then return to the oven for 10 minutes more until the potatoes have browned and the fish is cooked.
3 Remove the dish from the oven, scatter over the rest of the parsley and bring the dish to the table. When you serve up, don't forget the lovely white wine juices in the bottom of the dish.

■ Per serving 463 kcalories, protein 34g, carbohydrate 36g, fat 20g, saturated fat 3g, fibre 3g, sugar 6g, salt 0.81g

Sirloin steaks with pizzaiola sauce

This simple recipe is ideal for a special midweek supper, as it can be cooked quickly when you get home from work. Any leftover sauce is stunning saved and used on pizzas or folded through pasta.

■ **Takes 30 minutes** ■ **Serves 4**

50ml/2fl oz olive oil
1 garlic clove, roughly chopped
4 sirloin steaks, about 140g/5oz each
2 × 400g cans chopped tomatoes
2 tsp dried oregano
rocket leaves, to garnish
bread or new potatoes, to serve

1 Heat a heavy-based frying pan over a high heat, then add the olive oil and garlic. Season the meat and then, two at a time, quickly brown the steaks in the pan on both sides.
2 Put all four steaks in the pan, add the tomatoes, season with salt and pepper, then turn down the heat. Sprinkle the oregano over the meat and tomatoes, partially cover the pan, then simmer gently for 10 minutes.
3 Lift the tender pieces of meat from the pan, cover with foil, then set aside. Increase the heat, then simmer the tomato sauce for about 10 minutes, until it has reduced by half. Spoon the sauce over the steak, garnish with rocket leaves and serve with bread or new potatoes.

■ Per serving 415 kcalories, protein 33g, carbohydrate 5g, fat 29g, saturated fat 10g, fibre 2g, sugar 4g, salt 0.63g

Chunky chilli wraps

Once you're prepped, this dish only takes about 10 minutes to cook, so it's perfect for casual last-minute entertaining. Serve with a salad, if you like.

■ **Takes 35–45 minutes** ■ **Serves 6**

1 tbsp vegetable oil, plus a few extra drizzles
750g/1lb 10oz rump steak, sliced into thin strips
1 red onion, roughly chopped
4 mild green chillies, seeded and chopped
1 tsp cumin seeds
1 tsp cayenne or hot chilli powder
400g can chopped tomatoes
420g can red kidney beans, drained and rinsed
200g/8oz roasted peppers from a jar, cut into strips
1 tsp Worcestershire sauce

TO SERVE
12 flour tortillas, warmed
284ml pot soured cream
a handful of fresh mint, roughly chopped

1 Heat the oil in a wok until hot. Tip in a third of the beef and stir-fry for 2–3 minutes until it begins to brown. Scoop out the beef and put it on a plate. Repeat with the remaining beef, adding a drizzle more oil to the pan each time.
2 Toss the onion, chillies, cumin seeds and cayenne or chilli powder into the pan, stir and sizzle for 2 minutes. Lower the heat, tip in the tomatoes, kidney beans and roasted peppers. Return the beef to the pan and cook for 2 minutes, stirring occasionally, until bubbling. Add the Worcestershire sauce and continue to simmer gently for a further 2 minutes. Season to taste.
3 To serve, heat the tortillas according to the packet instructions. Pass round the warm tortillas for wrapping up the chilli, and bowls of soured cream and mint for drizzling and scattering over.

■ Per serving 644 kcalories, protein 38g, carbohydrate 54g, fat 32g, saturated fat 13g, fibre 6g, added sugar none, salt 2.89g

Feta-crusted lamb with rich tomato sauce

If you want to cook this irresistibly easy lamb for four, simply double the ingredients and make sure you use a large-enough pan.

■ **Takes 50 minutes, plus marinating and resting**
■ **Serves 2**

7- or 8-bone rack of lamb, trimmed of fat, then cut into two racks
2 tbsp extra-virgin olive oil, plus extra to drizzle
a few fresh thyme sprigs, left whole, plus extra to serve
4 garlic cloves, crushed
zest of 1 lemon
1 tsp dried oregano, plus a pinch
20g pack flat-leaf parsley, stalks finely chopped, leaves roughly chopped
400g can cherry tomatoes
50g/2oz feta, finely crumbled
½ slice white bread (day old if you can), whizzed into crumbs

1 Put the lamb racks into a food bag with 1 tablespoon of the oil, the thyme sprigs, half the garlic, zest and oregano. Chill for 30 minutes or up to 24 hours. Make sure the lamb has returned to room temperature before cooking.
2 Heat a casserole dish, add another tablespoon of oil, the remaining garlic and the parsley stalks; soften for 1 minute. Add the tomatoes and pinch of oregano; simmer for 5 minutes. Add half the parsley leaves. Heat the oven to 230C/210C fan/gas 8. Meanwhile, mix the remaining parsley, zest and oregano, plus the feta and crumbs to make a crust.
3 Season the meat, then press the crust on. Sit the racks in the sauce, crust-side up. Strew the extra thyme sprigs over, then drizzle with oil. Roast uncovered for 20 minutes until golden and the sauce thickened. Rest for 10 minutes, then serve.

■ Per serving 582 kcalories, protein 26g, carbohydrate 12g, fat 48g, saturated fat 18g, fibre 3g, sugar 6g, salt 1.47g

TOP: Sirloin steaks with pizzaiola sauce

BOTTOM LEFT: Chunky chilli wraps

BOTTOM RIGHT: Feta-crusted lamb with rich tomato sauce

TOP: Rhubarb, ginger and apple scrunch pie

BOTTOM LEFT: Broken-biscotti ice cream with hot mocha

BOTTOM RIGHT: Star anise and lemon pears

Rhubarb, ginger and apple scrunch pie

This is the ultimate cheat's dessert; it tastes every bit as gorgeous as a full-blown fruit pie, without all the work and washing up.

■ **Takes 1 hour** ■ **Serves 6**

butter, for greasing
375g pack ready-rolled shortcrust pastry
400g/14oz Bramley apples, sliced
400g bag trimmed rhubarb, cut into lengths
100g/4oz demerara sugar, plus extra for sprinkling
2 stem ginger in syrup, drained and chopped
2 tbsp cornflour
milk, for brushing
custard, to serve

1 Heat the oven to 180C/160C fan/gas 4 and grease a large baking sheet. Unroll the pastry and place it flat on the baking sheet.
2 Mix the apple slices and the rhubarb with the sugar, ginger and cornflour, then pile into the centre of the pastry. Gather up the sides of the pastry to enclose the fruit so that the pie looks like a rough tart (you need to work with the size and shape of the pastry, so it will be more of an oblong shape than round).
3 Brush the pastry with milk and scatter with demerara. Bake for 35 minutes until the pastry is golden and the fruit is tender. Cut into slices and serve with custard.

■ Per serving 397 kcalories, protein 4g, carbohydrate 59g, fat 18g, saturated fat 9g, fibre 4g, added sugar 18g, salt 0.27g

Broken-biscotti ice cream with hot mocha

Give ice cream an Italian twist with this easy coffee-flavoured chocolatey dessert. It's so good you might want to make double!

■ **Takes 10 minutes** ■ **Serves 4**

500ml tub good-quality vanilla ice cream
12 biscotti biscuits
100g bar good-quality dark chocolate
2 tbsp brandy
200ml/7fl oz (about 1 mug) freshly made strong coffee

1 Leave the ice cream out of the freezer for 5 minutes to soften, then tip into a bowl. Put six of the biscuits into a freezer bag, squeeze out the air, then bash the biscuits into crumbs. Fold into the ice cream then return to the freezer.
2 Break the chocolate into a pan, add the brandy and heat gently until melted. Stir (it will thicken), then pour in the hot coffee and carry on stirring until it becomes a smooth mocha.
3 Scoop the ice cream into heatproof glasses or bowls, then pour the mocha over. Serve straight away with the remaining biscotti on the side.

■ Per serving 349 kcalories, protein 6g, carbohydrate 38g, fat 19g, saturated fat 11g, fibre 2g, sugar 26g, salt 0.26g

Star anise and lemon pears

Gently infused spice transforms the humble pear into a wonderful winter dessert. Serve with scoops of ice cream or a drizzle of cream.

■ **Takes 1 hour** ■ **Serves 4**

zest and juice of 1 lemon
140g/5oz golden caster sugar
4 star anise
4 ripe pears

1 Thinly peel the zest from the lemon with a potato peeler and put the zest in a pan with the sugar, star anise and 1 litre water. Bring to the boil, then leave to infuse for 5 minutes.
2 Peel and core the pears, leaving the stem on, then lower into the syrup. Cover and leave to cook on a gentle heat for 10 minutes or until the pears are tender. Lift the pears from the pan, then boil the liquid over a high heat until syrupy. Squeeze the juice from the lemon into the syrup, then pour over the pears. Eat warm or chilled.

■ Per serving 205 kcalories, protein 1g, carbohydrate 53g, fat none, saturated fat none, fibre 3g, added sugar 37g, salt 0.02g

Pasta and noodle recipes

Storecupboard minestrone

Adapt this tasty and substantial winter soup according to what you've got in the freezer – try adding frozen broad beans, sweetcorn or spinach.

■ **Takes 30 minutes** ■ **Serves 2**

2 tbsp olive oil
1 onion, roughly chopped
2 × 400g cans chopped tomatoes
1 tbsp vegetable bouillon powder
1 tbsp pesto, plus extra to serve
pinch of sugar
50g/2oz dried mini pasta shapes for soup (such as farfalline), or spaghetti or other pasta, broken into small pieces
420g can mixed pulses, drained and rinsed
200g/8oz frozen green vegetables, such as sliced green beans and peas

1 Heat the oil in a large pan and cook the onion over a low heat until softened. Pour in the tomatoes and 4 canfuls of water. Sprinkle in the bouillon powder, then stir in the pesto, sugar and seasoning to taste.
2 Increase the heat and bring to the boil. Add the pasta and simmer for 10 minutes or until just tender, stirring occasionally.
3 Tip in the pulses and frozen vegetables, stir well and bring to the boil again. Cover and simmer for 10 minutes, stirring occasionally. Taste for seasoning. Serve with extra pesto.

■ Per serving 256 kcalories, protein 12g, carbohydrate 33g, fat 9g, saturated fat 2g, fibre 9g, added sugar 1g, salt 2.16g

Sizzled sausage pasta

This hearty dish tastes great cold, so pack any leftovers into your lunchbox.

■ **Takes 25 minutes** ■ **Serves 4**

400g/14oz short pasta shapes, such as trompetti
6 good-quality sausages
140g/5oz sun-dried tomatoes
4 tbsp oil from the sun-dried tomato jar
generous handful of parsley, coarsely chopped

1 Cook the pasta in a large pan of salted boiling water for 8–10 minutes, or according to the packet instructions.
2 Meanwhile, peel the skins off the sausages and chop the meat into small pieces. Chop the tomatoes into small chunks. Heat 1 tablespoon of the tomato oil in a large, deep frying pan or wok and sizzle the sausage chunks for 6–8 minutes until crumbly and golden. Stir in the tomato chunks and the remaining oil, then heat through.
3 Drain the pasta well and toss into the sausage mixture with the parsley. Season, make sure everything is well mixed and serve straight from the pan.

■ Per serving 775 kcalories, protein 28g, carbohydrate 86g, fat 38g, saturated fat 10g, fibre 5g, added sugar none, salt 3.24g

Tuna pasta niçoise

No microwave? Cook the oil, lemon juice or vinegar, tomatoes and anchovies in a pan over a low heat for 3–4 minutes, stirring once.

■ **Takes 20 minutes** ■ **Serves 4**

350g/12oz short pasta shapes, such as conchiglie or penne
4 tbsp olive oil
1 tbsp lemon juice or white wine vinegar
250g pack cherry tomatoes, halved
50g can anchovy fillets, drained and chopped
80g can tuna in olive oil, drained
handful of fresh herbs, such as chives, basil, parsley

1 Cook the pasta in a large pan of salted boiling water for 8–10 minutes, or according to the packet instructions.
2 Meanwhile, put the oil and lemon juice or vinegar into a medium microwave-proof bowl. Tip in the tomatoes and anchovies, and gently mix with the dressing. Microwave on High for 2–2 ½ minutes, stirring halfway through, until the tomatoes just start to burst and soften.
3 Drain the pasta and return it to the pan. Break the tuna into rough chunks, then toss into the pasta with the tomatoes and herbs. Season with black pepper and serve immediately.

■ Per serving 474 kcalories, protein 18g, carbohydrate 68g, fat 16g, saturated fat 2g, fibre 3g, added sugar none, salt 0.94g

TOP: Storecupboard minestrone

BOTTOM LEFT: Sizzled sausage pasta

BOTTOM RIGHT: Tuna pasta niçoise

TOP: Conchiglie with tomato sauce

BOTTOM LEFT: Creamy pasta with crispy bacon

BOTTOM RIGHT: Chicken with creamy bacon penne

Conchiglie with tomato sauce

This simple Italian dish with a kick is perfect for entertaining if you're short of time.

■ **Takes 20 minutes** ■ **Serves 6**

2 tbsp extra-virgin olive oil
2 garlic cloves, chopped
300ml/½ pint good-quality tomato passata
500g pack conchiglie or other short pasta shapes
50g/2oz butter
1 tbsp crushed black pepper
100ml/3½fl oz single cream
small handful of fresh basil leaves, roughly torn
2 tbsp vodka (optional)
3 tbsp freshly grated Parmesan

1 Heat the oil in a small pan and fry the garlic gently until golden. Stir in the passata, season and simmer for 10 minutes.
2 While the sauce is cooking, boil the pasta in salted water according to the packet instructions. Drain well.
3 Melt the butter in a large pan, add the pasta and black pepper, and toss well until the pasta is coated. With the heat high, continue tossing the pasta while adding the tomato sauce, cream and basil. Stir in the vodka, if using. Serve straight away, sprinkled with the Parmesan.

■ Per serving 476 kcalories, protein 13g, carbohydrate 69g, fat 17g, saturated fat 8g, fibre 3g, added sugar 1g, salt 0.6g

Creamy pasta with crispy bacon

Short pasta shapes are good for serving with this delicious sauce, as it gets trapped inside.

■ **Takes 25 minutes** ■ **Serves 2**

200g/8oz short pasta shapes, such as trompetti, conchiglie or penne
85g/3oz frozen peas
4 rashers back bacon
25g/1oz butter
1 small onion, finely chopped
142ml pot whipping or double cream
20g pack flatleaf parsley, roughly chopped

1 Cook the pasta in a large pan of salted boiling water for 8–10 minutes, or according to the packet instructions. Add the peas to the pasta for the last 3 minutes.
2 While the pasta is cooking, grill the bacon until crisp, then snip into strips with scissors. Melt the butter in a pan and fry the onion over a medium heat for about 5 minutes until soft and golden. Pour in the cream, season and simmer until thickened slightly.
3 Drain the pasta and peas, reserving some of the water, then return to the pan and pour in the sauce. Toss well to mix, adding some of the water if the sauce is too thick. Toss in the parsley and bacon, taste for seasoning and serve straight away.

■ Per serving 911 kcalories, protein 25g, carbohydrate 84g, fat 55g, saturated fat 30.1g, fibre 6.2g, added sugar none, salt 1.92g

Chicken with creamy bacon penne

This amazingly quick and tasty dish works well with fresh salmon, too. Just cook for 3 minutes on each side and leave out the bacon.

■ **Takes 10 minutes** ■ **Serves 2**

1 tbsp olive oil
2 boneless skinless chicken breasts
100g/4oz smoked lardons (chopped bacon)
4 tbsp dry white wine
100g/4oz frozen petits pois
5 tbsp double cream
220g pack 'instant' cooked penne

1 Heat the oil in a deep non-stick frying pan, add the chicken and scatter with the lardons. Leave to cook over a high heat for 4 minutes.
2 Turn the chicken over in the pan, give the lardons a stir, then pour in the wine and let it bubble over a high heat until it has virtually evaporated.
3 Now add the peas, cream and penne, season and stir well. Cover the pan and cook for 4 minutes more until the chicken is cooked all the way through. Serve straight away.

■ Per serving 639 kcalories, protein 48g, carbohydrate 24g, fat 38g, saturated fat 17g, fibre 3g, added sugar none, salt 1.86g

TOP: Home-from-work spaghetti

BOTTOM LEFT: Leek, pea and ham pasta

BOTTOM RIGHT: Spaghetti with chorizo

Home-from-work spaghetti

Use 100g/4oz frozen peas instead of the courgettes, if you prefer.

■ **Takes 20 minutes** ■ **Serves 4**

400g/14oz spaghetti
2 tbsp olive oil
4 rashers streaky bacon, chopped
2 courgettes, chopped
250g pack cherry tomatoes, halved
4 tbsp pesto
freshly grated Parmesan, to serve

1 Cook the spaghetti in a large pan of salted boiling water for 10–12 minutes, or according to the packet instructions.
2 Meanwhile, heat the oil in a large, deep frying pan and fry the bacon for 5 minutes until it starts to crisp. Tip in the courgettes and tomatoes, and cook for 2–3 minutes until the courgettes begin to brown round the edges and the tomatoes start to soften.
3 When the pasta is cooked, spoon a couple of tablespoons of the water into the vegetables, then drain the pasta and tip it into the vegetables too. Spoon in the pesto and toss until everything is coated. Serve with Parmesan.

■ Per serving 512 kcalories, protein 19g, carbohydrate 77g, fat 16g, saturated fat 4g, fibre 4g, added sugar none, salt 0.81g

Leek, pea and ham pasta

A cheap and easy supper made from readily available ingredients.

■ **Takes 15 minutes** ■ **Serves 4**

300g/10oz spaghetti
175g/6oz frozen peas
25g/1oz butter
1 large leek
4 eggs
140g/5oz thick slice smoked ham, cut into cubes
85g/3oz Cheddar or Lancashire cheese, grated

1 Bring a large pan of salted water to the boil. Add the spaghetti and cook for about 10–12 minutes, adding the peas for the last 3 minutes of the cooking time.
2 Meanwhile, heat the butter in a small pan. Wash and slice the leek. Add to the pan and cook over a medium heat for 3 minutes until softened.
3 Beat the eggs in a bowl and season. Drain the pasta and immediately return to the pan. Tip in the leeks, eggs, ham and half the cheese. Stir well. Adjust the seasoning and serve sprinkled with the remaining cheese.

■ Per serving 553 kcalories, protein 32g, carbohydrate 61g, fat 22g, saturated fat 10g, fibre 6g, added sugar none, salt 1.67g

Spaghetti with chorizo

A quick, tasty and filling pasta dish – just toss it together and serve.

■ **Takes 10 minutes** ■ **Serves 4**

80g pack sliced chorizo
good handful of flatleaf parsley
2 red peppers from a jar, in brine or oil
300g/10oz fresh spaghetti
2 tbsp olive oil
50g/2oz Parmesan, freshly grated, plus extra to serve

1 Put a pan of water on a high heat to boil. Meanwhile, snip the chorizo into strips with scissors and chop the parsley and red peppers.
2 When the water is boiling briskly, add the spaghetti with a good measure of salt, stir and return to the boil. Cook for 3 minutes.
3 In a large frying pan, heat the oil and add the chorizo, peppers and plenty of black pepper. Cook for a minute or so, until heated through and the juices are stained red from the paprika in the chorizo. Scoop half a mugful of pasta water from the pan, drain the remainder and tip the spaghetti into the frying pan.
4 Add the parsley and Parmesan, toss well and splash in the pasta water, to moisten. Hand round extra Parmesan at the table.

■ Per serving 444 kcalories, protein 18g, carbohydrate 46g, fat 22g, saturated fat 6g, fibre 3g, added sugar none, salt 2.21g

Chicken tarragon pasta

Use cooked, flaked salmon or white fish instead of the chicken, if you prefer.

■ **Takes 30 minutes** ■ **Serves 3**

250g/9oz pasta, such as pappardelle or tagliatelle
2 tbsp olive oil
2 boneless skinless chicken breasts, cut into small pieces
2 garlic cloves, chopped
142ml pot single cream
3 tbsp roughly chopped fresh tarragon leaves
100g/4oz spinach leaves, thick stalks removed
lemon wedges, to garnish

1 Cook the pasta in a large pan of salted boiling water for 8–10 minutes, or according to the packet instructions.
2 Meanwhile, heat the oil in a large frying pan and fry the chicken over a high heat for 4–5 minutes, until golden and cooked. Add the garlic, cream, tarragon and 3 tablespoons of the pasta cooking water. Heat through gently.
3 When the pasta is cooked, stir in the spinach (it will wilt in the hot water). Drain the spinach and pasta well, then toss into the creamy chicken. Season and serve with lemon wedges.

■ Per serving 560 kcalories, protein 35g, carbohydrate 65g, fat 19g, saturated fat 7g, fibre 3g, added sugar none, salt 0.58g

Pork with pappardelle

Serve this simple but impressive dish with a crisp green salad.

■ **Takes 25 minutes** ■ **Serves 4**

500g/1lb 2oz pork fillet, cut into 2cm/¾in-thick slices
seasoned flour, for coating
2 tbsp olive oil
300g/10oz pappardelle
25g/1oz pine nuts
grated zest of ½ lemon
juice of 1 lemon
1 tbsp clear honey
good handful of flatleaf parsley, chopped

1 Toss the pork in seasoned flour to coat very lightly. Shake off the excess. Heat 1 tablespoon of the oil in a large frying pan and fry the pork in a single layer until browned, about 3 minutes each side. Remove and keep warm.
2 Cook the pasta in a large pan of salted boiling water according to the packet instructions. Meanwhile, heat the remaining oil in the frying pan and fry the pine nuts until lightly browned. Stir in the lemon zest and juice and honey, then bubble Briefly, stirring, to make a sauce.
3 Return the pork to the pan and scatter with the parsley. Cook for 3 minutes, turning the pork halfway through, until hot. Drain the pasta and serve with the pork.

■ Per serving 566 kcalories, protein 38g, carbohydrate 64g, fat 19g, saturated fat 4.4g, fibre 2.7g, added sugar 2.9g, salt 0.44g

Spaghetti with hot-smoked salmon

You can fry the breadcrumbs several hours ahead and, by the time the spaghetti has cooked, the remaining ingredients will be ready as well.

■ **Takes 40 minutes** ■ **Serves 4–6**

125ml/4fl oz extra-virgin olive oil
25g/1oz fresh white breadcrumbs
500g/1lb 2oz spaghetti
2 garlic cloves, very finely chopped
2 tiny dried bird's eye chillies, finely crumbled, or ¼ tsp chilli flakes
finely grated zest of 1 lemon
4 tbsp capers in brine, drained
85g/3oz rocket leaves
200g/8oz hot-smoked salmon, flaked

1 Heat 2 tablespoons of the oil in a small frying pan and fry the breadcrumbs over a medium heat for 3–4 minutes until golden and crisp, turning often. Tip into a small bowl. Set aside.
2 Cook the pasta in plenty of salted boiling water for 10–12 minutes, or according to the packet instructions. Put the rest of the oil in a small pan with the garlic and chillies. Warm gently over a low heat so they flavour the oil – don't let the garlic fry.
3 Drain the pasta and tip it into a warmed, very large serving bowl. Quickly add the lemon zest and capers to the flavoured oil, then pour over the pasta. Toss well, add the rocket and salmon, and toss again, taking care not to break up the salmon too much. Scatter the breadcrumbs on top just before serving.

■ Per serving (4) 796 kcalories, protein 28g, carbohydrate 99g, fat 35g, saturated fat 5.3g, fibre 4.5g, added sugar none, salt 2.41g

TOP: Chicken tarragon pasta

BOTTOM LEFT: Pork with pappardelle

BOTTOM RIGHT: Spaghetti with hot-smoked salmon

TOP: Four-cheese pasta
florentine

BOTTOM LEFT: Sicilian lamb
with noodles

BOTTOM RIGHT: Spaghetti
bolognese

Four-cheese pasta florentine

Create something special using a storecupboard sauce.

■ **Takes 25 minutes** ■ **Serves 4**

400g/14oz penne
225g pack chestnut mushrooms, thickly
    sliced
1 tsp olive oil
350g jar four cheese sauce
250g bag baby spinach leaves
25g/1oz walnut halves, broken up roughly
50g/2oz blue cheese, crumbled

1 Heat the grill. Cook the pasta in a large pan of salted boiling water for 10 minutes, or according to the packet instructions. Meanwhile, fry the mushrooms in the oil for 5 minutes until golden and softened.
2 Tip the four cheese sauce and spinach into the mushroom pan and heat through until the spinach wilts. Drain the pasta, stir into the sauce and season with pepper.
3 Tip into a large baking dish, sprinkle the walnuts over, then scatter the blue cheese on top. Grill for 5–8 minutes until the cheese bubbles.

■ Per serving 639 kcalories, protein 24g, carbohydrate 83g, fat 25g, saturated fat 10g, fibre 6g, added sugar none, salt 1.31g

Sicilian lamb with noodles

Use home-grown or vine-ripened tomatoes for the sauce as an intense, sweet tomato flavour is at the heart of this dish.

■ **Takes about 1 hour** ■ **Serves 6**

1 large onion, roughly chopped
2 fresh red chillies, seeded and roughly
    chopped
1kg/2lb 4oz ripe tomatoes, halved
2 red peppers, seeded and chopped
2 garlic cloves, peeled
5 tbsp olive oil
1kg/2lb 4oz lamb fillet, trimmed of fat and
    cut into 2cm/¾in slices
500g pack egg pappardelle
50g/2oz pine nuts, toasted
5 tbsp chopped fresh mint
2 tbsp chopped fresh parsley

1 Heat the oven to 200C/180C fan/gas 6. Put the onion, chillies, tomatoes, peppers and garlic in a roasting tin. Drizzle with 2 tablespoons of the oil, season and roast for 25 minutes. Tip the vegetables and juices into a food processor and whizz to a chunky sauce.
2 Heat 2 more tablespoons of the oil in a large pan and fry the lamb over a high heat until browned. Lower the heat, stir in the tomato sauce and simmer, uncovered, for 20–30 minutes until the lamb is tender.
3 Cook the pasta according to the packet instructions. Drain and return to the pan with the pine nuts, herbs and remaining oil. Season and toss well before serving with the lamb.

■ Per serving 864 kcalories, protein 46g, carbohydrate 72g, fat 46g, saturated fat 14g, fibre 3.2g, added sugar none, salt 0.69g

Spaghetti bolognese

A new twist on a classic recipe. For an even healthier version, use turkey mince, as it's brilliantly low in fat.

■ **Takes about 1 hour** ■ **Serves 4**

2 tbsp olive oil
1 onion, finely chopped
1 celery stick, finely chopped
450g/1lb lean minced beef
2 garlic cloves, crushed
2 tbsp sun-dried tomato purée
400g can chopped tomatoes
150ml/¼ pint beef stock
350g/12oz spaghetti
50g/2oz pitted black olives, chopped
    (optional)
handful of basil leaves, torn

1 Heat the oil in a large pan and fry the onion and celery gently for 5 minutes or until softened. Add the beef and garlic, and fry for 3–4 minutes until the meat has browned, pressing with a spoon to remove any lumps. Stir in the tomato purée, then tip in the tomatoes. Swirl the stock in the tomato can, pour into the pan and bring to the boil. Season, cover and simmer gently for 35–40 minutes, stirring occasionally.
2 About 15 minutes before the end of cooking, boil the spaghetti according to the packet instructions.
3 Stir the olives, if using, and basil into the sauce and heat through. Drain the spaghetti, toss with the sauce and serve straight away.

■ Per serving 594 kcalories, protein 37g, carbohydrate 69g, fat 20g, saturated fat 5.7g, fibre 4g, added sugar none, salt 0.69g

TOP: Farfalle with chicken and asparagus

BOTTOM LEFT: Mediterranean chicken pasta

BOTTOM RIGHT: Stroganoff with parsley noodles

Farfalle with chicken and asparagus

The arrival of new-season English asparagus in May is the perfect excuse for cooking this impressive, creamy dish.

■ **Takes 35 minutes** ■ **Serves 4–6**

500g/1lb 2oz asparagus, trimmed
2 lemons
100g/4oz thinly sliced pancetta or rindless streaky bacon
500g/1lb 2oz farfalle (pasta bows)
50g/2oz butter
284ml pot double cream
2 cooked boneless skinless chicken breasts, torn into strips
50g/2oz Parmesan, freshly grated
few gratings of fresh nutmeg

1 Cut the asparagus into short lengths on the diagonal, keeping the tips separate. Cook the stems in salted boiling water for 4 minutes, add the tips and cook for 1 minute more. Drain and refresh under cold running water.
2 Peel and segment the lemons, removing the pith, then cut the segments into small pieces and put them in a bowl with any juice. Grill the pancetta or bacon for 3–4 minutes until crisp.
3 Cook the pasta in salted boiling water according to the packet instructions. Meanwhile, simmer the butter and half the cream in a large pan for 2–3 minutes until slightly thickened. Tip in the lemons and juice, chicken and asparagus. Turn off the heat.
4 Drain the pasta and add to the chicken with the rest of the cream. Toss well, adding the Parmesan and nutmeg. Season and serve topped with the pancetta or bacon.

■ Per serving (4) 1122 kcalories, protein 47g, carbohydrate 100g, fat 63g, saturated fat 33.4g, fibre 6g, added sugar none, salt 1.89g

Mediterranean chicken pasta

Vegetarians can omit the chicken and stir in a 400g can of chickpeas (drained) 5 minutes before the end of the roasting time.

■ **Takes 35–45 minutes** ■ **Serves 4**

2 boneless skinless chicken breasts, cut into chunks
1 red onion, cut into 8 wedges
1 red pepper, seeded and cut into 8 strips
2 garlic cloves, unpeeled
3 tbsp olive oil
300g/10oz short pasta shapes, such as rigatoni
4 tbsp pesto
200g/8oz cherry tomatoes, halved
100g/4oz firm goat's cheese or feta

1 Heat the oven to 200C/180C fan/gas 6. Put the chicken, onion, red pepper and garlic cloves in a roasting tin and drizzle with the oil. Season to taste. Mix with a spoon and roast for 20 minutes.
2 After the chicken has been cooking for 5 minutes, cook the pasta in a pan of salted boiling water according to the packet instructions. Drain well.
3 When the chicken and vegetables are cooked, remove from the oven. Slip the garlic out of its skin and mash in the tin with a spoon, then tip in the pasta, pesto and tomatoes, and carefully mix together. Crumble the cheese over the top, check the seasoning and serve.

■ Per serving 605 kcalories, protein 34g, carbohydrate 64g, fat 26g, saturated fat 9g, fibre 4g, added sugar none, salt 0.78g

Stroganoff with parsley noodles

Create an unusual supper for two using just a few simple ingredients.

■ **Takes 30 minutes** ■ **Serves 2**

2 tbsp olive oil
1 onion, thinly sliced
2 steaks (fillet, sirloin or rump – whatever you like best), cut into bite-sized chunks
1 garlic clove, crushed
1 tsp paprika, plus extra for sprinkling
1 tbsp tomato purée
300ml/½ pint beef stock
175g/6oz tagliatelle
knob of butter
handful of fresh flatleaf parsley, chopped
142ml pot soured cream

1 Heat the oil in a deep frying pan and cook the onion gently for about 5 minutes until softened but not coloured. Tip in the steak and garlic, increase the heat and cook briskly until the meat is browned on all sides. Lower the heat and stir in the paprika, tomato purée and stock. Season, then simmer gently until the pasta is ready.
2 Cook the tagliatelle in a large pan of salted boiling water, according to the packet instructions. Drain and return to the pan, then toss with the butter and parsley.
3 Stir all but 2 tablespoons of the soured cream into the stroganoff and heat through gently, then serve with the pasta, topped with the remaining soured cream and a sprinkling of paprika.

■ Per serving 895 kcalories, protein 58g, carbohydrate 77g, fat 42g, saturated fat 17.1g, fibre 4g, added sugar none, salt 0.91g

TOP: Spaghetti with broccoli and tomatoes

BOTTOM LEFT: Spaghetti with pea and mint pesto

BOTTOM RIGHT: Veggie pasta with goat's cheese

Spaghetti with broccoli and tomatoes

Cooking the broccoli with the pasta adds flavour to the finished dish.

■ **Takes 30 minutes** ■ **Serves 4**

400g/14oz spaghetti
300g/10oz broccoli, trimmed and cut into
   small florets
3 tbsp olive oil
1 onion, finely chopped
2 garlic cloves, crushed
1 fresh red chilli, seeded and finely chopped
2 SunBlush or sun-dried tomatoes, snipped
   into small pieces
4 ripe plum tomatoes, roughly chopped
freshly grated vegetarian Parmesan, to serve

1 Cook the spaghetti into a large pan of salted boiling water for 8 minutes. Add the broccoli florets and continue boiling for another 3–4 minutes or until the spaghetti is tender.
2 While the pasta is cooking, heat the oil in a separate pan and gently cook the onion, garlic and chilli for about 5 minutes until softened but not browned. Tip in both types of tomatoes, season and simmer for a further 5 minutes.
3 Drain the pasta and broccoli, reserving some of the water. Toss with the tomato mixture, moistening with water if necessary. Spoon into 4 warmed bowls and serve with Parmesan.

■ Per serving 474 kcalories, protein 17g, carbohydrate 82g, fat 11g, saturated fat 1.5g, fibre 6.4g, added sugar none, salt 0.11g

Spaghetti with pea and mint pesto

If you have any of this delicious pesto left over, try it on top of grilled or barbecued lamb chops.

■ **Takes 35–40 minutes** ■ **Serves 4**

250g/9oz shelled fresh peas, just under
   900g/2lb in their pods
2 fat garlic cloves, finely chopped
50g/2oz pine nuts, toasted
50g/2oz Parmesan, chopped into small
   chunks
good handful of fresh mint leaves (about
   20g/¾oz)
6 tbsp extra-virgin olive oil
350g/12oz spaghetti

TO SERVE
freshly grated vegetarian Parmesan
extra-virgin olive oil

1 Cook the peas in boiling water for 2–3 minutes until just tender, then drain and refresh under cold running water. Pat dry, then tip into a food processor and add the garlic, pine nuts, Parmesan, mint and oil. Season, then pulse very briefly until the ingredients are roughly chopped.
2 Cook the spaghetti according to the packet instructions. Drain, reserving some of the water, then toss with the pesto and about 2 tablespoons of the water.
3 Pile into warmed bowls and serve at once, with Parmesan and olive oil at the table.

■ Per serving 640 kcalories, protein 21g, carbohydrate 72g, fat 32g, saturated fat 6g, fibre 6g, added sugar none, salt 0.30g

Veggie pasta with goat's cheese

This simple and delicious supper dish for two combines larder ingredients in a slightly unusual way. Serve with a green salad.

■ **Takes 25 minutes** ■ **Serves 2**

200g/8oz farfalle (pasta bows)
100g/4oz frozen peas
finely grated zest of 1 lemon
2 tbsp extra-virgin olive oil
100g/4oz goat's cheese, crumbled
100g/4oz chargrilled (antipasto) peppers
   from a jar, torn into strips

1 Tip the pasta into a large pan of salted boiling water and cook according to the packet instructions. Three minutes before the pasta is ready, throw in the peas.
2 When the pasta and peas are cooked, drain, reserving some of the water, then tip the pasta and peas back into the pan. Over a low heat, stir in the lemon zest and 1 tablespoon of the oil, then 4 tablespoons pasta water, the goat's cheese and pepper strips.
3 Season and heat through until the cheese begins to melt. Spoon the pasta and veggies into warmed bowls and top with a grinding of black pepper and a drizzle of oil. Serve straight away.

■ Per serving 671 kcalories, protein 22g, carbohydrate 85g, fat 29g, saturated fat 3g, fibre 7g, added sugar none, salt 2.5g

Pumpkin pasta

You can make the mozzarella butter in advance and freeze it, so that you'll always be ready to whip up this delicious and unusual pasta dish.

■ **Takes about 1 hour** ■ **Serves 4**

3 tbsp olive oil
2 garlic cloves, crushed
125g ball mozzarella, roughly chopped
50g/2oz unsalted butter, softened
small handful of fresh sage leaves, plus extra to garnish
grated zest and juice of 1 lemon
500g/1lb 2oz piece pumpkin (unpeeled weight), peeled, seeded and cut into 2cm/¾in cubes
300g/10oz conchiglie
85g/3oz vegetarian Parmesan, freshly grated

1 Heat 1 tablespoon of the oil in a small pan and soften the garlic, then blend to a coarse paste in a food processor with the mozzarella, butter, sage, lemon zest and juice and seasoning. Transfer to a piece of parchment paper or cling film, roll into a cylinder and chill for at least 30 minutes.
2 Heat the oven to 200C/180C fan/gas 6. Heat the remaining oil in a roasting tin in the oven for 5 minutes. Toss in the pumpkin, season and roast for 25–30 minutes, turning occasionally.
3 Cook the pasta according to the packet instructions. Drain and return to the pan with the pumpkin and Parmesan. Slice the mozzarella butter, add to the pan and toss to mix and melt. Serve topped with sage.

■ Per serving 634 kcalories, protein 26g, carbohydrate 60g, fat 34g, saturated fat 17g, fibre 4g, added sugar none, salt 1.10g

Rigatoni with roasted squash

Roasting the squash brings out its sweet, nutty flavour and the onions add a savoury note.

■ **Takes 50 minutes** ■ **Serves 2 generously**

1 butternut squash, about 700g/1lb 9oz
2 red onions
2 garlic cloves, sliced
2 tbsp olive oil
175g/6oz rigatoni or penne
3 rounded tbsp crème fraîche
freshly grated vegetarian Parmesan, to serve (optional)

1 Heat the oven to 200C/180C fan/gas 6. Peel, halve and seed the squash, then cut into bite-sized chunks and tip into a roasting tin. Peel the onions, leaving the roots intact, then cut each one lengthways into 8 wedges and add them to the tin with the garlic, oil and seasoning. Toss until all the ingredients are glistening, then roast for 30 minutes.
2 Meanwhile, cook the pasta in salted boiling water for 8–10 minutes, or according to the packet instructions, until tender. Drain, reserving 4 tablespoons of the water.
3 Remove the tin from the oven and stir in the 4 tablespoons water and the crème fraîche, then toss in the pasta. Serve sprinkled with black pepper and Parmesan, if you like.

■ Per serving 572 kcalories, protein 16.7g, carbohydrate 102g, fat 13.8g, saturated fat 7.6g, fibre 9.2g, added sugar none, salt 0.16g

Roasted vegetable and feta pasta

Tossing the spinach into the hot ingredients just before serving preserves both its vitamins and texture.

■ **Takes 45–55 minutes** ■ **Serves 2**

1 small butternut squash, peeled, seeded and cut into chunks
1 large red pepper, seeded and cut into chunks
2 garlic cloves, roughly chopped
60g/2½oz feta, crumbled
1 tsp finely chopped fresh rosemary
1 tbsp olive oil
200g/8oz penne or other short pasta shape
100g/4oz baby spinach leaves

1 Heat the oven to 200C/180C fan/gas 6. Put the squash, pepper, garlic, feta and rosemary into a large roasting tin. Sprinkle over the oil and plenty of freshly ground black pepper. Toss until lightly coated, then roast for 30–40 minutes, tossing again after 15 minutes.
2 Meanwhile, cook the pasta in a large pan of salted boiling water for 8 minutes, or according to the packet instructions.
3 Take the tin from the oven. Scoop out about half a mugful of the pasta water. Drain the pasta and toss it into the tin with the spinach. Stir until the spinach starts to wilt, adding a splash of the reserved water to moisten if necessary. Serve straight away.

■ Per serving 605 kcalories, protein 22g, carbohydrate 104g, fat 14g, saturated fat 5g, fibre 10g, added sugar none, salt 1.34g

Tagliatelle with goat's cheese

Mushrooms add a deliciously nutty flavour and juicy texture to this veggie-friendly pasta.

■ **Takes 20 minutes** ■ **Serves 2 (easily doubled)**

250g/9oz chestnut mushrooms
1 small onion
2 garlic cloves
175g/6oz tagliatelle
25g/1oz butter
1 tbsp olive oil, plus extra for drizzling
100g/4oz firm goat's cheese
freshly shaved vegetarian Parmesan, to serve

1 Slice the mushrooms and finely chop the onion and garlic. Cook the pasta in plenty of salted boiling water according to the packet instructions.
2 Heat the butter and oil in a frying pan until the butter has melted. Add the onion and cook until golden, about 3–4 minutes. Stir in the garlic and mushrooms, and cook, stirring, until the mushrooms are golden brown.
3 Drain the pasta, reserving 4 tablespoons of the water. Return the pasta to its pan with the reserved water and stir in the mushroom mixture. Roughly break the goat's cheese into pieces and gently stir it into the pasta so it starts to melt. Serve sprinkled with a grinding of black pepper, a drizzle of olive oil and a few shavings of Parmesan.

■ Per serving 598 kcalories, protein 20g, carbohydrate 71g, fat 28g, saturated fat 8g, fibre 5g, added sugar none, salt 0.88g

Pasta Primavera

A seasonal celebration of fresh summer vegetables that makes the perfect weekend lunch.

■ **Takes 30 minutes** ■ **Serves 4**

85g/3oz unsalted butter
1½ tbsp each chopped parsley, mint and chives
400g/14oz tagliatelle
200g/8oz baby carrots, preferably with a little stalk left on
400g/14oz shelled garden peas, about 1.25kg/2lb 12oz in their pods
200g/8oz fine green beans, trimmed
200g/8oz baby or regular-sized courgettes, thickly sliced
splash of olive oil
finely grated zest and juice 1 lemon
basil leaves, to garnish

1 Gently melt the butter with the herbs. Set aside. Bring 2 large pans of salted water to the boil (one for the pasta, the other for the vegetables). Tip the pasta into one pan and cook according to the packet instructions.
2 While the pasta cooks, cook the carrots in the other pan for 2 minutes. Add the peas, beans and courgettes and cook for 3 minutes more.
3 Drain both pasta and vegetables well. Return the pasta to its pan and toss with the oil, half the herb butter and the lemon zest and juice. Return the vegetables to their pan, toss with the rest of the butter and season to taste. Spoon the pasta into bowls, grind black pepper over and top with the vegetables and basil.

■ Per serving 634 kcalories, protein 21g, carbohydrate 93g, fat 22g, saturated fat 12g, fibre 11g, added sugar none, salt 0.09g

Cheesy leek and spinach pasta

A creamy, all-in-one sauce that smells delicious – this is comfort food at its best.

■ **Takes 25–35 minutes** ■ **Serves 4**

good knob of butter
1 tbsp olive oil
2 large leeks, about 450g/1lb total, thinly sliced
500g pack penne rigate or your favourite pasta shape
200g pot crème fraîche
1 tbsp wholegrain mustard
125g pack Danish blue, roughly diced
8 sun-dried tomatoes in oil, drained and thinly sliced
225g bag baby spinach leaves

1 Melt the butter with the oil in a large pan, tip in the leeks and splash in a little hot water. Cover and cook over a low heat, stirring occasionally, for about 10 minutes until no longer squeaky.
2 While the leeks are cooking, cook the pasta in salted boiling water according to the packet instructions. Meanwhile, tip the crème fraîche and mustard into the leeks, add three-quarters of the cheese and season well. Stir until the cheese melts. Take off the heat.
3 Drain the pasta, reserving the water. Stir the pasta into the cheesy sauce, adding enough cooking water to make the sauce coat the pasta, and add the tomatoes. Stir in the spinach, a handful at a time, until it wilts, splashing in a little more water if needed. Toss in the remaining cheese and serve.

■ Per serving 808 kcalories, protein 27g, carbohydrate 103g, fat 35g, saturated fat 18g, fibre 9g, added sugar none, salt 2.03g

Veggie bolognese

This vegetarian version of the classic Bolognese sauce is cheap to make and superhealthy too – it's particularly high in iron.

■ **Takes 35–45 minutes** ■ **Serves 4**

1 onion
1 carrot
1 celery stick
1 red pepper, cored and seeded
2 tbsp olive oil
100g/4oz red lentils
400g can tomatoes
600ml/1 pint vegetable stock
2 tsp dried oregano
½ tsp ground cinnamon
350g/12oz spaghetti
freshly grated vegetarian Parmesan, to serve

1 Roughly chop the vegetables, then whizz in a food processor until finely chopped.
2 Heat the oil in a large pan and fry the vegetables for about 8 minutes until soft. Stir in the lentils, tomatoes, stock, oregano and cinnamon. Bring to the boil and season to taste, then reduce the heat, cover and simmer for 20 minutes.
3 Cook the spaghetti in a large pan of salted boiling water according to the packet instructions. Drain well and serve with the sauce and grated cheese.

■ Per serving 484 kcalories, protein 19g, carbohydrate 90g, fat 8g, saturated fat 1g, fibre 6g, added sugar none, salt 0.66g

Broccoli pesto pasta

An unusual alternative to the classic Italian pesto. If you don't like broccoli, try making it with frozen peas.

■ **Takes 20 minutes** ■ **Serves 4**

400g/14oz rigatoni or other short pasta shape
250g/9oz broccoli florets
1 garlic clove, grated
finely grated zest of 1 lemon
½ tsp chilli flakes
3 tbsp pine nuts
juice of ½ lemon
5 tbsp extra-virgin olive oil
3 tbsp freshly grated vegetarian Parmesan

1 Cook the pasta according to the packet instructions. Meanwhile, cook the broccoli in salted boiling water for 4 minutes, then drain and return to the pan. Mash the broccoli lightly, add the garlic, lemon zest, chilli flakes and pine nuts, and toss to mix.
2 Drain the pasta and return it to the pan. Stir in the broccoli pesto, lemon juice and oil, then add seasoning and toss through the Parmesan. Serve straight away.

■ Per serving 604 kcalories, protein 19g, carbohydrate 79g, fat 26g, saturated fat 4g, fibre 5g, added sugar none, salt 0.47g

Macaroni cheese with mushrooms

This is a lighter version of the traditional dish. Try adding other appropriate ingredients from your storecupboard.

■ **Takes 20 minutes** ■ **Serves 2**

200g/8oz macaroni
2 tbsp olive oil
2 leeks, sliced
6 mushrooms, quartered
4 tomatoes, roughly chopped
100g/4oz garlic and herb soft cheese

1 Cook the macaroni in a large pan of salted boiling water for 8–10 minutes, or according to the packet instructions.
2 Meanwhile, heat the oil in a wok or deep frying pan and cook the leeks and mushrooms for 4–6 minutes or until the leeks are tender. Toss in the tomatoes, season well and cook for another minute.
3 Drain the macaroni, tip into the leek mixture and toss well to mix. Crumble the cheese on top and serve as soon as it starts to melt.

■ Per serving 664 kcalories, protein 20g, carbohydrate 85g, fat 30g, saturated fat 11.7g, fibre 7.9g, added sugar none, salt 0.5g

TOP: Veggie bolognese

BOTTOM LEFT: Broccoli pesto pasta

BOTTOM RIGHT: Macaroni cheese with mushrooms

Two-cheese lasagne with pesto

Enjoy the rich flavours of Italy in this easy, all-in-one tomato and basil lasagne – perfect for relaxed entertaining on a summer evening.

■ **Takes about 1½ hours** ■ **Serves 6**

250g pack fresh lasagne sheets

FOR THE SAUCE
1.2 litres/2 pints milk
100g/4oz butter
100g/4oz plain flour
pinch of freshly grated nutmeg

FOR THE FILLING
500g/1lb 2oz baby spinach leaves
3 rounded tbsp good-quality pesto
500g/1lb 2oz cherry tomatoes on the vine
good handful of basil leaves, plus extra to garnish
175g/6oz Parmesan, freshly grated
2 × 125–150g balls mozzarella (preferably buffalo), torn into pieces

1 Heat the oven to 200C/180C fan/gas 6. Put all the sauce ingredients in a pan and simmer, whisking, until thick and smooth. Season and cool.
2 Pour a kettleful of boiling water over the spinach in a large bowl. Leave for 30 seconds, then drain. Rinse, drain and squeeze dry.
3 Spread 1–2 spoonfuls of sauce over the base of an ovenproof dish 30 × 20 × 6cm. Lay a third of the lasagne on top and spread with a third of the sauce, then swirl a spoonful of pesto through with a knife. Scatter over half the spinach, then a third of the tomatoes, some basil and a third of the cheeses. Season. Repeat these layers, then finish with a layer of lasagne, sauce, pesto, tomatoes and cheeses. Season and bake for 35–40 minutes. Serve scattered with basil.

■ Per serving 711 kcalories, protein 38g, carbohydrate 46g, fat 43g, saturated fat 25g, fibre 4g, added sugar none, salt 2.5g

Rigatoni sausage bake

You can prepare this dish several hours ahead, so it's ideal for when you're having friends round for supper.

■ **Takes about 1¼ hours** ■ **Serves 6**

1 tbsp olive oil
1 onion, chopped
400g/14oz good-quality pork sausages, skins discarded and meat chopped
1 large carrot, grated
150ml/¼ pint red wine
300ml/½ pint vegetable stock
3 tbsp tomato purée
500g pack rigatoni
200g/8oz fresh spinach
140g/5oz mature Cheddar, grated

FOR THE WHITE SAUCE
50g/2oz butter
50g/2oz plain flour
600ml/1 pint milk
good pinch of freshly grated nutmeg

1 Heat the oven to 190C/170C fan/gas 6. Heat the oil in a large pan and fry the onion for 5 minutes until softened. Stir in the sausagemeat and fry until lightly coloured. Add the carrot, wine, stock, purée and seasoning. Bring to the boil and simmer uncovered for 15 minutes until thickened.
2 Put all the sauce ingredients in a pan with some seasoning and simmer, whisking all the time, until thick and smooth.
3 Cook the pasta according to the packet instructions, remove from the heat and stir in the spinach until just wilted, then drain. Spread half the pasta and spinach in a shallow 2.2-litre ovenproof dish. Cover with the sausage sauce, then the remaining pasta mix and the white sauce. Sprinkle with the cheese and bake for 25 minutes until golden brown.

■ Per serving 749 kcalories, protein 31g, carbohydrate 84g, fat 33g, saturated fat 16g, fibre 5g, added sugar none, salt 2.32g

Pasta parmigiana

Don't be put off by the time it takes to roast the tomatoes and aubergines – it's well worth it for the extra flavour.

■ **Takes 2½ hours** ■ **Serves 6**

1.25kg/2lb 12oz small vine or plum tomatoes, halved widthways
sprinkling of golden caster sugar
4 tbsp extra-virgin olive oil, plus extra for drizzling and brushing
1 large aubergine, about 450g/1lb
500g/1lb 2oz rigatoni or penne
2 garlic cloves, crushed
2 good handfuls of basil leaves, plus extra for serving
450g/1lb buffalo mozzarella (3 balls), drained and very thinly sliced
50g/2oz Parmesan, freshly grated

1 Heat the oven to 160C/140C fan/gas 3. Stand the tomatoes cut-side up on a large baking tray and sprinkle with the sugar and seasoning. Drizzle with oil and roast for 45 minutes.
2 Meanwhile, slice the aubergine into rounds, brush both sides with oil and spread out on another tray. When the tomatoes have been roasting for 45 minutes, put the aubergine in the oven and roast for another 45 minutes.
3 Cook the pasta, drain well and mix in a bowl with 4 tablespoons oil and the garlic. Remove the vegetables from the oven and turn it up to 200C/180C fan/gas 6. Layer the pasta and vegetables with the basil and mozzarella in a 2.5-litre ovenproof dish, finishing with a layer of tomatoes and mozzarella and then the Parmesan. Bake for 25 minutes and serve sprinkled with basil.

■ Per serving 722 kcalories, protein 29g, carbohydrate 73g, fat 37g, saturated fat 16g, fibre 7g, added sugar 2g, salt 2.07g

TOP: Two-cheese lasagne with pesto

BOTTOM LEFT: Rigatoni sausage bake

BOTTOM RIGHT: Pasta parmigiana

Cauli-macaroni cheese

In this new twist on a family favourite, the white sauce is replaced with crème fraîche, giving it a luxurious creamy touch.

■ **Takes 30 minutes** ■ **Serves 4**

300g/10oz rigatoni or penne
1 small cauliflower, cut into florets
200g pot crème fraîche
2 tsp wholegrain mustard
175g/6oz Red Leicester, grated
2 tomatoes, cut into wedges

1 Bring a large pan of salted water to the boil. Toss in the pasta and bring back to the boil, then cook for a couple of minutes. Tip in the cauliflower and cook for a further 8–10 minutes until both are tender. Drain well.
2 Put the crème fraîche, mustard and most of the cheese into the pasta pan. Stir over a low heat just until the cheese starts to melt.
3 Heat the grill to hot. Tip the pasta and cauliflower into the sauce and gently stir together. Season. Transfer to a flameproof dish, scatter the tomatoes on top, then the rest of the cheese and a grinding of black pepper. Grill for 5 minutes until brown and bubbling.

■ Per serving 636 kcalories, protein 25g, carbohydrate 64g, fat 33g, saturated fat 18g, fibre 5g, added sugar none, salt 0.98g

Creamy fish lasagne

This is a rich and luscious pasta bake, so a little goes a long way.

■ **Takes 1–1¼ hours** ■ **Serves 4**

250g tub mascarpone
250g tub ricotta
284ml pot single cream
3 tbsp chopped fresh dill
2 tbsp lemon juice
300g/10oz broccoli, cut into small florets
250g/9oz fresh lasagne sheets
450g/1lb salmon fillet, skinned and cut into small chunks
3 rounded tbsp freshly grated Parmesan

1 Heat the oven to 180C/160C fan/gas 4. Beat together the mascarpone, ricotta, cream, dill, lemon juice and seasoning.
2 Cook the broccoli in salted boiling water for 3 minutes, then drain and cool under running cold water. Drain well again.
3 Spread a little cream mixture over the base of an oiled shallow rectangular dish, about 25cm long. Cover with a layer of lasagne, cutting it to fit and not overlapping. Spread with more cream mixture, then sprinkle over a third of the salmon and broccoli. Repeat twice more, then finish with lasagne and the remaining sauce. Sprinkle with Parmesan and bake for 35–40 minutes until deep golden.

■ Per serving 914 kcalories, protein 45g, carbohydrate 36g, fat 66g, saturated fat 35g, fibre 4g, added sugar none, salt 0.77g

Salmon and broccoli pasta bake

The perfect dish for a spoil-yourself Saturday-night supper – it's easy to cook, tastes really special and only needs a simple salad to go with it.

■ **Takes about 1 hour** ■ **Serves 4**

250g/9oz penne
300g/10oz broccoli florets
25g/1oz butter
25g/1oz plain flour
600ml/1 pint milk
100g/4oz mascarpone
8 sun-dried tomatoes (preserved in oil), drained and thickly sliced
10 large fresh basil leaves, roughly torn
4 skinless salmon fillets, halved widthways
50g/2oz mature Cheddar, finely grated

1 Heat the oven to 190C/170C fan/gas 5. Cook the pasta in salted boiling water for 6 minutes, add the broccoli and boil for another 4 minutes.
2 Meanwhile, put the butter, flour and milk in a pan and simmer, whisking, to make a thick, smooth sauce. Remove from the heat and stir in the mascarpone, tomatoes and basil.
3 Drain the pasta and broccoli, mix with the sauce and season well. Put the salmon in a single layer in an ovenproof dish 30 × 20 × 6cm, spoon the pasta mixture on top and scatter with the cheese. Bake for 30 minutes until golden.

■ Per serving 817 kcalories, protein 49g, carbohydrate 64g, fat 42g, saturated fat 18g, fibre 5g, added sugar none, salt 1.3g

TOP: Cauli-macaroni cheese

BOTTOM LEFT: Creamy fish lasagne

BOTTOM RIGHT: Salmon and broccoli pasta bake

TOP: Cheeseboard pasta bake

BOTTOM LEFT: Pork and rosemary lasagne

BOTTOM RIGHT: Ricotta pasta pockets

Cheeseboard pasta bake

A couple of handfuls of crushed crisps will give the topping extra crunch. Use whatever cheese you have to hand.

■ **Takes about 1 hour** ■ **Serves 4**

500g pack rigatoni or penne
850ml/1½ pints milk
50g/2oz butter
50g/2oz plain flour
½ nutmeg (or ¼ tsp ready ground)
200g/8oz cooked ham, chopped
85g/3oz mature Cheddar
85g/3oz dolcelatte or other blue cheese
85g/3oz garlic and herb soft cheese
85g/3oz mixed nuts, such as cashews, blanched almonds and hazelnuts, roughly chopped
handful of parsley, roughly chopped

1 Cook the pasta in a large pan of salted boiling water for 8–10 minutes, or according to the packet instructions. Heat the oven to 190C/170C fan/gas 5.
2 Pour the milk into a pan and add the butter, flour and seasoning. Grate in the nutmeg half (or sprinkle in the ground). Bring to the boil over a medium heat, whisking until it makes a smooth, creamy sauce.
3 Drain the pasta and tip it into the sauce. Stir in the ham and grate in the Cheddar, then taste for seasoning, and tip into a shallow ovenproof dish. Dice the remaining cheeses and swirl into the pasta to make cheesy pockets. Scatter the nuts and parsley over the top, then bake for 30 minutes.

■ Per serving 840 kcalories, protein 55g, carbohydrate 26g, fat 44g, saturated fat 21g, fibre 6g, added sugar none, salt 2.61g

Pork and rosemary lasagne

Quark and skimmed milk replace the conventional calorific béchamel sauce in this lean, yet tasty lasagne.

■ **Takes about 1½ hours** ■ **Serves 4**

1 tsp olive oil, plus extra for greasing
400g/14oz lean minced pork
1 onion, finely chopped
2 celery sticks, finely chopped
1 tsp dried rosemary
150ml/¼ pint white wine
425ml/¾ pint chicken stock
2 tbsp tomato purée
400g can chopped tomatoes
1 tsp cornflour, mixed to a paste with a little cold water
2 × 250g cartons Quark
250ml/9fl oz skimmed milk
freshly grated nutmeg
10 dried lasagne sheets (no pre-cooking required type)
15g/½oz freshly grated Parmesan (about 5 tbsp)

1 Heat the oil in a non-stick pan and fry the pork until brown and crumbly. Add the onion, celery, rosemary and wine, simmer for 10 minutes, then stir in the stock, purée and tomatoes. Season, cover and simmer for 30 minutes. Stir in the cornflour paste until slightly thickened, then remove from the heat.
2 Heat the oven to 190C/170C fan/gas 5. Mix the quark with the milk, nutmeg and seasoning. Spoon a third of the meat over the base of a 1.4-litre oblong baking dish. Cover with 2 lasagne sheets, avoiding overlapping. Top with a third of the sauce and a little Parmesan, then 2 more lasagne sheets. Repeat the layers twice more, omitting the last layer of lasagne and finishing with sauce. Sprinkle with the remaining Parmesan and bake for 30–35 minutes.

■ Per serving 425 kcalories, protein 41g, carbohydrate 45g, fat 7g, saturated fat 2g, fibre 3g, added sugar none, salt 1.03g

Ricotta pasta pockets

This surprisingly light pasta bake is quick and straightforward, and makes an impressive veggie supper.

■ **Takes 30 minutes** ■ **Serves 4**

250g pack fresh lasagne sheets
1 tbsp olive oil
250g tub ricotta
50g bag rocket leaves
2 × 350g jars tomato and chargrilled vegetable sauce, or your favourite tomato sauce
50g/2oz mature vegetarian Cheddar, grated

1 Put the lasagne sheets in a large bowl and pour over boiling water to cover. Leave to soak for 5 minutes. Meanwhile, heat the oven to 200C/180C fan/gas 6 and lightly oil a shallow baking tray.
2 Drain the lasagne in a colander. Take one sheet and put a large spoonful of ricotta in the centre. Scatter over a few rocket leaves and season well, then fold the sheet in half and press the edges together to form a pocket. Continue to fill all the pasta sheets, then lay them on the baking tray so they overlap slightly.
3 Cover the pasta pockets with the sauce, sprinkle over the cheese and bake for 10–12 minutes until hot and bubbly.

■ Per serving 440 kcalories, protein 19g, carbohydrate 57g, fat 17g, saturated fat 8g, fibre 4g, added sugar 5g, salt 3.5g

Spicy prawn noodle soup

This fragrant Thai soup, known as *tom yum*, can be made with pieces of shredded chicken instead of prawns, if you prefer.

■ Takes 25 minutes ■ Serves 4

850ml/1½ pints chicken stock
2 lemon grass stalks, bruised with
   a rolling pin
2.5cm/1in piece of ginger, peeled and finely
   chopped
1 fresh green chilli, seeded and
   finely chopped
2 garlic cloves, finely chopped
100g/4oz medium egg noodles
2 tbsp Thai fish sauce, plus extra to taste
juice of ½ lime
pinch of sugar
12 peeled raw tiger prawns, with tail
   shells on
1 small bunch fresh coriander, roughly
   chopped, 4 sprigs reserved
lime wedges, to serve

1 Bring the stock to the boil in a large pan with the lemongrass, ginger, chilli and garlic, then add the noodles and simmer for 4 minutes.
2 Now stir in the 2 tablespoons fish sauce, lime juice and sugar followed by the prawns. Simmer for 3–4 minutes until the prawns turn pink.
3 Remove the pan from the heat and throw in the chopped coriander. Stir and taste for seasoning, adding more fish sauce if you like. Serve straight away, with the reserved coriander sprigs as a garnish and lime wedges for squeezing.

■ Per serving 145 kcalories, protein 12g, carbohydrate 20g, fat 2g, saturated fat 0.1g, fibre 0.1g, added sugar 0.7g, salt 2.51g

Chinese noodle soup

Stir-fry rice noodles are soft, silky and delicate once cooked.

■ Takes 20 minutes ■ Serves 4

100g/4oz (2 bundles) stir fry noodles
1.2 litres/2 pints good-quality chicken stock
2 kaffir lime leaves, finely shredded
1 tsp grated ginger
2 tbsp finely chopped coriander
418g can creamed-style corn
2 cooked chicken breasts, skinned, boned
   and shredded

1 Soak the noodles in boiling water for 4 minutes. Drain, rinse and drain again, then divide among four soup bowls.
2 Heat the stock to boiling in a pan with the lime leaves, ginger and coriander.
3 Add the sweetcorn and chicken to the pan, stir and heat through for 2 minutes, then ladle over the noodles.

■ Per serving 350 kcalories, protein 24g, carbohydrate 59g, fat 3g, saturated fat 0.9g, fibre 1.7g, added sugar 7.7g, salt 2.68g

Oriental beef and mushroom soup

Dried mushrooms give the same deep taste as soy sauce but, as they are virtually salt-free, they are much healthier.

■ Takes 20–30 minutes ■• Serves 2

25g/1oz dried ceps or porcini mushrooms
½ beef stock cube
1 tbsp sunflower oil
1 extra-lean sirloin steak, about 140g/5oz
1 fresh red chilli, seeded and finely chopped
2 garlic cloves, crushed
1 tsp finely grated ginger
100g/4oz small broccoli florets, halved
2 tbsp dry sherry
100g/4oz fine egg noodles
100g/4oz fresh beansprouts
25g/1oz watercress, roughly chopped

1 Snip the mushrooms into a large measuring jug, pour over 1 litre/1¾ pints boiling water and crumble in the stock cube. Set aside.
2 Heat the oil in a large non-stick pan. Add the steak and cook over a high heat for 2 minutes on each side. Lift on to a plate.
3 Add the chilli, garlic and ginger to the pan with the broccoli and stir fry for about a minute. Spoon in the sherry and stir to remove any sediment from the pan. Pour in the stock and mushrooms, and simmer for 4 minutes.
4 Pour a kettleful of boiling water over the noodles in a large bowl and leave to soften. Add the beansprouts and watercress to the soup, and cook for 2 minutes. Drain the noodles, divide between two soup bowls, then ladle over the soup. Thinly slice the beef and pile on top.

■ Per serving 488 kcalories, protein 30g, carbohydrate 48g, fat 15g, saturated fat 2g, fibre 2g, added sugar none, salt 2.26g

TOP: Spicy prawn noodle soup

BOTTOM LEFT: Chinese noodle soup

BOTTOM RIGHT: Oriental beef and mushroom soup

Pad Thai

A wonderful, authentic Thai classic. If there are two thicknesses of noodle on offer, go for the thicker ones for this recipe.

■ **Takes 25–30 minutes** ■ **Serves 2–3**

125g (½ × 250g pack) rice noodles
3 tbsp lime juice (about 2 limes)
½ tsp cayenne pepper
2 tsp light muscovado sugar
2 tbsp Thai fish sauce
2 tbsp vegetable oil
200g/8oz cooked peeled tiger prawns, tail shells on
4 spring onions, sliced
140g/5oz beansprouts
25g/1oz salted peanuts, finely chopped
small handful of coriander leaves

TO SERVE
1–2 limes, cut into wedges
sweet chilli sauce

1 Put the noodles in a large heatproof bowl, pour boiling water over them and leave for 4 minutes, then drain and refresh under cold running water.
2 Put the lime juice, cayenne, sugar and fish sauce in a bowl and mix well. Have all the other ingredients ready by the stove
3 Heat the oil and fry the prawns until warmed through. Add the spring onions and noodles, and toss to mix. Tip in the lime-juice mixture, then stir in the beansprouts and half the peanuts and coriander. Cook for 1 minute until everything is heated through.
4 Pile into a large dish, scatter with the rest of the peanuts and coriander, and serve with lime wedges and chilli sauce.

■ Per serving (2) 531 kcalories, protein 27g, carbohydrate 62g, fat 20g, saturated fat 3g, fibre 2g, added sugar 5g, salt 3g

Tiger prawn spring rolls

Try to buy ricepaper wrappers from oriental stores – supermarket ones tend to be smaller, so you'll need twice as many.

■ **Takes about 1 hour** ■ **Serves 6**

4 large iceberg lettuce leaves, halved lengthways, with crunchy cores cut out
8 round sheets rice paper, 23cm/9in diameter
8 each fresh mint and coriander leaves
soy sauce, for dipping

FOR THE FILLING
25g/1oz rice vermicelli noodles
175g/6oz peeled raw tiger prawns
2.5cm/1in piece of ginger, peeled and finely chopped
1 garlic clove, finely chopped
1 tbsp vegetable oil
1 medium carrot, grated
50g/2oz beansprouts
handful each of fresh mint and coriander leaves, chopped

1 First make the filling. Soak the noodles until soft, then drain. Chop the prawns, then stir fry them with the ginger and garlic in hot oil for 2–3 minutes until the prawns turn pink. Tip into a bowl and stir in the remaining filling ingredients, then pile into the lettuce halves and roll them up.
2 One at a time, dip the rice paper sheets in hot water for 30–40 seconds until soft. Lay them on damp tea towels and put a mint and coriander leaf on each one. Now put a lettuce roll just off centre on each rice paper sheet and roll it up, tucking in the sides halfway.
3 Keep the rolls wrapped, seam-side down, in the damp tea towels. Just before serving, unwrap and cut each roll at an angle. Serve with soy sauce for dipping.

■ Per serving 75 kcalories, protein 7g, carbohydrate 8g, fat 2g, saturated fat 0.2g, fibre 0.7g, added sugar 0.1g, salt 1.55g

Oriental leaf and noodle broth

A salad mix that includes carrot, pepper and cabbage will add crunch to this tasty and healthy soup.

■ **Takes 10 minutes** ■ **Serves 4**

2 litres/3½ pints vegetable stock
1 tsp grated ginger
100g/4oz button mushrooms, thinly sliced
100g/4oz rice noodles
4 spring onions, trimmed and sliced
250g bag sweet and crunchy salad (white cabbage, carrots, lettuce, red and green peppers)
juice of 1 lime

1 Bring the stock and ginger to the boil in a large pan. Stir in the mushrooms and noodles, and simmer gently for 2 minutes until the noodles are almost tender.
2 Tip in the spring onions and salad, and simmer for 30 seconds, then stir in the lime juice and seasoning to taste. Serve straight away.

■ Per serving 117 kcalories, protein 6g, carbohydrate 23g, fat 1g, saturated fat 0.1g, fibre 1.4g, added sugar none, salt 1.66g

TOP: Pad Thai

BOTTOM LEFT: Tiger prawn spring rolls

BOTTOM RIGHT: Oriental leaf and noodle broth

Tofu and vegetable stir fry

Alternatively you can use peeled raw tiger prawns, but only sauté for 30 seconds–1 minute until they turn pink.

■ **Takes 30 minutes** ■ **Serves 2**

350g/12oz firm tofu, cut into 2cm/¾in cubes
1 tbsp light soy sauce
1 tbsp chilli sauce
1 tsp sesame oil
50g/2oz egg noodles
1 tbsp vegetable oil
200g/8oz pak choi or spinach leaves
1 red pepper, seeded and cubed
6 spring onions, trimmed and cut into 5cm/2in lengths
85g/3oz mangetout
1 tbsp cashew nuts, roughly chopped

1 Marinate the tofu with the soy, chilli sauce and sesame oil. Cook the noodles in a large pan of salted boiling water for 4 minutes or until tender, drain then return to the pan.
2 Heat the vegetable oil in a wok or large frying pan until really hot, then stir fry the tofu for 2–3 minutes until golden. Tip into the noodles.
3 Cut off the pak choi leaves and chop the stems on a slant. Add the stems to the wok with the pepper, spring onions, mangetout and cashew nuts and stir fry for 3–4 minutes until softened.
4 Return the noodles and tofu to the wok. Throw in the pak choi leaves or spinach, toss thoroughly and serve.

■ Per serving 403 kcalories, protein 23g, carbohydrate 33g, fat 21g, saturated fat 2g, fibre 3g, added sugar 1g, salt 3.89g

Noodles with black bean pork

Add this simple but tasty dish to your repertoire and you'll never have to rely on takeaways again.

■ **Takes 35 minutes** ■ **Serves 4**

2 tbsp vegetable oil
2 garlic cloves, crushed
2cm/¾in piece of ginger, peeled and grated
1 large fresh red chilli, seeded and finely chopped
450g/1lb minced pork
350g jar black bean sauce
100g/4oz rice noodles
6 spring onions, trimmed and shredded

1 Heat the oil in a large pan and cook the garlic, ginger and chilli gently for 1–2 minutes until softened. Add the pork and cook for 4–5 minutes until browned, pressing with a spoon to remove any lumps. Pour in the black bean sauce and stir well, then cook for another 4–5 minutes, stirring occasionally.
2 Meanwhile, cook or soak the rice noodles according to the packet instructions. Drain and toss into the pork with the spring onions. Serve straight away.

■ Per serving 405 kcalories, protein 31g, carbohydrate 31g, fat 18g, saturated fat 5.3g, fibre 2g, added sugar 3.9g, salt 5.78g

Pork and ginger noodles

Make the most of quick-cooking ingredients to create an appetizing stir fry. For vegetarians, replace the pork with mushrooms.

■ **Takes 25 minutes** ■ **Serves 4**

2 tbsp sunflower oil
450g/1lb pork fillet, cut into thin strips about 1cm/½in wide
2.5cm/1in piece of ginger, grated
2 garlic cloves, finely chopped
½ Savoy cabbage, about 250g/9oz, shredded
300ml/½ pint vegetable or chicken stock
1 tbsp soy sauce
100g/4oz frozen peas
2 × 150g packs straight-to-wok noodles
2 tbsp chopped fresh coriander, to serve

1 Heat the oil in a wok over a high heat, add the pork and stir fry for 3–4 minutes until just cooked. Stir in the ginger and garlic, and continue to fry for 1–2 minutes.
2 Add the cabbage and stir fry with the pork until well combined. Pour over the stock and soy sauce.
3 Add the peas and noodles, stir well, then simmer for 5 minutes, until the cabbage is cooked but still crunchy. Scatter with coriander and serve.

■ Per serving 337 kcalories, protein 31g, carbohydrate 28g, fat 12g, saturated fat 2g, fibre 4g, added sugar none, salt 1.84g

TOP: Tofu and vegetable
stir fry

BOTTOM LEFT: Noodles with
black bean pork

BOTTOM RIGHT: Pork and
ginger noodles

Zesty noodle stir fry

You'll find flat rice noodles with the oriental foods in the supermarket. Change the vegetables to suit your taste.

■ **Takes 40 minutes** ■ **Serves 4 (easily halved)**

140g/5oz flat rice noodles
6 tbsp soy sauce
5 tbsp fresh orange juice
½ tsp finely grated orange zest
1 tsp sugar
½ tsp cornflour
1 tbsp vegetable or sunflower oil
½ tbsp grated ginger
2 garlic cloves, finely chopped
2 tbsp dry sherry
2 red peppers, seeded and sliced
2 carrots, cut into fine strips
2 courgettes, cut into fine strips
100g/4oz mangetout, sliced
220g can water chestnuts, sliced
1 bunch spring onions, shredded

1 Put the noodles in a large bowl, cover with boiling water for 4 minutes, then drain and rinse under cold running water.
2 Mix the soy sauce, orange juice and zest, sugar and cornflour. Heat the oil in a wok, add the ginger and garlic, and fry for 1 minute. Add the sherry and peppers and fry for 1 minute. Add the carrots, courgettes and mangetout, and fry for 3 minutes. Stir in the water chestnuts and spring onions, and fry for 1 minute.
3 Add the soy-sauce mix and noodles, and stir fry until hot. Serve straight away.

■ Per serving 240 kcalories, protein 6g, carbohydrate 47g, fat 3g, saturated fat none, fibre 4g, added sugar 1.6g, salt 2.77g

Broccoli and anchovy spaghetti

If you love garlic, add a couple of chopped cloves with the breadcrumbs.

■ **Takes 25–30 minutes** ■ **Serves 4**

350g/12oz spaghetti
350g/12oz broccoli
5 tbsp olive oil
6 canned anchovy fillets, drained and chopped
2 fresh red chillies, seeded and finely chopped
100g/4oz white breadcrumbs, made from stale bread

1 Cook the spaghetti in a large pan of salted boiling water for 10–12 minutes, or according to the packet instructions. Cut the broccoli into small florets, thinly slice the thick stalks and throw into the pan of pasta for the last 3 minutes.
2 Meanwhile, heat 3 tablespoons of the oil in a frying pan, add the anchovies and chillies, and fry Briefly. Add the breadcrumbs and cook, stirring, for about 5 minutes until the crumbs are crunchy and golden.
3 Drain the spaghetti and broccoli, and return to the pan. Toss with three-quarters of the crumb mixture, some seasoning and the remaining oil. Serve sprinkled with the remaining crumbs.

■ Per serving 400 kcalories, protein 17g, carbohydrate 78g, fat 4g, saturated fat 0.5g, fibre 5g, added sugar none, salt 0.8g

Sweet pepper pasta

Sweet cherry peppers are available in some larger supermarkets – if you can't find them, use sliced peppers from a jar.

■ **Takes 20 minutes** ■ **Serves 4**

350g/12oz trompetti or fusilli
2 tsp olive oil
1 large onion, roughly chopped
2 plump garlic cloves, crushed
375g jar mild Peppadew sweet cherry peppers
85g bag rocket or watercress, roughly torn

1 Cook the pasta in a large pan of salted boiling water for 8–10 minutes, or according to the packet instructions.
2 Meanwhile, heat the oil in a large pan and fry the onion over a medium–high heat for 5–6 minutes, until golden and softened. Stir in the garlic and cook for a further 2–3 minutes. Drain the peppers, reserving their juice, and stir them into the onion. Cook for 2–3 minutes. Blitz the mixture in a food processor with 5 tablespoons each reserved pepper juice and pasta cooking water.
3 Drain the pasta and return it to the pan with the pepper mixture and seasoning to taste. Toss in the rocket or watercress and heat through Briefly until it just begins to wilt. Serve straight away.

■ Per serving 375 kcalories, protein 13g, carbohydrate 77g, fat 4g, saturated fat 1g, fibre 6g, added sugar none, salt trace

TOP: Zesty noodle stir fry

BOTTOM LEFT: Broccoli and anchovy spaghetti

BOTTOM RIGHT: Sweet pepper pasta

Good-for-you pasta

You could use spinach leaves or shredded, leftover cooked Brussels sprouts instead of the chard in this recipe.

■ **Takes 50 minutes** ■ **Serves 4**

150ml/¼ pint tomato sauce (homemade or from a jar)
350g/12oz pasta ribbons, such as pappardelle
175g/6oz cauliflower, cut into bite-sized florets
175g/6oz broccoli, cut into bite-sized florets
120g bag baby chard
a little olive oil
freshly grated Parmesan cheese, to serve

1 First purée the tomato sauce, if it is not already smooth.
2 Bring a large pan of salted water to the boil and cook the pasta for 8–10 minutes, or according to the packet instructions, until just tender.
3 Meanwhile, cook the cauliflower in another pan for 6 minutes, add the broccoli and cook for a further 3–4 minutes, until both are just tender. Drain well and keep warm. Heat through the tomato sauce.
4 Drain the pasta and stir in the chard with a little olive oil and seasoning. Toss in the broccoli, cauliflower and hot tomato sauce, and serve with Parmesan.

■ Per serving 498 kcalories, protein 20g, carbohydrate 99g, fat 5g, saturated fat 1g, fibre 9g, added sugar 1g, salt 0.72g

Spaghetti with peas and Parmesan

Transform this simple dish into a posh supper by adding thin slices of smoked salmon with the peas, and substituting dill for the parsley.

■ **Takes 20–30 minutes** ■ **Serves 2**

140g/5oz spaghetti
100g/4oz frozen petits pois or garden peas
2 tsp olive oil
1 small onion, finely chopped
100g/4oz low-fat soft cheese with chives and onion
finely grated zest of 1 lemon
3 tbsp freshly grated Parmesan
1 tbsp chopped parsley

1 Cook the spaghetti in a large pan of salted boiling water for 10–12 minutes, or according to the packet instructions. Add the peas for the last 2–3 minutes.
2 While the spaghetti is cooking, heat the oil in a pan and fry the onion gently until softened. Stir in the soft cheese and warm it through, adding 3 tablespoons of the pasta water to thin it down. Stir in the lemon zest and 2 tablespoons of the Parmesan.
3 Drain the spaghetti and peas really well, return them to the pan and gently stir in the sauce. Season, then pile into serving bowls and sprinkle the parsley and remaining Parmesan over the top.

■ Per serving 420 kcalories, protein 22g, carbohydrate 61g, fat 11g, saturated fat 3g, fibre 5g, added sugar none, salt 0.83g

Summer veggie pasta

This makes a great vegetarian family supper, but it can easily be halved to serve two.

■ **Takes 25–35 minutes** ■ **Serves 4**

200g/8oz farfalle (pasta bows)
175g/6oz fresh or frozen broad beans, about 650g/1lb 7oz in their pods
1 tbsp good-quality olive oil
1 large onion, finely chopped
2 garlic cloves, chopped
2 large courgettes, cut into sticks
6 ripe plum tomatoes, cut into wedges
generous shot of Tabasco sauce
handful of fresh basil, shredded

1 Cook the pasta in a large pan of salted boiling water according to the packet instructions, adding the fresh broad beans for the last 3 minutes (frozen for the last 2 minutes).
2 While the pasta is cooking, heat the oil in a large frying pan and cook the onion over a medium heat for 1–2 minutes. Stir in the garlic and courgettes, toss over a medium heat for 2–3 minutes, then stir in the tomatoes and shake in the Tabasco. Stir for 2–3 minutes to soften the tomatoes a little (not too much or they will go mushy).
3 Drain the pasta and beans. Toss the courgette mixture and basil into the pasta and season, to taste. Serve in a large bowl.

■ Per serving 284 kcalories, protein 12g, carbohydrate 51g, fat 5g, saturated fat 1g, fibre 7g, added sugar none, salt 0.1g

TOP: Good-for-you pasta

BOTTOM LEFT: Spaghetti with peas and Parmesan

BOTTOM RIGHT: Summer veggie pasta

TOP: 15-minute chicken pasta

BOTTOM LEFT: Spaghetti with salmon and peas

BOTTOM RIGHT: Minestrone pasta pot

15-minute chicken pasta

If you have a nut allergy, replace the almonds with pine nuts.

■ Takes 15 minutes ■ Serves 4

350g/12oz farfalle (pasta bows)
300g/10oz broccoli, cut into small florets
1 tbsp olive oil
3 large skinless boneless chicken breasts, cut into bite-sized chunks
2 garlic cloves, crushed
2 tbsp wholegrain mustard
juice of 1 large or 2 small oranges
25g/1oz flaked almonds, toasted

1 Cook the pasta in a large pan of salted boiling water for 8–10 minutes, or according to the packet instructions. Three minutes before the pasta is cooked, throw in the broccoli and continue to boil.

2 While the pasta is cooking, gently heat the oil in a large frying pan or wok and fry the chicken, stirring occasionally, until cooked and golden, for about 5–7 minutes, adding the garlic for the last 2 minutes.

3 Mix the mustard with the orange juice in a small bowl. Pour the mixture over the chicken and simmer gently for a minute or two.

4 Drain the pasta and broccoli, reserving 3 tablespoons of the water. Toss the pasta and broccoli with the chicken, stir in the water and almonds, and season well before serving.

■ Per serving 531 kcalories, protein 43g, carbohydrate 70g, fat 11g, saturated fat 1g, fibre 6g, added sugar none, salt 0.52g

Spaghetti with salmon and peas

Hot-smoked salmon usually comes ready flaked in tubs or vacuum packed as steaks. It has a juicy texture and delicious smoky flavour.

■ Takes 20 minutes ■ Serves 4

400g/14oz spaghetti
100g/4oz frozen petits pois
150–160g pack hot-smoked salmon, flaked into bite-sized chunks
20g pack fresh dill, roughly chopped (tough stalks removed)
3 rounded tbsp crème fraîche

1 Cook the spaghetti in salted water according to the packet instructions. When the pasta is almost done, throw in the peas.

2 Reserve about 4 tablespoons of the pasta water, then drain the pasta and peas, and return them to the pan with the reserved water.

3 Set the pan over a very low heat and toss in the salmon, dill, crème fraîche and some seasoning. Heat through briefly, then serve.

■ Per serving 470 kcalories, protein 24g, carbohydrate 77g, fat 10g, saturated fat 4g, fibre 4g, added sugar none, salt 1.85g

Minestrone pasta pot

A great storecupboard standby that's brimming with goodness and is a great family favourite.

■ Takes 25–35 minutes ■ Serves 4

2 tbsp olive oil
1 small onion, finely chopped
2 tbsp tomato purée
300g/10oz frozen mixed vegetables (including peas, sweetcorn, carrots and broccoli, but not the chunky stewpacks)
700ml/1¼ pints hot vegetable stock
175g/6oz small pasta shapes, such as conchigliette
220g can baked beans
grated Cheddar, to serve

1 Heat the olive oil in a pan over a medium heat and gently fry the onion for a few minutes until it starts to soften. Stir in the tomato purée, then tip in the frozen vegetables and pour in the stock.

2 Bring to the boil, add the pasta and stir. Cover and simmer for 12–14 minutes or until the pasta is cooked.

3 Stir in the beans and heat through, then taste for seasoning. Serve hot, with a bowl of grated Cheddar for sprinkling over the top.

■ Per serving 294 kcalories, protein 11g, carbohydrate 49g, fat 7g, saturated fat 1g, fibre 4g, added sugar 2g, salt 1.58g

Family food
on a budget

Cheese and onion pork chops

A tasty topping of melting cheese and tangy onions transforms chops into something far more exciting.

■ **Take 20 minutes** ■ **Serves 4**

4 pork chops
2 tsp olive oil
1 tsp English mustard
4 tbsp caramelized onions, from a jar
50g/2oz Cheshire cheese, grated
1 tsp thyme, chopped

1 Heat grill to high, then place the chops on a grill pan, rub with oil and season. Grill for about 6 minutes on each side, until golden.
2 Spread a little mustard over one side of each chop, then top each one with 1 tablespoon of onions. Mix together the cheese and thyme, sprinkle over the chops, then grill until golden and bubbly.

■ Per serving 378 kcalories, protein 36g, carbohydrate 8g, fat 23g, saturated fat 9g, fibre none, sugar 6g, salt 0.56g

Pesto chicken kebabs with roasted veg pasta

You can sneak a few vegetables that might normally be refused into this scrumptious supper, which won't break the bank.

■ **Takes 1 hour** ■ **Serves 4**

about 350g/12oz butternut squash, halved, seeded and cubed
2 courgettes, cubed
1 onion, chopped
1 red pepper, seeded and cut into small pieces
4 thyme sprigs, leaves removed
2 tbsp olive oil
4 boneless skinless chicken breasts, cut into bite-sized pieces
juice of 1 lemon
4 tbsp pesto
16 cherry tomatoes
400g/14oz dried penne pasta

1 Heat oven to 200C/180C fan/gas 6. Put all the vegetables into a large roasting tin, scatter with the thyme and season. Drizzle with the oil and roast for 40 minutes, turning halfway through.
2 Meanwhile, leave 8 wooden skewers to soak in water. Put the chicken into a shallow dish and mix with the lemon juice and pesto.
3 Thread the chicken pieces and whole tomatoes on to the skewers, then put them on a baking sheet. Drizzle with a little more olive oil and roast for 20 minutes, turning once, until the chicken is cooked through. Cook the pasta according to the packet instructions.
4 Toss the roasted vegetables and pasta together and serve with the pesto chicken kebabs.

■ Per serving 668 kcalories, protein 51.8g, carbohydrate 90.6g, fat 13.5g, saturated fat 3.1g, fibre 6.5g, sugar 12.6g, salt 0.45g

Fruity pork meatballs

Pork meatballs make a welcome change to beef – and they cost less to make, too.

■ **Takes 20–25 minutes** ■ **Serves 4**

300g pack mince pork
1 small onion, chopped
1 tsp dried mixed herbs
3 tbsp caramelized onion marmalade or onion chutney
300ml/½ pint hot vegetable stock
2 red apples, cored and thickly sliced
mash or jacket potatoes, to serve

1 Combine the mince, onion and herbs. Wet your hands and divide the mixture into 16 balls. Heat a large, non-stick frying pan, then brown the meatballs for 2 minutes over a high heat.
2 Stir in the onion marmalade, stock and apples, then bring to the boil. Simmer for about 15 minutes until the apples and pork are cooked and the sauce has thickened. Spoon the meatballs and sauce over mash or a jacket potato to serve.

■ Per serving 235 kcalories, protein 11g, carbohydrate 19g, fat 13g, saturated fat 6g, fibre 3g, sugar 13g, salt 1.54g

TOP: Cheese and onion pork chops

BOTTOM LEFT: Pesto chicken kebabs with roasted veg pasta

BOTTOM RIGHT: Fruity pork meatballs

TOP: Sticky apple, sausages and bacon

BOTTOM LEFT: Chilli con carne

BOTTOM RIGHT: Herby lamb cobbler

Sticky apple, sausages and bacon

Apples, sausages and bacon are a marriage made in heaven – just think about roast pork with apple sauce!

■ **Takes 35 minutes** ■ **Serves 4**

8 rashers smoked streaky bacon
8 good-quality pork sausages
1 tbsp sunflower oil
2 red-skinned apples, each cut into 8 wedges
mashed potatoes, to serve

1 Heat oven to 220C/200C fan/gas 7. Wrap a piece of bacon around each sausage. Heat the oil in a flameproof roasting tin on the hob, then brown the bacon-wrapped sausages in the tin. Place in the oven and roast for 20 minutes.
2 Toss in the apple wedges and roast everything for another 10 minutes until the sausages are cooked and the apples are sticky and caramelized. Serve with mashed potatoes.

■ Per serving 442 kcalories, protein 22g, carbohydrate 14g, fat 34g, saturated fat 11g, fibre 1g, sugar 10g, salt 2.72g

Chilli con carne

A spicy, slowly simmered chilli is hard to beat on top of a fluffy jacket potato or pile of rice. You could even use it for a spicy cottage pie.

■ **Takes 1½ hours** ■ **Serves 4**

2 tbsp olive oil
1 onion, finely chopped
1 carrot, finely chopped
1 celery stick, finely chopped
500g pack lean minced beef
½–1 tsp chilli powder or chilli flakes
2 garlic cloves, crushed
2 tsp dried mixed herbs
small glass of milk
2 × 400g cans chopped tomatoes
large glass of white wine or stock
2 tbsp tomato purée
2–3 roasted red peppers from a jar or deli counter, chopped (optional)
400g can red kidney beans, drained and rinsed

1 Heat the oil in a large pan with a well-fitting lid. Add the onion, carrot and celery, cover and fry for 5 minutes until the vegetables are softened and lightly coloured. Remove the lid and tip in the beef, breaking it up with a wooden spoon, then fry over a fairly high heat, stirring all the time until it is evenly coloured. Add the chilli, garlic and herbs, and fry for 1 minute more.
2 Reduce the heat, pour in the milk, stir well, then simmer for a few minutes, stirring occasionally, until the milk has almost evaporated. Stir in the tomatoes, wine (or stock) and the tomato purée with some seasoning, then bring to the boil. Reduce the heat then simmer for 1 hour. Stir in the peppers (if using) and kidney beans, simmer for 5 minutes more, then serve.

■ Per serving 447 kcalories, protein 37g, carbohydrate 27g, fat 20g, saturated fat 7g, fibre 8g, sugar 14g, salt 2.17g

Herby lamb cobbler

Cooked slowly, stewing cuts give far more flavour than any quick-cook steaks or expensive joints.

■ **Takes about 3 hours** ■ **Serves 6**

1 tbsp sunflower oil
200g/8oz smoked streaky bacon, chopped
900g/2lb stewing lamb, cut into large chunks
350g/12oz baby onions, peeled
5 carrots, cut into large chunks
350g/12oz button mushrooms
3 tbsp plain flour
3 bay leaves
small bunch thyme
350ml/12fl oz red wine
350ml/12fl oz lamb or beef stock
large splash of Worcestershire sauce

FOR THE COBBLER TOPPING
350g/12oz self-raising flour
4 tbsp chopped mixed herbs, including thyme, rosemary and parsley
200g/8oz chilled butter, cubed
juice of 1 lemon
5 bay leaves
1 beaten egg, to glaze

1 Heat oven to 180C/160C fan/gas 4. In a flameproof casserole, heat the oil, then sizzle the bacon for 5 minutes. Turn up the heat, then brown the lamb in batches. Remove with a slotted spoon. Fry the onions, carrots and mushrooms for 5 minutes, then stir in the flour. Return the meat to the pan with the herbs, wine, stock and Worcestershire sauce. Season, cover and braise for 1 hour 20 minutes.
2 Make the topping just before the lamb is cooked. Tip the flour, herbs and seasoning into a large bowl. Rub in the butter. Make a well, then add the lemon juice and 3 tablespoons water. Form a soft dough then roll out to about 5mm thick, then cut into rounds with a 7cm cutter. Overlap the circles of dough and bay leaves on the top of the stew. Brush with egg and bake for 45 minutes until golden.

■ Per serving 963 kcalories, protein 45g, carbohydrate 59g, fat 60g, saturated fat 31g, fibre 5g, sugar 9g, salt 2.89g

Butter bean and squash crumble

This flavour-packed beany bake will make your meat-eating guests as happy as the veggies.

■ **Takes 2¼ hours** ■ **Serves 6**

350g/12oz dried butter beans, soaked
   overnight in cold water
4 tbsp olive oil
2 onions, chopped
4 garlic cloves, finely chopped
1–2 red chillies, seeded and finely chopped
700g jar passata
1 dried bouquet garni
425ml/¾ pint white wine
425ml/¾ pint vegetable stock
700g/1lb 9oz squash, peeled,
   seeded and cut into chunks

FOR THE CRUMBLE
50g/2oz breadcrumbs
25g/1oz walnuts, finely chopped
1 tbsp chopped rosemary
4 tbsp chopped parsley

1 Rinse the beans and put in a large pan with plenty of water to cover. Bring to the boil, reduce the heat and cook, partly covered, for about 1 hour until tender. Drain well.
2 Heat 2 tablespoons of the oil in a large pan, add the onions, fry for 10 minutes until lightly browned. Add the garlic, chillies, passata, bouquet garni, wine, stock, salt and pepper, and bring to the boil. Reduce the heat and simmer, uncovered, for 20 minutes, then add the squash and cook for a further 20 minutes. Taste and add more seasoning, if necessary.
3 Heat oven to 180C/160C fan/gas 4. Stir the beans into the sauce, then transfer to a 2.5-litre gratin dish, or two smaller ones. Mix together all the crumble ingredients, plus the remaining oil, then sprinkle over the beans. Bake for 30 minutes until the topping is golden and crisp.

■ Per serving 428 kcalories, protein 17g, carbohydrate 62g, fat 12g, saturated fat 2g, fibre 13g, sugar 18g, salt 0.93g

Chilli chicken one-pot

This tasty chicken one-pot with chorizo can be prepared ahead and just reheated and plonked on the table. Serve this with garlic bread and a big salad, or a few slices of avocado and a squeeze of lime.

■ **Takes 1½ hours** ■ **Serves 8**

2 large onions, halved and sliced
2 tbsp olive oil
265g chorizo ring, skinned and thickly sliced
4 red peppers, seeded and cut into large
   chunks
2 × 400g cans chopped tomatoes
2 chicken stock cubes
½–1 tsp dried chilli flakes
2 tsp dried oregano
16 large boneless skinless chicken thighs
3 × 410g cans red kidney beans, drained
small pack coriander, chopped, to serve

1 Heat oven to 180C/160C fan/gas 4. Fry the onions in the oil for 5 minutes. Add the chorizo and fry for 2 minutes more. Stir in the peppers, tomatoes, a can of water, the stock cubes, chilli and oregano.
2 Sit the chicken thighs in the sauce, bring to a simmer then remove from the heat. Cover and bake in the oven for 40 minutes. Add the beans, stir, then return to the oven for 20 minutes more. Top with a sprigs of coriander, to serve.

■ Per serving 501 kcalories, protein 58g, carbohydrate 30g, fat 18g, saturated fat 6g, fibre 9g, sugar 14g, salt 3.16g

Quorn and carrot pilaf

Quorn is a great please-all choice if you have vegetarians and meat-eaters in the same household.

■ **Takes 45 minutes** ■ **Serves 4 generously**

3 tbsp vegetable oil
1 large onion, chopped
1 large aubergine, cubed
1 garlic clove, crushed
3 tbsp balti curry paste
1 large sweet potato, cubed
250g/9oz carrots, grated
250g/9oz frozen beans
350g/12oz basmati rice
300ml/½ pint reduced-fat coconut milk
200g bag spinach leaves
2 × 140g packs low-fat Quorn fajita strips

1 Heat the oil in a large pan. Add the onion and cook for 5 minutes until softened but not browned. Stir in the aubergine and cook for 5 minutes, adding the garlic and curry paste 1 minute before the end of the cooking time.
2 Stir in the sweet potato, carrots, beans, rice, 700ml/1¼pints water and the coconut milk. Bring to the boil, cover and simmer for 15 minutes.
3 Add the spinach and Quorn strips to the pan, stir everything together, then cover and leave off the heat for 5 minutes. Fork through to fluff up the rice, then serve.

■ Per serving 699 kcalories, protein 22.7g, carbohydrate 106.2g, fat 23.6g, saturated fat 8.8g, fibre 12.6g, sugar 18.5g, salt 2.26g

TOP: Butter bean and squash crumble

BOTTOM LEFT: Chilli chicken one-pot

BOTTOM RIGHT: Quorn and carrot pilaf

TOP: Chicken with roots and chickpeas

BOTTOM LEFT: Quick sausage Bolognese

BOTTOM RIGHT: Lamb meatball and pea pilaf

Chicken with roots and chickpeas

Whole chicken legs are substantially cheaper than breast meat – and are full of flavour, too. Serve this filling supper with warm flatbreads or plain rice.

■ **Takes 1 hour** ■ **Serves 4**

4 chicken legs
2 tbsp olive oil
4 carrots, cut into large chunks
3 parsnips, cut into large chunks
1 onion, cut into large chunks
1 tbsp Moroccan seasoning or mix
1tsp each of ground cumin, coriander and cinnamon
440g can chickpeas, drained and rinsed
400g can chopped tomatoes
chopped coriander leaves (optional)

1 Heat oven to 220C/200C fan/gas 7. Toss the chicken, oil, vegetables and Moroccan seasoning or mixed spices with some salt and pepper. Roast for 40 minutes, shaking the pan every so often.
2 When the chicken and vegetables are cooked, lift the chicken on to four plates and keep warm, then put the roasting tin over a high heat on the hob. Tip in the chickpeas and tomatoes, and bring to a simmer. Cook for a few minutes, then stir in the coriander, if using. Serve with the chicken.

■ Per serving 590 kcalories, protein 40g, carbohydrate 37g, fat 32g, saturated fat 8g, fibre 10g, sugar 17g, salt 2.12g

Quick sausage Bolognese

Using the meat from good-quality sausages is an easy way to get lots of flavour into mince dishes without having to add extra herbs, spices and seasoning.

■ **Takes 20 minutes** ■ **Serves 4**

6 good-quality sausages, skins removed
1 tsp fennel seeds (optional)
250g pack mushrooms, sliced
150ml/¼ pint red wine (optional)
660g jar tomato pasta sauce
300g/10oz penne or other pasta shapes
grated or shaved Parmesan, to serve (optional)

1 Heat a large, wide frying pan, then crumble in the sausagemeat and fennel seeds, infusing (there's no need to add any oil). Fry for a few minutes until golden and the fat is released, stirring well to break up the meat. Add the mushrooms and fry for a few minutes until beginning to soften. Stir in the wine, if using, bubble for 1 minute, then add the tomato sauce and heat through until bubbling.
2 Meanwhile, cook the pasta according to the packet instructions. When ready, drain and tip into the sauce. Mix well until completely coated, then divide among four plates, sprinkling with a little Parmesan, if you like, before serving.

■ Per serving 657 kcalories, protein 27g, carbohydrate 75g, fat 30g, saturated fat 8g, fibre 5g, sugar 15g, salt 2.98g

Lamb meatball and pea pilaf

If you haven't made lamb meatballs before, experiment with this tasty pilaf. For an even healthier version, substitute the lamb for turkey mince – it's a good source of protein and low in saturated fat.

■ **Takes 30 minutes** ■ **Serves 4**

400g pack lean minced lamb
3 garlic cloves, crushed
2 tsp ground cumin
300g/10oz basmati rice
enough lamb or vegetable stock to cover the rice (from a cube is fine)
300g/10oz frozen peas
zest of 2 lemons, juice of 1

FOR THE CUCUMBER YOGURT
½ cucumber, finely chopped or grated
150g pot mild natural yogurt
small bunch of mint, leaves torn

1 Mix the lamb with half the garlic and 1 teaspoon of the cumin, then season and shape into about 16 balls (it's easier to do if you wet your hands) Heat a large frying pan then fry the meatballs for about 8 minutes until golden and cooked through. Remove from the pan, set aside, then tip in the rice and the remaining cumin and garlic. Fry for 30 seconds, stirring, then pour in enough stock to cover. Cover and simmer for 10 minutes or until almost all of the liquid is absorbed.
2 Stir in the peas, return the meatballs to the pan, then warm through for a few minutes until the peas are tender. Meanwhile, mix the cucumber, yogurt and half the mint together, then season. To finish the pilaf, stir in the lemon zest and juice with some seasoning and the remaining mint. Serve with a good dollop of the cooling cucumber yogurt.

■ Per serving 496 kcalories, protein 33g, carbohydrate 72g, fat 10g, saturated fat 4g, fibre 4g, sugar 5g, salt 1.34g

Toad in the hole with onion gravy

Toad in the hole is a classic money-saving recipe, the cheap-to-make batter making sausages go further. The trick to a good rise is to get the pan really hot before you add the batter.

■ **Takes 1 hour** ■ **Serves 4**

100g/4oz plain flour, plus 1 tbsp for gravy
½ tsp English mustard powder
1 egg
300ml/½ pint milk
3 thyme sprigs, leaves only
8 plain pork sausages
2 tbsp sunflower oil
2 onions, peeled and sliced
500ml/18fl oz beef stock

1 Heat oven to 220C/200C fan/gas 7. Mix together the flour, mustard powder and a good pinch of salt in a large bowl. Make a well in the flour and crack the egg into it, then pour in 100ml of the milk. Stir slowly to make a smooth batter – beating out any lumps. Stir in the remaining milk and the thyme leaves.
2 Tip the sausages into a 20cm x 30cm roasting tin. Add 1 tablespoon of the oil, tossing the sausages in it thoroughly to coat the base, then roast for 15 minutes.
3 Quickly pour the batter into the hot tin. Bake for 40 minutes until the batter is cooked through, well risen and crisp at the edges.
4 In a pan, cook the onions in the remaining oil over a medium heat for 20 minutes until golden brown. Add the remaining flour, then cook, stirring, for 2 minutes. Gradually stir in the stock to make a smooth gravy. Bubble to thicken, then season and serve with the toad in the hole.

■ Per serving 520 kcalories, protein 25g, carbohydrate 37g, fat 31g, saturated fat 9g, fibre 2g, sugar 11g, salt 2.22g

Tasty cottage pies

A classic family recipe that the kids will love. Serve with your favourite green veg for a complete meal.

■ **Takes 1½ hours** ■ **Serves 4**

FOR THE FILLING
2 onions, sliced
2 tbsp olive oil
500g/1lb 2oz lean minced beef
2 beef stock cubes
3 tbsp brown sauce
415g can reduced sugar and salt baked beans

FOR THE TOPPING
900g/2lb large potatoes, quartered
3 medium carrots, thickly sliced
25g/1oz butter
a good splash of milk
40g/1½oz mature Cheddar, grated
4 small tomatoes, quartered
broccoli florets or peas, to serve

1 Heat oven to 200C/180C fan/gas 6. Fry the onions in the oil for 5 minutes until soft and golden. Add the mince, breaking it up well, and fry until it has browned. Add a mug of water, the stock cubes and brown sauce. Cover and simmer over a low heat for 10 minutes, stirring every now and then.
2 Boil the potatoes and carrots together in salted water for 15 minutes or until tender. Drain and return to the pan with the butter and milk, then mash until smooth with an electric whisk or potato masher.
3 Stir the beans into the meat mix, simmer for 2 minutes, then spoon into 4 mini pie dishes. Spoon the mash over the top. Put the pie dishes on a baking sheet and top with the cheese and the tomatoes. Bake for 35 minutes or until the tops are golden. Serve with broccoli or peas.

■ Per serving 634 kcalories, protein 42g, carbohydrate 57g, fat 28g, saturated fat 12g, fibre 9g, sugar 15g, salt 3.65g

Sausage casserole with garlic toasts

You can't beat sausage casserole – it's comfort food at its best.

■ **Takes 45 minutes** ■ **Serves 4**

8 reduced-fat sausages
1 yellow pepper, seeded and chopped
4 red onions, cut into wedges
400g can chopped tomatoes
250ml/9fl oz hot vegetable stock
1 tbsp sugar
½ × 20g pack basil

FOR THE TOASTS
400g/14oz bloomer loaf
25g/1oz low-fat soft cheese
1 tbsp butter
2 garlic cloves, crushed
½ × 20g pack basil, chopped

1 Heat oven to 220C/200C fan/gas 7. Put the sausages, pepper and onions into a roasting tin, then roast for 20 minutes.
2 Lower the oven to 200C/180C fan/gas 6, then tip the tomatoes and stock over the sausages. Add the sugar and most of the basil leaves season, then stir well. Roast for another 20 minutes.
3 To make the toasts, lightly toast the bread on both sides. Mix together the cheese, butter, garlic and chopped basil then spread one side of the toast with this herby mix and grill Briefly until melted and golden.
4 Serve the garlic toasts with the sausage casserole, sprinkled with the remaining basil leaves.

■ Per serving (with toasts) 568 kcalories, protein 28g, carbohydrate 78g, fat 18g, saturated fat 7g, fibre 6g, sugar 19g, salt 4.24g

TOP: Toad in the hole with onion gravy

BOTTOM LEFT: Tasty cottage pies

BOTTOM RIGHT: Sausage casserole with garlic toasts

TOP: Braised chicken and beans

BOTTOM LEFT: Simple pasta with tomato and basil sauce

BOTTOM RIGHT: Tasty veg tagine

Braised chicken and beans

Canned beans take on masses of flavour in this French-style dish. To make it that bit more special, chuck in a glass of wine with the stock.

■ **Takes 1 hour** ■ **Serves 4**

2 tbsp olive oil
8 boneless skinless chicken thighs
2 onions, chopped
2 garlic cloves, chopped
1 tsp dried thyme
600ml/1 pint chicken or vegetable stock
2 × 400g cans flageolet, cannellini or butter beans
a handful of parsley leaves

1 Heat the oil in a large frying pan with a lid, add the chicken, then quickly brown it all over. Tip in the onions, garlic and thyme, then fry for a further 2 minutes. Pour in the stock, 150ml /¼ pint water and a little salt and pepper. Bring to the boil, then simmer for 40 minutes, covering halfway through the cooking time, until the chicken is tender.
2 Stir the beans into the pan and Briefly warm through. Roughly chop the parsley, then scatter over to serve.

■ Per serving 444 kcalories, protein 54.4g, carbohydrate 29g, fat 13.2g, saturated fat 2.7g, fibre 8.2g, sugar 6.9g, salt 2.48g

Simple pasta with tomato and basil sauce

You'll love the fresh flavour of this sauce. Adapt it with chillies, mushrooms, bacon, anchovies or olives – the choice is yours.

■ **Takes 20 minutes** ■ **Serves 4**

400g/14oz pasta
1 tbsp olive oil
1 garlic clove, crushed
400g can chopped tomatoes
1 tsp vegetable stock powder or ½ crumbled stock cube
1 tbsp tomato purée
1 tsp sugar
a few basil leaves

1 Boil the pasta according to the packet instructions.
2 Heat the oil in a pan, add the garlic, then gently fry for 1 minute. Tip in all the other ingredients, except the basil, and bring to the boil. Reduce the heat, then simmer uncovered for 5 minutes, stirring occasionally. To finish, roughly tear the basil leaves and stir them into the sauce.
3 Drain the pasta, reserving a little of the cooking water. Stir the pasta and reserved water into the sauce and serve.

■ Per serving 394 kcalories, protein 13.6g, carbohydrate 79g, fat 4.0g, saturated fat 0.7g, fibre 4.1g, sugar 7.5g, salt 0.29g

Tasty veg tagine

Tagines are a type of classic Moroccan stew – just perfect for serving with a steaming mound of couscous or over crisp jacket potatoes.

■ **Takes 45 minutes** ■ **Serves 4**

4 carrots, cut into chunks
4 small parsnips or 3 large, cut into chunks
3 red onions, cut into wedges
2 red peppers, seeded and cut into chunks
2 tbsp olive oil
1 tsp each ground cumin, paprika, cinnamon and mild chilli powder
400g can chopped tomatoes
2 small handfuls of soft dried apricots
2 tsp clear honey
couscous or jacket potatoes, to serve

1 Heat oven to 200C/180C fan/gas 6. Scatter the veg over a couple of baking sheets, drizzle with half the oil, season, then, using your hands, rub the oil over the veg to coat. Roast for 30 minutes until tender and beginning to brown.
2 Meanwhile, in a frying pan, cook the spices in the remaining oil for 1 minute – they should sizzle and start to smell aromatic. Tip in the tomatoes, apricots, honey and a can of water. Simmer for 5 minutes until the sauce is slightly reduced and the apricots plump, then stir in the veg and some seasoning. Serve with couscous or jacket potatoes.

■ Per serving 272 kcalories, protein 7g, carbohydrate 45g, fat 8g, saturated fat 1g, fibre 12g, sugar 32g, salt 0.35g

Gnocchi and tomato bake

Gnocchi is a delicious change from pasta and potatoes. It's available in most supermarkets and makes a filling family meal.

■ **Takes 30 minutes** ■ **Serves 4**

1 tbsp olive oil
1 onion, chopped
1 red pepper, seeded and finely chopped
1 garlic clove, crushed
400g can chopped tomatoes
500g pack gnocchi
a handful of basil leaves, torn
½ × 125g ball mozzarella, torn into chunks

1 Heat grill to high. Heat the oil in a large frying pan, then soften the onion and pepper for 5 minutes. Stir in the garlic, fry for 1 minute, then tip in the tomatoes and gnocchi and bring to a simmer. Bubble for 10–15 minutes, stirring occasionally, until the gnocchi is soft and the sauce has thickened. Season, stir through the basil, then transfer to a large ovenproof dish.
2 Scatter with the mozzarella and grill for 5–6 minutes until the cheese is bubbling and golden.

■ Per serving 285 kcalories, protein 10g, carbohydrate 50g, fat 7g, saturated fat 3g, fibre 4g, sugar 8g, salt 1.64g

Chorizo chicken with chilli wedges

Add some Spanish spice to chicken with a little chorizo. The sausage bastes the chicken as it roasts and gives the whole dish a delicious, garlicky paprika flavour.

■ **Takes 35 minutes** ■ **Serves 4**

4 large sweet potatoes, peeled and cut into wedges
1 tsp olive oil
1 tsp dried chilli flakes
12 thin chorizo slices
4 boneless skinless chicken breasts
a few thyme sprigs, leaves stripped, or 1 tsp dried thyme

1 Heat oven to 220C/200C fan/gas 7. Put the sweet potatoes on a large baking sheet, then toss with the oil and chilli flakes, and season. Roast for 10 minutes, then remove and reduce the oven temperature to 200C/180C fan/gas 6.
2 Lay 3 slices of chorizo over each chicken breast, and secure with a cocktail stick. Lift the chicken on to the baking sheet next to the potato wedges. Scatter the wedges with thyme leaves, then roast for another 20 minutes until the chicken is golden, turning it halfway through cooking.

■ Per serving 422 kcalories, protein 39g, carbohydrate 54g, fat 7g, saturated fat 2g, fibre 6g, sugar 15g, salt 0.66g

Creamy aubergine curry

Here's proof that creamy curries don't have to be bad for your waistline. Serve with basmati rice scattered with coriander and almonds.

■ **Takes 30 minutes** ■ **Serves 4**

2 onions, roughly chopped
4cm piece ginger, chopped
4 tbsp toasted flaked almonds, plus 1 tbsp to serve
1 tbsp curry powder
small bunch coriander, stalks and leaves separated
2 tsp olive oil
2 aubergines, chopped into large wedges
200g pot thick Greek yogurt
400ml/14oz hot water
basmati rice, to serve

1 Whizz the onions, ginger, almonds, curry powder and coriander stalks in a mini food processor until pulpy (add a splash of water if needed). Boil a kettle full of water.
2 Heat the oil in a pan, then fry the aubergines for 5 minutes until browned. Scoop them out using a slotted spoon and set aside. Add the onion paste to the pan and cook for a few minutes, stirring, until the onions soften. Return the aubergine to the pan with the yogurt and the hot water. Stir, then simmer for 10–15 minutes until the aubergine is tender. Season well, scatter with extra almonds and the chopped coriander leaves, and serve with basmati rice.

■ Per serving 190 kcalories, protein 8g, carbohydrate 11g, fat 13g, saturated fat 4g, fibre 6g, sugar 8g, salt 0.15g

TOP: Gnocchi and tomato bake

BOTTOM LEFT: Chorizo chicken with chilli wedges

BOTTOM RIGHT: Creamy aubergine curry

TOP: Lemon fish with basil bean mash

BOTTOM LEFT: Paella fried rice

BOTTOM RIGHT: Cottage pie potatoes

Lemon fish with basil bean mash

Fish is a healthy choice for the whole family. This tasty twist on fish and mushy peas is high in omega 3 and counts as two of your 5-a-day.

■ **Takes 25 minutes** ■ **Serves 4**

4 small bunches cherry tomatoes on the vine
1 tbsp olive oil
4 × 140g/5oz chunks white fish fillet (frozen is good value)
zest of 1 lemon, plus juice of ½
480g pack frozen soya beans
2 garlic cloves
bunch basil, leaves and stalks separated
200ml/7fl oz chicken or vegetable stock

1 Heat oven to 200C/180C fan/gas 6. Put the tomatoes on to a baking sheet, rub with a little of the oil and some seasoning, then roast for 5 minutes until the skins are starting to split. Add the fish, top with most of the lemon zest and some more seasoning, then drizzle with a little more oil. Roast for 8–10 minutes until the fish flakes easily.
2 Meanwhile, cook the beans in a pan of boiling water for 3 minutes until just tender. Drain, then tip into a food processor with the remaining oil, the garlic, basil stalks, lemon juice and stock, then pulse to a thick, slightly rough purée. Season to taste.
3 Divide the tomatoes and bean mash among four plates, top with the fish, then scatter with basil leaves and the remaining lemon zest to serve.

■ Per serving 372 kcalories, protein 44g, carbohydrate 17g, fat 15g, saturated fat 3g, fibre 6g, sugar 3g, salt 0.5g

Paella fried rice

A little chorizo transforms some very ordinary storecupboard ingredients into a main meal you'll make again and again!

■ **Takes 35 minutes** ■ **Serves 4**

300g/10oz basmati rice
1 tbsp vegetable oil
2 small chorizo sausages, sliced
1 onion, sliced
1 garlic clove, chopped
½ tsp ground turmeric
200g/8oz frozen cooked peeled prawns
100g/4oz frozen peas
150ml/¼ pint boiling water
lemon wedges, to serve

1 Rinse the rice until the water runs clear, tip into a pan, cover with cold water to a fingertip's depth and bring to the boil. Season, then cover and simmer for 10 minutes or until all of the liquid has been absorbed, then take off the heat and let it rest for 10 minutes. Fluff up with a fork.
2 Heat the oil in a frying pan. Tip in the chorizo, onion and garlic, then cook until softened. Stir through the turmeric, followed by the rice, prawns, peas and the boiling water. Keep stirring until everything is warmed through. Serve with lemon wedges.

■ Per serving 347 kcalories, protein 20g, carbohydrate 50g, fat 9g, saturated fat 2g, fibre 2g, sugar 3g, salt 1.19g

Cottage pie potatoes

If your family like cottage pie, they'll love these special baked spuds. You could make these the night before, then simply bake them for 20 minutes when you get in.

■ **Takes 1 hour** ■ **Serves 4**

2 tbsp butter
1 large onion, chopped
500g pack lean minced beef
500ml/18fl oz hot beef stock
1 tbsp Worcestershire sauce
2 tbsp tomato purée
4 large jacket potatoes, baked or microwaved
2 good handfuls of grated Cheddar
your favourite veg, to serve

1 Heat oven to 200C/180C fan/gas 6. Melt half the butter in a non-stick pan. Cook the onion for 3–4 minutes, then increase the heat and add the mince. Fry for a further 3–4 minutes until the beef has browned. Stir in the stock, Worcestershire sauce, tomato purée and some seasoning. Gently bubble for 15–20 minutes until the mince is tender and the sauce has thickened.
2 To assemble, cut the jacket potatoes in half lengthways and scoop the flesh into a small bowl, leaving the skin intact. Mash the potato with the remaining butter and season well. Divide the mince among the potato skins, then cover with the mash. Transfer the potatoes to a baking dish, sprinkle with cheese, then bake for 20 minutes until golden. Serve with your favourite veg.

■ Per serving 779 kcalories, protein 50g, carbohydrate 79g, fat 31g, saturated fat 15g, fibre 7g, sugar 9g, salt 2.43g

BBQ pork steaks with smoky corn

Barbecue sauce is dead easy to make yourself and tastes fabulous with pork and juicy buttered corn.

■ **Takes 20 minutes** ■ **Serves 4**

4 tbsp tomato ketchup
2 tbsp dark muscovado sugar
1 tbsp white wine vinegar
1 tsp paprika
4 pork loin steaks, trimmed of any fat
4 corn cobs
1 tbsp butter
green salad, to serve

1 Boil a large pan of water for the corn and make the sauce by mixing together the ketchup, sugar and vinegar with half the paprika.
2 Heat a non-stick frying pan, then brown the pork for 3–4 minutes on each side. Spoon over the sauce halfway through cooking and turn the steaks in it until the pork is cooked through and sticky.
3 Meanwhile, tip the corn into the boiling water and cook for 5–8 minutes until tender. Stir the remaining paprika into the butter in a heatproof bowl and microwave on High for 15–20 seconds until the paprika is sizzling in the melted butter (alternatively, just melt the smoky butter in a small pan). Drain the corn, brush over the butter, then serve with the sticky pork steaks and a green salad.

■ Per serving 320 kcalories, protein 30g, carbohydrate 30g, fat 10g, saturated fat 4g, fibre 2g, sugar 14g, salt 0.88g

Better-than-baked beans with spicy wedges

Good-for-you baked beans that are cheap but taste brilliant. The wedges are a complete winner – they go with so many meals.

■ **Takes 45 minutes** ■ **Serves 2 (easily doubled)**

1 tsp oil
1 onion, halved and thinly sliced
2 rashers streaky bacon, cut into large-ish pieces
1 tsp sugar (brown, if you have it)
400g can chopped tomatoes
200ml/7fl oz vegetable stock (from a cube)
410g can cannellini, butter or haricot beans in water

FOR THE WEDGES
1 tbsp white flour (plain or self-raising)
½ tsp cayenne, paprika or mild chilli powder
1 tsp dried mixed herbs (optional)
2 baking potatoes, each cut into 8 wedges
2 tsp oil

1 Heat oven to 200C/180C fan/gas 6. For the wedges, mix the flour, cayenne, paprika or chilli powder, and herbs (if using), add some salt and pepper, then toss with the potatoes and oil until well coated. Tip into a roasting tin, then bake for about 35 minutes until crisp and cooked through.
2 Meanwhile, heat the oil in a non-stick pan, then gently fry the onion and bacon together for 5–10 minutes until the onions are softened and just starting to turn golden. Stir in the sugar, tomatoes, stock and seasoning to taste, then simmer the sauce for 5 minutes. Add the beans, then simmer for another 5 minutes until the sauce has thickened. Serve with the wedges.

■ Per serving 399 kcalories, protein 19g, carbohydrate 60g, fat 11g, saturated fat 2g, fibre 12g, sugar 15g, salt 1.14g

Crunchy fish fingers

Homemade fish fingers are quick to prepare, good for you and convenient – you can even cook them from frozen. Try great-value pollack as a sustainable and tasty alternative to cod.

■ **Takes 25 minutes** ■ **Serves 4**

250g/9oz pollack fillets
juice of ½ lemon
½ tsp fish seasoning (we used Schwartz)
50g/2oz polenta
50g/2oz dried breadcrumbs
1 egg, lightly beaten
2 tbsp olive oil, to drizzle
your favourite veg, to serve

1 Heat oven to 200C/180C fan/gas 6. Cut the fish into 8 pieces, then squeeze over the lemon juice.
2 Mix the fish seasoning, polenta and breadcrumbs on a plate. Dip the fish into the beaten egg, then turn several times in the polenta and breadcrumb mixture to coat. Repeat with all the pieces of fish, then put on a baking sheet lined with non-stick baking paper.
3 Drizzle the fish fingers with olive oil and bake for 15 minutes, turning halfway through cooking. Serve with your favourite veg.

■ Per serving 205 kcalories, protein 15g, carbohydrate 20g, fat 8g, saturated fat 1g, fibre none, sugar 1g, salt 0.32g

TOP: BBQ pork steaks with smoky corn

BOTTOM LEFT: Better-than-baked beans with spicy wedges

BOTTOM RIGHT: Crunchy fish fingers

TOP: Sticky chicken stir fry with sesame seeds

BOTTOM LEFT: Spiced tortilla

BOTTOM RIGHT: All-in-one baked mushrooms

Sticky chicken stir fry with sesame seeds

With stand-bys in your cupboard, you can make a stir fry quickly and cheaply. For even better value, switch the chicken for turkey.

■ **Takes 20 minutes** ■ **Serves 2**

175g/6oz egg noodles
2 tsp sunflower oil
2 boneless, skinless chicken breasts, sliced into strips
3 carrots, cut into matchsticks
2 tbsp clear honey
1 tbsp soy sauce
juice of 2 limes
3 tbsp sesame seeds, toasted
small bunch coriander, roughly chopped

1 Cook the noodles according to the packet instructions, then drain and toss with 1 teaspoon of the oil to stop them sticking together.
2 Meanwhile, heat the remaining teaspoon of oil in a large wok, add the chicken, then stir-fry over a high heat for a few minutes. Tip in the carrot sticks, then continue stir-frying for about 4 minutes until the chicken is cooked and starting to brown.
3 Quickly stir in the honey, soy sauce and lime juice, allow to bubble for 30 seconds, then add the sesame seeds and cooked noodles. (At this stage it's easier to use tongs to mix everything together.) Warm everything through Briefly, then toss through the coriander just before serving.

■ Per serving 799 kcalories, protein 53.4g, carbohydrate 10.9g, fat 18.9g, saturated fat 2.7g, fibre 7.9g, sugar 25g, salt 3.42g

Spiced tortilla

Indian spices and eggs work together brilliantly in this filling veggie meal.

■ **Takes 25 minutes** ■ **Serves 4**

1 tbsp sunflower oil
1 onion, sliced
1 red chilli, seeded and shredded
2 tsp curry spices (we mixed ground coriander, cumin and turmeric)
300g/10oz cherry tomatoes
500g/1lb 2oz cooked potatoes, sliced
bunch coriander, stalks finely chopped, leaves roughly chopped
8 eggs, beaten
green salad, to serve

1 Heat the oil in a large frying pan. Fry the onion and half the chilli for 5 minutes until softened. Tip in the curry spices, fry for 1 minute more, then add the cherry tomatoes, potatoes and coriander stalks to the pan. Season the eggs well, pour over the top of the veg and leave the tortilla to cook gently for 8–10 minutes until almost set.
2 Heat the grill and flash the tortilla underneath it for 1–2 minutes until the top is set. Scatter the coriander leaves and remaining chilli over the top, slice into wedges and serve with a green salad.

■ Per serving 327 kcalories, protein 19g, carbohydrate 27g, fat 17g, saturated fat 4g, fibre 3g, sugar 5g, salt 0.69g

All-in-one baked mushrooms

Roast some potato wedges and heat up some baked beans to go with this easy breakfast-come-dinner dish.

■ **Takes 30 minutes** ■ **Serves 2 (easily doubled)**

2 tbsp olive oil
4 very large field mushrooms
4 slices good-quality cooked ham
4 eggs

1 Heat oven to 220C/200C fan/gas 7. Drizzle a little olive oil over the base of a ceramic baking dish, then pop in the mushrooms. Drizzle with the remaining oil and season. Bake for 15 minutes until soft, then remove from the oven.
2 Tuck the ham slices around the mushrooms to create little pockets. Crack the eggs into the pockets, then return to the oven for 10 minutes until the egg white is set and the yolk is still a little runny. Serve scooped straight from the dish.

■ Per serving 379 kcalories, protein 30g, carbohydrate 1g, fat 28g, saturated fat 6g, fibre 3g, sugar 1g, salt 1.79g

Smoked salmon with grapefruit salad

If you think you can't stretch to smoked salmon, think again. Packs of trimmings contain the same fish, only in smaller pieces. This salad goes brilliantly with prawns, too.

■ Takes 30 minutes ■ Serves 4

3 grapefruit (a selection of yellow and pink, if you like)
100ml/3½fl oz olive oil
1 lemon
12 slices smoked salmon
a large handful of coriander sprigs, to garnish
brown bread and butter, to serve (optional)

1 Peel the grapefruit then cut away the pith and cut into segments over a pan, to catch any juice. Put the segments on a plate to one side. Squeeze the juice out of the membrane you are left with as well. Boil the juice in the pan for about 10 minutes until reduced to a few syrupy tablespoons. Mix with the olive oil and set aside.
2 Peel the lemon and cut away the pith then segment and carefully mix with the grapefruit segments. Drape the smoked salmon over 4 plates and scatter with the fruit segments. Spoon over the dressing and garnish with the coriander sprigs. Delicious served with slices of brown bread and butter.

■ Per serving 354 kcalories, protein 20g, carbohydrate 10g, fat 26g, saturated fat 4g, fibre 2g, sugar 10g, salt 3.6g

Velvety liver parfait

Pâtés and parfaits are the ultimate in economical entertaining, as they cost little but taste fabulous. Serve with toast, chutney and gherkins.

■ Takes 45 minutes, plus cooling ■ Serves 6 with leftovers

250g pack butter, diced and slightly softened
2 shallots, finely sliced
1 garlic clove, sliced
600g/1lb 5oz chicken livers, any sinews cut away
a good splash of brandy
1 tbsp tomato purée
toast, sliced gherkins and chutney, to serve

FOR THE TOPPING
100g/4oz butter
1 tbsp thyme leaves
1 tsp cracked black peppercorns

1 Heat about a third of the butter in a large frying pan, then gently fry the shallots and garlic for 3–4 minutes until soft. Turn up the heat, add the livers, then fry until just browned on all sides. Add the brandy then boil down – if the sauce catches light for an instant, all the better. Cool completely.
2 Season generously, then tip into a processor with the tomato purée and remaining butter, and blitz until smooth. Push through a fine sieve, then tip into a serving dish and smooth the top. Chill for at least 4 hours until set.
3 For the topping, melt the butter then leave for a minute to separate. Scatter the thyme and peppercorns over the parfait, then pour the yellow layer of butter on top. Chill to set. Serve with plenty of toast, sliced gherkins and chutney. Will keep for 2 days in the fridge.

■ Per serving 535 kcalories, protein 18g, carbohydrate 2g, fat 50g, saturated fat 31g, fibre none, sugar 1g, salt 1.11g

Make-ahead mushroom soufflés

Not all soufflés are scary. Keep your cool in the kitchen and serve this sensational dish as an elegant wintry starter or lunch.

■ Takes 40–45 minutes, plus cooling ■ Makes 8

140g/5oz button mushrooms, sliced
50g/2oz butter, plus extra for greasing
25g/1oz plain flour
325ml/11fl oz milk
85g/3oz Gruyère, finely grated, plus a little extra for baking
3 eggs, separated
6 tsp crème fraîche
snipped chives, to serve

1 Fry the mushrooms in the butter for 3 minutes. Remove from the heat and reserve a good spoonful. Add the flour, blend with milk and return to the heat, stirring to make a thick sauce. Stir in the cheese, season and leave to cool.
2 Heat oven to 200C/180C fan/gas 6. Butter 8 x 150ml soufflé dishes and line the bases with non-stick baking paper. Stir the egg yolks into the cheese mixture. In a separate bowl, whisk the whites until stiff then fold into the soufflé mixture. Spoon into the dishes and place in a roasting tin. Fill with water to halfway up the dishes' sides. Bake for 15 minutes until golden. Leave to cool (they will sink). They can be baked up to 2 days ahead.
3 To serve, heat the oven to 190C/170C fan/gas 5. Turn the soufflés out and peel off the lining paper. Put them on a baking sheet lined with squares of baking paper. Top with crème fraîche, a little cheese and the reserved mushrooms. Bake for 10–15 minutes until risen and warmed through. Sprinkle with chives and serve.

■ Per soufflé 170 kcalories, protein 8g, carbohydrate 5g, fat 14g, saturated fat 8g, fibre none, sugar 2g, salt 0.41g

TOP: Smoked salmon with grapefruit salad

BOTTOM LEFT: Velvety liver parfait

BOTTOM RIGHT: Make-ahead mushroom soufflés

TOP: Sardines with Sicilian fennel salad

BOTTOM LEFT: Tomato and curd cheese tart

BOTTOM RIGHT: Tomato and crispy crumb chicken

Sardines with Sicilian fennel salad

Sardines are inexpensive and widely available because their stocks are sustainable. They're packed with health-giving oils and a perfect match for this punchy summer salad.

■ **Takes 30 minutes** ■ **Serves 2 (easily doubled)**

zest and juice of 1 lemon
bunch parsley, half the leaves finely
    chopped, half left whole
1 small garlic clove, finely chopped
1 fennel bulb, with fronds
50g/2oz toasted pine nuts
50g/2oz raisins
a handful of green olives, chopped
3 tbsp olive oil, plus extra for drizzling
4 large sardines, scaled and gutted
a handful of flaky sea salt

1 Mix the lemon zest, chopped parsley and garlic together, then set aside. Pick the fronds from the fennel and set aside. Halve the fennel bulb and finely slice. Make the salad by mixing the sliced fennel and fronds with the pine nuts, raisins, olives and whole parsley leaves. Dress with the olive oil and lemon juice.

2 Heat the barbecue or a griddle pan over a medium heat. Season the fish with the salt (this stops them sticking). Griddle or barbecue for 2–3 minutes on each side until the eyes turn white. Sprinkle the fish with the parsley mix and lift on to plates. Drizzle with oil and serve with the salad.

■ Per serving 663 kcalories, protein 34g, carbohydrate 20g, fat 50g, saturated fat 7g, fibre 3g, sugar 20g, salt 1.49g

Tomato and curd cheese tart

A fabulous tart that's perfect as a starter or light lunch. Curd cheese is a soft, very creamy cheese, available at most deli counters. You could use cream cheese or mascarpone instead.

■ **Takes 1½ hours** ■ **Serves 8**

200g/8oz plain flour, plus extra for dusting
100g/4oz butter, cold and cubed
50g/2oz mature Cheddar, grated
small bunch of basil, leaves roughly chopped
175g/6oz curd cheese
8 ripe medium tomatoes, thinly sliced
a little olive oil, to drizzle
a handful of mixed soft herbs (we used
    chervil, mint, and flat-leaf parsley), to
    garnish

1 Put the flour, ½ teaspoon salt and the butter into a food processor, and blend until roughly mixed. Tip into a bowl, stir in two-thirds of the Cheddar, then 100ml ice-cold water. Knead quickly, then chill the pastry for 30 minutes. In a bowl, mix together the basil, the remaining Cheddar and the curd cheese, then season.

2 Roll the pastry out to a long rectangle. Fold the top third down, then the bottom third up. Repeat 3 times. Chill for another 10 minutes.

3 Heat oven to 220C/200C fan/gas 7. Roll out the pastry again until large enough to cut a circle about the size of a dinner plate. Place on a floured baking sheet, prick all over with a fork, then bake for 15 minutes. Cool, then spread over the herby cheese mix, almost to the edge. Lay the tomatoes on top, overlapping.

4 Season and bake for 15 minutes. Turn down to 150C/130C fan/gas 2 and bake for 40 minutes. Cool a little, then drizzle with oil. Toss the herbs with more oil, then pile on to the tart to serve.

■ Per serving 278 kcalories, protein 8g, carbohydrate 24g, fat 17g, saturated fat 10g, fibre 2g, sugar 4g, salt 0.58g

Tomato and crispy crumb chicken

Chicken with a tasty tomato sauce makes an easy Friday-night supper for friends.

■ **Takes 40 minutes** ■ **Serves 4**

4 boneless skinless chicken breasts
2 thick slices wholemeal bread
2 tsp dried mixed herbs
400g can chopped tomatoes
1 garlic clove, crushed
1 tsp balsamic vinegar (optional)
2 tsp tomato purée
350g/12oz green beans

1 Heat the oven to 190C/170C fan/gas 5. Split the chicken breasts almost in half and open them out like a book. Put them in a non-stick roasting tin.

2 Whizz the bread in a food processor to make breadcrumbs and mix with the herbs. Drain the tomatoes and mix with the garlic, vinegar (if using) and tomato purée. Spread the sauce over the chicken and sprinkle with the breadcrumbs. Bake for 20–25 minutes until the chicken is tender.

3 Meanwhile, steam the beans for 5–7 minutes until just tender. Serve the chicken on a bed of beans.

■ Per serving 238 kcalories, protein 39g, carbohydrate 16g, fat 3g, saturated fat 1g, fibre none, sugar 5g, salt 0.66g

Asparagus and Parmesan pastries

These look special but are incredibly simple to make, especially as the pastry is ready-rolled. Asparagus is an inexpensive luxury when in season.

■ **Takes 35 minutes** ■ **Serves 4**

6 tbsp mascarpone
40g/1½oz grated Parmesan, plus
    shavings to serve
3 tbsp finely chopped basil
zest of ½ lemon
375g pack ready-rolled puff pastry,
    quartered, then cut to the length of
    the asparagus
350g pack asparagus spears
1 tbsp olive oil
a good handful of pretty salad
    leaves tossed in vinaigrette,
    to serve

1 Heat oven to 200C/180C fan/gas 6. Mix the mascarpone with the Parmesan, basil and lemon zest, then season.
2 Lift the pastry on to 2 baking sheets, then score around the edges of each piece to make a thin border. Spread over the cheese mixture, within the borders.
3 Toss the asparagus in the oil, then arrange in bundles on top of the pastry (these can be stacked a bit for height). Bake the pastries for 20–25 minutes until golden. Serve warm topped with the dressed salad leaves and a few shavings of Parmesan.

■ Per serving 535 kcalories, protein 12g, carbohydrate 37g, fat 39g, saturated fat 18g, fibre 1g, sugar 4g, salt 0.99g

Crisp Chinese pork

If you find the name of this cut off-putting, consider that, when cured and sliced, this is what we know as streaky bacon. Belly is the cheapest pork roasting joint; it's rich, so a little goes a long way.

■ **Takes 2 hours 10 minutes, plus salting**
■ **Serves 4**

1.3kg/3lb piece boned pork belly,
    skin on and scored (ask the butcher for
    the thin end if you can)
2 tsp Chinese five spice powder
2 tsp sea salt
boiled rice and steamed greens, to serve
    (optional)

FOR THE DIPPING SAUCE
4 tbsp soy sauce
a small piece ginger, grated
1 tbsp Thai sweet chilli sauce
1 spring onion, finely chopped

1 Rub the pork with the five-spice and sea salt then leave, uncovered, in the fridge for at least 2 hours, but preferably overnight.
2 Heat the oven to its maximum setting then lay the pork on a rack over a roasting tin, making sure the skin is exposed. Roast for 10 minutes before turning down the heat to 180C/160C fan/gas 4, then leave to cook for a further 1½ hours. Have a look at the pork; if the skin isn't crisp, turn up the heat to 220C/200C fan/gas 7, then cook for another 30 minutes until it is. Remove from the oven and leave to rest on a board for at least 10 minutes before cutting.
3 To make the dipping sauce, mix all the ingredients together with 2 tablespoons water. Cut the pork into small pieces, then serve with the sauce, plus boiled rice and steamed greens, if you like.

■ Per serving 696 kcalories, protein 59g, carbohydrate 3g, fat 50g, saturated fat 19g, fibre none, sugar 2g, salt 5.83g

Herb and Parmesan risotto

The perfect dish for relaxed entertaining: bring a pan of oozing risotto to the table, break some crusty bread and tuck in.

■ **Takes 50 minutes** ■ **Serves 4**

50g/2oz butter
1 onion, finely chopped
300g/10oz risotto rice
1 small glass white wine
1.5 litres/2¾ pints hot vegetable stock
50g/2oz Parmesan (half finely grated, half
    shaved)
2 handfuls of soft herbs (including basil and
    chives), half chopped and half left whole
2 tbsp olive oil
1 tbsp balsamic vinegar
crusty bread, to serve

1 Melt half the butter over a medium heat. Stir in the onion and sweat for 8–10 minutes until soft, stirring occasionally. Add the rice to the onion, and stir continuously until the edges of the grains start to look transparent.
2 Pour in the wine and simmer until totally evaporated. Add the stock, a ladleful at a time, stirring with each addition. Continue doing this for 25–30 minutes, until the rice is cooked but has a firm bite.
3 When the rice is cooked, turn off the heat, stir in the grated Parmesan, the remaining butter, the chopped herbs and half the oil, then season. Roughly chop the remaining chives, then mix with the whole herb leaves, remaining olive oil and the balsamic vinegar. Serve the risotto in bowls topped with some of the herb salad and Parmesan shavings.

■ Per serving 496 kcalories, protein 13g, carbohydrate 67g, fat 21g, saturated fat 10g, fibre 4g, sugar 7g, salt 0.93g

TOP: Asparagus and Parmesan pastries

BOTTOM LEFT: Crisp Chinese pork

BOTTOM RIGHT: Herb and Parmesan risotto

Squash, ricotta and sage pasta bake

This veggie main course can be put together a day ahead and left in the fridge, ready to cook at a moment's notice, or frozen well in advance.

■ **Takes 1 hour 20 minutes** ■ **Serves 6**

1 squash, about 1kg/2lb 4oz, chopped into chunks
2 tbsp olive oil
200ml pot crème fraîche
50g/2oz Parmesan, finely grated
12 dried lasagne sheets
250g pot ricotta
a small bunch of sage leaves, half chopped and half left whole

1 Heat the oven to 220C/200C fan/gas 7. Toss the squash with the olive oil in a roasting tin, then roast for 30 minutes until soft and golden. Meanwhile, mix the crème fraîche with half the Parmesan. Boil the lasagne sheets for 5 minutes and toss in a little oil.
2 Leave the squash to cool slightly, then peel away the skin from the flesh. In a separate bowl, beat the ricotta with the chopped sage and remaining Parmesan, then gently fold through the squash.
3 Assemble the bake. Spread a little of the crème fraîche mix over the bottom of a gratin dish, then lay some lasagne sheets over, then some ricotta and squash mix and more crème fraîche. Repeat saving some crème fraîche for the top. Spread the crème fraîche over the top layer of lasagne, then scatter with the sage leaves. Bake for 25 minutes until bubbling and golden.

■ Per serving 445 kcalories, protein 15g, carbohydrate 40g, fat 26g, saturated fat 14g, fibre 3g, sugar 8g, salt 0.36g

Roast chicken with lemon, garlic and rosemary

No one will ever turn down a roast chicken – especially not one roasted with garlic, herbs and lemon. Delicious.

■ **Takes 1¾ hours** ■ **Serves 4**

2 lemons
1 chicken, about 1.8kg/4lb
6 bay leaves
small bunch rosemary, broken into sprigs
2 whole garlic heads, cut across the middle
1.5kg/3lb 5oz potatoes, peeled and quartered
2 tbsp sunflower oil
50g/2oz butter, very soft
green vegetables, to serve

1 Heat oven to 200C/180C fan/gas 6. Halve a lemon and prick one half all over with a knife. Cut the rest into wedges. Put the lemon half, a bay leaf, a few sprigs of rosemary and one half head of garlic inside the chicken cavity.
2 Tip the potatoes and remaining garlic into the roasting tin, toss with the oil and season. Push the potatoes to the edges and sit the chicken in the middle. Brush the chicken all over with some of the butter and make sure the potatoes are evenly spaced.
3 Roast for 1 hour 20 minutes, brushing twice with more butter during cooking. Lift the bird out of the tin, cover, then leave to rest.
4 Turn the oven up to 220C/200C fan/gas 7. Toss the potatoes, remaining herbs and lemon wedges in the pan juices, then roast for 15–20 minutes, turning once, until golden. Serve your roast with simple green vegetables, such as broccoli.

■ Per serving 800 kcalories, protein 50g, carbohydrate 67g, fat 39g, saturated fat 13g, fibre 5g, sugar 4g, salt 1.93g

Braised beef with red onions and wild mushrooms

Rich, sticky, dark and packed with flavour, this is the kind of dish that puts a smile on everyone's face, even on the bleakest winter day.

■ **Takes 3½ hours** ■ **Serves 6–8**

1.5kg/3lb 5oz beef braising steak, thickly sliced
600ml/1 pint boiling water
15g/½oz dried porcini mushrooms
3 tbsp olive oil
3 red onions, thinly sliced
1 tbsp plain flour
425ml/¾ pint port or red wine
250g/9oz chestnut mushrooms, whole, or halved if large
handful of chopped parsley, to serve

1 Heat oven to 160C/140C fan/gas 3. Pat the beef dry with kitchen paper and season both sides. Pour the boiling water over the dried mushrooms. Soak for 30 minutes then strain, reserving the juices.
2 Heat half the oil in a casserole, then add the meat in batches and fry on both sides until browned. Remove the meat from the pan, pour in the remaining oil, fry the onions for 10 minutes until softened. Return the meat to the pan, sprinkle in the flour and cook for 1 minute.
3 Add the port or wine, mushroom liquid and strained mushrooms. Bring to the boil, season, then cover and cook for 1½–2 hours until tender. Check after 1 hour. If the sauce looks like it's getting too thick, add a splash of boiling water.
4 Taste and season, then add the chestnut mushrooms and cook for a further 10 minutes. Serve, sprinkled with chopped parsley.

■ Per serving (8) 570 kcalories, protein 54g, carbohydrate 17g, fat 28g, saturated fat 10g, fibre 2g, sugar 13g, salt 0.4g

Duck tagine with clementines

The longer you cook duck legs, the more meltingly tender they become, so it's almost impossible to overcook them. They go well with mellow Moroccan spicing and the sweet flavours of honey and fresh fruit.

■ **Takes 2½ hours** ■ **Serves 6**

6 duck legs
200g/8oz shallots, peeled
2 tsp each ground coriander, cumin, ginger, and paprika
600ml/1 pint vegetable stock
2 tsp clear honey
juice of 1 lemon
6 small firm clementines, peeled
3 tbsp chopped coriander
2 tbsp toasted sesame seeds
couscous, to serve (optional)

1 Heat oven to 190C/170C fan/gas 5. Put the duck legs in one layer in a large roasting tin or in two smaller ones. Sprinkle with salt, then roast for 45 minutes. Remove the duck legs to a dish and spoon 3 tablespoons of the duck fat into a large pan (reserve the remainder of fat).
2 Add the shallots to the pan and fry Briefly until just starting to colour. Sprinkle in the spices and mix well. Add the stock, honey, lemon juice, salt and pepper then bring to the boil. Sit the duck legs on top, cover tightly and cook over a gentle heat for 1–1¼ hours until the meat is tender.
3 Meanwhile, heat 1 tablespoon of the reserved duck fat in a frying pan, add the whole clementines and fry all over until glistening and starting to brown. Add to the pan with the duck and cook for a further 15 minutes, then sprinkle with the coriander and sesame seeds. This dish goes really well with couscous.

■ Per serving 437 kcalories, protein 48g, carbohydrate 9g, fat 23g, saturated fat 6g, fibre 2g, sugar 7g, salt 0.62g

Slow-cooked pork and red cabbage

This is a wonderful dish for winter. Serve with a big bowl of mashed potatoes, and a seasonal salad of bitter leaves such as chicory or curly endive, which will cut through the richness of the pork.

■ **Takes 2 hours 40 minutes** ■ **Serves 6**

1.5kg/3lb 5oz pork shoulder
1 rounded tsp black peppercorns, crushed
1 tbsp thyme leaves
3 tbsp olive oil
2 onions, chopped
1kg/2lb 4oz red cabbage, finely shredded
2 apples, peeled, cored and cut into eighths
425ml/¾ pint red wine
200g pack vacuum-packed chestnuts
2 tbsp cranberry or redcurrant jelly
mashed potatoes and green salad, to serve (optional)

1 Heat oven to 160C/140C fan/gas 3. Cut the pork into 3cm slices. Sprinkle with the crushed peppercorns, thyme and some salt.
2 Heat 2 tablespoons of the oil in a large flameproof casserole, then add the onions and fry until lightly browned. Add the cabbage, stir well, then add the apples and wine, and cook until the cabbage starts to soften. Finally, add the chestnuts, 1 tablespoon of the jelly, some seasoning, and bring to the boil. Cover and simmer for 5 minutes.
3 Meanwhile, heat the remaining oil in a frying pan, add the pork and fry on both sides until browned, then stir in the remaining jelly. Cook for a few minutes until the pork is deeply brown. Arrange over the cabbage in the casserole. Pour a little boiling water into the frying pan, stir well and scrape off any bits on the bottom of the pan, then pour over the pork.
4 Cover the casserole tightly with a lid and cook for 1¼–1½ hours until the pork is very tender.

■ Per serving 770 kcalories, protein 49g, carbohydrate 33g, fat 48g, saturated fat 17g, fibre 7g, sugar 21g, salt 0.48g

Moroccan lamb

Just five ingredients meld into one delicious stew – that's clever entertaining. Serve with rice or couscous.

■ **Takes 45 minutes** ■ **Serves 4**

500g/1lb 2oz lamb neck fillet, cut into bite-sized pieces
2 tsp paprika
3 tsp ground cinnamon
2 × 400g cans chopped tomatoes with olive oil and garlic
1 tbsp finely chopped parsley, plus extra to serve
rice or couscous, to serve

1 Heat a large, non-stick frying pan. Brown the lamb well on all sides without adding oil. Tip in the spices, then fry for 1 minute more until aromatic.
2 Tip in the chopped tomatoes and parsley, bring to the boil, then simmer gently, with a lid on, for 30 minutes or until the lamb is tender. Serve sprinkled with more parsley, and with the rice and couscous.

■ Per serving 350 kcalories, protein 27g, carbohydrate 13g, fat 22g, saturated fat 9g, fibre 2g, sugar 9g, salt 1.47g

TOP: Cheese, leek and potato tortilla

BOTTOM LEFT: Fridge or freezer tarts

BOTTOM RIGHT: Honey-mustard chicken pasta

Cheese, leek and potato tortilla

This classic combination of flavours works really well in a tortilla – a thick omelette that's quick to make and a brilliant way to use up leftover potatoes and cheese.

■ **Takes 15 minutes** ■ **Serves 4**

a knob of butter, for frying
1 leek, thinly sliced
200g/8oz cooked and cooled potatoes
6 eggs
85g/3oz Cheddar
1 tbsp finely chopped sage, or 1 tsp dried (optional)
green salad, to serve

1 Melt a knob of butter in a medium, non-stick frying pan, then gently cook the leek for 5 minutes until softened. Meanwhile, cut the potatoes in half, then into slices about ½cm thick. Beat the eggs, season, then stir in the cheese and the sage (if using).
2 Add a little extra butter to the pan if needed, tip in the potatoes, then the egg mixture. Gently stir the potato and leek together, then turn the heat to low and cook for 10 minutes until nearly set. Put under a hot grill to cook for a couple of minutes more until the top is set and golden. Slice into wedges and serve with a green salad.

■ Per serving 277 kcalories, protein 16g, carbohydrate 11g, fat 19g, saturated fat 9g, fibre 1g, sugar 1g, salt 0.81g

Fridge or freezer tarts

It's amazing what you can throw together with a pack of pastry and a bit of imagination. We've used peppers, artichokes and mozzarella, but you can use ham, any cheese, anchovies or olives.

■ **Takes about 30 minutes** ■ **Serves 4**

375g pack ready-rolled puff pastry
4 tbsp green pesto or other pasta sauce
140g/5oz frozen sliced roasted peppers
140g/5oz artichokes, from a jar or frozen (about 3 wedges per serving)
125g ball mozzarella, torn or 85g/3oz hard cheese, grated
green salad, to serve

1 Heat oven to 200C/180C fan/gas 6. Unroll the pastry and cut into 4 rectangles. Take a sharp knife and lightly score a 1cm edge inside each rectangle, taking care that you don't cut all the way through the pastry. Put on a baking sheet.
2 Spread 1 tablespoon of pesto or pasta sauce on to each pastry slice, staying inside the border, then pile up the peppers and artichokes on top. Bake in the oven for 15 minutes until the pastry is starting to brown.
3 Scatter the cheese over the veg. Return to the oven for 5–7 minutes until the pastry is crisp and the cheese has melted. Serve with a green salad.

■ Per serving 515 kcalories, protein 16g, carbohydrate 42g, fat 33g, saturated fat 14g, fibre 3g, sugar 6g, salt 1.98g

Honey-mustard chicken pasta

There's a chance you'll already have most of the ingredients for this low-fat salad in your storecupboard and fridge.

■ **Takes 20 minutes** ■ **Serves 4 (easily halved)**

300g/10oz farfalle or other pasta shape
3 tbsp reduced-fat mayonnaise (use full fat, if you prefer)
1 heaped tsp wholegrain mustard
1 tsp clear honey
300g/10oz cooked chicken, torn into rough pieces
4 spring onions, thinly sliced (or use ½ red onion, thinly sliced)
a small bunch of basil, leaves roughly torn
4 tomatoes, quartered then halved

1 Cook the pasta according to the packet instructions, drain and cool under running water.
2 Mix the mayonnaise with the mustard and honey in a large bowl and loosen with a little water to make a dressing the consistency of double cream. Add the pasta, chicken, spring onions or red onion, basil and tomatoes, season to taste, then gently mix together to serve.

■ Per serving 450 kcalories, protein 31g, carbohydrate 62g, fat 11g, saturated fat 3g, fibre 3g, sugar 6g, salt 0.55g

Turkey and bacon club

Pre-packed sandwiches can be expensive and disappointing, so why not take your own classic club to work instead. You can grill the bacon the night before, then assemble and eat the next day.

■ **Takes 10 minutes** ■ **Serves 1**

2 rashers streaky bacon
butter, for spreading
3 slices bread (white or brown, or a mix)
1 thick slice cooked turkey
a little mayonnaise and mustard
a few lettuce leaves, shredded
½ avocado, sliced

1 Grill the bacon until crisp, then drain on kitchen paper (do this the night before, if you like).
2 Butter one slice of bread on one side, then cover with the turkey, a little mayonnaise and the lettuce. Butter both sides of the next slice of bread, and put on top of the turkey. Spread a little mustard over the bread, then arrange the bacon on top with the sliced avocado. Butter the last slice of bread on one side and put on top, buttered-side down.
3 Press the sandwich down lightly, then cut in half on the diagonal.

■ Per serving 745 kcalories, protein 31g, carbohydrate 54g, fat 46g, saturated fat 19g, fibre 4g, sugar 4g, salt 3.44g

Cheese stackers

Kids love these tasty little biscuits – pack some up with a few slices of ham, carrot sticks and cherry tomatoes for a healthy snack and happy faces.

■ **Takes 30 minutes** ■ **Makes about 30**

100g/4oz olive oil spread
50g/2oz Emmenthal or Cheddar, finely grated
85g/3oz mozzarella, grated
200g/8oz malted grain flour
1 tsp baking powder
pinch of English mustard powder (optional)
1 tbsp mixed seeds

1 Heat oven to 190C/170C fan/gas 5. Line two baking sheets with non-stick baking parchment. Put the olive oil spread into a bowl and mix in the cheeses. Add the flour, baking powder, mustard powder, if using, a pinch of salt and the mixed seeds, then stir to combine. Squeeze the mixture together with your hands. Roll the mixture into balls the size of cherry tomatoes. Space out on the baking sheet, then flatten each one with the palm of your hand (or roll out the dough and use a cookie cutter to make fun shapes).
2 Prick each biscuit several times with a fork, then bake for 12–15 minutes until golden. Cool, then store in an airtight container for up to a week.

■ Per stacker 70 kcalories, protein 2g, carbohydrate 5g, fat 5g, saturated fat 1g, fibre 1g, sugar none, salt 0.10g

Best bean spread

Versatile and tasty, this spread is brilliant stuffed into pitta with carrot, celery and cucumber sticks, or used as you would houmous.

■ **Takes 10 minutes** ■ **Serves 4**

410g can butter beans, drained
2 tbsp olive oil
2 tbsp lemon juice
125g light garlic and herb soft cheese

1 Put the butter beans into a food processor, then pour in the olive oil and lemon juice. Add a pinch of salt and some freshly ground black pepper. Whizz together to make a smooth paste.
2 Add the garlic and herb cheese, blend until smooth, then put into a sealable container and chill. Will keep for up to 3 days in the fridge.

■ Per serving 151 kcalories, protein 5.7g, carbohydrate 8.8g, fat 10.6g, saturated fat 3.8g, fibre 2.8g, sugar 1.8g, salt 0.97g

TOP: Turkey and bacon club

BOTTOM LEFT: Cheese stackers

BOTTOM RIGHT: Best bean spread

Chicken hoisin wraps

If you like duck and hoisin sauce but worry about the high fat content, try these easy wraps instead. With no lettuce to turn soggy, they make great food to go and are equally good using turkey too.

■ **Takes 5 minutes** ■ **Serves 2**

2 tortilla wraps
4 tsp hoisin sauce
100g/4oz cooked chicken, shredded
¼ cucumber, cut into sticks
4 spring onions, shredded

1 Warm the tortillas in the microwave or in a dry frying pan.
2 Thinly spread each tortilla with 2 teaspoons of the hoisin sauce. Scatter with the chicken, cucumber and shredded spring onion, then wrap and eat.

■ Per serving 182 kcalories, protein 18.6g, carbohydrate 20.1g, fat 3.6g, saturated fat 0.9g, fibre 1.4g, sugar 4.7g, salt 0.85g

Turkey and ham salad

Take what's left of the fruit bowl and some leftover ham or turkey, and you've got a great family salad in 15 minutes flat. If you're taking the salad to work, keep the dressing separate until you want to eat.

■ **Takes 15 minutes** ■ **Serves 4 (easily halved)**

180g bag Continental salad
2 ripe pears or crisp apples
a good handful of chopped walnuts (or use hazelnuts or pine nuts)
3 slices each turkey and ham

FOR THE DRESSING
1 small red onion, finely chopped
1 tbsp wine vinegar, any type
2 tsp clear honey
125g pot low-fat natural yogurt

1 Tip the bag of salad on to a large platter. Quarter, core and slice the pears or apples, then scatter over the salad leaves with the walnuts.
2 Cut the turkey and ham into strips, and scatter over the top.
3 Mix together all the dressing ingredients in a small bowl, then drizzle over the salad just before serving.

■ Per serving 240 kcalories, protein 27g, carbohydrate 14g, fat 9g, saturated fat 2g, fibre 3g, sugar 14g, salt 1.67g

Houmous avocado with tomato salad

A ripe avocado makes a fab lunch instead of the usual salad or sandwiches. Rub the cut and stoned avocado with a little lemon juice if you're not planning to tuck in straight away.

■ **Takes 5 minutes** ■ **Serves 2**

1 small red onion, sliced
2 tomatoes, chopped
a handful of pitted olives
a squeeze of lemon juice
olive oil, for drizzling
1 avocado
2 tbsp houmous
toasted bread, to serve

1 Combine the onion, tomatoes and olives with the lemon juice. Drizzle with oil and season to taste.
2 Halve and stone the avocado, then spoon the houmous into the space where the stone was. Scatter with the tomato salad, drizzle with a little more oil, then serve with toasted bread.

■ Per serving 436 kcalories, protein 4.6g, carbohydrate 8.8g, fat 42.7g, saturated fat 5.4g, fibre 7g, sugar 5.3g, salt 0.46g

TOP: Chicken hoisin wraps

BOTTOM LEFT: Turkey and ham salad

BOTTOM RIGHT: Houmous avocado with tomato salad

Speedy sweet potato soup with coconut

Sweet potatoes cook down to make a silky soup that tastes luxurious but costs very little.

■ **Takes 20 minutes** ■ **Serves 4**

1 tbsp vegetable oil
1 onion, chopped
1–2 tsp Thai curry paste (red or green)
750g/1lb 10oz sweet potatoes, peeled and grated
1 litre/1¾ pints hot vegetable stock
½ sachet creamed coconut (or use ¼ can reduced-fat coconut milk)
a handful of coriander leaves, roughly chopped, to garnish
mini naan breads, to serve

1 Heat the oil in a deep pan, then add the onion and soften it over a low heat for 4–5 minutes. Stir in the curry paste and cook for 1 minute more until fragrant. Add the grated sweet potatoes and stock, then bring quickly to the boil, simmering for 5 minutes until the potatoes are tender.
2 Remove the soup from the heat, stir in the coconut and some seasoning, then blend until smooth. Sprinkle with coriander and serve with warm mini naan breads.

■ Per serving 240 kcalories, protein 4g, carbohydrate 45g, fat 6g, saturated fat 3g, fibre 6g, sugar 15g, salt 0.56g

Springtime minestrone

This simple soup will become a favourite standby for a quick spring lunch. In any other season, use frozen mixed green veg instead of fresh.

■ **Takes 10 minutes** ■ **Serves 4**

200g/8oz mixed green vegetables (we used asparagus, broad beans and spring onions)
700ml/1¼ pints hot vegetable stock
140g/5oz cooked pasta (spaghetti chopped into small pieces works well)
215g can butter beans, drained and rinsed
3 tbsp green pesto

1 Place the green vegetables in a medium-sized pan, then pour over the stock. Bring to the boil, then reduce the heat and simmer until the vegetables are cooked through, about 3 minutes.
2 Stir in the cooked pasta, beans and 1 tablespoon of the pesto. Warm through, then ladle into bowls and top each with another drizzle of pesto.

■ Per serving 125 kcalories, protein 8g, carbohydrate 16g, fat 4g, saturated fat 1g, fibre 4g, sugar 3g, salt 0.7g

Creamy chicken soup

Although creamy in both name and texture, this soup actually has no cream added. The generous chunks of chicken and vegetables make it a real meal in a bowl.

■ **Takes 40 minutes** ■ **Serves 4**

85g/3oz butter
1 small onion, roughly chopped
1 large carrot, cut into small chunks
300g/10oz floury potatoes, cut into small chunks
1 large leek, trimmed and thinly sliced
1 heaped tbsp fresh thyme leaves or 1 tsp dried
50g/2oz plain flour
1.3 litres/2¼ pints hot chicken stock
200g/8oz cooked chicken, torn into big chunks
crusty bread, to serve

1 Melt 25g of the butter in a large, wide pan and heat until bubbling. Add the onion and fry for 3–4 minutes until just starting to colour. Stir in the carrot and potatoes, and fry for 4 minutes, then add the leek and thyme, and cook for 3 more minutes.
2 Melt the remaining butter in a medium pan. When bubbling, stir in the flour and keep stirring for 3–4 minutes until pale golden. With the pan still on the heat, gradually pour in the hot stock, stirring constantly as you go. When all the stock has been added, pour it into the pan of vegetables, simmer, then cook gently for 8–10 minutes, giving it all an occasional stir.
3 Stir in the chicken and seasoning, to taste. Warm through, and serve with crusty bread.

■ Per serving 449 kcalories, protein 28g, carbohydrate 32g, fat 24g, saturated fat 13g, fibre 4g, sugar 8g, salt 1.10g

TOP: Speedy sweet potato soup with coconut

BOTTOM LEFT: Springtime minestrone

BOTTOM RIGHT: Creamy chicken soup

Carrot and coriander soup

Everyone loves this soup and it's simplicity itself to make a batch using just a few low-cost ingredients.

■ **Takes 40 minutes** ■ **Serves 4**

1 tbsp vegetable oil
1 onion, chopped
1 tsp ground coriander
1 potato, peeled and chopped
450g/1lb carrots, peeled and chopped
1.2 litres/2 pints hot vegetable or chicken stock
a handful of coriander (about ½ a supermarket pack)

1 Heat the oil in a large pan, add the onion, then fry for 5 minutes until softened. Stir in the ground coriander and potato, then cook for 1 minute. Add the carrots and stock, bring to the boil, then lower the heat. Cover and cook for 20 minutes until the carrots are tender.
2 Tip into a food processor with most of the coriander and blitz until smooth (you may need to do this in two batches). Return the soup to the pan, taste, add salt if necessary, then reheat to serve. Garnish with the remaining coriander leaves.

■ Per serving 115 kcalories, protein 3g, carbohydrate 19g, fat 4g, saturated fat 1g, fibre 5g, sugar 12g, salt 0.46g

Sweetcorn and haddock chowder

Keep smoked haddock fillets and sweetcorn in the freezer, and add a few storecupboard staples for this tasty chowder.

■ **Takes 30 minutes** ■ **Serves 2**

a knob of butter
2 rashers streaky bacon, chopped
1 onion, finely chopped
500ml/18fl oz milk
350g/12oz potatoes (about 2 medium), cut into small cubes
300g/10oz frozen smoked haddock fillets (about 2)
140g/5oz frozen sweetcorn
chopped parsley, to garnish (optional)
crusty bread, to serve

1 Heat the butter in a large pan. Tip in the bacon, then cook until starting to brown. Add the onion, cook until soft, then pour over the milk and stir through the potatoes. Bring to the boil, then simmer for 5 minutes.
2 Add the haddock, then leave to cook gently for another 10 minutes. By now the fish should have defrosted so you can break it up into large chunks. Stir through the sweetcorn, then cook for another few minutes until the fish is cooked through and the sweetcorn has defrosted. Scatter over the parsley, if using. Serve with plenty of crusty bread.

■ Per serving 550 kcalories, protein 47g, carbohydrate 59g, fat 16g, saturated fat 7g, fibre 4g, sugar 18g, salt 3.92g

British onion soup

Although French in origin, onion soup feels very British too, and we've added cider and Cheddar to this one to make it even more so.

■ **Takes 1¾ hours** ■ **Serves 4**

50g/2oz butter or 2 tbsp dripping
1kg/2lb 4oz onions, finely sliced
1 tbsp golden caster sugar
a few thyme sprigs
3 bay leaves
150ml/¼ pint cider
1 litre/1¾ pints hot vegetable or chicken stock

FOR THE TOP
4 thick slices from a round country loaf
100g/4oz mature Cheddar, grated
a large handful of parsley, chopped

1 Heat most of the butter or dripping in a pan, then add the onions, sugar and herbs. Season and cook, uncovered, over a low heat, stirring occasionally, for up to 40 minutes until sticky and brown. Pour in the cider and simmer until reduced by half. Pour in the stock, bring to the boil, then cook for 20 minutes.
2 To serve, heat the grill to high. Spread the bread on both sides with the remaining butter or dripping, then toast under the grill until golden. Scatter with the cheese and put back under the grill until melted. Serve the soup in bowls with a slice of the toast floating in it, scattered generously with parsley.

■ Per serving 451 kcalories, protein 15g, carbohydrate 51g, fat 21g, saturated fat 12g, fibre 6g, sugar 22g, salt 1.75g

TOP: Carrot and coriander soup

BOTTOM LEFT: Sweetcorn and haddock chowder

BOTTOM RIGHT: British onion soup

TOP: Spiced parsnip bubble and squeak cake

BOTTOM LEFT: Red cabbage and fennel coleslaw

BOTTOM RIGHT: Roast sweet potato, squash and garlic mash

Spiced parsnip bubble and squeak cake

This leftover classic makes a great side dish at Christmas or any time of the year, and a delicious vegetarian main in its own right.

■ **Takes 45 minutes** ■ **Serves 4 as a main or 8 as a side dish**

800g/1lb 12oz parsnips, chopped into chunks
1 tsp turmeric
½ Savoy cabbage or 300g/10oz
   Brussels sprouts, finely shredded
a large handful of frozen peas
juice of ½ lemon
50g/2oz butter
1 tsp cumin seeds
1 tbsp garam masala
bunch fresh coriander, chopped, plus extra
   to garnish
1 red chilli, seeded and chopped

1 Tip the parsnips and turmeric into a pan of cold water. Bring to the boil for 12 minutes or until the parsnips are on the brink of collapsing. Blanch the cabbage or sprouts in another pan of boiling water for 3 minutes until tender. Add the peas for the final minute, then drain well.
2 Drain the parsnips, then tip back into the pan and roughly mash with the lemon juice and half the butter. Beat in all the other ingredients except the remaining butter and coriander sprigs then season.
3 Heat the remaining butter in a large non-stick frying pan and press the parsnip mixture down into it. Cook until crisp underneath, then turn with a fish slice. (Don't worry if it breaks at this point, it will hold eventually.) Keep cooking until crisp on the other side, then slide on to a plate and flip back into the pan. Keep on doing this until you have a crisp cake. Serve cut into wedges and garnished with coriander leaves.

■ Per serving 277 kcalories, protein 7g, carbohydrate 33g, fat 14g, saturated fat 7g, fibre 12g, sugar 15g, salt 0.27g

Red cabbage and fennel coleslaw

Add a little crunch to your plate with our fresh twist on coleslaw. If you like, you can replace the fennel and shallots with a finely sliced Spanish onion.

■ **Takes 15 minutes** ■ **Serves 4**

½ small red cabbage, shredded
2 medium carrots, coarsely grated
1 fennel bulb, cut into quarters and
   shredded
2 shallots, thinly sliced
50g/2oz mayonnaise

1 Put all the vegetables in a bowl and toss well
2 Stir in the mayonnaise to coat the salad, then season with lots of black pepper and a little salt, and serve. Any leftovers can be stored in a sealed container in the fridge for up to 2 days.

■ Per serving 117 kcalories, protein 1g, carbohydrate 6g, fat 10g, saturated fat 2g, fibre 3g, sugar 6g, salt 0.19g

Roast sweet potato, squash and garlic mash

Roasting brings out the best in root veg. This full-flavoured mash goes particularly well with roast chicken, chorizo and blue cheese.

■ **Takes 1 hour** ■ **Serves 4**

1kg/2lb 4oz butternut squash, peeled and
   cut into chunks
1kg/2lb 4oz sweet potatoes, peeled and cut
   into chunks
2 garlic bulbs
1 red chilli
3 tbsp olive oil, plus extra for drizzling

1 Heat oven to 200C/180C fan/gas 6. Divide the squash and potatoes between 2 roasting tins. Halve the garlic bulbs and put them and the whole chilli into one of the tins. Toss with the olive oil and roast for 45 minutes.
2 Once the squash and potatoes are soft and golden, halve and seed the roasted chilli, then chop, discarding the seeds. Squeeze out the garlic from the cut cloves and mash everything together. Season and drizzle with a little more oil to serve.

■ Per serving 434 kcalories, protein 6.8g, carbohydrate 76.1g, fat 13.6g, saturated fat 2.1g, fibre 10.5g, sugar 25.8g, salt 0.28g

Chicken noodle soup

This fragrant noodle soup is just the thing when you crave something light and healthy.

■ **Takes 30 minutes** ■ **Serves 4**

1.3 litres/2¼ pints chicken stock
2 star anise
3cm piece ginger, sliced (no need to peel)
2 garlic cloves in skins, bruised
2 bok choi, shredded
85g/3oz medium egg noodles
4 spring onions, finely sliced
100g/4oz cooked chicken, torn into very thin shreds
a splash of soy sauce
a handful of basil leaves
1 mild plump red chilli, seeded and finely sliced
sesame oil, to serve (optional)

1 Pour the stock into a medium pan. Add the star anise, ginger and garlic, and gently simmer, without boiling, for 10 minutes. For the last 2 minutes, put the bok choi into a colander or sieve, suspend it over the pan and cover to steam the greens.
2 Drop the egg noodles into the stock, stirring to separate, then simmer for 4 minutes until tender. Throw in the spring onions and chicken. Season to taste with a splash of soy sauce. Ladle into bowls and scatter over the bok choi, basil leaves and chilli. Shake over a few drops of sesame oil, if you like.

■ Per serving 132 kcalories, protein 19g, carbohydrate 5g, fat 4g, saturated fat 1g, fibre 1g, sugar 3g, salt 1.08g

Leek, bacon and potato soup

With this homemade soup in the freezer, you're never short of a starter, a casual lunch, or even a late-night supper.

■ **Takes 40 minutes** ■ **Serves 4–6**

25g/1oz butter
3 rashers streaky bacon, chopped, plus 4 rashers crisp streaky bacon, to serve
1 onion, chopped
400g pack trimmed leeks, sliced and well washed
3 medium potatoes, peeled and diced
1.4 litres/2½ pints hot vegetable stock
142ml pot single cream (or use milk)
toasted or warm crusty bread, to serve

1 Melt the butter in a large pan, then fry the bacon and onion, stirring until they start to turn golden. Tip in the leeks and potatoes, stir well, then cover and turn down the heat. Cook gently for 5 minutes, shaking the pan every now and then to make sure the mixture doesn't catch.
2 Pour in the stock, season well then bring to the boil. Cover and simmer for 20 minutes until the vegetables are soft. Leave to cool for a few minutes, then blend in a food processor in batches until smooth. Return to the pan, pour in the cream or milk and stir well. Taste and season if necessary. Serve scattered with tasty crisp bacon and toasted or warm crusty bread on the side.

■ Per serving (6) 175 kcalories, protein 6g, carbohydrate 15g, fat 11g, saturated fat 6g, fibre 4g, sugar 5g, salt 0.68g

Pumpkin soup

Silky-smooth pumpkin soup is a doddle to make. Try topping it with your own croûtons – a thrifty way to use up stale bread.

■ **Takes 45 minutes** ■ **Serves 6**

4 tbsp olive oil, plus extra to drizzle (optional)
2 onions, finely chopped
1kg/2lb 4oz pumpkin or squash, peeled, seeded and chopped into chunks
700ml/1¼ pints vegetable or chicken stock
142ml pot double cream
4 slices wholemeal seeded bread, crusts removed
a handful of pumpkin seeds

1 Heat half the oil in a large pan, then gently cook the onions for 5 minutes until soft. Add the pumpkin or squash to the pan and cook for 8–10 minutes more, stirring occasionally until it starts to soften and turn golden.
2 Pour the stock into the pan and season. Bring to the boil, then simmer for 10 minutes until the pumpkin or squash is very soft. Pour the cream into the pan, bring back to the boil, then whizz with an electric hand blender.
3 While the soup is cooking, cut the bread into small croûtons. Heat the remaining oil in a frying pan and fry the bread until crisp.
4 Add the pumpkin seeds to the pan, then cook for a few minutes more until toasty. Reheat the soup if necessary, taste for seasoning, then serve with croûtons and seeds, and drizzle with more oil, if you like.

■ Per serving 317 kcalories, protein 6g, carbohydrate 20g, fat 24g, saturated fat 9g, fibre none, sugar 6g, salt 0.54g

TOP: Chicken noodle soup

BOTTOM LEFT: Leek, bacon and potato soup

BOTTOM RIGHT: Pumpkin soup

TOP: Rich tomato soup with pesto

BOTTOM LEFT: Hearty sausage soup

BOTTOM RIGHT: Spicy prawn soup

Rich tomato soup with pesto

When you've got rich tinned tomatoes and intense, fruity sun-dried tomatoes, there's no reason not to enjoy a home-made tomato soup in the depths of winter.

■ **Take 25 minutes** ■ **Serves 4**

a knob of butter or 1 tbsp olive oil
2 garlic cloves, crushed
5 soft sun-dried tomatoes in oil, or SunBlush, roughly chopped
3 × 400g cans plum tomatoes
500ml/18fl oz chicken or vegetable stock
1 tsp sugar (any type), or to taste
142g pot soured cream
4–5 tbsp basil pesto
basil leaves, to garnish (optional)

1 Heat the butter or oil in a large pan, then add the garlic and soften for a few minutes over a low heat. Add the sun-dried or SunBlush tomatoes, canned tomatoes, stock, sugar and seasoning, then bring to a simmer. Let the soup bubble for 10 minutes until the tomatoes have broken down a little.
2 Whizz with a stick blender, adding half the soured cream as you do so. Taste and adjust the seasoning – add more sugar if you need to. Serve in bowls with 1 tablespoon or so of the pesto swirled on top and a little more soured cream, and a scattering of basil leaves, if you like.

■ Per serving 213 kcalories, protein 8g, carbohydrate 14g, fat 14g, saturated fat 7g, fibre 4g, sugar 13g, salt 1.15g

Hearty sausage soup

Polish food is becoming increasingly popular in British supermarkets, so why not experiment with some new ingredients in this filling family soup.

■ **Takes 40 minutes** ■ **Serves 4**

2 large onions, sliced
2 tbsp olive oil
2 garlic cloves, thinly sliced
200g/8oz Polish Kabanos sausages, chopped
1 tsp paprika, sweet or smoked
85g/3oz brown basmati rice
1 tbsp chopped fresh thyme
2 litres/3½ pints beef stock
3 carrots, thickly sliced
100g/4oz shredded kale or cabbage
crusty bread, to serve

1 Fry the onions in the oil for 5 minutes. Add the garlic and sausage, fry for a few minutes more, then stir in the paprika, rice and thyme.
2 Pour in the stock, bring to the boil, add the carrots and some salt and pepper, cover, then simmer for 20 minutes. Stir in the kale or cabbage, and cook for 10 minutes more. Serve with crusty bread.

■ Per serving 433 kcalories, protein 21g, carbohydrate 34g, fat 24g, saturated fat 6g, fibre 5g, sugar 12g, salt 3.83g

Spicy prawn soup

Blast away the cobwebs with this spicy broth. The best Thai curry pastes come in large pots and can seem costly, but they last ages and taste fantastic, so your taste buds will thank you for it!

■ **Takes 20 minutes** ■ **Serves 4 (easily halved)**

1 tbsp sunflower oil
300g bag crunchy stir-fry vegetables
140g/5oz mushrooms, sliced
2 tbsp Thai green curry paste
400ml can reduced-fat coconut milk
200ml/7fl oz vegetable or fish stock
300g/10oz medium straight-to-wok noodles
200g bag cooked peeled prawns

1 Heat a wok, add the oil, then stir-fry the veg and mushrooms for 2–3 minutes. Remove with a slotted spoon and set aside.
2 Tip the curry paste into the wok and fry for 1 minute. Pour in the coconut milk and stock. Bring to the boil, drop in the noodles and prawns, then reduce the heat and simmer for 4 minutes until the prawns are cooked through. Stir in the veg and serve.

■ Per serving 327 kcalories, protein 16g, carbohydrate 32g, fat 17g, saturated fat 10g, fibre 4g, sugar 4g, salt 0.97g

Banana cake with nutty crumble crunch

Don't chuck out over-ripe bananas – make a delicious banana cake instead. Perfect with a cup of tea, any time of day.

■ **Takes 1 hour 20 minutes** ■ **Serves 10**

250g/9oz golden caster sugar
250g/9oz self-raising flour
140g/5oz pecan nuts, walnuts or hazelnuts, roughly chopped
1 tbsp butter, chopped
2 eggs, beaten, plus 2 egg whites
3 large ripe bananas or 4 small, mashed
150ml/¼ pint sunflower oil
100ml/3½fl oz milk
1 tsp ground cinnamon
1 tsp baking powder

1 Heat oven to 180C/160C fan/gas 4, and line the base and sides of a deep 20cm cake tin with non-stick baking paper. Stir together 2 tablespoons each of the sugar, flour and nuts, then add the butter and rub in to make sticky crumbs for the topping.
2 Mix the whole eggs with the bananas, oil and milk. In a clean, dry bowl, whisk the egg whites until just stiff. In another bowl, mix the remaining sugar, flour and nuts with the cinnamon and baking powder. Tip the banana mix into the dry ingredients and quickly stir. Fold in the egg whites, then pour the mixture into the tin. Scatter over the topping and bake for 1 hour until a skewer inserted in the centre comes out clean. After 45 minutes, if the surface is browning too quickly, cover with baking paper.
3 Leave in the tin for 5 minutes, then finish cooling on a wire rack.

■ Per serving 476 kcalories, protein 6.6g, carbohydrate 56.2g, fat 26.6g, saturated fat 3.9g, fibre 1.9g, sugar 36g, salt 0.5g

Spiced apple cake

An old-fashioned homely bake, perfect with tea or for dessert.

■ **Takes 2 hours** ■ **Serves 12**

140g/5oz softened butter, plus extra for greasing
200g/8oz caster sugar
2 eggs, beaten
200g/8oz self-raising flour
½ tsp ground cloves
¼ tsp grated nutmeg
450g/1lb Bramley apples, peeled, cored and thickly sliced
icing sugar, for dusting

1 Heat oven to 180C/160C fan/gas 4, then butter and line a deep 20cm round cake tin. Put the butter and sugar into a large bowl and beat together until pale and creamy. Beat in the eggs, a little at a time, until light and fluffy. Mix the flour with the cloves and nutmeg, then fold into the eggy mixture.
2 Spread half the mix over the bottom of the tin, then cover with the apple slices. Dot the rest of the mix over the apples, then bake for 1½ hours or until a skewer inserted into the centre comes out clean. It will get quite dark on the top before it's done in the middle. Leave the cake in the tin to cool (it might sink a bit), then dust with icing sugar to serve.

■ Per serving 238 kcalories, protein 3g, carbohydrate 34g, fat 11g, saturated fat 6g, fibre 1g, sugar 22g, salt 0.37g

Toffee pecan cake

This special cake will go perfectly with coffee or makes a dessert to die for when served warm with ice cream. If maple syrup seems a little extravagant, use a little squeezy toffee sauce instead.

■ **Takes 55 minutes** ■ **Serves 8**

300g/10oz pecan nut halves
140g/5oz stoned dates
200g/8oz butter, softened, plus extra for greasing
200g/8oz light muscovado sugar
1 tsp ground mixed spice
4 eggs, beaten
140g/5oz self-raising flour
maple syrup, to serve

1 Tip 100g/3½oz of the pecans into a food processor and whizz until fine. Tip out into a bowl and set aside.
2 Put the dates into a small pan with enough water to cover, boil for 5 minutes until very soft, then drain, discarding the liquid, and whizz in the food processor until smooth.
3 Heat oven to 160C/140C fan/gas 4. Butter and line the base of a 20cm-round cake tin. Beat together the butter, sugar and spice until light and creamy, then tip in the dates, ground pecans, eggs and a pinch of salt, and beat Briefly until smooth.
4 Fold in the flour with a metal spoon, then spoon into the tin and level the top. Sprinkle the remaining nuts over the top (don't press them in) then bake for 40 minutes or until risen and golden and a skewer inserted into the centre comes out clean. Serve warm, with generous drizzles of maple syrup.

■ Per serving 692 kcalories, protein 10g, carbohydrate 53g, fat 51g, saturated fat 16g, fibre 3g, sugar 39g, salt 0.68g

TOP: Banana cake with nutty crumble crunch

BOTTOM LEFT: Spiced apple cake

BOTTOM RIGHT: Toffee pecan cake

TOP: Gluten-free lemon drizzle cake

BOTTOM LEFT: Chocolate marble cake

BOTTOM RIGHT: Smarties cookies

Gluten-free lemon drizzle cake

It can be hard to find special gluten-free ingredients, so this cake uses a cheap and starchy staple that almost everyone has knocking about in the kitchen.

■ Takes 1 hour 10 minutes ■ Serves 8–10

200g/8oz butter, softened, plus extra for greasing
200g/8oz golden caster sugar
4 eggs
175g/6oz ground almonds
250g/9oz mashed potatoes, cold
zest of 3 lemons
2 tsp gluten-free baking powder

FOR THE DRIZZLE
4 tbsp granulated sugar
juice of 1 lemon

1 Heat oven to 180C/160C fan/gas 4. Butter and line a deep, 20cm-round cake tin. Beat the butter and sugar together until light and fluffy, then gradually add the eggs, beating after each addition. Fold in the almonds, cold mashed potato, lemon zest and baking powder.
2 Tip the mixture into the tin, level the top, then bake for 40–45 minutes or until golden and a skewer inserted into the centre of the cake comes out clean. Turn out on to a wire rack after 10 minutes' cooling.
3 Mix the granulated sugar and the lemon juice together, then spoon over the top of the cake, letting it drip down the sides. Allow the cake to cool completely before slicing.

■ Per serving (10) 514 kcalories, protein 9g, carbohydrate 41g, fat 36g, saturated fat 2g, fibre 2g, sugar 35g, salt 0.88g

Chocolate marble cake

Good old cocoa powder makes this family cake as chocolatey as it needs to be – and works out a lot cheaper than using 70 per cent dark chocolate.

■ Takes 1 hour 10 minutes ■ Serves 8

225g/8oz butter, softened, plus extra for greasing
225g/8oz caster sugar
4 eggs
225g/8oz self-raising flour
3 tbsp milk
1 tsp vanilla extract
2 tbsp cocoa powder, sifted

1 Heat oven to 180C/160C fan/gas 4. Grease and line a round 20cm cake tin. Beat the butter and sugar together. Add the eggs, one at a time, mixing well after each addition. Fold through the flour, milk and vanilla extract until the mixture is smooth.
2 Divide the mixture between 2 bowls. Stir the cocoa powder into the mixture in one of the bowls. Dollop the chocolate and vanilla cake mixes into the cake tin alternately. When all the mixture has been used up, tap the bottom of the tin on the work surface to remove any air bubbles. Take a skewer and swirl it around the mixture in the tin a few times to create a marbled effect.
3 Bake the cake for 45–55 minutes until a skewer inserted into the centre comes out clean. Turn out on to a cooling rack and leave to cool.

■ Per serving 468 kcalories, protein 6g, carbohydrate 52g, fat 27g, saturated fat 16g, fibre 1g, sugar 31g, salt 0.81g

Smarties cookies

Kids absolutely adore these colourful biscuits!

■ Takes 30 minutes ■ Makes 10 large cookies

350g/12oz plain flour
1 tsp bicarbonate of soda
1 tsp baking powder
250g/9oz butter, softened
300g/10oz caster sugar
1 egg, beaten
1 tsp vanilla extract
2 × 40g tubes Smarties

1 Heat oven to 180C/160C fan/gas 4. Sift the flour, bicarbonate of soda, baking powder and a pinch of salt into a mixing bowl, then set aside. Cream together the butter and sugar until pale and fluffy, then beat in the egg and vanilla extract. Gradually beat in the sifted dry ingredients to form a stiff dough.
2 Roll the dough into 10 balls, then place on baking sheets, spaced well apart. Press several Smarties into each ball, flattening them slightly. Bake for 15 minutes until pale golden brown. Leave for 2 minutes to firm up a little, then transfer to wire racks to cool completely. Will keep in an airtight tin for up to 3 days.

■ Per cookie 253 kcalories, protein 3g, carbohydrate 35g, fat 12g, saturated fat 7g, fibre 1g, sugar 22g, salt 0.47g

Low-fat feasts

TOP: Hearty Tuscan bean soup

BOTTOM LEFT: Cauliflower, pumpkin and bean soup

BOTTOM RIGHT: Crab and noodle soup

Hearty Tuscan bean soup

The ham and crispy bacon turn this deliciously thick soup into something a bit special. It's healthy too, as it is high in fibre and contains two of your 5-a-day.

■ **Takes 30 minutes** ■ **Serves 4**

2 tbsp olive oil, plus extra to drizzle
1 celery stick, chopped
1 onion, chopped
1 large carrot, chopped
700ml/1¼ pint stock
400g can cannellini beans in water, drained
400g can borlotti beans in water, drained
1 rosemary sprig
1 thyme sprig
1 bay leaf
140g/5oz cooked ham, shredded
8 slices prosciutto or rashers streaky bacon, fried or grilled, to garnish

1 Heat the oil in a large pan, then add the chopped vegetables and some salt and pepper. Cook very gently for 10 minutes until softened but not coloured.
2 Add the stock, beans, rosemary and thyme sprigs and the bay leaf. Bring to the boil, then simmer for 10 minutes.
3 Lift out the herbs then, using a stick blender, whizz to a roughly chunky but creamy soup. Stir in the ham and bring to a simmer. Serve garnished with a few crisp prosciutto slices or bacon rashers and a swirl of olive oil.

■ Per serving 248 kcalories, protein 17g, carbohydrate 28g, fat 8g, saturated fat 1g, fibre 8g, sugar 8g, salt 1.33g

Cauliflower, pumpkin and bean soup

This healthy, fill-you-up soup contains five of your 5-a-day in one bowl. You can use whatever vegetables are in season – just choose your favourites. Delicious served with granary bread.

■ **Takes 55 minutes** ■ **Serves 4**

1 tbsp olive oil
2 onions, chopped
2 garlic cloves, chopped
500g/1lb 2oz pumpkin or squash, peeled, seeded and chopped
1 potato, chopped
several thyme sprigs, leaves stripped
1 litre/1¾ pints vegetable stock
500g/1lb 2oz cauliflower, cut into small florets
400g can haricot beans, drained and rinsed
a handful of chopped parsley
crusty bread, to serve

1 Heat the oil in a large pan, add the onions, then fry for about 10 minutes until soft and lightly coloured. Stir in the garlic, pumpkin or squash, potato and thyme, then cook for 1 minute.
2 Pour in the stock, then bring to the boil. Reduce the heat, cover, simmer for around 20 minutes, then add the cauliflower and beans, and cook for a further 10 minutes until all the vegetables are tender.
3 Remove about two ladlefuls of soup and pour into a food processor, then add the parsley and process until smooth – taking good care not to splash yourself with the hot liquid. Return to the pan, then reheat and serve with some crusty bread.

■ Per serving 215 kcalories, protein 13g, carbohydrate 31g, fat 5g, saturated fat none, fibre 10g, sugar 12g, salt 1.01g

Crab and noodle soup

If you don't want to buy ready-prepared veg, make your own mix from some of these sliced vegetables: broccoli, sugar snap peas, mushrooms, spring onions, carrots, beansprouts or peppers.

■ **Takes 8 minutes** ■ **Serves 2**

50g/2oz thin rice noodles
100g/4oz Chinese-style stir-fry mixed vegetables
2 tsp fish sauce
2 tsp sweet chilli sauce
600ml/1 pint vegetable stock
170g can white crabmeat in brine
a handful of coriander leaves, roughly chopped, to garnish

1 Put the noodles and vegetables into a bowl, then pour over boiling water. Leave to soak for 4 minutes until the noodles are tender and the vegetables are just softened.
2 Heat together the fish sauce, chilli sauce and stock in a pan. Drain the noodles and veg from their soaking water and divide between two serving bowls. Add the crabmeat and pour over the hot stock. Scatter with coriander to serve.

■ Per serving 184 kcalories, protein 17g, carbohydrate 28g, fat 1g, saturated fat none, fibre 3g, sugar 5g, salt 2.66g

Superfood pasta salad

The aromatic Asian-style sesame, lime and ginger dressing in this recipe goes brilliantly with pasta, which is, after all, the European equivalent of the noodle.

■ **Takes 20 minutes** ■ **Serves 4**

300g/10oz wholewheat penne
250g/9oz frozen soya beans
250g pack green beans, trimmed and halved
1 tsp sesame oil
1 tbsp soy sauce
thumb-sized piece of ginger, grated
juice of 1 lime
50g/2oz alfalfa sprouts or cress
2 carrots, grated
1 small bunch coriander, leaves roughly chopped

1 Cook the pasta according to the packet instructions, adding the soya beans and green beans 3 minutes before the end of cooking. Drain, tip into a colander, then cool quickly under cold running water.
2 Whisk together the oil, soy sauce, ginger and lime juice in a large bowl, then tip in the pasta, cooked beans, alfalfa sprouts or cress, carrots and coriander. Toss the salad well, then serve.

■ Per serving 379 kcalories, protein 20g, carbohydrate 63g, fat 7g, saturated fat 1g, fibre 12g, sugar 8g, salt 0.96g

Crunchy prawn noodle salad

The flavourful Vietnamese-style dressing for this crunchy salad is best made just before serving to preserve the vibrant colour of the mint.

■ **Takes 20 minutes** ■ **Serves 2**

100g/4oz rice noodles
100g/4oz sugar snap peas, shredded
2 carrots, coarsely grated
100g/4oz baby leaf spinach
85g/3oz cooked peeled prawns (defrosted if frozen)

FOR THE DRESSING
1 red chilli, seeded and finely chopped
3 tbsp rice vinegar
1 tsp caster sugar
1 tsp fish sauce
1 tbsp roughly chopped mint

1 Pour boiling water over the noodles to cover, leave for 4 minutes, then cool under cold running water. Drain well.
2 Mix the sugar snaps, carrots, spinach, noodles and prawns in a shallow bowl. Mix together the dressing ingredients until the sugar has dissolved, pour over the salad, then toss everything together. Serve it up straight away.

■ Per serving 278 kcalories, protein 15g, carbohydrate 55g, fat 1g, saturated fat none, fibre 4g, sugar 13g, salt 1.43g

Roasted peppers with tomatoes and anchovies

These full-of-flavour peppers make a great low-fat side dish with just about anything, or serve them on their own with chunks of bread.

■ **Takes 1 hour 20 minutes** ■ **Serves 4**

4 red peppers, halved and seeded
50g can anchovies in oil, drained and oil reserved
8 smallish tomatoes, halved
2 garlic cloves, thinly sliced
2 rosemary sprigs
2 tbsp olive oil
bread or focaccia, to serve

1 Heat the oven to 160C/140C fan/gas 3. Put the peppers into a large baking dish, toss with a little of the oil from the anchovy can, then turn cut-side up. Roast for 40 minutes, until soft but not collapsed.
2 Slice 8 of the anchovies along their length. Put 2 halves of tomato, several garlic slices, a few little rosemary sprigs and 2 pieces of anchovy into the hollow of each pepper. Drizzle over the olive oil, then roast again for 30 minutes until the tomatoes are soft and the peppers are filled with pools of tasty juice. Leave to cool and serve warm or at room temperature, with some bread or focaccia on the side, if you like.

■ Per serving 162 kcalories, protein 4g, carbohydrate 13g, fat 11g, saturated fat 1g, fibre 3g, sugar 12g, salt 1.44g

TOP: Superfood pasta salad

BOTTOM LEFT: Crunchy prawn noodle salad

BOTTOM RIGHT: Roasted peppers with tomatoes and anchovies

TOP: Lemony potato, broccoli and goat's cheese salad

BOTTOM LEFT: Quinoa, lentil and feta salad

BOTTOM RIGHT: Asian prawn and pineapple salad

Lemony potato, broccoli and goat's cheese salad

This fresh-tasting salad is perfect for making ahead, but take it out of the fridge a good hour before serving to allow the flavours to develop.

■ **Takes 35 minutes, plus cooling** ■ **Serves 4**

500g bag new potatoes
1 tbsp extra-virgin olive oil
zest and juice of 1 lemon
1 broccoli head, cut into florets
200g/8oz green beans, trimmed
20g pack dill, leaves roughly chopped
100g/4oz goat's cheese
2 tbsp toasted pine nuts

1 Boil the potatoes for 12–15 minutes until tender. Mix together the oil, lemon zest and juice in a serving bowl. Lift out the potatoes with a slotted spoon, leaving the pan of water on the hob. Drain the potatoes well, then place them in the serving bowl. Leave on one side to cool.
2 Add the broccoli and beans to the pan of boiling water. Cook for 4 minutes until tender but still with some bite. Drain, then cool under cold running water.
3 Stir the drained broccoli and beans into the cooled potatoes with the dill and some seasoning. Break the goat's cheese into chunks and scatter over the vegetables with the pine nuts and serve.

■ Per serving 237 kcalories, protein 10g, carbohydrate 24g, fat 12g, saturated fat 3g, fibre 4g, sugar 4g, salt 0.35g

Quinoa, lentil and feta salad

Quinoa is a wonderful ingredient and makes a great substitute for rice or couscous. It's a seed, not a grain, so it is an excellent source of protein and has a satisfying texture.

■ **Takes 30 minutes** ■ **Serves 4**

200g/8oz quinoa
1 tsp olive oil
1 shallot or ½ onion, finely chopped
2 tbsp tarragon leaves, roughly chopped
400g can Puy or green lentils, drained and rinsed
¼ cucumber, peeled and diced
100g/4oz feta, crumbled
6 spring onions, thinly sliced
zest and juice of 1 orange
1 tbsp red or white wine vinegar

1 Cook the quinoa in a large pan of boiling water for 10–15 minutes until tender, drain well, then set aside to cool.
2 Meanwhile, heat the oil in a small pan, then cook the shallot or onion for a few minutes until softened. Add the tarragon, stir well, then remove from the heat.
3 Stir the softened shallot and tarragon into the cooled quinoa along with the lentils, cucumber, feta, spring onions, orange zest and juice and vinegar. Toss well together and chill until ready to serve.

■ Per serving 286 kcalories, protein 16g, carbohydrate 39g, fat 9g, saturated fat 3g, fibre 2g, sugar 6g, salt 1.48g

Asian prawn and pineapple salad

Just toss this together and serve on its own or with steamed rice or boiled noodles, if you like. As well as prawns you could flake leftover roast chicken through the salad.

■ **Takes 20 minutes** ■ **Serves 4**

1 small pineapple or 350g/12oz pineapple chunks
140g/5oz beansprouts
250g/9oz cooked peeled king prawns
½ cucumber, peeled, seeded and sliced on the angle
200g/8oz cherry tomatoes, halved
a handful of mint leaves, roughly chopped
50g/2oz unsalted cashew nuts, toasted

FOR THE DRESSING
½ red chilli, seeded and sliced
1 garlic clove
1 tsp golden caster sugar
juice of 2 limes
1½ tsp fish sauce

1 Mash the chilli, garlic and sugar for the dressing to a paste using a pestle and mortar or small food processor. Stir in the lime juice and fish sauce, then set the dressing aside.
2 Peel, quarter, core and slice the pineapple at an angle. Toss with beansprouts, prawns, cucumber and tomatoes and some of the dressing. Pile into bowls and scatter with mint and cashews. Drizzle with the rest of the dressing and serve.

■ Per serving 202 kcalories, protein 19g, carbohydrate 17g, fat 7g, saturated fat 1g, fibre 3g, sugar 14g, salt 1.5g

Potato and chorizo pizza breads

An easy-to-cook, healthy pizza-style dish topped with a peppery tomato salad makes a speedy and satisfying lunch that's on the table in 20 minutes.

■ Takes 20 minutes ■ Serves 4

3 medium–large potatoes, very thinly sliced
4 wholemeal tortillas
6 tbsp half-fat crème fraîche
½ onion, thinly sliced
8 thin slices chorizo from a pack, diced
25g/1oz mature Cheddar, grated
3 tomatoes, roughly chopped
2 tsp balsamic dressing
½ × 50g bag rocket leaves

1 Heat the oven to 200C/180C fan/gas 6. Bring a pan of water to the boil, then blanch the potato slices in it for 2 minutes until almost cooked. Drain well, then tip on to kitchen paper to dry.
2 Put the tortillas on to baking sheets. Season the crème fraîche, then spread over the tortillas. Top with the potato slices, onion and chorizo, then scatter over the grated cheese. Bake for 8 minutes until golden.
3 Meanwhile, mix the tomatoes with the dressing and ½ teaspoon coarsely ground black pepper, then toss through the rocket.
4 Pile a quarter of the salad in the middle of each cooked tortilla and serve.

■ Per serving 287 kcalories, protein 11g, carbohydrate 37g, fat 12g, saturated fat 5g, fibre 5g, sugar 5g, salt 1.01g

Smoked trout and potato wedges

As well as supplying omega-3 fats, trout is an excellent source of vitamin D, which is vital for strong bones.

■ Takes 40 minutes ■ Serves 4

500g/1lb 2oz Maris Piper potatoes, peeled and cubed
100g bag baby leaf spinach
zest and juice of 1 lemon
140g/5oz smoked trout fillet, flaked
1 tbsp capers
1 tbsp chopped dill
140g/5oz breadcrumbs, from stale bread
1 tbsp sunflower oil
lemon wedges, tartare sauce and green salad, to serve

1 Boil the potatoes in salted water for 15 minutes. Meanwhile, tip the spinach into a large colander in the sink. Drain the potatoes over the spinach so the cooking water wilts it, then spoon the potatoes back into the pan. Mash, stirring in the lemon zest and juice and some seasoning, then fold through the trout flakes, squeezed-out spinach, capers and dill.
2 Tip half the breadcrumbs on to a large plate, then tip the potato mixture on to another plate and shape into a large disc. Flip the potato cake on to the crumbs, pressing the remaining crumbs on to the top.
3 Heat the grill and pour the oil into a large frying pan. Carefully slide the potato cake into the pan, then cook for 5 minutes. Now grill for 4–5 minutes until golden and the cake is hot through. Serve with lemon wedges, tartare sauce and a green salad.

■ Per serving 294 kcalories, protein 15g, carbohydrate 49g, fat 6g, saturated fat 1g, fibre 3g, sugar 2g, salt 1.74g

Two bean, potato and tuna salad

This recipe makes a great lunchbox salad to take to work. Soya beans are packed with nutrients; you'll find them in the vegetable section of the supermarket freezer cabinet.

■ Takes 25 minutes ■ Serves 4

300g/10oz new potatoes, cut into chunks
175g/6oz green beans, trimmed and halved
175g/6oz frozen soya beans
160g can tuna in water, drained well
a good handful of rocket or watercress leaves, to garnish

FOR THE DRESSING
2 tsp harissa paste
1 tbsp red wine vinegar
2 tbsp olive oil

1 Put the potatoes in a pan of boiling water and cook for 6–8 minutes until almost tender. Add both types of beans, then boil for a further 5 minutes until everything is cooked.
2 Meanwhile, make the dressing. Whisk together the harissa and vinegar in a small bowl with a little seasoning. Whisk in the oil until the dressing is thickened. Drain the potatoes and beans well, toss with half of the dressing and leave to cool.
3 Flake the tuna, then fold into the potatoes and beans. Add the remaining dressing, then gently toss. Divide among four bowls and serve each portion with a handful of rocket or watercress leaves on top. Serve warm or cold.

■ Per serving 211 kcalories, protein 15g, carbohydrate 19g, fat 9g, saturated fat 1g, fibre 4g, sugar 2g, salt 0.14g

TOP: Potato and chorizo pizza breads

BOTTOM LEFT: Smoked trout and potato wedges

BOTTOM RIGHT: Two bean, potato and tuna salad

TOP: Grilled pork with apple and sage

BOTTOM LEFT: Smoky chicken with warm corn and potato salad

BOTTOM RIGHT: Thai beef stir-fry

Grilled pork with apple and sage

Fresh sage and apple is a classic flavour combination for pork, and choosing a quick-cook lean cut means this impressive-looking dish is ready in just 20 minutes. Serve with your favourite green veg.

■ Takes 20 minutes ■ Serves 4

1 lemon
4 pieces pork tenderloin, about 140g/5oz each
2 tbsp roughly chopped sage leaves
3 eating apples, peeled, cored and chopped
1 rounded tbsp light muscovado sugar
green veg, to serve

1 Heat the grill to high. Grate the zest from half the lemon and squeeze the juice from both halves. Split the pork fillets down the centre, cutting almost all the way through, and open each one out like a book. Lift on to a baking sheet and season with salt, pepper and the lemon zest. Sprinkle with 1 tablespoon of the sage. Grill for 8–10 minutes, turning once, until cooked through.
2 Meanwhile, pour the lemon juice into a small pan. Add the apples to the pan with the remaining sage, the sugar and salt and pepper to taste. Bring to the boil, stirring, then simmer until soft, about 6 minutes. Serve the pork and apples with a green veg of your choice.

■ Per serving 269 kcalories, protein 31g, carbohydrate 16g, fat 9g, saturated fat 3g, fibre 1g, sugar 16g, salt 0.2g

Smoky chicken with warm corn and potato salad

You can make this tasty low-fat salad all year round – just use a 198g can of drained sweetcorn instead of the fresh corn cobs.

■ Takes 20 minutes ■ Serves 4

500g bag new potatoes
2 large corn cobs
½ red onion, thinly sliced
juice of 1 lime
2 tbsp olive oil
2 garlic cloves, crushed
½–1 tsp sweet smoked paprika
4 boneless, skinless chicken breasts, each halved horizontally through the middle to make 2 thin escalopes
1 small bunch coriander, leaves roughly chopped
lime wedges, to serve

1 Bring to the boil a pan of water big enough to hold all the potatoes and corn. Cook the potatoes for 12 minutes, add the corn after 6 minutes, and boil until both are tender. Drain well.
2 Meanwhile, mix the onion with the lime juice and half the oil in a large salad bowl. Mix the remaining oil with the garlic, paprika and some seasoning in a shallow bowl, then toss in the chicken until thoroughly coated.
3 Heat a griddle pan and cook the chicken for 3 minutes on each side until cooked through. Tip the potatoes into the bowl with the onions. Stand a corn cob on one end on a chopping board, then slice down the length, cutting off the kernels in strips. Mix into the potato salad with the coriander and seasoning to taste, then serve with the griddled chicken and lime wedges.

■ Per serving 343 kcalories, protein 38g, carbohydrate 31g, fat 8g, saturated fat 1g, fibre 2g, sugar 4g, salt 0.25g

Thai beef stir-fry

Just five simple ingredients, easy to cook and on the table in 10 minutes – what more could you want for a delicious home-from-work supper?

■ Takes 10 minutes ■ Serves 4

2 tbsp vegetable oil
400g/14oz beef strips or steak cut into thin strips
1 red chilli, seeded and finely sliced
2 tbsp oyster sauce
a handful of basil leaves, to garnish
plain rice, to serve

1 Heat a wok or a large frying pan until smoking hot. Pour in the oil and swirl around the pan, then tip in the beef strips and chilli. Cook, stirring all the time, until the meat is lightly browned, about 3 minutes, then pour over the oyster sauce.
2 Cook until heated through and the sauce coats the meat. Garnish with the basil leaves and serve with plain rice.

■ Per serving 178 kcalories, protein 22g, carbohydrate 1g, fat 10g, saturated fat 2g, fibre none, sugar 1g, salt 0.55g

Lamb kebabs with fennel and cucumber slaw

The crunchy cucumber and fennel salad mixed with Greek yogurt makes a perfect accompaniment to the juicy grilled kebabs.

■ **Takes 20 minutes** ■ **Serves 4**

400g can green lentils, drained and rinsed
250g pack lean minced lamb
1 tsp ground coriander
1 cucumber, chopped
1 fennel bulb, shredded
200g pot reduced-fat Greek yogurt
1 small garlic clove, crushed (optional)
1 mild red chilli, seeded and chopped

1 Heat the grill to high. Put the lentils into the bowl of a food processor, then whizz to a rough paste. Tip into a bowl, add the mince, coriander and plenty of seasoning, then mix well. Roll into 16 balls, divide them among 4 skewers and thread them on, then grill for 10 minutes, turning halfway through, until golden and juicy in the middle.
2 Meanwhile, mix the cucumber and fennel with the yogurt, garlic (if using), chilli and salt and pepper to taste. Serve with the kebabs.

■ Per serving 202 kcalories, protein 21g, carbohydrate 12g, fat 8g, saturated fat 4g, fibre 3g, sugar 4g, salt 1.02g

Sticky chicken with mango couscous

Full of delicious sweetness, this healthy dish is a good source of vitamin C and iron. You can use vegetable stock instead of water for the couscous.

■ **Takes 20 minutes** ■ **Serves 4**

1 large mango
4 spring onions, sliced
1 heaped tsp ground cumin
3 tbsp white wine vinegar
250g/9oz couscous
3 tbsp thick-cut marmalade
4 tsp grainy mustard
4 chicken breasts, each sliced into 3–4 strips

1 Heat the grill to high. Peel and dice the mango, toss with most of the spring onions, and the cumin and vinegar, then set aside. Put the couscous in a large heatproof bowl, pour over 400ml/14fl oz boiling water, then cover with cling film and set aside.
2 Mix together the marmalade and mustard. Lay the chicken strips in a roasting tin, then brush over half of the marmalade glaze. Grill for 4–5 minutes, then turn the chicken over and brush with the remaining glaze. Grill for a further 4–5 minutes until the chicken is cooked through, and the glaze is bubbling.
3 The couscous should now be ready. Stir in the mango mixture and serve with the hot chicken strips and the remaining spring onions sprinkled over.

■ Per serving 369 kcalories, protein 35g, carbohydrate 53g, fat 3g, saturated fat 1g, fibre 3g, sugar 21g, salt 0.43g

Zesty lentil and haddock pilaf

This fish pilaf is packed with goodness and makes a tasty and quick midweek supper.

■ **Takes 20 minutes** ■ **Serves 4**

250g/9oz easy-cook basmati rice
3 red onions, finely sliced
2 tbsp olive oil
140g/5oz smoked haddock fillet
140g/5oz haddock fillet
250g pack ready-cooked Puy lentils
zest of 1 lemon (then cut the lemon into wedges, to serve)
1 large bunch flatleaf parsley, leaves roughly chopped
25g/1oz toasted flaked almonds, to garnish

1 Cook the rice in boiling water until just tender, then drain.
2 Meanwhile, fry the onions in the oil in a large non-stick frying pan over a medium heat for 10–12 minutes until golden.
3 Bring some water to the boil in a shallow pan. Add the haddock fillets, poach for 4 minutes until the fish is just cooked, then drain and break into large flakes.
4 Spoon half the onions on to a plate, then set aside. Stir the drained rice and lentils into the onion pan, then fold through the fish, lemon zest and parsley to heat through. Serve topped with the reserved onions and the almonds, with the lemon wedges on the side for squeezing over.

■ Per serving 468 kcalories, protein 27g, carbohydrate 70g, fat 11g, saturated fat 1g, fibre 7g, sugar 6g, salt 1.39g

TOP: Lamb kebabs with fennel and cucumber slaw

BOTTOM LEFT: Sticky chicken with mango couscous

BOTTOM RIGHT: Zesty lentil and haddock pilaf

TOP: Tuna sweetcorn
burgers

BOTTOM LEFT: Mustardy pork
and apples

BOTTOM RIGHT: Beef strips
with crunchy Thai salad

Tuna sweetcorn burgers

Adding corn to these healthy fish burgers makes them a hit with children and adults alike. Top with a good dollop of spicy tomato salsa for a scrummy supper.

■ **Takes 15 minutes** ■ **Serves 4**

85g/3oz white bread, torn into pieces
198g can sweetcorn, drained and rinsed
2 × 185g cans tuna in water, drained well
25g/1oz grated Cheddar
3 spring onions, finely chopped
1 egg, beaten
2 tbsp vegetable oil
wholemeal buns, lettuce and salsa, to serve

1 Whizz the bread to crumbs in a food processor, tip into a bowl, then whizz half the sweetcorn until finely chopped. Add the chopped corn, remaining whole corn, tuna, cheese, spring onions and some seasoning to the bowl and mix well. Add the egg, bit by bit (you may not need it all), until the mixture is sticky enough to be shaped into four even-sized burgers.
2 Heat the oil in a non-stick pan, then cook the burgers for 5 minutes on each side until golden and hot through the middle.
3 Stuff into wholemeal buns with your favourite lettuce and some salsa to serve.

■ Per serving 262 kcalories, protein 22g, carbohydrate 21g, fat 11g, saturated fat 3g, fibre 1g, sugar 5g, salt 0.87g

Mustardy pork and apples

The subtle hint of mustard complements the pork in this dish. A good supper idea for family or friends and great served with mash and vegetables.

■ **Takes 25 minutes** ■ **Serves 4**

4 pork steaks, about 140g/5oz each, trimmed of excess fat
1 tbsp oil
2 eating apples, cored and cut into 8 (red-skinned look good)
1 onion, halved and sliced
a small handful of sage leaves, torn, or 2 tsp dried
100ml/3½fl oz chicken stock (from a cube is fine)
2 tsp wholegrain or Dijon mustard
mash and green veg, to serve

1 Rub the pork steaks with a little oil and season with pepper and salt to taste. Heat a large frying pan and fry the steaks for 2 minutes on both sides until golden. Transfer to a plate.
2 Adding a little more oil to the pan, fry the apples, onion and sage for 5 minutes or until the apples have softened. Pour in the stock and spoon in the mustard, then return the pork to the pan and simmer for 10 minutes until the sauce has reduced by about a third and the pork is cooked through. Serve with mash and some green veg.

■ Per serving 248 kcalories, protein 35g, carbohydrate 9g, fat 8g, saturated fat 2g, fibre 2g, sugar 8g, salt 0.42g

Beef strips with crunchy Thai salad

Rump steak is a good choice for this dish as it's not too expensive and has plenty of flavour. Trim off any excess fat after grilling. Some steamed rice flavoured with rice vinegar is a good accompaniment.

■ **Takes 10 minutes** ■ **Serves 4**

2 thick-cut lean steaks, about 600g/1lb 5oz total
4 tbsp fresh lime juice
1 tbsp Thai fish sauce
1 tbsp light muscovado sugar
1 red chilli, seeded and finely chopped
200g bag crunchy salad mix
50g/2oz carrot, grated
a handful of beansprouts

1 Heat the grill to high. Lightly season the steaks, then grill on each side for 2–3 minutes for medium–rare, or longer if you prefer your meat more well done.
2 Mix the lime juice, fish sauce, sugar and chilli together in a jug.
3 Tip the salad, carrot and beansprouts into a bowl, then add the dressing, tossing everything together. Divide among four plates.
4 Thinly slice the beef and add to the salad, to serve.

■ Per serving 242 kcalories, protein 33g, carbohydrate 6g, fat 10g, saturated fat 4g, fibre 1g, sugar 6g, salt 0.92g

Mustard chicken with celeriac and carrot mash

Root vegetables make a healthy alternative to potato. Celeriac is rich in vitamin C and carrots in beta-carotene, which we convert to vitamin A.

■ **Takes 20 minutes** ■ **Serves 4**

1 large celeriac, about 1kg/2lb 4oz, peeled
500g/1lb 2oz carrots
500g/1lb 2oz boneless, skinless chicken breasts
1 tbsp plain flour, seasoned with salt and pepper
1 tbsp sunflower oil
2 tbsp wholegrain mustard
300ml/½ pint vegetable or chicken stock
steamed green beans, to serve

1 Slice the celeriac and carrots in a food processor, then put in a pan and pour over boiling water to cover. Add a little salt, then cover and boil for 10–12 minutes until tender.
2 Meanwhile, cut the chicken into strips and toss in the seasoned flour. Heat the oil in a large frying pan, add the chicken and fry quickly on all sides until lightly browned. Stir in the mustard and stock, then bring to the boil. Simmer uncovered, stirring occasionally, for 5–6 minutes until the chicken is cooked and the sauce thickened.
3 Drain the veg and whizz to a rough mash. Divide among four plates with the chicken and sauce. Serve with steamed green beans.

■ Per serving 248 kcalories, protein 34g, carbohydrate 16g, fat 6g, saturated fat 1g, fibre 9g, sugar 12g, salt 1.01g

Smoky prawns with green couscous

For a change, try swapping the couscous for bulghar wheat. It's just as quick to prepare and has a lovely nutty flavour that goes really well with citrusy dressings.

■ **Takes 25 minutes** ■ **Serves 4**

200g/8oz large raw peeled prawns
zest and juice of 2 lemons, plus extra wedges to serve
2 garlic cloves, crushed
2 tsp paprika
2 tbsp olive oil
175g/6oz couscous
4 courgettes, sliced on the diagonal
large bunch coriander, leaves only, chopped

1 Tip the prawns into a small bowl. Add all the lemon zest, plus the juice from 1 lemon, the garlic, paprika and 1 tablespoon of oil. Mix, then set aside. Put the couscous into a large bowl, pour over 250ml/9fl oz boiling water, cover and set aside for 10 minutes.
2 Heat a non-stick frying pan, and then add 1 tablespoon of the prawn marinade, the courgettes and a splash of water. Stir-fry for 4–5 minutes until the courgettes are golden, then tip on to a plate and set aside. Add the prawns to the pan with their marinade, then fry for 1 minute until just pink.
3 Fluff up the couscous with a fork, then mix in the courgettes, coriander, remaining oil and lemon juice and some seasoning. Lastly, scrape in the prawns with all the pan juices and toss Briefly before serving with extra lemon wedges for squeezing.

■ Per serving 219 kcalories, protein 14g, carbohydrate 26g, fat 7g, saturated fat 1g, fibre 1g, sugar 3g, salt 0.26g

Lemon and cumin koftas

Make the koftas and then freeze half of them, uncooked, for supper or lunch on another day. Children love these meatballs served with wraps and a crunchy salad.

■ **Takes 30 minutes** ■ **Makes 16**

1kg/2lb 4oz lean minced lamb
zest and juice of 2 lemons
small bunch mint, leaves only, roughly chopped (save a little for the salad)
4 tsp ground cumin
1 garlic clove, crushed

FOR THE CABBAGE SALAD
½ small red cabbage
1 red onion
1 tsp sugar
wraps or flatbreads and ready-made raita or tzatziki, to serve

1 Heat the grill to medium. Put the mince in a large bowl and add the lemon zest, half of the juice, most of the mint, the cumin, garlic and seasoning to taste. Use your hands to mix well, then shape into 16 evenly sized balls, and set aside on a plate. (Freeze half at this stage.)
2 Grill the koftas for 12–15 minutes on a grill rack, turning once, until well browned.
3 Meanwhile, make the salad: shred the cabbage and finely slice the onion, then toss with the remaining lemon juice, sugar, reserved mint and seasoning to taste.
4 Serve two koftas per person, in wraps or flatbreads, with the salad and some raita or tzatziki.

■ Per serving 217 kcalories, protein 27g, carbohydrate 4g, fat 11g, saturated fat 5g, fibre 1g, sugar 3g, salt 0.24g

TOP: Mustard chicken with celeriac and carrot mash

BOTTOM LEFT: Smoky prawns with green couscous

BOTTOM RIGHT: Lemon and cumin koftas

TOP: Coriander cod with carrot pilaf

BOTTOM LEFT: Asian beef and watercress salad

BOTTOM RIGHT: Chicken with orange and avocado salsa

Coriander cod with carrot pilaf

Increase your veg count by adding a handful of any of the following to the pilaf: broad beans, peas, grated courgette, shredded leeks, sweetcorn or some chopped red pepper.

■ **Takes 25 minutes** ■ **Serves 4**

2 tbsp olive oil
4 skinless cod fillets, about 175g/6oz each
2 tbsp chopped coriander
zest and juice of 1 lemon
1 onion, chopped
2 tsp cumin seeds
2 large carrots, grated
200g/8oz basmati rice
600ml/1 pint vegetable stock

1 Heat the grill to high, then line the grill pan with a double thickness of foil and curl up the edges to catch the juices. Brush lightly with a little of the oil and put the cod on top. Sprinkle over the coriander, lemon zest and juice, and drizzle with a little more of the oil. Season with salt and pepper, then grill for 10–12 minutes until the fish flakes easily.
2 Meanwhile, heat the remaining oil in a pan. Add the onion and cumin seeds, and fry for a few minutes. Add the carrots and stir well, then stir in the rice until glistening. Add the stock and bring to the boil. Cover and cook gently for about 10 minutes until the rice is tender and the stock absorbed. Spoon the rice on to four warm plates, top with the cod and pour over the pan juices.

■ Per serving 305 kcalories, protein 14g, carbohydrate 50g, fat 7g, saturated fat 1g, fibre 3g, sugar 8g, salt 0.31g

Asian beef and watercress salad

The pepperiness of watercress works extremely well with Asian flavours, and this main-dish salad is a good example. If you like cucumber, add some chunks to give extra low-fat crunchiness.

■ **Takes 30 minutes** ■ **Serves 4**

500g/1lb 2oz lean stir-fry beef, cubed
3 tsp Thai fish sauce
juice of 2 limes
thumb-sized piece ginger, peeled and finely chopped
1 garlic clove, crushed
1 small red chilli, seeded and finely chopped
2 tbsp soft brown sugar
2 bunches watercress
1 mango, peeled and cut into medium chunks
1 small red onion, thinly sliced into half moons
1 tsp vegetable oil

1 Season the beef with some pepper and 1 teaspoon of the fish sauce and set aside.
2 In a small bowl, mix together the lime juice, ginger, garlic, chilli, brown sugar and remaining fish sauce. Taste for extra fish sauce or sugar – it should be sweet, salty and sour without any one being dominant.
3 Place a handful of watercress on each serving plate, then divide the mango chunks and red onion among them.
4 Just before serving, set a wok over a high heat and tip in the oil. Sear the meat, turning often until browned all over. Divide among the plates of salad and pour the dressing over. Serve while warm.

■ Per serving 255 kcalories, protein 30g, carbohydrate 20g, fat 6g, saturated fat 2g, fibre 3g, sugar 19g, salt 0.98g

Chicken with orange and avocado salsa

To make sure the avocado you buy is ripe for this fresh-tasting salad, look for one with dark green skin and gently squeeze to check it is soft.

■ **Takes 20 minutes** ■ **Serves 4**

2 tsp olive oil
4 boneless, skinless chicken breasts, cut in half on the diagonal
zest and juice of 1 lime
1 avocado
2 oranges
1 red chilli, seeded and diced (optional)
3 spring onions, finely sliced
1 tbsp chopped coriander or basil

1 Heat the oil in a non-stick frying pan, season the chicken and fry for 10 minutes, turning once. Add the lime juice for the final minute of cooking.
2 Meanwhile, halve the avocado and remove the stone. Peel away the skin and use a small knife to cut the flesh into small chunks. Tip into a bowl. Cut away the skin and pith of the oranges, cut out the segments, then add to the avocado with the remaining ingredients, not forgetting the lime zest. Toss gently, then serve alongside the chicken.

■ Per serving 240 kcalories, protein 35g, carbohydrate 8g, fat 8g, saturated fat 1g, fibre 3g, sugar 7g, salt 0.23g

Sticky lemon pork

The citrus zest and juice adds a refreshing zing to this casserole. Serve with a bowl of fluffy mash sprinkled with chopped parsley.

■ **Takes 1 hour 40 minutes** ■ **Serves 4**

3 tbsp plain flour
1 tbsp paprika
800g/1lb 12oz leg or shoulder of pork, diced into large chunks
2 tbsp olive oil
2 rosemary sprigs, leaves stripped
4 garlic cloves, chopped
3 bay leaves
300ml/½ pint white wine
peeled zest and juice of 1 lemon

1 Tip the flour, paprika, salt and pepper into a food bag and toss in the pork until coated. Heat the oil in a flameproof casserole and fry the pork until brown on all sides. Add the rosemary, garlic and bay leaves, then fry for 1 minute more. Pour in the wine and bring to the boil, scraping the bottom of the casserole to remove any bits. Lower to a simmer and throw in the lemon zest.
2 Cover the casserole, place on the lowest heat and simmer for 1 hour until the pork is tender. Add a splash of water if the sauce becomes too thick. Just before serving, stir in the lemon juice and check the seasoning.

■ Per serving 356 kcalories, protein 46g, carbohydrate 14g, fat 11g, saturated fat 3g, fibre 1g, sugar 4g, salt 0.34g

Spanish rice and prawn one-pot

With a flavour and look of the sunny Med, this wonderful one-pot can be on the table in just 20 minutes. It's a healthy choice too, because it counts as two of your 5-a-day.

■ **Takes 20 minutes** ■ **Serves 4**

1 onion, sliced
1 red and 1 green pepper, seeded and sliced
50g/2oz chorizo, sliced
2 garlic cloves, crushed
1 tbsp olive oil
250g/9oz easy-cook basmati rice
400g can chopped tomatoes
200g/8oz raw peeled prawns, (defrosted if frozen)

1 Boil the kettle. In a non-stick frying or shallow pan with a lid, fry the onion, peppers, chorizo and garlic in the oil over a high heat for 3 minutes. Stir in the rice and chopped tomatoes with 500ml/18fl oz boiling water, cover, then cook over a high heat for 12 minutes.
2 Uncover, then stir – the rice should be almost tender. Stir in the prawns, with a splash more water if the rice is looking dry, then cook for another minute until the prawns are just pink and the rice is tender. Serve at the table, straight from the pot.

■ Per serving 356 kcalories, protein 19g, carbohydrate 59g, fat 7g, saturated fat 2g, fibre 4g, sugar 7g, salt 0.85g

All-in-one chicken, squash and new potato casserole

Courgette slices or broccoli florets can be used instead of the French beans for a change in this healthy casserole for two.

■ **Takes 45 minutes** ■ **Serves 2**

¼ small butternut squash, about 200g/8oz, peeled, seeded and diced
8 small new potatoes
1 tsp ground coriander
1 tbsp thyme leaves
600ml/1pt chicken stock
1 garlic clove, crushed
2 boneless, skinless chicken breasts
175g/6oz French beans
25g/1oz pitted green olives in brine, drained

1 Heat the oven to 190C/170C fan/gas 5. Put the butternut squash, potatoes, ground coriander, thyme, stock and garlic into a flameproof casserole. Season and bring to the boil, then simmer gently for 10 minutes.
2 Tuck in the chicken breasts, making sure that they are submerged. Cover and transfer to the oven for 15 minutes until the chicken is cooked through. Lift out the chicken and vegetables, set aside and keep warm, then boil the stock on the hob until reduced by half. Add the beans and olives, simmer until cooked. Season and serve.

■ Per serving 413 kcalories, protein 41g, carbohydrate 50g, fat 6.5g, saturated fat 1.5g, fibre 8g, sugar 13g, salt 1g

TOP: Sticky lemon pork

BOTTOM LEFT: Spanish rice and prawn one-pot

BOTTOM RIGHT: All-in-one chicken, squash and new potato casserole

TOP: Sticky lemon chicken

BOTTOM LEFT: Beef stir-fry with broccoli and oyster sauce

BOTTOM RIGHT: Prawn, pea and tomato curry

Sticky lemon chicken

Coating the chicken in cornflour before frying helps not only to crisp it up, but also to thicken the sauce.

■ Takes 30 minutes ■ Serves 4

1 tbsp clear honey
juice of 1 lemon
250ml/9fl oz chicken stock
1 tbsp soy sauce
4 boneless, chicken breasts, cut into chunks
1 tbsp cornflour
1 tsp vegetable oil
2 carrots, finely sliced
1 red pepper, seeded and cut into chunks
140g/5oz sugar snap peas
noodles, to serve

1 In a jug, mix together the honey, lemon, stock and soy sauce, then set aside. Toss the chicken with the cornflour so it is completely coated. Heat the oil in a non-stick frying pan, then fry the chicken until it changes colour and starts to become crisp around the edges.
2 Add the carrots and red pepper, then fry for 1 minute more. Pour the stock mixture into the pan, bring to a simmer, then add the sugar snap peas and bubble everything together for 5 minutes until the chicken is cooked and the vegetables are tender. Serve with noodles.

■ Per serving 236 kcalories, protein 38g, carbohydrate 15g, fat 3g, saturated fat 1g, fibre 2g, sugar 10g, salt 1.25g

Beef stir-fry with broccoli and oyster sauce

Beef stir-fry strips are handy, but you can also slice your own steaks instead. Put them in the freezer for 10 minutes then cut into slices.

■ Takes 15 minutes ■ Serves 2

1–2 tbsp sunflower oil
200g/8oz beef stir-fry strips
200g pack Tenderstem broccoli
1 onion, sliced
2 garlic cloves, sliced
2 tbsp oyster sauce

1 Heat a wok until smoking, pour in the oil then add the beef. Stir-fry for 2 minutes, then tip the beef on to a plate. Add the broccoli with a splash of water then cook until it turns bright green.
2 Add the onion and stir-fry for 1 minute, then add the garlic and cook for 1 minute more. Pour in the oyster sauce and 125ml/4fl oz water. Bring to the boil and cook until reduced to a sticky sauce. Stir in the beef, along with any juices from the plate, then serve straight away.

■ Per serving 256 kcalories, protein 30g, carbohydrate 10g, fat 12g, saturated fat 2g, fibre 4g, sugar 8g, salt 1.78g

Prawn, pea and tomato curry

A clean, fresh-tasting dish that's packed with flavour and includes three of your 5-a-day.

■ Takes 20 minutes ■ Serves 4

1 tbsp vegetable oil
2 onions, halved, each cut into 6 wedges
6 ripe tomatoes, each cut into 8 wedges
thumb-sized piece of ginger, peeled and chopped
6 garlic cloves, roughly chopped
3 tbsp curry paste (we used tikka masala paste)
400g/14oz peeled raw king prawns
250g/9oz frozen peas
1 small bunch coriander, leaves chopped, to garnish
basmati rice or chapatis, to serve

1 Heat the oil in a frying pan, then fry the onions over a medium heat until soft and beginning to brown, for about 5 minutes. Meanwhile, reserve 8 of the tomato wedges, then whizz the remainder in a food processor with the ginger and garlic.
2 Add the curry paste to the pan for around 30 seconds. Stir through the tomato mix and remaining tomato wedges, then bubble over a high heat for 5 minutes, stirring so the sauce doesn't catch. Mix in the prawns and peas; simmer until the prawns are pink and cooked through. Scatter with coriander, then serve with rice or chapatis.

■ Per serving 236 kcalories, protein 24g, carbohydrate 18g, fat 8g, saturated fat 1g, fibre 6g, sugar 10g, salt 1.24g

Oven-baked red pepper risotto

This easy risotto is baked in the oven rather than stirred on the hob while you add the stock bit by bit – the result tastes just as good.

■ **Takes 35 minutes** ■ **Serves 4**

1 tbsp oil
1 onion, chopped
300g/10oz risotto rice
100ml/3½fl oz white wine (optional) or use
  more stock
400g can chopped tomatoes
200g/8oz frozen roasted peppers
500ml/18fl oz vegetable stock
a handful of flatleaf parsley, chopped
Parmesan, to garnish (optional)

1 Heat the oven to 200C/180C fan/gas 6. Heat the oil in an ovenproof pan, then fry the onion for a few minutes until softened. Turn up the heat, tip in the rice, stir, then fry for 1 minute more.
2 Pour in the wine, if using, or more stock, stirring until absorbed, then tip in the tomatoes, peppers and 400ml/14fl oz of the stock. Cover and bake in the oven for 25 minutes until the rice is tender and creamy.
3 Stir in the remaining stock and the parsley, season and scatter with Parmesan shavings, if you like.

■ Per serving 334 kcalories, protein 9g, carbohydrate 70g, fat 4g, saturated fat 1g, fibre 5g, sugar 9g, salt 1.36g

Chicken with wine and mushrooms

If you take the skin off chicken before cooking it dramatically reduces the saturated-fat content. Removing the skin also shaves 10 minutes off the cooking time.

■ **Takes 20 minutes** ■ **Serves 4**

4 boneless, skinless chicken breasts
1 tbsp plain flour, seasoned
150ml/¼ pint chicken stock (use ½ a cube)
1 tbsp mild olive or vegetable oil
250g pack chestnut mushrooms, halved
a few thyme sprigs
150ml/¼ pint red wine
mash, to serve

1 Toss the chicken in the flour, then tap off the excess. Mix 1 teaspoon of the excess flour with a little stock and set aside. Heat the oil in a frying pan, then add the chicken, mushrooms and thyme. Cook over a medium–high heat for about 5 minutes, turning the chicken breasts once until golden all over.
2 Lift the chicken out, then set aside. Pour in the wine and the remaining stock, and boil for 5 minutes or until reduced by half. Add the flour-and-stock mix, stirring until the sauce thickens a little. Put the chicken back into the pan, along with any juices from the plate, then simmer for 5 minutes or until cooked through and the sauce is glossy. Serve the chicken with mash.

■ Per serving 216 kcalories, protein 35g, carbohydrate 5g, fat 5g, saturated fat 1g, fibre 1g, sugar 2g, salt 0.99g

Creamy crab and pea pasta

Fresh crab is one of summer's real treats and its delicate flavour means it needs only minimal cooking. This pasta dish is ready on the table in just 15 minutes.

■ **Takes 15 minutes** ■ **Serves 4**

400g/14oz spaghetti
200g/8oz fresh or frozen peas
300g/10oz fresh crabmeat
5 tbsp half-fat crème fraîche
juice of ½ lemon
1 red chilli, seeded and chopped, plus extra
  to garnish
a handful of parsley leaves, chopped
zest of 1 lemon, to garnish

1 Boil a large pan of salted water. Tip in the pasta, then cook for about 7 minutes. Add the peas, then cook for 2–3 minutes more or until both are cooked through.
2 Drain in a colander, reserving a little cooking water, then tip back into the pan with the crabmeat and crème fraîche. Stir it all together well with the lemon juice, most of the chilli and parsley and a little of the pasta cooking water if the mixture seems dry. Serve sprinkled with the remaining chilli and parsley and the lemon zest.

■ Per serving 512 kcalories, protein 31g, carbohydrate 81g, fat 10g, saturated fat 3g, fibre 5g, sugar 5g, salt 0.83g

TOP: Oven-baked red pepper risotto

BOTTOM LEFT: Chicken with wine and mushrooms

BOTTOM RIGHT: Creamy crab and pea pasta

TOP: Goulash in a dash

BOTTOM LEFT: White fish with spicy beans and chorizo

BOTTOM RIGHT: Baked porcini and thyme risotto

Goulash in a dash

Ultra-thin minute steak is great for weeknight suppers because it's quick to cook. It is also very lean, so lower in fat than other cuts of beef.

■ **Takes 30 minutes** ■ **Serves 4**

1 tbsp vegetable oil
300g/10oz stir-fry beef strips or minute steak, cut into strips
100g/4oz chestnut mushrooms, quartered
2 tsp paprika
500g/1lb 2oz potatoes, peeled and cut into smallish chunks
600ml/1 pint hot beef stock (a cube is fine)
500g jar tomato-based cooking sauce
a handful of parsley leaves, roughly chopped
natural low-fat yogurt, to garnish
crusty bread or rice, to serve

1 Heat half the oil in a large non-stick pan and fry the beef for 2 minutes, stirring once halfway through. Tip the meat on to a plate. Heat the remaining oil in the pan (there is no need to clean it) and fry the mushrooms for 2–3 minutes until they start to colour.
2 Sprinkle the paprika over the mushrooms, fry Briefly, then tip in potatoes, stock and tomato sauce. Give it all a good stir, then cover and simmer for 20 minutes until the potatoes are tender. Return the beef to the pan along with any juices, and warm through. Stir in the parsley and a swirl of yogurt, then serve straight from the pan. Crusty bread or rice make a good accompaniment.

■ Per serving 299 kcalories, protein 23g, carbohydrate 33g, fat 9g, saturated fat 2g, fibre 3g, sugar 5g, salt 1.59g

White fish with spicy beans and chorizo

When using bottled passata or canned tomatoes, try adding a pinch of sugar – it will help to bring out the natural sweetness of the tomatoes.

■ **Takes 20 minutes** ■ **Serves 4**

1 tbsp olive oil
1 onion, chopped
1 small rosemary sprig, leaves finely chopped
25g/1oz chorizo or other spicy sausage, chopped
2 fat garlic cloves, crushed
700g bottle passata
410g can cannellini beans in water, drained and rinsed
200g/8oz shredded green cabbage
a pinch of sugar
4 × skinless chunky haddock or cod fillets
crusty bread, to serve

1 Heat the oil in a large frying pan, then soften the onion for 5 minutes. Add the rosemary, chorizo and garlic, then fry for 2 minutes more until the chorizo is starting to crisp. Tip in the passata, beans, cabbage and sugar, season, then simmer for 5 minutes.
2 Add the fish to the pan, leaving the tops of the fillets peeking out of the sauce, then cover with a lid and leave to cook for 3–5 minutes or until the flesh flakes easily. Delicious served with crusty bread.

■ Per serving 304 kcalories, protein 36g, carbohydrate 27g, fat 6g, saturated fat 1g, fibre 6g, sugar 11g, salt 1.23g

Baked porcini and thyme risotto

The dried mushrooms give a real depth of flavour to this dish. Keep a pack in the storecupboard and this will be a supper you can always rustle up in half an hour.

■ **Takes 30 minutes** ■ **Serves 4**

25g pack dried porcini mushrooms
2 tbsp olive oil
1 small onion, finely chopped
2 garlic cloves, crushed
2 tsp thyme leaves, plus extra to garnish
350g/12oz risotto rice
700ml/1¼ pints hot vegetable stock
100ml/3½fl oz white wine
a handful of grated Parmesan, plus shavings, to garnish

1 Put the mushrooms in a bowl, pour over 400ml/14fl oz boiling water and leave to soak for 10 minutes. Meanwhile, heat the oil in an ovenproof pan and fry the onion for 2 minutes until starting to soften. Add the garlic and cook for another minute.
2 Heat the oven to 190C/170C fan/gas 5. Drain the mushrooms, reserving the liquid, and chop. Add the mushrooms, thyme and rice to the pan, then stir well. Strain over the mushroom liquid, pour in the stock and wine, and bring to the boil.
3 Season to taste, cover and bake for 25 minutes or until the rice is just cooked and all the liquid has been absorbed. Stir in the grated Parmesan, check the seasoning and sprinkle with extra thyme leaves and Parmesan shavings to serve.

■ Per serving 374 kcalories, protein 9g, carbohydrate 75g, fat 6g, saturated fat 1g, fibre 2g, sugar 5g, salt 0.64g

Lemon-spiced chicken with chickpeas

The combination of cinnamon, coriander and cumin with the lemon, chickpeas and chicken makes this a perfectly balanced meal. Serve with lots of crusty bread to mop up the sauce.

■ **Takes 20 minutes** ■ **Serves 4**

1 tbsp sunflower oil
1 onion, halved and thinly sliced
4 boneless, skinless chicken breasts, cut into chunks
1 cinnamon stick, broken in half
1 tsp each ground coriander and cumin
zest and juice of 1 lemon
400g can chickpeas, drained and rinsed
200ml/7fl oz chicken stock
250g bag spinach leaves

1 Heat the oil in a large frying pan, then fry the onion gently for 5 minutes. Turn up the heat and add the chicken, frying for about 3 minutes until golden.
2 Stir in the spices and lemon zest, fry for 1 more minute, then tip in the chickpeas and stock. Put the lid on and simmer for 5 minutes. Season to taste, then tip in the spinach and re-cover. Leave to wilt for 2 minutes, then stir through. Squeeze over the lemon juice just before serving.

■ Per serving 290 kcalories, protein 42g, carbohydrate 14g, fat 7g, saturated fat 1g, fibre 4g, sugar 3g, salt 1.03g

Red flannel hash

Use roasted or boiled beetroot for this dish; if buying it cooked, go for vac-packed, but make sure it's not pickled in vinegar. Serve with fried eggs for brunch.

■ **Takes 35 minutes** ■ **Serves 4**

800g/1lb 12oz boiled potatoes
3 tbsp sunflower oil
140g/5oz corned beef, shredded
3 cooked beetroots, peeled and diced
horseradish sauce, to serve

1 Break up the potatoes. Heat the oil in a heavy-based frying pan, then add the potatoes and corned beef, and cook, turning the potato chunks over with a fish slice every time they become crisp.
2 After about 10 minutes, when the potatoes are crisp all over, stir through the beetroots, then season. Turn down the heat, pat the potatoes into a cake, then leave to brown on the bottom. Invert on to a plate, then return to the pan until the other side is browned.
3 Serve straight from the pan, or turn out on to a board and cut into wedges. Serve with the horseradish sauce.

■ Per serving 303 kcalories, protein 13g, carbohydrate 37g, fat 12g, saturated fat 3g, fibre 3g, sugar 4g, salt 1.17g

Chunky chicken and ham chowder

You can also make this chowder with fish – cut 300g/10oz skinned smoked haddock or cod into chunks and add at the same time as the peas and sweetcorn, replacing the chicken and ham.

■ **Takes 30 minutes** ■ **Serves 4**

1 tbsp sunflower oil
2 leeks, thinly sliced
3 medium potatoes, peeled and cut into small cubes
1 tbsp plain flour
700ml/1¼ pints skimmed milk
2 ready-roasted chicken breasts, skin removed and cut into chunks
2 thick slices ham, chopped
175g/6oz each frozen sweetcorn and frozen peas

1 Heat the oil in a large pan and fry the leeks over a low heat for 3 minutes until softened. Stir in the potatoes and flour, then slowly blend in the milk, stirring with a wooden spoon. Bring to the boil and simmer, uncovered, for 10–12 minutes until the potatoes are soft.
2 Add the chicken, ham, sweetcorn and peas, then stir over a medium heat for 5 minutes or until hot and bubbling. Season to taste and serve with crusty bread.

■ Per serving 341 kcalories, protein 34g, carbohydrate 37g, fat 7g, saturated fat 2g, fibre 5g, sugar 12g, salt 0.66g

TOP: Lemon-spiced chicken with chickpeas

BOTTOM LEFT: Red flannel hash

BOTTOM RIGHT: Chunky chicken and ham chowder

TOP: Gremolata couscous-stuffed peppers

BOTTOM LEFT: Roast veggie moussaka with feta

BOTTOM RIGHT: Puy lentil salad with soy beans, sugar snaps and broccoli

Gremolata couscous-stuffed peppers

These make peppers a light and colourful lunch or supper. Packed with goodness, this dish counts as three of your 5-a-day.

■ Takes 55 minutes ■ Serves 2

85g/3oz couscous
2 tbsp raisins
50ml/2fl oz hot vegetable stock
1 tsp clear honey
zest and juice of 1 lemon
2 garlic cloves
1 small bunch flatleaf parsley
150g pot low-fat natural yogurt
2 tomatoes, roughly chopped
2 red peppers, halved and seeded
1 tbsp olive oil
simple green salad, to serve

1 Heat the oven to 190C/170C fan/gas 5. Put the couscous and raisins in a heatproof bowl. Stir together the stock, honey and lemon juice, then pour over the couscous. Cover and leave to absorb for 5 minutes.
2 Meanwhile, make the gremolata. Put the lemon zest, garlic and parsley in a mini food processor, then whizz until fine (or finely chop everything together). Stir 1 tablespoon of this mixture into the yogurt, then set aside. Stir the remaining mixture into the couscous with the tomatoes and some seasoning.
3 Spoon the couscous mixture into each pepper half, then sit them in a small roasting tin. Drizzle with oil, then bake for 40 minutes until the peppers are tender. Serve with the yogurt and a simple green salad on the side.

■ Per serving 302 kcalories, protein 9g, carbohydrate 52g, fat 8g, saturated fat 1g, fibre 4g, sugar 30g, salt 0.23g

Roast veggie moussaka with feta

Bubbling and golden brown straight from the oven, moussaka is always a firm favourite, and this one has all of your 5-a-day in just one portion.

■ Takes 55 minutes ■ Serves 4

2 yellow peppers, seeded and cut into chunks
2 red onions, cut into wedges
2 medium courgettes, thickly sliced
1 large aubergine, cut into chunks
1 tbsp olive oil
85g/3oz feta
1 egg
200g pot Greek yogurt
700g bottle passata
2 tbsp chopped fresh oregano or 2 tsp dried
crusty bread, to serve

1 Heat the oven to 200C/180C fan/gas 6. Scatter the vegetables in a large roasting tin. Toss with the oil, season, then roast for 25 minutes until softened.
2 Break up the feta in a small bowl with a fork, then mix well with the egg, yogurt and seasoning. When the vegetables are ready, tip them into an ovenproof dish, then stir in the passata and oregano. Spoon over the creamy feta topping, turn up the oven to 220C/200C fan/ gas 7, then bake for around 20–25 minutes until the filling is hot and the topping is beginning to brown and bubble. Serve the moussaka with crusty bread.

■ Per serving 223 kcalories, protein 11g, carbohydrate 24g, fat 10g, saturated fat 4g, fibre 5g, sugar 17g, salt 1.74g

Puy lentil salad with soy beans, sugar snaps and broccoli

An exciting new idea for a salad that can be served as a main meal. The delicious sesame dressing adds zing to the vibrant veg.

■ Takes 25 minutes ■ Serves 4

200g/8oz Puy lentils
1 litre/1¾ pints hot vegetable stock
200g/8oz Tenderstem broccoli
140g/5oz frozen soy beans, thawed
140g/5oz sugar snap peas
1 red chilli, seeded and sliced

FOR THE DRESSING
2 tbsp sesame oil
juice of 1 lemon
1 garlic clove, chopped
2½ tbsp reduced-salt soy sauce
3cm piece ginger, finely grated
1 tbsp clear honey

1 Boil the lentils in the stock for about 15 minutes until just cooked. Drain, then tip into a large bowl. Bring a pan of salted water to the boil, throw in the broccoli for 1 minute, add the beans and peas for 1 minute more. Drain, then cool under cold water. Pat dry, then add to the bowl with the lentils.
2 Mix together the dressing ingredients with some seasoning. Pour the dressing over the lentils and vegetables, then thoroughly stir through with the sliced chilli. Pile on to a serving platter or divide among four plates and serve.

■ Per serving 302 kcalories, protein 22g, carbohydrate 42g, fat 7g, saturated fat 1g, fibre 8g, sugar 9g, salt 1.41g

Butternut and rosemary pizza

Make your own pizza and you can tailor it to your choice – this one is low fat, low cost, meat free and truly delicious.

■ **Takes 45 minutes** ■ **Serves 4–6**

500g pack white bread mix
flour, for rolling
1 tbsp olive oil, plus extra to drizzle
  (optional)
1 large butternut squash, peeled, seeded
  and cut into small cubes
2 red onions, sliced
3 rosemary sprigs, leaves chopped,
  plus extra small sprigs to garnish
1 tbsp caster sugar
2 tbsp balsamic vinegar
100g/4oz feta
salad, to serve

1 Make the bread dough according to the packet instructions, knead for a few minutes, then, using flour to prevent sticking, roll into two large rounds and lift on to baking sheets.
2 Heat the oil in a large frying pan, then fry the squash with the onions and chopped rosemary for 5 minutes until beginning to soften and brown. Splash in about 200ml/7fl oz water, then cook over a fierce heat for 10 minutes, stirring until the squash is tender and almost all the liquid has gone. Heat the oven to 220C/200C fan/gas 7.
3 Stir the sugar, vinegar and some seasoning into the squash mix, then spread over the pizza dough. Top with a few small rosemary sprigs, crumble over the feta, then drizzle with a little more oil, if you like. Bake one at a time for 15 minutes until the pizzas are golden and crisp. Serve with salad.

■ Per serving (4) 630 kcalories, protein 24g, carbohydrate 115g, fat 11g, saturated fat 4g, fibre 9g, sugar 20g, salt 2.92g

Halloumi kebabs with thyme and lemon baste

The secret to keeping down the fat content is to use low-fat halloumi cheese bulked out with plenty of vegetables.

■ **Takes 25 minutes** ■ **Serves 4**

2 medium courgettes
1 large red onion
250g/9oz low-fat halloumi, cut into
  16 chunks
16 cherry tomatoes
warm pitta bread, to serve

FOR THE LEMON BASTE
1 tbsp olive oil
2 tbsp fresh lemon juice
2 tsp thyme leaves (preferably lemon thyme)
1 tsp Dijon mustard

1 Halve the courgettes lengthways, then thickly slice. Cut the onion into wedges and separate into pieces. Thread the halloumi, cherry tomatoes, courgettes and onion on to eight skewers. Cover and chill the kebabs until you are ready to cook.
2 To make the baste, mix together the olive oil, lemon juice, thyme, mustard and a little seasoning, to taste.
3 Heat the barbecue or grill and arrange the kebabs on the rack. Brush with the baste, stirring it first to make sure the ingredients are blended. Cook for 4–5 minutes, turning often, until the cheese begins to turn golden and the vegetables are just tender. Serve while still hot with warm pitta bread.

■ Per serving 194 kcalories, protein 17g, carbohydrate 7g, fat 11g, saturated fat 5g, fibre 1g, sugar none, salt 2.4g

Summer courgette risotto

This soft, delicious low-fat risotto makes the most of the summer's fresh produce. It's a great way to get kids to eat their vegetables, especially if you grate over a little cheese.

■ **Takes 45 minutes** ■ **Serves 4**

1 tbsp olive oil
1 onion, finely chopped
2 garlic cloves, finely chopped
3 ripe tomatoes, roughly chopped
350g/12oz carnaroli or other risotto rice
1 tsp chopped rosemary
1.5 litres/2¾ pints hot vegetable stock
3 courgettes, finely diced
140g/5oz peas, fresh or frozen
a large handful of basil leaves, lightly torn

1 Heat the oil in a large pan. Cook the onion and garlic for 5 minutes until the onion has softened. Add the tomatoes and cook for 3–4 minutes until softened and pulpy, then add the rice and rosemary.
2 Pour in half the stock and leave to cook for 10 minutes or until the liquid has evaporated, stirring from time to time. Add the rest of the stock, then continue to cook for a further 5 minutes.
3 Stir in the courgettes and peas, then cook for another 5 minutes or so, stirring until the rice is tender but the mixture is still a bit saucy. Season with plenty of black pepper, then add the basil and stir until wilted. Serve immediately.

■ Per serving 406 kcalories, protein 14g, carbohydrate 82g, fat 5g, saturated fat 1g, fibre 7g, sugar 9g, salt 0.51g

TOP: Butternut and rosemary pizza

BOTTOM LEFT: Halloumi kebabs with thyme and lemon baste

BOTTOM RIGHT: Summer courgette risotto

TOP: Biryani-stuffed peppers

BOTTOM LEFT: Vitality veggie pasta

BOTTOM RIGHT: Microwave butternut squash risotto

Biryani-stuffed peppers

This Indian-inspired rice stuffing can also be used in large beefsteak tomatoes, but they will take less time to cook than the peppers – roast for just 20 minutes without adding the water or foil.

■ **Takes 1¼ hours** ■ **Serves 6**

4 tbsp olive oil
1 onion, chopped
2 garlic cloves, chopped
1 cinnamon stick
1 tsp each ground turmeric, ground cumin, ground coriander and cardamom pods
250g/9oz basmati rice
a handful of parsley leaves, roughly chopped
a handful of coriander leaves, roughly chopped
zest and juice of 1 lemon
50g/2oz each pine nuts and raisins
6 red peppers

1 Heat the oven to 200C/180C fan/gas 6. Heat half the oil in a pan and fry the onion and garlic. Add the spices and cook for a few minutes more. Stir the rice through. Cover the rice with water, put a lid on the pan and bring to the boil. Turn down the heat and simmer for 10 minutes until just cooked. Stir the herbs, lemon zest and juice, pine nuts and raisins through the rice.
2 Cut around the stalks of the peppers and discard. Use a teaspoon to scrape out the pith and seeds. Stuff the peppers with the rice and sit them in a small roasting tin. Pour 100ml/3½fl oz water into the tin and drizzle with the remaining oil. Cover the tin with foil, then roast for 20 minutes. Remove the foil, then continue to cook for 20 minutes until the peppers are soft and just starting to fall apart.

■ Per serving 274 kcalories, protein 6g, carbohydrate 46g, fat 9g, saturated fat 1g, fibre 3g, sugar 11g, salt 0.02g

Vitality veggie pasta

The pine nuts add a nice toasty crunch to this meal in a bowl. You can ring the changes by using tomatoes instead of the mushrooms.

■ **Takes 25 minutes** ■ **Serves 4**

250g pack pappardelle pasta
1 small butternut squash, peeled, seeded and chopped into chunks
2 tbsp olive oil
a small handful of pine nuts
1 plump garlic clove, finely chopped
4 large field mushrooms, sliced
250g bag spinach leaves
grated Parmesan and chilli flakes, to serve (optional)

1 Cook the pasta according to the packet instructions. When the pasta has 5 minutes left to cook, tip in the squash and cook with the pasta for the remaining time.
2 Meanwhile, heat half the oil in a large frying pan. Sizzle the pine nuts until they start to colour, stir in the garlic and cook for a moment just to soften. Add the remaining oil, turn up the heat, add the mushrooms and cook for 2–3 minutes until they start to soften. Turn the heat to maximum, add the spinach to the pan and cook for 1–2 minutes until completely wilted.
3 Drain the pasta and squash, then mix in with the vegetables until everything is nicely combined and serve. You could also pass round grated Parmesan and chilli flakes.

■ Per serving 377 kcalories, protein 13g, carbohydrate 62g, fat 10g, saturated fat 1g, fibre 7g, added sugar none, salt 0.27g

Microwave butternut squash risotto

Just five ingredients make a terrific-tasting risotto that's easy to cook in the microwave. The squash adds a sweetness to this ultimate comfort food.

■ **Takes 25 minutes** ■ **Serves 4**

250g/9oz risotto rice
700ml/1¼ pint hot vegetable stock
1 medium butternut squash
a big handful of grated Parmesan, plus extra to garnish
a handful of sage leaves, roughly chopped

1 Tip the rice into a large bowl, then add 500ml/18fl oz of the hot vegetable stock. Cover with cling film and microwave on High for 5 minutes.
2 Meanwhile, peel and seed the squash then cut into medium chunks. Stir the rice, then add the squash and the rest of the stock. Re-cover with cling film, then microwave for another 15 minutes, stirring halfway, until almost all the stock is absorbed and the rice and squash are tender.
3 Leave the risotto to sit for 2 minutes, then stir in the cheese and sage leaves. Serve topped with more grated Parmesan.

■ Per serving 313 kcalories, protein 10g, carbohydrate 66g, fat 3g, saturated fat 1g, fibre 4g, sugar 9g, salt 1.04g

Easy oven frittata

A golden pasta bake is always a popular choice with the family. The only accompaniment you need is a crisp green salad and some crusty bread.

■ **Takes 1 hour** ■ **Serves 4**

½ tsp olive oil
85g/3oz fusilli or macaroni
1 leek or 1 bunch spring onions, chopped
85g/3oz frozen or canned sweetcorn
85g/3oz frozen peas
1 red pepper, seeded and chopped
2 eggs
150ml/¼ pint semi-skimmed milk
1 tbsp thyme leaves (preferably lemon
   thyme)
50g/2oz extra-mature Cheddar, grated
2 tbsp finely grated Parmesan

1 Heat the oven to 190C/170C fan/gas 5. Grease a 1.2-litre baking dish with the olive oil.
2 Cook the pasta in salted boiling water in a large pan for 8 minutes. Add all the vegetables and cook for another 2–3 minutes until the pasta is tender and the vegetables slightly softened. Drain, then tip into the baking dish and mix well.
3 Beat together the eggs and milk in a jug, and add the thyme. Mix the two cheeses together and add most of it to the egg mixture, then season. Pour into the baking dish, mix gently, then scatter the rest of the cheese on top. Bake for 35–40 minutes until set and golden. Cool for just a few minutes, then serve.

■ Per serving 277 kcalories, protein 16g, carbohydrate 29g, fat 12g, saturated fat 6g, fibre 3g, sugar 2g, salt 0.7g

Roasted spring vegetable pizza

By using low-fat mozzarella, just a little olive oil and plenty of vegetables, a pizza can make a healthy meal!

■ **Takes 1 hour** ■ **Serves 4**

200g/8oz strong plain flour
½ tsp salt
1 tsp easy-blend dried yeast
150ml/¼ pint warm water
olive oil, for brushing

FOR THE TOPPING
2 red peppers
1 leek
1 tsp olive oil
4 tbsp passata
125g pack light mozzarella
12 cherry tomatoes
3 tbsp frozen peas
2 tbsp freshly grated Parmesan

1 Heat the oven to 220C/200C fan/gas 7. Tip the flour, salt and yeast into a bowl, and mix well. Add the warm water and mix to a soft dough. Knead for 2–3 minutes, then roll out to a 30-cm round. Brush a large baking sheet with a thin slick of oil, then add the pizza base. Cover with a clean tea towel.
2 Cut the peppers into rings and slice the leek. Toss the leek and red peppers in the oil, and season with salt and pepper. Spread over a baking sheet and roast for 10 minutes.
3 Spread the pizza base with the passata. Scatter over the leek and red pepper. Thinly slice the mozzarella and arrange over the vegetables. Scatter over the whole cherry tomatoes and peas, and sprinkle with the Parmesan. Bake for 15–20 minutes, until the crust is crisp and lightly browned.

■ Per serving 290 kcalories, protein 15g carbohydrate 47g, fat 6g, saturated fat 3g, fibre 4g, added sugar none, salt 0.84g

Chilli bean open lasagne

An attractive and quick way of serving lasagne. The bean mixture is simply stacked with the cooked lasagne sheets on individual plates.

■ **Takes 30 minutes** ■ **Serves 4**

1 tbsp olive oil
1 onion, chopped
2 garlic cloves, crushed
1 red chilli, seeded and finely sliced
1 small aubergine, chopped
1 large courgette, chopped
410g can borlotti beans, drained and rinsed
400g can chopped tomatoes
2 tbsp tomato purée
250g pack fresh lasagne sheets
a handful of basil leaves, torn, plus extra
   to garnish
100g/4oz Cheddar, grated

1 Heat the oil, then fry the onion for around 2–3 minutes. Add the garlic, chilli, aubergine and courgette, then fry for a further 2–3 minutes. Stir in the beans, tomatoes, purée and some seasoning. Bring to the boil, then simmer for 5 minutes.
2 Meanwhile, cook the lasagne according to the packet instructions. Drain, then halve each sheet diagonally. Stir the torn basil leaves into the beans.
3 Place a spoonful of the bean mixture on each of four warmed serving plates, and top each with a quarter of the lasagne triangles. Top with the remaining bean mixture and a quarter of the cheese per plate. Garnish with the extra basil.

■ Per serving 400 kcalories, protein 17g, carbohydrate 73g, fat 6g, saturated fat 1g, fibre 11g, sugar none, salt 1.21g

Spring-into-summer pasta

The fresh, simple flavours of lemon and mint work perfectly together for a light full-of-summer lunch that's low in fat.

■ **Takes 15 minutes** ■ **Serves 4**

350g/12oz tagliatelle
500g/1lb 2oz courgettes
190g bag shelled fresh peas, or use frozen
zest and juice of 1 lemon
a handful of mint leaves, chopped
250g pot ricotta

1 Cook the tagliatelle according to the packet instructions.
2 Meanwhile, cut the courgettes into thin finger-length sticks. When the pasta has 2 minutes left to cook, tip the courgettes and peas into the pan, then cook until just tender. Drain and return to the pan.
3 Toss in the lemon juice, zest and most of the mint, then season to taste. Divide among four bowls, spoon small dollops of ricotta over each and sprinkle with the remaining mint.

■ Per serving 457 kcalories, protein 22g, carbohydrate 75g, fat 10g, saturated fat 5g, fibre 6g, sugar none, salt 0.19g

Greek baked beans

Serve this dish at room temperature with a Greek salad and crusty bread for a light lunch, or on top of some toasted sourdough as a snack.

■ **Takes 2 hours 20 minutes, plus overnight soaking** ■ **Serves 4**

400g/14oz dried butter beans
3 tbsp Greek extra-virgin olive oil, plus extra to drizzle
1 Spanish onion, finely chopped
2 garlic cloves, finely chopped
2 tbsp tomato purée
800g/1lb 12oz ripe tomatoes, skinned and roughly chopped
1 tsp sugar
1 tsp dried oregano
a pinch of ground cinnamon
2 tbsp chopped flatleaf parsley, plus extra to garnish

1 Soak the beans overnight in plenty of water. Drain, rinse, then place in a pan covered with water. Bring to the boil, reduce the heat, then simmer for about 50 minutes until tender but not soft. Drain, then set aside.
2 Heat the oven to 180C/160C fan/gas 4. Heat the olive oil in a large frying pan, tip in the onion and garlic, then cook over a medium heat for 10 minutes until softened. Add the tomato purée, cook for 1 minute, add remaining ingredients, then simmer for 2–3 minutes. Season, then stir in the beans.
3 Tip the beans into a large ovenproof dish, then bake for 1 hour, uncovered and without stirring, until tender. The beans will absorb all the fabulous flavours and the sauce will thicken. Allow to cool, then scatter with the extra parsley and drizzle with a little more oil to serve.

■ Per serving 431 kcalories, protein 22g, carbohydrate 66g, fat 11g, saturated fat 1g, fibre 19g, sugar 15g, salt 0.2g

Sweet and hot vegetable curry

Using a ready-made curry paste means you have all the authentic flavour without having to buy a long list of spices.

■ **Takes 35 minutes** ■ **Serves 6**

1 tbsp sunflower oil
3 tbsp vindaloo curry paste
1 tbsp soft brown sugar
juice of ½ lemon
2 courgettes, thickly sliced
300g/10oz cauliflower florets (about ½ a head)
400g/14 oz passata
400g can chickpeas, drained and rinsed
250g bag spinach leaves
basmati rice, to serve

1 Heat the oil in a large pan, add the curry paste and fry for 1 minute. Add the sugar and lemon juice, cook for 1 minute, then tip in the courgettes and cauliflower, and cook for 2 minutes. Now stir in the passata, plus 100ml/3½fl oz water and the chickpeas, and season to taste. Bring to the boil, cover with a lid and simmer for 15 minutes.
2 Just before serving, throw in the spinach, give it a stir and remove from the heat once the leaves have just wilted. Serve with boiled basmati rice.

■ Per serving 142 kcalories, protein 8g, carbohydrate 16g, fat 6g, saturated fat none, fibre 4g, sugar 8g, salt 1.01g

Moroccan-spiced fish with ginger mash

Sweet potatoes can become waterlogged when boiled, so mash them over a low heat and any excess water will evaporate, leaving fluffy spuds.

■ **Takes 30 minutes** ■ **Serves 2**

2 large sweet potatoes, peeled and cut into chunks
2 tsp butter, softened
1 garlic clove, crushed
½–1 tsp harissa paste
zest of 1 lemon
a small handful of coriander, chopped
thumb-size piece of ginger, finely grated
2 skinless white fish fillets
green veg, to serve

1 Heat the oven to 200C/180C fan/gas 6. Cook the sweet potatoes in boiling salted water for about 10 minutes or until just tender when pierced with a knife.
2 Meanwhile, mix together the butter with the garlic, harissa, lemon zest, coriander and some seasoning. Set aside.
3 When the potatoes are ready, drain thoroughly and mash with the ginger and some seasoning, then keep warm.
4 Put the fish in a roasting tin, season, then spread half the flavoured butter over each fillet. Roast for about 8 minutes until just cooked through. Serve with the ginger mash and some green veg.

■ Per serving 445 kcalories, protein 36g, carbohydrate 65g, fat 7g, saturated fat 3g, fibre 7g, sugar 17g, salt 0.67g

Teriyaki steak with fennel slaw

A new way to serve steak – marinated in a soy-and-honey mix then griddled and served with a crunchy salad.

■ **Takes 20 minutes, plus marinating** ■ **Serves 4**

2 tbsp reduced-salt soy sauce
1 tbsp red wine vinegar
1 tsp clear honey
4 sirloin or rump steaks, trimmed of all visible fat, about 125g/4½oz each

FOR THE FENNEL SLAW
1 large carrot, coarsely grated
1 fennel bulb, halved and thinly sliced
1 red onion, halved and thinly sliced
a handful of coriander leaves
juice of 1 lime

1 Mix the soy, vinegar and honey, add the steaks, then marinate for 10–15 minutes.
2 Toss together the carrot, fennel, onion and coriander, then chill until ready to serve.
3 Remove the steaks from the marinade, reserving the liquid. Cook the steaks in a griddle pan for a few minutes on each side, depending on the thickness and how well done you like them. Set the meat aside to rest on a plate, then add the reserved marinade to the pan. Bubble the marinade until it reduces a little to make a sticky sauce.
4 Dress the slaw with the lime juice, then pile on to plates and serve with the steaks. Spoon the sauce over the meat.

■ Per serving 188 kcalories, protein 29g, carbohydrate 7g, fat 5g, saturated fat 2g, fibre 2g, sugar 6g, salt 1.05g

Chicken stir-fry

Asian cooking can be light, healthy and so quick that you'll think twice before ever ordering a takeaway again. Sprinkle with sesame seeds, if you have some in your storecupboard.

■ **Takes 35 minutes, plus marinating** ■ **Serves 4**

1 egg white
1 tbsp cornflour, plus 1 tsp extra
4 boneless, skinless chicken breasts, sliced
350g/12oz Thai fragrant rice
1 tbsp vegetable oil
1 red pepper, seeded and cut into chunks
1 tbsp finely chopped ginger
1 shallot, thinly sliced
1 garlic clove, thinly sliced
1 red chilli, seeded and sliced (optional)
1 tbsp Thai fish sauce
juice of 1 lime
a handful of basil leaves

1 Beat together the egg white and the 1 tablespoon of cornflour. Mix in the chicken and marinate for 15–30 minutes.
2 Rinse and drain the rice, tip into a pan and pour over 600ml/1 pint water and a pinch of salt. Bring to the boil, then cook for 10 minutes or so until the water has almost boiled away. Cover, turn the heat down low and cook for 10 minutes more.
3 Remove the chicken from the marinade and pat dry. Heat the oil in a wok and cook the chicken for 7–10 minutes, tossing until cooked. Remove from the pan and set aside. Add the pepper and cook for 1 minute, then add the ginger, shallot, garlic and chilli, if using, for 1–2 minutes more.
4 Combine the fish sauce, lime juice, 50ml/2fl oz water and the extra teaspoon of cornflour. Tip into the wok with the chicken. Cook for 1 minute, stir through the basil, then serve with the rice.

■ Per serving 501 kcalories, protein 42g, carbohydrate 76g, fat 5g, saturated fat 1g, fibre 2g, sugar 3g, salt 1.02g

TOP: Moroccan-spiced fish with ginger mash

BOTTOM LEFT: Teriyaki steak with fennel slaw

BOTTOM RIGHT: Chicken stir-fry

TOP: Sticky pork

BOTTOM LEFT: Sesame chicken with soy dip

BOTTOM RIGHT: Butternut squash with spicy chilli

Sticky pork

This pork is wonderful with some plain boiled rice and steamed greens. The pork can be tossed in the marinade just before cooking or marinated overnight.

- **Takes 35 minutes, plus marinating (optional)**
- **Serves 4**

500g/1lb 2oz piece pork fillet
rice and steamed greens, to serve

FOR THE MARINADE
4 tbsp soy sauce
1 tbsp clear honey
finely grated zest and juice of 1 orange
thumb-sized piece of ginger, finely grated

1 Tip all the marinade ingredients into a shallow dish and stir to combine. Coat the pork in the marinade and, if you have time, leave for 1 hour or, even better, overnight.
2 Heat the oven to 200C/180C fan/gas 6. Heat an ovenproof pan and take the pork out of the marinade. Brown in the pan on all sides, then baste over the rest of the marinade and roast the pork in the oven for 20 minutes until cooked all the way through, basting with its juices every 5 minutes or so. Serve the pork sliced with the juices drizzled over, with rice and your favourite steamed greens.

- Per serving 165 kcalories, protein 28g, carbohydrate 3g, fat 5g, saturated fat 2g, fibre none, sugar 3g, salt 1.56g

Sesame chicken with soy dip

Perfect for a Saturday-night supper with the family. The children will love the crispy-coated chicken and zesty dip.

- **Takes 35 minutes** ■ **Serves 4**

140g/5oz breadcrumbs
3 tbsp sesame seeds
1 tsp Chinese five-spice
4 boneless, skinless chicken breasts, flattened a little
1 egg, lightly beaten
300g/10oz Tenderstem broccoli
3 tbsp soy sauce
juice of 1 lemon
juice of 1 lime, plus extra wedges to serve
1 tbsp caster sugar

1 Heat the oven to 200C/180C fan/gas 6 and line a baking sheet with baking parchment. Mix the breadcrumbs, sesame seeds, five-spice and a little seasoning on a plate. Pat dry the chicken, dip into the egg, then roll in the breadcrumb mix. Arrange on the baking sheet, then bake for 25–30 minutes until crisp and cooked through.
2 When the chicken is almost ready, cook the broccoli in salted water for a few minutes until just tender. Mix the soy sauce with the citrus juices and sugar to make a dipping sauce. Serve the crispy chicken with the broccoli and little dishes of the sauce for dipping, plus lime wedges for squeezing over.

- Per serving 398 kcalories, protein 44g, carbohydrate 34g, fat 10g, saturated fat 2g, fibre 4g, sugar 8g, salt 3.01g

Butternut squash with spicy chilli

Turn chilli into something special by serving it in roasted butternut-squash halves. The chilli combines beautifully with the sweet squash flesh.

- **Takes 55 minutes** ■ **Serves 4**

2 small butternut squash, halved lengthways and seeds scraped out
1 tbsp olive oil, plus extra to serve
1 red onion, chopped
2 red chillies, seeded and finely chopped
2 tsp ground cumin
250g/9oz lean minced beef
2 tbsp tomato purée
410g can kidney beans, drained and rinsed
½ × 20g bunch coriander, leaves chopped
50g/2oz baby leaf spinach

1 Heat the oven to 200C/180C fan/gas 6. Rub the squash halves with a little of the oil, then roast them on a baking sheet for 45 minutes until soft.
2 Meanwhile, heat the remaining oil in a large frying pan, then fry the onion for a few minutes until soft. Stir in the chillies and cumin, fry for 1 minute more, then add the mince, browning for 3–4 minutes. Stir in the tomato purée and beans with a splash of water and season. Warm through and keep warm.
3 Scoop out a little of the soft squash flesh to make a hollow, then stir this into the chilli with half the coriander. Fill the cavity of each squash with a quarter of the mix, then scatter with the remaining coriander. Dress the spinach with a drop more olive oil, season and serve alongside the squash.

- Per serving 318 kcalories, protein 23g, carbohydrate 37g, fat 10g, saturated fat 3g, fibre 9g, sugar 16g, salt 0.92g

Soy tuna with wasabi mash

Wasabi is a Japanese root vegetable that is finely grated to make a hot paste a little like horseradish sauce. You could use English mustard or freshly grated horseradish instead, if you prefer.

■ **Takes 25 minutes, plus marinating** ■ **Serves 2**

3 tbsp soy sauce
1 tbsp rice wine vinegar
1 tbsp caster sugar
2 tuna steaks, about 140g/5oz each
500g/1lb 2oz potatoes, peeled and halved
100ml/3½fl oz semi-skimmed milk
2 tsp wasabi paste
1 spring onion, finely sliced
broad beans or soya beans, to serve

1 Mix together the soy sauce, vinegar and sugar. Pour over the tuna and marinate for at least 20 minutes or up to 2 hours in the fridge. Put the potatoes in a pan of lightly salted boiling water, then cook for 10–15 minutes until soft. Drain well. Heat the milk in the pan and mix in the wasabi, return the potatoes to the pan, then mash until smooth. Stir through the spring onion and keep warm.
2 Heat a non-stick griddle pan until smoking hot. Remove the tuna from the marinade. Cook on the griddle for 2–3 minutes on each side until seared on the outside but still pink inside. Serve the tuna alongside the wasabi mash with broad beans or soya beans.

■ Per serving 439 kcalories, protein 43g, carbohydrate 51g, fat 9g, saturated fat 2g, fibre 3g, sugar 7g, salt 1.38g

Summer seafood simmer

This tomato-based spicy fish stew is so simple to cook yet looks really impressive for a special dinner for two.

■ **Takes 40 minutes** ■ **Serves 2**

8 large raw prawns, shells on
1 tbsp olive oil
1 small onion, finely chopped
2 garlic cloves, crushed
1 tsp hot smoked paprika
200ml/7fl oz dry white wine
400g can chopped tomatoes
1 roasted red pepper, from a jar, sliced
200g/8oz boneless, skinless white fish fillets, cut into chunks
a handful of chopped parsley
crusty bread, to serve

1 Peel the prawns and de-vein them by simply scoring down the back and removing the black vein. Set aside.
2 Heat the olive oil in a heavy-based pan, then add the onion. Cook gently for 3–4 minutes until softened, then add the garlic and paprika. Cook for a further minute, then pour in the wine. Allow to bubble for a minute or so, then tip in the tomatoes. Season, then leave to simmer for 20 minutes.
3 Stir the red pepper, fish and prawns into the stew. Simmer gently for 4–5 minutes, or until the fish and prawns are cooked through. Stir in the chopped parsley, then serve with crusty bread.

■ Per serving 353 kcalories, protein 38g, carbohydrate 16g, fat 12g, saturated fat 2g, fibre 4g, sugar 13g, salt 1.74g

Easy Indian chicken with coleslaw

This great-tasting dish is full of fresh, warm flavours. It's a perfect recipe for a spicy, casual supper with friends.

■ **Takes 1 hour, plus marinating** ■ **Serves 4**

a large handful of coriander, stems finely chopped, leaves separated
2 tsp ground cumin
zest and juice of 2 limes
2 tbsp vegetable oil
4 skinless chicken quarters
1 tbsp ground turmeric
½ small head purple cabbage, shredded
2 carrots, finely shredded
naan bread or rice, to serve (optional)

1 Mix the coriander stems with the cumin, lime zest and juice, and oil. Make three slashes in each chicken quarter, then sprinkle over the turmeric and half the lime mixture. Season well, then leave to marinate for 10 minutes or up to 24 hours in the fridge.
2 Heat the oven to 200C/180C fan/gas 6 a little while before you are ready to cook the chicken. Remove the chicken from the marinade and roast on a baking sheet for 50 minutes until it is golden and cooked through.
3 Tip the cabbage and carrots into a bowl, then pour over the remaining lime dressing. Add the coriander leaves and toss. Sit the chicken on top of the salad to serve, with some warm naan bread or rice, if you like.

■ Per serving 147 kcalories, protein 11g, carbohydrate 9g, fat 8g, saturated fat 1g, fibre 2g, sugar 5g, salt 0.16g

TOP: Soy tuna with wasabi mash

BOTTOM LEFT: Summer seafood simmer

BOTTOM RIGHT: Easy Indian chicken with coleslaw

TOP: Baked fish with Thai spices

BOTTOM LEFT: Garlic beef

BOTTOM RIGHT: Steamed bass with pak choi

Baked fish with Thai spices

Snapper or sea bass would also work well in this recipe, though as they can be quite expensive, use trout, which works a treat with gentle, aromatic flavours.

■ **Takes 20 minutes** ■ **Serves 4**

4 trout fillets, about 200g/8oz each
1 lemongrass stalk, finely chopped
thumb-sized piece of ginger, peeled and finely chopped
1 red chilli, seeded and finely chopped
1 garlic clove, finely chopped
1 tbsp Thai fish sauce
juice of 2 limes
1 tsp golden caster sugar
a handful of coriander, roughly chopped

1 Heat the oven to 200C/180C fan/gas 6. Tear off two large sheets of foil and put one fillet, skin-side down, in the centre of each sheet. Make a sauce by mixing together the remaining ingredients. Spoon half of this mixture over the fillets, setting aside the remainder.
2 Put the other two fish fillets on top of each fillet to make a sandwich, skin-side up, then tightly seal the foil to create two packages. Bake in the oven for 12–15 minutes. Bring the packages to the table to open and serve with the rest of the sauce.

■ Per serving 236 kcalories, protein 40g, carbohydrate 2g, fat 8g, saturated fat 2g, fibre none, sugar 1g, salt 1.02g

Garlic beef

Beef skirt has an excellent flavour and is best served rare to medium rare or it becomes tough. Skirt can also be used for braising.

■ **Takes 25 minutes, plus marinating** ■ **Serves 4**

1 tbsp black peppercorns
6 garlic cloves
4 tbsp red wine vinegar
600g/1lb 5oz piece well-trimmed beef skirt
chips and mustard, to serve (optional)

1 In a pestle and mortar, crush the peppercorns and garlic with a pinch of salt until you have a smooth-ish paste, then stir in the vinegar. Sit the beef in a non-metallic dish, then rub all over with the paste. Leave in the fridge to marinate for a few hours, but no longer.
2 To cook, put a griddle pan over a very high heat. Rub the marinade off the meat, then season with a little more salt. Cook the meat until charred on each side – about 5 minutes per side for rare, longer if you prefer it medium or well done. If the cut is very thick, you may want to roast it in a hot oven for 5 minutes after searing.
3 Lift on to a chopping board, then rest for 5 minutes before carving into slices and serving with chips and mustard, if you like.

■ Per serving 205 kcalories, protein 34g, carbohydrate 3g, fat 6g, saturated fat 2g, fibre none, sugar none, salt 0.24g

Steamed bass with pak choi

This is a one-pot dish, as everything is cooked in a Chinese bamboo steamer. If you don't have a steamer, cook it in a foil parcel in a medium oven for 30 minutes.

■ **Takes 15 minutes** ■ **Serves 2**

thumb-sized piece of ginger, peeled and sliced
2 garlic cloves, finely sliced
3 spring onions, finely sliced
2 tbsp soy sauce
1 tbsp sesame oil
splash of sherry (optional)
2 sea bass fillets, about 140g/5oz each
2 pak choi heads, quartered

1 In a small bowl, combine all of the ingredients, except the fish and the pak choi, to make a soy mix. Line one tier of a two-tiered bamboo steamer loosely with foil. Lay the fish, skin-side up, on the foil and spoon over the soy mix. Set the steamer over a pan of simmering water and throw the pak choi into the second tier then cover it with a lid. Alternatively, add the pak choi to the fish layer after 2 minutes of cooking – the closer the tier is to the steam, the hotter it is.
2 Leave everything to steam for 6–8 minutes until the pak choi has wilted and the fish is cooked. Divide the greens between two plates, then carefully lift out the fish and set it on top of the greens. Lift the foil up and drizzle the tasty juices back over the fish.

■ Per serving 217 kcalories, protein 30g, carbohydrate 5g, fat 9g, saturated fat 1g, fibre none, sugar 2g, salt 4.58g

Healthy fish and chips with tartare sauce

A great Saturday-night supper – fresh, light and tangy fish served with crunchy chips.

■ **Takes 40–45 minutes** ■ **Serves 2**

450g/1lb potatoes, peeled and cut into chips
1 tbsp olive oil, plus a little extra for brushing
2 white fish fillets, about 140g/5oz each
grated zest and juice of 1 lemon
a small handful of parsley leaves, chopped
1 tbsp capers, chopped
2 heaped tbsp 0% fat Greek yogurt

1 Heat the oven to 200C/180C fan/gas 6. Toss the prepared chips in the oil. Spread over a baking sheet in an even layer and bake for 40 minutes until browned and crisp.
2 Put the fish in a shallow dish, brush lightly with oil, salt and pepper. Sprinkle with half the lemon juice and bake for 12–15 minutes. After 10 minutes, sprinkle over the lemon zest and a little of the parsley to finish cooking.
3 Meanwhile, mix the capers, yogurt, remaining parsley and lemon juice together, set aside, and season to taste.
4 To serve, divide the chips between plates, lift the fish on to the plates and serve with a little side dish of the tartare sauce.

■ Per serving 373 kcalories, protein 35g, carbohydrate 41g, fat 9g, saturated fat 1g, fibre 3g, added sugar none, salt 0.96g

Must-make moussaka

Softening the aubergine in the microwave cuts down the amount of oil that's usually used when frying them for this dish. Remember to prick holes in the aubergine with a fork so that it doesn't explode!

■ **Takes 30 minutes** ■ **Serves 4**

500g pack lean minced beef
1 large aubergine
150g pot 0% fat Greek yogurt
1 egg, beaten
3 tbsp finely grated Parmesan
400g can chopped tomatoes with garlic and herbs
4 tbsp sun-dried tomato purée
400g/14oz leftover boiled potatoes or 350g/12oz uncooked weight, boiled

1 Heat the grill to high. Brown the beef in a deep ovenproof frying pan over a high heat for 5 minutes.
2 Meanwhile, prick the aubergine with a fork, then microwave on High for 3–5 minutes until soft. Mix the yogurt, egg and Parmesan together, then add a little seasoning. Set aside.
3 Stir the tomatoes, tomato purée and potatoes in with the beef with some seasoning, and heat through. Smooth the surface of the beef mixture with the back of a spoon, then slice the cooked aubergine and arrange on top. Pour the yogurt mixture over the aubergines, smooth out evenly, then grill until the topping has set and turned golden.

■ Per serving 342 kcalories, protein 41g, carbohydrate 25g, fat 9g, saturated fat 4g, fibre 4g, sugar 6g, salt 0.97g

Leanburgers with rocket and peppers

These tasty homemade burgers use extra-lean beef mince lightened with couscous and flavoured with herbs and chilli. Serve on a slice of French bread.

■ **Takes 25–35 minutes** ■ **Serves 6**

50g/2oz couscous
500g/1lb 2oz extra-lean minced beef
1 small onion, finely chopped
2 tsp mixed dried herbs
3 tbsp snipped chives
¼ tsp hot chilli powder
6 slices French bread
6 tsp Dijon mustard
175g/6oz roasted red peppers from a jar, cut into large pieces (choose ones in brine, or rinse them if they're packed in oil)
a couple of handfuls of rocket leaves

1 Tip the couscous into a medium bowl, pour over 75ml/2½fl oz boiling water and leave it for a few minutes to swell and absorb all the water.
2 Add the mince, onion, dried herbs, chives and chilli powder, then grind in plenty of salt and pepper. Mix thoroughly then shape into six oval burgers that are slightly larger than the bread slices. Cover with foil and chill until ready to cook.
3 Heat the grill or barbecue, then cook the burgers for 5–6 minutes on each side, or more if you like them well cooked.
4 Grill or lightly toast the slices of bread and spread with the mustard. Top with the peppers, rocket and a burger, and serve.

■ Per serving 260 kcalories, protein 23g, carbohydrate 30g, fat 6g, saturated fat 2g, fibre 2g, sugar none, salt 1.1g

TOP: Healthy fish and chips with tartare sauce

BOTTOM LEFT: Must-make moussaka

BOTTOM RIGHT: Leanburgers with rocket and peppers

TOP: Banana rice pudding with cinnamon sugar

BOTTOM LEFT: Strawberry cheesecakes

BOTTOM RIGHT: Maple pears with pecans and cranberries

Banana rice pudding with cinnamon sugar

Rice pudding can be made in the microwave in under 20 minutes. For a change, stir in a handful of blueberries instead of the banana.

■ Takes 17 minutes ■ Serves 2

1 tbsp custard powder
400ml/14fl oz skimmed milk
2 tbsp demerara sugar
1 large banana, thinly sliced
85g/3oz pudding rice
¼ tsp ground cinnamon

1 Put the custard powder into a large, deep microwave-proof dish with a lid, then mix to a paste with a dribble of the milk. Stir in the rest of the milk gradually so you have no custardy lumps, then add 1 tablespoon of the sugar and half the banana. Cover tightly with the lid and microwave for 3 minutes on High. Stir in the rice, cover again, then microwave on High for 6 minutes, stirring halfway through.
2 Carefully stir in the remaining banana – take care as the rice will be very hot. Cover and microwave for 4 minutes more, stirring at 1-minute intervals to check if the rice is cooked. Cooking times will vary a little, depending on your microwave.
3 Meanwhile, mix the remaining sugar and cinnamon together. Spoon the creamy banana rice into two bowls and serve sprinkled with the crunchy cinnamon sugar.

■ Per serving 347 kcalories, protein 11g, carbohydrate 78g, fat 1g, saturated fat none, fibre 1g, sugar 37g, salt 0.29g

Strawberry cheesecakes

Top these little puds with whatever fruit you've got at home. For a delicious banoffee version, slice bananas and toss with a squeeze of fresh lemon juice and a spoonful of caramel sauce.

■ Takes 10 minutes ■ Serves 4

85g/3oz low-fat biscuits
200g pack extra-light soft cheese
200g pot 0% fat Greek yogurt
4 tbsp caster sugar
a few drops vanilla extract
2 tbsp good-quality strawberry jam
100g/4oz strawberries, hulled and sliced

1 Put the biscuits in a plastic bag and bash with a rolling pin until you have chunky crumbs. Divide among four glasses or small bowls.
2 Beat the soft cheese, yogurt, sugar and vanilla together until smooth, then spoon over the crumbs, and chill until ready to serve.
3 Stir the jam in a bowl until loose, then gently stir in the strawberries. Divide the strawberries among the cheesecakes and serve.

■ Per serving 263 kcalories, protein 12g, carbohydrate 43g, fat 6g, saturated fat 3g, fibre 1g, sugar 31g, salt 0.93g

Maple pears with pecans and cranberries

Serve warm for pudding or cool the pears in the fridge overnight, then enjoy with muesli or crunchy oat cereal and yogurt for breakfast.

■ Takes 10 minutes ■ Serves 4

4 ripe pears
a handful of dried cranberries
2 tbsp maple syrup, plus extra to drizzle (optional)
50g/2oz pecan nuts, roughly chopped
0% fat Greek yogurt, to serve

1 Peel and halve the pears, and scoop out the core with a teaspoon. Lay the halves in a shallow microwave-proof dish, cut-side down, along with the cranberries. Pour the maple syrup over and cover with cling film. Microwave on High for 3 minutes until softened, stirring halfway through. Uncover and leave to cool for a few minutes. Stir the pecan nuts through the syrup.
2 Spoon into serving dishes, drizzle with the extra maple syrup, if you like, and serve with Greek yogurt.

■ Per serving 208 kcalories, protein 2g, carbohydrate 32g, fat 9g, saturated fat 1g, fibre 4g, sugar 9g, salt none

Fruity summer Charlotte

This is a great way of using over-ripe summer fruits and makes a delicious low-fat pud with its crunchy fruit-loaf topping.

■ **Takes 20 minutes** ■ **Serves 4**

500g/1lb 2oz summer fruits (we used raspberries, blackberries and blueberries)
4 tbsp demerara sugar
7 slices from a small cinnamon and raisin loaf
25g/1oz butter, softened
half-fat crème fraîche or fromage frais, to serve

1 Heat the oven to 220C/200C fan/gas 7. Tumble three-quarters of the berries into a medium baking dish. Whizz the remainder of the berries in a food processor to make a purée, then stir this into the dish along with 2 tablespoons of the sugar.
2 Spread the loaf slices with butter, then cut into triangles. Cover the top of the fruit with the bread slices, then scatter over the rest of the sugar. Cover with foil, bake for 10 minutes, uncover the dish, then bake for 5 minutes more until the fruit is starting to bubble and the bread is toasty. Serve with dollops of crème fraîche or fromage frais.

■ Per serving 262 kcalories, protein 6g, carbohydrate 47g, fat 7g, saturated fat 4g, fibre 5g, sugar 33g, salt 0.43g

Poached apricots with rosewater

The cooking time will vary depending on the ripeness of the fruit, so keep an eye on the pan. Peaches would also work well in this recipe.

■ **Takes 20 minutes, plus cooling** ■ **Serves 2**

50g/2oz golden caster sugar
400g/14oz ripe apricots, halved and stoned
a few drops of rosewater
Greek yogurt and a handful of pistachios, roughly chopped, to decorate

1 Put the sugar into a medium pan with 150ml/¼ pint water. Heat gently until the sugar dissolves, then add the apricots and simmer for 15 minutes until soft.
2 Take off the heat, splash in the rosewater and leave to cool. Spoon into two glasses and serve topped with a few dollops of the yogurt and a scattering of nuts.

■ Per serving 161 kcalories, protein 2g, carbohydrate 41g, fat none, saturated fat none, fibre 3g, sugar 41g, salt 0.01g

Cranberry sunrise

This show-stopper jelly makes a great finale to a meal. For a grown-up dinner party add 100ml/3½fl oz vodka to both of the fruit juices.

■ **Takes 10 minutes, plus overnight setting**
■ **Serves 8–10**

10 sheets leaf gelatine
700ml/1¼ pints smooth-style orange juice, warmed through
700ml/1¼ pints cranberry juice, warmed through

1 Soak 5 leaf gelatine sheets in cold water for at least 5 minutes until soft. Drain the gelatine and squeeze to get rid of any excess water. Dissolve the soaked gelatine in 100ml/3½fl oz hot water from the kettle. Add to the warm orange juice and set aside. Repeat the process, this time using the warm cranberry juice.
2 Pour half of the orange juice into a large jelly mould and chill in the fridge until set completely – about 4 hours. Cover the orange jelly with half the cranberry juice and chill to set. Repeat the process until both juices are used. Leave to set overnight.

■ Per serving (8) 110 kcalories, protein 5g, carbohydrate 24g, fat none, saturated fat none, fibre none, added sugar 10g, salt 0.1g

TOP: Fruity summer Charlotte

BOTTOM LEFT: Poached apricots with rosewater

BOTTOM RIGHT: Cranberry sunrise

TOP: Sugar plums

BOTTOM LEFT: Sweet and fruity Yorkshire

BOTTOM RIGHT: Crunchy spiced rhubarb trifles

Sugar plums

Roasting the plums gives them a deliciously juicy flavour, and the cinnamon sugar adds a crisp coating. Serve warm with low-fat crème fraîche, ice cream or custard.

■ **Takes 25 minutes** ■ **Serves 4**

140g/5oz white granulated sugar
¼ tsp ground cinnamon
1 egg white
12 red plums

1 Heat the oven to 200C/180C fan/gas 6. Mix the sugar and cinnamon in a bowl. Whisk the egg white in a second bowl, then roll the plums first in egg white, then the cinnamon sugar until very well coated in a sugary crust.
2 Space apart in a buttered baking dish, then bake for 15 minutes or until the plums are crusty, cooked through and starting to be juicy. To test, poke the plums with a cocktail stick; if it goes in easily, they are ready to serve.

■ Per serving 207 kcalories, protein 2g, carbohydrate 53g, fat none, saturated fat none, fibre 3g, sugar 53g, salt 0.06g

Sweet and fruity Yorkshire

Use any kind of canned fruit in this comfort-food pud. We used a mixture of cherries and apricot halves.

■ **Takes 30 minutes** ■ **Serves 4**

2 × 400g cans fruit in juice, drained
85g/3oz plain flour
50g/2oz caster sugar
3 eggs, beaten
300ml/½ pint skimmed milk
icing sugar, to dust (optional)

1 Heat the oven to 220C/200C fan/gas 7. Spread the fruit out in a medium baking dish. Combine the flour and caster sugar in a bowl, make a well in the centre, and stir in the eggs until smooth. Gradually stir in the milk until you have a smooth batter, the consistency of pouring cream.
2 Pour the batter over the fruit and bake for 20–25 minutes until golden and set. Dust with icing sugar, if you like, and serve hot or warm.

■ Per serving 363 kcalories, protein 11g, carbohydrate 69g, fat 7g, saturated fat 2g, fibre 2g, sugar 53g, salt 0.26g

Crunchy spiced rhubarb trifles

Ginger is a delicious partner to rhubarb, and this put-together dessert takes just 5 minutes to layer into pretty serving glasses.

■ **Takes 5 minutes** ■ **Serves 4**

540g can rhubarb
a pinch of ground ginger
500g tub fresh custard
6 ginger nut biscuits, roughly crushed

1 Mix the rhubarb and ginger together, and divide among four serving glasses.
2 Spoon the custard on top (you will have some left over) and finish with a sprinkling of crushed biscuit.

■ Per serving 254 kcalories, protein 5g, carbohydrate 42g, fat 10g, saturated fat 5g, fibre 1g, sugar 18g, salt 0.3g

Delicious
desserts and
brilliant bakes

Banoffee trifles

This is an excellent cheat's recipe as there's no cooking involved; it makes the most of ready-made cakes and sauces, and looks spectacular.

■ **Takes 15 minutes** ■ **Serves 4**

6 tbsp tropical fruit juice (from a carton)
2 tbsp rum or brandy
2 firm bananas
8 thin slices from a bought Madeira cake
2 tbsp Belgian chocolate sauce
4 heaped tbsp dulce de leche, or other toffee sauce
225g tub mascarpone
250ml/9fl oz chilled custard (from a tub)
a block of dark chocolate (any type or size will do)

1 In a large bowl, stir the tropical fruit juice with the rum or brandy. Slice the bananas into the fruit juice mixture and toss together. Sandwich the slices of Madeira cake with the chocolate sauce, dice it into squares and pile in the bottom of four pretty glasses.
2 Top with the bananas and rum mixture then add a heaped spoonful of dulce de leche to make another layer. Beat the mascarpone and custard together until smooth, then spoon on top of the mixture.
3 Chill for up to 2 hours until ready to serve. Before serving, run a potato peeler down the flat back of the bar of chocolate to make shavings and scatter indulgently on top of the trifles.

■ Per serving 787 kcalories, protein 9g, carbohydrate 87g, fat 46g, saturated fat 25.1g, fibre 1.6g, added sugar 50.2g, salt 0.82g

Gratin of summer berries

The combination of hot caramelised sauce and still-chilly fruits is irresistible in this simple, yet sophisticated dessert.

■ **Takes 15 minutes, plus cooling** ■ **Serves 4**

140g/5oz strawberries, hulled and cut into halves or quarters
140g/5oz each fresh raspberries and blueberries
finely grated zest of 1 small lemon
100g/4oz white chocolate
142ml pot double cream
2 tbsp icing sugar

1 Scatter the berries between four medium ramekins or one large, shallow heatproof dish, preferably in a single layer. Sprinkle with the lemon zest, cover and chill until ready to serve.
2 Meanwhile, break up the chocolate into a small heatproof bowl. Heat the cream in a small pan until almost boiling, then pour on to the chocolate. Leave for 3 minutes, then stir slowly until dissolved. Allow to cool to room temperature until thickened.
3 To serve, heat the grill for a good 5 minutes until glowing hot. Spoon the chocolate cream over the berries, sprinkle over the icing sugar and grill for 2–3 minutes, until the sauce begins to brown, turning the dish if necessary. Remove and serve immediately.

■ Per serving 356 kcalories, protein 3g, carbohydrate 27g, fat 27g, saturated fat 11g, fibre 1g, added sugar 20g, salt 0.10g

Blackberry honey creams

You can sprinkle crushed ginger nut biscuits between the layers if you want more of a crunch.

■ **Takes 5 minutes** ■ **Serves 4**

500g pot Greek yogurt
2–3 tbsp clear honey
300g/10oz blackberries
225g bottle fruit coulis

1 Beat the yogurt with honey to taste.
2 Divide half the berries among four glasses, drizzle with some coulis and spoon the yogurt over.
3 Top with the remaining berries and some coulis. Serve immediately with the rest of the coulis.

■ Per serving 242 kcalories, protein 9g, carbohydrate 27g, fat 12g, saturated fat 7.1g, fibre 3.2g, added sugar 15.9g, salt 0.23g

TOP: Banoffee trifles

BOTTOM LEFT: Gratin of summer berries

BOTTOM RIGHT: Blackberry honey creams

TOP: Mars bar mousses

BOTTOM LEFT: Quick chocolate-nut slice

BOTTOM RIGHT: Lemon cheesecake tartlets

Mars bar mousses

These chocolate mousses are mild and fudgy so children will love them, too. Put the mousse in one large bowl for everyone to dive into.

■ **Takes 20–25 minutes, plus setting** ■ **Serves 6**

4 standard (58g) Mars bars, chopped into pieces
50ml/2fl oz milk
4 tbsp cocoa powder
3 egg whites
chocolate shavings, to decorate

1 Put the Mars bars, milk and cocoa in a heavy-based pan. Cook over a very gentle heat, stirring constantly, until the chocolate has melted. Transfer to a bowl and leave to cool for 15 minutes, whisking frequently with a wire whisk to blend in any pieces of fudge that rise to the surface, to leave a smooth mixture.
2 Whisk the egg whites in a separate bowl to soft peaks. Using a metal spoon, fold a quarter of the whites into the chocolate sauce to lighten it, then fold in the remainder.
3 Turn the mixture into six small cups, glasses or ramekins and chill in the fridge to set, for at least 2 hours, before serving. Serve topped with chocolate shavings.

■ Per serving 369 kcalories, protein 8g, carbohydrate 50g, fat 17g, saturated fat 9g, fibre 1g, added sugar 39g, salt 0.60g.

Quick chocolate-nut slice

The perfect, speedy no-cook treat for a get-together. Simply melt, mix and stick in the fridge.

■ **Takes 20 minutes, plus chilling** ■ **Serves 6**

100g/4oz butter
400g/14oz dark chocolate, broken in pieces
50g/2oz golden caster sugar
½ tsp ground cinnamon
200g/8oz macaroons or coconut biscuits, broken into pieces
100g/4oz Brazil nuts, roughly chopped
desiccated coconut, to decorate
fresh fruit or ice cream, to serve (optional)

1 Line a 900g/2lb loaf tin with a double layer of cling film. Melt the butter, chocolate and sugar in the microwave on Medium for 2–3 minutes, or in a bowl set over a pan of simmering water over a low heat. Stir in the cinnamon, macaroons or coconut biscuits, and the nuts.
2 Pour the mixture into the prepared tin, smooth over the surface with a knife and cover completely with cling film. Leave in the fridge to set for at least 2 hours.
3 To serve, turn out on to a plate, remove the cling film and sprinkle with desiccated coconut. This dessert is fairly rich, so slice into thin pieces. Serve with fresh fruit or ice cream, if you like.

■ Per serving 759 kcalories, protein 9g, carbohydrate 73g, fat 50g, saturated fat 22g, fibre 3g, added sugar 70g, salt 0.32g

Lemon cheesecake tartlets

A pretty, summery idea that looks like 2 hours' work, but only takes 15 minutes!

■ **Takes 15 minutes** ■ **Serves 4**

4 tbsp lemon curd
2 x 200g tubs Philadelphia Light soft cheese
6 tbsp summer fruit sauce, from a bottle
8 sweet dessert tartlet cases (from a pack)
100g/4oz blueberries
100g/4oz raspberries
1 tbsp cassis (blackcurrant liqueur)
icing sugar, for dusting
fresh mint sprigs, to decorate

1 Beat the lemon curd into the soft cheese until smooth and creamy. Pour 1 teaspoon of summer fruit sauce into each dessert tartlet, then top with a spoonful of the cheese mixture (set aside the remainder).
2 Carefully mix the berries together, then pile on to the cheese mixture. Stir the cassis into the remaining sauce. (You can make the tarts and sauce up to this stage and chill for 2–3 hours.)
3 Dust the tartlets with icing sugar. Drizzle lines of the sauce over half of four dinner plates with a teaspoon and spoon the remaining cheesecake mixture in the centre. Put two tarts on each plate, propping one of the tarts against the cheesecake mixture. Add a sprig of mint for an extra flourish.

■ Per serving 599 kcalories, protein 14g, carbohydrate 58g, fat 35g, saturated fat 12.9g, fibre 2.8g, added sugar 13.3g, salt 1.76g

Raspberry and mango salad

For a tropical version, scoop the seeds and juice from 2 ripe passion fruit into the syrup.

■ **Takes 10 minutes** ■ **Serves 4**

200ml/7fl oz cranberry juice
1 tbsp caster sugar
1 large ripe mango
150g punnet raspberries
a dash of vodka (optional)
vanilla ice cream or yogurt, to serve

1 In a small pan, bring the cranberry juice and sugar to a rolling boil, then remove from the heat and leave to cool.
2 Meanwhile, peel and thinly slice the mango, then tip into a large bowl with the raspberries.
3 Add a dash of vodka, if using, to the syrup, then pour the cranberry syrup over the fruit and spoon into bowls. Serve with scoops of ice cream or spoonfuls of yogurt.

■ Per serving 106 kcalories, protein 1g, carbohydrate 27g, fat 1g, saturated fat none, fibre 3g, added sugar 11g, salt 0.02g

Amaretti biscuits with ice cream

A clever and easy last-minute dessert that is wonderful served with coffee.

24 soft amaretti biscuits
good-quality vanilla ice cream
Amaretto liqueur, to drizzle (optional)

■ **Takes 10 minutes** ■ **Serves 6**

1 Sandwich a small scoop of ice cream between two amaretti biscuits.
2 Put two filled biscuits on each plate.
3 Serve drizzled with a little Amaretto, if you wish.

■ Per serving 262 kcalories, protein 4g, carbohydrate 46g, fat 7g, saturated fat 4g, fibre 1g, added sugar 17g, salt 0.49g

Iced berries with hot-choc sauce

This is a great idea for using frozen berries. And it's so quick you can whip it up in an instant if you have unexpected guests.

■ **Takes 10 minutes** ■ **Serves 4**

500g/1lb 2oz mixed frozen berries
   (blackberries, blueberries, raspberries,
   redcurrants)

FOR THE SAUCE
142ml pot double cream
140g/5oz white chocolate
1 tbsp white rum (optional)

1 Make the sauce. Pour the cream into a small pan and break in the chocolate. Heat gently, stirring, until the chocolate melts into a smooth sauce. Take care not to overheat or the chocolate will seize into a hard lump.
2 Remove from the heat and stir in the rum, if using. Scatter the frozen berries on four dessert plates or in shallow bowls.
3 Pour the hot chocolate sauce over the fruits and serve immediately, as the fruits start to defrost.

■ Per serving 377 kcalories, protein 5g, carbohydrate 28g, fat 28g, saturated fat 11g, fibre 3g, added sugar 17g, salt 0.14g

TOP: Raspberry and mango salad

BOTTOM LEFT: Amaretti biscuits with Ice cream

BOTTOM RIGHT: Iced berries with hot-choc sauce

TOP: Melba sundaes

BOTTOM LEFT: Lemon
meringue ice cream

BOTTOM RIGHT: Chocolate
berry cups

Melba sundaes

You don't have to use vanilla ice cream – try scoops of your favourite flavour.

■ **Takes 10 minutes** ■ **Serves 2**

150g punnet raspberries
1–2 tsp icing sugar, to sweeten
1 peach
4–6 scoops vanilla ice cream

1 Blitz half the raspberries in a blender with enough icing sugar to sweeten (or mash well with a fork). Set aside.
2 Halve, stone and thinly slice a peach. Divide it between two tall glasses, layering it with the remaining whole berries and scoops of ice cream.
3 Finish off with a drizzle of the raspberry sauce.

■ Per serving 260 kcalories, protein 6g, carbohydrate 34g, fat 12g, saturated fat 7.8g, fibre 2.7g, added sugar 22.2g, salt 0.19g

Lemon meringue ice cream

This recipe is not only easy to make, but also looks and tastes so good it's hard to believe it only takes 20 minutes to put together.

■ **Takes 25 minutes, plus freezing** ■ **Serves 8**

1 shopbought slab Madeira cake
8 meringue nests
500ml pot crème fraîche
325g jar good quality lemon curd
red summer berries, to decorate

1 Line the base of a 20cm round spring-form cake tin with greaseproof paper. Cut the Madeira cake into 1cm slices and use to line the base of the tin. Fill in the gaps between the slices with small pieces of cake.
2 Break the meringues into pieces and put into a large bowl. Fold in the crème fraîche. Dollop large spoonfuls of the meringue mixture and lemon curd into the tin. Don't stir. Level with a palette knife, then tap the tin to pack down the mixture. Freeze for at least 4 hours.
3 When ready to serve, remove the cake from the tin and put on a serving plate. (If made a day or more ahead, put in the fridge for 20 minutes before serving.) Decorate with red summer berries and serve.

■ Per serving 464 kcalories, protein 5g, carbohydrate 57g, fat 26g, saturated fat 14g, fibre 1g, added sugar 37g, salt 0.51g

Chocolate berry cups

Perfect served with a glass of Asti Spumante at the end of a summer meal.

■ **Takes 15 minutes, plus chilling** ■ **Serves 4**

284ml pot double cream
100g/4oz dark chocolate, broken into pieces
1 tbsp icing sugar
550g/1lb 4oz mixed summer fruits (raspberries, strawberries, cherries, blueberries), stoned and halved if necessary

1 Heat the cream in a pan until just coming to the boil. Remove from the heat, tip in the chocolate pieces, then stir until melted. Cool slightly.
2 Tip the icing sugar and most of the fruit into the pan and mix gently.
3 Spoon into four glasses or cups, top with the remaining fruit, then chill in the fridge until needed (up to 3 hours ahead of serving).

■ Per serving 503 kcalories, protein 4g, carbohydrate 31g, fat 41g, saturated fat 25g, fibre 3g, added sugar 20g, salt 0.08g

Apple and blueberry cobbler

This sumptuous American dessert makes a luscious change to crumble. You can substitute other fruits, if you like – try fruits of the forest.

■ **Takes 30 minutes** ■ **Serves 4**

1 Bramley cooking apple, about
  175g/6oz
250g punnet blueberries
50g/2oz light muscovado sugar
250g tub mascarpone

FOR THE COBBLER TOPPING
85g/3oz butter, cut into pieces
225g/8oz self-raising flour
50g/2oz light muscovado sugar
grated zest of 1 lemon
150g carton natural yogurt

1 Heat the oven to 220C/200C fan/gas 7. Peel, core and thinly slice the apple and put into a 1.5 litre pint ovenproof dish. Scatter over the blueberries, sprinkle with the sugar and gently stir. Spoon over the mascarpone.
2 To make the topping, rub the butter into the flour and whizz in a food processor until it looks like fine breadcrumbs. Stir in the sugar and lemon zest. Make a well in the centre and tip in the yogurt. Stir until evenly combined, but do not overmix.
3 Spoon the cobbler mixture on to the fruit and mascarpone. Bake for 20 minutes until the topping is risen and golden and the filling is bubbling.

■ Per serving 323 kcalories, protein 5g, carbohydrate 49g, fat 13g, saturated fat 8g, fibre 2g, added sugar 17g, salt 0.66g

Baked plums with mascarpone

An irresistible combination, perfect for cheering up cold winter days.

■ **Takes 1 hour** ■ **Serves 6**

400g tub mascarpone
2 tbsp icing sugar
50g/2oz golden caster sugar
4 clementines
175ml/6fl oz madeira
900g/2lb plums, halved and stoned

1 Heat the oven to 200C/180C fan/gas 6. Beat the mascarpone and icing sugar until smooth. Put in a serving bowl. Cover. Chill.
2 Tip the caster sugar into a pan, add 300ml/½ pint water, the pared zest of one of the clementines and the juice of all four. Slowly bring to the boil and simmer for 5 minutes. Stir in the Madeira. Remove from the heat. Arrange the plums in a single layer in a roasting tin, cut side up. Drizzle with the Madeira syrup. Bake, uncovered, for 10–12 minutes until just tender.
3 Lift the plums out of the cooking liquid with a slotted spoon and put them in a serving dish. Put the roasting tin on the hob, bring the liquid to the boil and simmer until lightly syrupy – about 10 minutes. Pour the syrup over the plums, leaving the zest behind in the tin. Serve warm, with the mascarpone.

■ Per serving 457 kcalories, protein 3g, carbohydrate 35g, fat 31g, saturated fat 19g, fibre 3g, added sugar 14g, salt 0.19g

Hot clementines with brandy sauce

You can get the clementines ready before the meal. Simply reheat them gently just before serving.

■ **Takes 20 minutes** ■ **Serves 4**

25g/1oz butter
2 tbsp light muscovado sugar
150ml/¼ pint smooth orange juice from
  a carton
6 clementines, peeled and halved
  horizontally
3 tbsp brandy
good-quality vanilla ice cream and thin,
  crisp biscuits, to serve

1 Melt the butter in a heavy-based frying pan, sprinkle in the sugar and stir well until dissolved, then pour in the orange juice and boil for 2–3 minutes until beginning to go syrupy.
2 Add the clementines and brandy, and boil for 3–5 minutes, spooning the sauce over until it is really syrupy.
3 To serve, put 3 clementine halves on four dessert plates, spoon the sauce over and finish with a scoop of ice cream with a biscuit broken over the top. Serve at once.

■ Per serving 142 kcalories, protein 1g, carbohydrate 17g, fat 5g, saturated fat 3g, fibre 1g, added sugar 6g, salt 0.14g

TOP: Apple and blueberry cobbler

BOTTOM LEFT: Baked plums with mascarpone

BOTTOM RIGHT: Hot clementines with brandy sauce

TOP: Cinnamon
blueberry tart

BOTTOM LEFT: Apricot
crème brûlée tart

BOTTOM RIGHT: Strawberry
toffee tart

Cinnamon blueberry tart

This has got to be the simplest summer tart ever – a must for anyone who loves blueberries.

■ **Takes 30 minutes** ■ **Serves 6–8**

2 tsp ground cinnamon
6 tbsp golden caster sugar
375g pack ready-made shortcrust pastry
200g tub soft cheese
finely grated zest and juice 1 orange
2 tbsp icing sugar, plus extra for dusting
2 × 150g punnets blueberries

1 Heat the oven to 200C/180C fan/gas 6. Line a baking sheet with baking parchment. Mix the cinnamon and caster sugar. Scatter the cinnamon sugar over a work surface, then roll out the pastry on top of the sugar, to the thickness of 2 x £1 coins. Using a large dinner plate, cut out a round, about 23cm, and lift onto the baking sheet. Prick the pastry all over with a fork and crimp round the edge with finger and thumb. Chill for 15 minutes.
2 Bake the pastry for 10–12 minutes until dry and biscuity. Cool, then transfer to a plate.
3 Beat the soft cheese with the orange juice and zest. Stir in the icing sugar. Spread this over the pastry base, leaving a 2.5cm border around the edge. Top with the blueberries and dust with extra icing sugar. Serve.

■ Per serving (6) 487 kcalories, protein 6g, carbohydrate 56g, fat 28g, saturated fat 15g, fibre 2.1g, added sugar 22.7g, salt 0.54g

Apricot crème brûlée tart

Don't be put off by the long method and cooking time – you'll adore the sensational flavours.

■ **Takes a staggered 3 hours** ■ **Serves 10**

140g/5oz butter
100g/4oz golden caster sugar
250g/9oz plain flour
25g/1oz ground almonds
1 egg, beaten

FOR THE FILLING
250g pack ready-to-eat dried apricots
175ml/6fl oz sweet dessert wine such as Sauternes
100g/4oz golden caster sugar, plus 4 tbsp to brûlée
284ml pot double cream
1 vanilla pod, split and seeds scraped
4 eggs, whisked

1 Beat the butter and sugar until pale. Mix in the flour, almonds and egg to make a dough. Wrap and chill for 30 minutes. Put the apricots in a bowl. Bring the wine and sugar to a boil in a pan, pour over the apricots and set aside. Bring the cream and vanilla to a boil in a clean pan. Remove from the heat and leave to infuse. Heat oven to 220C/200C fan/gas 7.
2 Roll the pastry to line a 23cm fluted tart tin. Freeze for 10 minutes. Cook for 20 minutes with foil and beans, 5 minutes without. Remove. Reduce oven to 160C/140C fan/gas 3.
3 Strain the vanilla mix over the eggs. Whisk. Drain the apricots. Stir the liquid into the eggs. Pull the apricots apart. Put the sticky sides down on the pastry. Pour the egg mix over. Bake for 30 minutes until set. Cool. Scatter the rest of the sugar over. Caramelise with a blowtorch.

■ Per serving 510 kcalories, protein 8g, carbohydrate 52g, fat 30g, saturated fat 17g, fibre 3g, added sugar 20g, salt 0.42g

Strawberry toffee tart

It's so easy to make this deconstructed strawberry tart. If you can't get strawberries, try other summer berries, or use sliced peaches or nectarines instead.

■ **Takes 45 minutes** ■ **Serves 6**

175g/6oz crunchy biscuits, such as Hobnobs
85g/3oz butter, melted
400g/14oz strawberries
284ml pot double cream
200g pot Greek yogurt
5 soft toffees (such as Werther's Original)
icing sugar, for dusting

1 Line a 20cm flan tin with baking parchment. Put the biscuits in a strong food bag and bash with a rolling pin to crush them finely. Tip into a bowl and mix in the melted butter. Press over the base of the tin. Chill for about 30 minutes until it feels firm. Slice or halve the strawberries, depending on their size.
2 Remove the biscuit base from the flan tin and slide it on to a flat serving plate. Whip the cream, reserving 2 tablespoons, until it just holds its shape in soft folds. Fold in the yogurt, then spoon over the biscuit base and pile on the strawberries.
3 Melt the toffees and reserved cream in the microwave on Medium for 30 seconds–1 minute, then stir until they form a sauce. Drizzle over the tart. Dust with icing sugar before serving.

■ Per serving 559 kcalories, protein 6g, carbohydrate 32g, fat 46g, saturated fat 24g, fibre 2g, added sugar 12g, salt 0.75g

Caramelized passion fruit and lime tart

This zingy tart has a wonderful flavour and is a great way to cook with passion fruit.

■ **Takes 1¼ hours, plus cooling**
■ **Serves 8**

500g pack dessert pastry
8 passion fruit
finely grated zest and juice of 1 lime
200g/8oz golden caster sugar
6 egg yolks
142ml pot double cream
icing sugar, for dusting (optional)

1 Roll out the pastry and line a 23cm tart case, then chill for at least 20 minutes. Heat the oven to 180C/160C fan/gas 4. Line the tart with baking parchment and baking beans, then bake for 15 minutes. Remove the parchment, bake for a further 5–10 minutes or until golden, then remove from the oven and turn it down to 140C/120C fan/gas 1.
2 Cut the passion fruit in half, scoop out the flesh into a bowl, then blitz with a hand blender. Push the pulp through a sieve and mix with the lime zest and juice. Beat the sugar and egg yolks until pale, then beat in the cream and fruit juice. Carefully pour into the tart case, then bake for 40 minutes or until set with a very slight wobble. Remove from the oven, then leave to cool completely.
3 Serve the tart as it is, or dust the top with icing sugar and caramelize the sugar using a blowtorch.

■ Per serving 546 kcalories, protein 6g, carbohydrate 57g, fat 34g, saturated fat 13g, fibre 2g, sugar 34g, salt 0.36g

Chocolate tart with raspberries

Prepare this dessert up to a day ahead. It's lovely to make and even better to eat.

■ **Takes 1½ hours, plus chilling** ■ **Serves 6–8**

FOR THE PASTRY
100g/4oz plain flour
50g/2oz ground almonds
85g/3oz butter, cut into small pieces
25g/1oz golden caster sugar
1 egg yolk

FOR THE FILLING
150g bar dark chocolate, in pieces
2 egg whites
100g/4oz golden caster sugar
142ml pot double cream
2 tbsp brandy or Tia Maria

TO SERVE
284ml pot double cream, whipped
300g/10oz raspberries
125g punnet blueberries
icing sugar, for dusting

1 Put the flour, almonds and butter in a processor and process into crumbs. Add the sugar, egg yolk and 1 tablespoon cold water. Wrap in cling film. Chill for 15–20 minutes.
2 Heat the oven to 190C/170C fan/gas 5. Roll out the dough and use to line a 24cm flan tin. Bake blind (with foil and beans) for 15 minutes, then remove the foil and beans and cook for 7–10 minutes more. Cool.
3 For the filling, melt the chocolate in a microwave. Put the egg whites and sugar in a bowl over a pan of simmering water. Whisk for 5 minutes until thick and glossy. Remove from the heat and whisk for 2 more minutes. Fold in the chocolate, cream and brandy or Tia Maria. Pour into the pastry case. Chill until set, then serve with the whipped cream, berries and icing sugar.

■ Per serving (6) 794 kcalories, protein 8g, carbohydrate 59g, fat 59g, saturated fat 34g, fibre 3g, added sugar 39g, salt 0.42g

Apricot and almond bistro tart

You do need to stone the apricots here, but after that everything is easy. The icing sugar caramelises deliciously over the fruit.

■ **Takes 30–40 minutes** ■ **Serves 8**

370g pack ready-rolled puff pastry
50g/2oz ground almonds
900g/2lb ripe fresh apricots, halved and stoned
2 tbsp icing sugar
maple syrup and clotted or single cream, to serve (optional)

1 Heat the oven to 220C/200C fan/gas 7. Unroll the pastry on to a lightly dampened baking sheet (this creates steam, which helps puff up the pastry), then sprinkle over the ground almonds. Lay the apricot halves over the top, nestling them close together, right up to the edge of the pastry.
2 Dust with the icing sugar and bake for 20–25 minutes until the sugar starts to caramelise a little.
3 If you like, drizzle with maple syrup and serve hot, warm or cold. If you really want to indulge, serve with a spoonful of clotted cream or a pouring of single cream.

■ Per serving 258 kcalories, protein 5g, carbohydrate 29g, fat 14g, saturated fat none, fibre 2g, added sugar 4g, salt 0.37g

TOP: Caramelized passion fruit and lime tart

BOTTOM LEFT: Chocolate tart with raspberries

BOTTOM RIGHT: Apricot and almond bistro tart

TOP: Flat apple and vanilla tart

BOTTOM LEFT: Rhubarb and custard pie

BOTTOM RIGHT: Tarte Tatin with brandy cream

Flat apple and vanilla tart

Vanilla sugar is widely used in France to give a subtle flavour to baking and desserts. You'll find it with the baking ingredients in supermarkets.

■ **Takes 25–30 minutes** ■ **Serves 6**

375g pack puff pastry, preferably all-butter
5 large eating apples – Cox's, russets
    or Elstar
juice of 1 lemon
25g/1oz butter, cut into small pieces
3 tsp vanilla sugar or 1 tsp vanilla extract
1 tbsp caster sugar
3 rounded tbsp apricot conserve
vanilla ice cream or crème fraîche, to serve

1 Heat the oven to 220C/200C fan/gas 7. Roll out the pastry and trim to a round about 35cm across. Transfer to a baking sheet lined with parchment paper.
2 Peel, core and thinly slice the apples and toss in the lemon juice. Spread over the pastry to within 2cm of the edge. Curl up the edge slightly to stop the juices running off.
3 Dot the top with the butter and sprinkle with the vanilla and caster sugar. Bake for 15–20 minutes until the apples are tender and the pastry crisp.
4 Warm the conserve (you can sieve it, if you like) and brush over the apples and pastry edge. Serve hot with vanilla ice cream or crème fraîche.

■ Per serving 356 kcalories, protein 4g, carbohydrate 47g, fat 18g, saturated fat 8g, fibre 2g, added sugar 10.7g, salt 0.58g

Rhubarb and custard pie

This is a great mix of two classic rhubarb puds. It's particularly good served warm with chilled crème fraîche or single cream.

■ **Takes 1¾–2 hours** ■ **Serves 8**

350g/12oz rhubarb, cut into bite-sized pieces
100g/4oz golden caster sugar
350g pack sweet shortcrust pastry
1 egg and 1 egg yolk
1 tsp vanilla extract
1 tbsp plain flour
284ml pot single cream

FOR THE TOPPING
50g/2oz butter, melted
50g/2oz demerara sugar
50g/2oz porridge oats
½ tsp ground ginger

1 Put the rhubarb in a frying pan with half the sugar. Warm until the sugar dissolves. Tip into a bowl and cool. Heat the oven to 180C/160C fan/gas 4. Roll the pastry quite thinly and line a deep, loose-based 24cm fluted flan tin. Bake blind for 20 minutes until the pastry is pale golden.
2 Beat together the egg and egg yolk, vanilla extract, remaining caster sugar and flour. Gradually whisk in the cream with a spoonful or two of juice from the rhubarb. Spoon the rhubarb into the pastry case and pour the cream mixture over. Turn up the oven to 200C/180C fan/gas 6 and bake for 20 minutes, or until the custard is lightly set.
3 Mix the topping ingredients and sprinkle over the top of the pie. Return the pie to the oven for 15 minutes until the top is golden and the custard just set.

■ Per serving 456 kcalories, protein 6g, carbohydrate 49g, fat 28g, saturated fat 13g, fibre 2g, added sugar 24g, salt 0.43g

Tarte Tatin with brandy cream

This updated version of the original apple recipe couldn't be simpler – it uses ready-rolled pastry so you don't even need a rolling pin.

■ **Takes 50 minutes** ■ **Serves 4**

50g/2oz butter
50g/2oz golden caster sugar
½ tsp ground cinnamon
6 medium Cox's or Egremont Russet apples,
    peeled, quartered and cored
375g pack fresh ready-rolled puff pastry

FOR THE BRANDY CREAM
200ml pot crème fraîche
2 tbsp icing sugar
1 tbsp brandy or calvados

1 Heat the oven to 220C/200C fan/gas 7. Melt the butter in a 20cm tarte tatin tin over a medium heat on the hob. Stir in the sugar and heat until starting to caramelise. Stir in the cinnamon. Pile in the apples and cook over a medium heat for about 10 minutes, stirring occasionally, until thickened and saucy. Remove from the heat.
2 Unroll the pastry. Prick it all over with a fork. Lay the pastry over the apples. Trim off any excess, leaving a 2cm rim. Tuck the pastry round the apples, down the inside of the tin. Bake for 20–30 minutes until risen and golden.
3 Mix the ingredients for the brandy cream. When the tart is cooked, leave in the tin for 5 minutes, then run the blade of a knife around the edge. Invert a plate on top and turn out the tart and juices. Serve with the brandy cream.

■ Per serving 761 kcalories, protein 8g, carbohydrate 77g, fat 48g, saturated fat 15g, fibre 3g, added sugar 21g, salt 1.12g

Limoncello plum tart

You can prepare this melt-in-the-mouth pud the morning or afternoon before you intend to serve it.

■ **Takes 1–1¼ hours** ■ **Serves 12**

500g pack ready-made shortcrust pastry
zest and juice of 2 unwaxed lemons
4 tbsp double cream
100g pack ground almonds
200g/8oz golden caster sugar
5 eggs
100g/4oz butter, melted
8 tbsp limoncello liqueur
6 plums, stoned and cut into wedges
icing sugar, to dust

1 Roll out the pastry and use to line a loose-bottomed tart tin, 25cm in diameter and about 3–4cm deep. Chill for at least 30 minutes.
2 Heat the oven to 180C/160C fan/gas 4. Line the pastry with foil, fill with baking beans and bake blind for 15 minutes. Remove beans and foil.
3 Put the lemon zest and juice, cream, almonds, sugar, eggs and melted butter in a large bowl and whisk until smooth, then stir in the limoncello. Put the plums in the pastry case, then pour the custard mixture over. Bake for about 20–30 minutes until the custard is just set. Allow to cool, then dredge with icing sugar before serving.

■ Per serving 924 kcalories, protein 14g, carbohydrate 83g, fat 57g, saturated fat 25g, fibre 4g, added sugar 38g, salt 0.86g

Treacle tart hearts

Make a sweet heart for your sweetheart – it doesn't matter if it's not Valentine's Day!

■ **Takes 45 minutes** ■ **Makes 8**

200g/8oz cold unsalted butter, cubed
350g/12oz plain flour, plus extra for rolling
½ tsp ground ginger (optional)
100g/4oz golden caster sugar
1 egg yolk

FOR THE FILLING
400g/14oz golden syrup
zest of 1 lemon and juice of ½
100g/4oz white breadcrumbs

1 Blitz the butter, flour and ginger (if using) to fine crumbs in a food processor. Stir in the sugar. Add the egg yolk and 2 teaspoons cold water. Pulse until the dough clumps together. Turn out on to a floured surface. Press into a round and chill, wrapped in clingfilm for 30 minutes.
2 Roll the pastry to the thickness of two £1 coins and stamp out eight 11cm circles. Line eight 10cm-wide heart-shaped tins with pastry. Re-roll the trimmings and stamp out eight small hearts. Chill the tins and hearts for 15 minutes or until firm. Heat the oven to 170C/150C fan/gas 3. Put in a baking sheet.
3 Stir the syrup, lemon juice and zest together. Divide the breadcrumbs among the tins. Spoon over the syrup slowly. Top with the hearts. Put the tins on to the hot sheet. Bake for 25 minutes or until the pastry is golden. Cool for 15 minutes, then turn out on to a wire rack. Serve just warm.

■ Per tart 452 kcalories, protein 5g, carbohydrate 78g, fat 16g, saturated fat 10g, fibre 2g, sugar 47g, salt 0.59g

Deep-filled Bramley apple pie

Everyone loves good old-fashioned apple pie, served just warm with cream or ice cream.

■ **Takes 1 hour 10 minutes** ■ **Serves 8**

5 tbsp brandy
200g/8oz sultanas
2 x 375g packs all-butter shortcrust pastry, squashed together
plain flour, for dusting
5 medium Bramley apples, peeled, cored and finely sliced
¼ tsp each ground cinnamon, nutmeg and allspice
140g/5oz golden caster sugar
1 egg, beaten with a splash of milk
vanilla ice cream or clotted cream, to serve

1 Heat the oven to 200C/180C fan/gas 6. Heat sultanas with the brandy in the microwave until plump. Cut off one-third of the pastry, dust the surface with flour, then roll the rest into a large circle and use to line a 23cm shallow, springform cake tin, overhanging the rim. Chill.
2 Toss the apples with the sultanas, spices and all but 2 tablespoons sugar. Roll out the rest of the pastry, then cut it into a circle, using the base of the tin as a guide. Arrange the apple in the tin. Cover with the pastry and tuck down the sides. Fold the overhanging pastry back over and pinch to seal. Brush with egg, slash the top and sprinkle with sugar.
3 Bake for 30–35 minutes or until golden. Cool for 1 hour, then run a knife around the pie's edge. Unclip the side of the tin and remove the pie.

■ Per serving 646 kcalories, protein 8g, carbohydrate 93g, fat 27g, saturated fat 11g, fibre 4g, sugar 48g, salt 1g

TOP: Limoncello plum tart

BOTTOM LEFT: Treacle tart hearts

BOTTOM RIGHT: Deep-filled Bramley apple pie

TOP: Apricot and pistachio pavlova

BOTTOM LEFT: Pear and chocolate pavlovas

BOTTOM RIGHT: Strawberries and cream meringue cake

Apricot and pistachio pavlova

Pavlovas are always popular. This is the one to try if you're looking for a fresh idea – it's simply bursting with Mediterranean flavours.

■ **Takes 1¾–2 hours, plus cooling** ■ **Serves 6**

2 tsp cornflour
2 tsp vanilla extract
2 tsp white wine or cider vinegar
300g/10oz golden caster sugar
5 egg whites, whisked until stiff
50g/2oz shelled pistachio nuts, roughly chopped
650g/1lb 7oz ripe fresh apricots
3 tbsp Cointreau or other orange-flavoured liqueur
4 tbsp icing sugar, plus extra to taste
568ml pot double cream, lightly whipped

1 Heat the oven to 140C/120C fan/gas 1. Line a baking sheet with non-stick parchment. Mix the cornflour, vanilla extract and vinegar. In separate bowls, slowly whisk in the sugar with the eggs until thick. Whisk in the cornflour paste.
2 Spoon the mixture on to the paper. Spread to a 23cm round. Swirl the edges. Scatter half the pistachios over and bake for 1 hour, until crisp. Turn off the oven and leave the pavlova to cool with the oven door open.
3 Reserve 450g/1lb of the apricots. Roughly chop and purée the rest then push them through a sieve. Stir in the liqueur and add icing sugar to taste. Spoon the cream over the pavlova. Slice the reserved apricots and scatter over the cream with the remaining pistachios. Dust with icing sugar and serve with the apricot purée.

■ Per serving 789 kcalories, protein 7g, carbohydrate 78g, fat 50g, saturated fat 29g, fibre 2g, added sugar 65g, salt 0.26g

Pear and chocolate pavlovas

These dinky pavlovas are sure to prove a family favourite.

■ **Takes 1½ hours** ■ **Serves 8**

2 medium egg whites
175g/6oz caster sugar
1 tsp cornflour
½ tsp white wine vinegar

FOR THE PEARS
8 small pears, peeled
2 tbsp clear honey
300ml/½ pint apple juice
1 cinnamon stick

FOR THE CHOCOLATE SAUCE
142ml pot double cream
100g bar dark chocolate, broken into pieces

FOR THE FILLING
284ml pot whipping cream
200g/8oz half-fat Greek yogurt

1 Heat the oven to 140C/120C fan/gas 1. Line two large baking sheets with parchment. Whisk the egg whites until stiff. Slowly whisk in the sugar until stiff. Beat in the cornflour and the vinegar. Spoon 8 mounds on the parchment. Spread each to a 9cm circle, with a dip in the centre. Bake for 40–50 minutes until crisp. Remove the paper and cool.
2 Scoop out the cores from the pears, leaving the stalks on. Fit the pears in a pan. Add the honey, apple juice and cinnamon. Boil, reduce the heat, cover and simmer for 35–40 minutes. Remove the lid, increase the heat and bubble briefly to a glaze then allow to cool.
3 Melt the chocolate and cream in a pan to make a sauce. For the filling, stir the cream and yogurt until thick. Top the meringues with the filling, pears and sauce.

■ Per serving 441 kcalories, protein 4.9g, carbohydrate 43g, fat 28.9g, saturated fat 17.5g, fibre 1.8g, added sugar 28.2g, salt 0.18g

Strawberries and cream meringue cake

An unusual pudding, where the sponge and meringue bake together.

■ **Takes 1¼ hours** ■ **Serves 8**

FOR THE CAKE
100g/4oz butter, at room temperature, plus extra for greasing
100g/4oz golden caster sugar
1 egg, plus 2 egg yolks (keep the whites for the meringue)
85g/3oz self-raising flour
25g/1oz shelled pistachios, finely ground
2 tbsp milk

FOR THE MERINGUE
2 egg whites
100g/4oz golden caster sugar

FOR THE TOPPING
284ml pot double cream, softly whipped
200g/8oz strawberries, hulled, sliced or left whole

1 Heat the oven to 180C/160C fan/gas 4. For the cake, butter and line the base of a 20cm-round, loose-bottomed tin with greaseproof paper. Beat the butter and sugar for 3–4 minutes until pale and creamy. Beat in the egg and egg yolks. Gently stir in the flour and nuts alternately with the milk. Spoon into the tin and level it smooth.
2 Make the meringue. Whisk the egg whites until stiff. Whisk in the sugar, a couple of spoonfuls at a time, until smooth and glossy. Spoon into the tin and spread it evenly. Bake for 45 minutes until the meringue feels crisp.
3 Leave in the tin to cool, then loosen the edges with a knife and remove. Peel off the paper and leave until cold. Spoon the cream over the meringue, then the strawberries and serve straight away.

■ Per serving 446 kcalories, protein 5g, carbohydrate 37g, fat 32g, saturated fat 18g, fibre 1g, added sugar 26g, salt 0.46g

TOP: Poached pears with blackberries

BOTTOM LEFT: Hot chocolate soufflés

BOTTOM RIGHT: Cappuccino tiramisu

Poached pears with blackberries

For a special occasion, substitute half the apple juice with 150ml/¼ pint red wine.

■ **Takes 40 minutes** ■ **Serves 4**

4 medium pears
zest of 1 lemon (peel off with a potato peeler)
1 tbsp lemon juice
250g/9oz blackberries
300ml/½ pint unsweetened apple juice
50g/2oz golden caster sugar
8 tbsp 0% fat natural Greek yogurt

1 Peel the pears but don't remove their stalks. Place the pears in a pan with the lemon zest and juice, half the blackberries, the apple juice and caster sugar. Heat until simmering, then cover and cook gently for 20–25 minutes until the pears are tender, turning them once.
2 Remove the pears from the liquid and cool for a few minutes. Halve each, core with a teaspoon or melon baller, and transfer to four dishes.
3 Strain the liquid through a sieve, into a pan. Add the remaining blackberries and warm gently. Serve the pears and blackberries with the yogurt.

■ Per serving 180 kcalories, protein 5g, carbohydrate 41g, fat none, saturated fat none, fibre 5g, added sugar 13g, salt trace

Hot chocolate soufflés

Always a popular pudding, but such a simple method!

■ **Takes 1 hour** ■ **Serves 6**

butter, for greasing
2 tbsp ground almonds
150g bar dark chocolate, broken into pieces
4 tbsp strong black coffee, Tia Maria or Frangelico
2 tsp plain flour
100g/4oz golden caster sugar
4 eggs, separated
6 scoops good-quality vanilla ice cream

FOR THE SAUCE
142ml pot double cream
100g/4oz dark chocolate, broken into pieces
2 tbsp strong black coffee, Tia Maria or Frangelico

1 Heat the oven to 190C/170C fan/gas 5. Butter six 200ml ramekin dishes. Dust the insides with ground almonds. Melt the chocolate with the coffee or liqueur in a pan, stir until smooth and leave to cool slightly.
2 Stir the flour, half the sugar and the egg yolks into the melted chocolate. Whisk the egg whites to soft peaks. Whisk in the remaining sugar, until the mix is thick. Gently fold into the chocolate mixture in four batches. Divide among the ramekins.
3 Bake for 15–25 minutes until risen and the crusts feel firm.
4 Meanwhile, make the sauce. Heat the cream in a small pan. When it simmers, remove from the heat and stir in the chocolate until smooth. Stir in the coffee or liqueur. Split the tops of the soufflés open, add a scoop of ice cream and a drizzle of sauce, and serve.

■ Per serving 503 kcalories, protein 10g, carbohydrate 39g, fat 35g, saturated fat 17g, fibre 3g, added sugar 28g, salt 0.17g

Cappuccino tiramisu

A quick way of turning a tub of ice cream into an indulgent treat.

■ **Takes 10 minutes** ■ **Serves 4**

8 sponge fingers
cold coffee, for soaking
142ml pot double cream
1 tbsp icing sugar
3 tbsp Baileys
8 scoops Baileys ice cream
1 chocolate flake

1 Halve the sponge fingers and press them into four glasses. Pour over enough cold coffee to soak the sponge. Whisk the cream with the icing sugar and the Baileys until it goes into soft peaks.
2 Spoon the ice cream into each glass, then top with the whipped Baileys cream.
3 Break up the chocolate flake and scatter over the cream to serve.

■ Per serving 566 kcalories, protein 7g, carbohydrate 40g, fat 42g, saturated fat 22.8g, fibre 0.2g, added sugar 30g, salt 0.27g

Blush meringues

Ideal for a girls' night in – try serving these with a glass of rosé wine or pink champagne.

■ **Takes 2 hours** ■ **Makes 9**

4 egg whites
edible pink food colouring
200g/8oz caster sugar

FOR THE FILLING
250g/9oz tub mascarpone
284ml pot double cream
1 tbsp icing sugar
couple of handfuls of fresh or frozen
    (thawed) mixed berries, lightly crushed

1 Heat the oven to 140C/120C fan/gas 1. Line two baking sheets with parchment. Whisk the egg whites and a generous dash of pink food colouring, until stiff. Continue whisking as you sprinkle in the sugar, a tablespoon at a time, then whisk until the mixture is thick and glossy.
2 Using two tablespoons, make 18 large 'quenelle' shapes, spaced well apart on the baking sheets. Bake for about 1½ hours until they are crisp and peel easily from the parchment. Cool in the oven for 30 minutes with the door slightly ajar.
3 Beat the mascarpone for the filling until smooth. Pour in the cream, add the sugar and whisk to soft peaks. Stir in the fruit lightly so it's rippled through the cream. Sandwich the meringues together with fruit cream and eat straight away.

■ Per meringue 380 kcalories, protein 3g, carbohydrate 25g, fat 30g, saturated fat 19g, fibre none, added sugar 24g, salt 0.3g

Lemon ice and minty strawberries

This is a really refreshing, palate-cleansing iced dessert – perfect for a hot, sunny day. And it contains absolutely no fat!

■ **Takes 30 minutes, plus freezing** ■ **Serves 4**

2 unwaxed lemons, each chopped into 8
140g/5oz golden caster sugar
400g/14oz strawberries, hulled and sliced
small handful of mint leaves, roughly
    chopped

1 Tip the lemons into a blender with the sugar and 500ml/18fl oz water. Blitz for a minute or two until the lemon is chopped to a pulp. Strain the juice into a shallowish freezer container, pressing down on the lemon pulp with the back of a spoon to release its flavour. Discard the pulp.
2 Reserve 2 tablespoons of the juice in a bowl. Cover the rest with cling film and freeze for 4 hours or until firm. When the lemon ice is frozen, break it into chunks and tip it back into the blender. Blitz until it's a smooth sorbet consistency. Tip it back into the freezer container and freeze for another 30 minutes to firm up.
3 While the ice is freezing, toss the strawberries and mint in the reserved lemon juice. When the ice is scoopable, spoon it into bowls and top with the strawberries.

■ Per serving 174 kcalories, protein 1g, carbohydrate 44g, fat none, saturated fat none, fibre 1g, added sugar 37g, salt 1.3g

Raspberry and amaretti crunch cake

If you're lucky enough to have any left over, this wonderfully moist cake is fantastic with coffee the next morning.

■ **Takes 1½ hours** ■ **Serves 6**

175g/6oz soft butter, plus extra for greasing
175g/6oz golden caster sugar
3 eggs
140g/5oz self-raising flour
85g/3oz ground almonds
140g/5oz amaretti biscuits, roughly broken
250g punnet raspberries
icing sugar, to dust
142ml pot single cream

1 Heat the oven to 160C/140C fan/gas 3. Butter and line the base of a loose-bottomed 20cm-round cake tin. Beat the butter, caster sugar, eggs, flour and ground almonds in a large bowl. Spread half the cake mixture into the lined tin and level. Scatter over half of the amaretti biscuits, then a third of the raspberries. Very lightly press into the cake mixture.
2 Dollop spoonfuls of the remaining cake mixture over the amaretti and raspberries and spread evenly. Scatter the remaining amaretti and half the remaining raspberries over the top. Bake for 55–60 minutes, until a skewer inserted into the centre comes out clean.
3 Cool for 15 minutes in the tin then run a knife round the edge and turn out on to a plate. Serve warm or cooled, lightly dusted with icing sugar, with the remaining raspberries and some single cream.

■ Per serving 640 kcalories, protein 12g, carbohydrate 68g, fat 37g, saturated fat 17g, fibre 4g, added sugar

TOP: Blush meringues

BOTTOM LEFT: Lemon ice and minty strawberries

BOTTOM RIGHT: Raspberry and amaretti crunch cake

TOP: Strawberry and cream layer

BOTTOM LEFT: Blueberry, coconut and lime ice cream

BOTTOM RIGHT: Creamy saffron yogurt

Strawberry and cream layer

Turn strawberries and cream into a pudding to remember with the simple addition of puff pastry sheets. Perfect for a sunny summer's day.

■ **Takes 35 minutes** ■ **Serves 4**

375g block all-butter puff pastry
4 tbsp icing sugar
400g/14oz ripe strawberries, halved
   or quartered
1 vanilla pod or 1 tsp vanilla extract
284ml pot double cream
140g/5oz golden caster sugar

1 Heat the oven to 220C/200C fan/gas 7. Roll out the pastry to a 30cm square. Lay it on a large baking sheet, place another sheet on top and bake for about 20 minutes or until golden.
2 Heat the grill to high, dust the pastry liberally with some of the icing sugar and carefully caramelize under the grill. Dust with another layer of icing sugar and return to the grill to caramelize again. While warm, cut the pastry into 12 neat rectangles, trimming the edges as you go.
3 Dust the strawberries with the remaining icing sugar and set aside. Split the vanilla pod and scrape the seeds into the cream, then whip lightly with the caster sugar until it just holds its shape.
4 To assemble, place a blob of vanilla cream on each plate and stack the biscuits, the remaining vanilla cream and strawberries at jaunty angles.

■ Per serving 931 kcalories, protein 7g, carbohydrate 96g, fat 60g, saturated fat 30g, fibre 1g, sugar 62g, salt 0.81g

Blueberry, coconut and lime ice cream

You can store this ice cream for up to 1 month in the freezer.

■ **Takes 20–25 minutes, plus freezing**
■ **Serves 4–6**

2 limes
140g/5oz golden caster sugar
125g punnet blueberries
200ml pot coconut cream
284ml pot double cream
extra blueberries and lime wedges,
   to serve

1 Finely grate the zest from one of the limes. Squeeze the juice from both. Put in a small pan with the sugar. Heat gently, stirring to dissolve the sugar. Add the blueberries and simmer for 2 minutes, until the skins start to split.
2 Pour the blueberry mixture into a bowl. Stir in the coconut cream. Cool. In a separate bowl, whip the cream until it just holds its shape, then gradually stir in the blueberry mixture. Put the bowl in the freezer for about 1 hour, until the mixture is set about 3cm in from the edges.
3 Remove from the freezer and whisk it all together. When it's fairly smooth, return to the freezer for 1 hour. Repeat the whisking. Transfer the ice cream to a rigid container, cover and freeze until firm. Before serving, move to the fridge for 30 minutes to soften. Serve with the extra blueberries and lime wedges.

■ Per serving (6) 429 kcalories, protein 3g, carbohydrate 29g, fat 35g, saturated fat 24g, fibre 1g, added sugar 25g, salt 0.05g

Creamy saffron yogurt

You'll love the flavours and textures of this healthy, but creamy Indian dessert.

■ **Takes 35 minutes** ■ **Serves 6**

700g/1lb 9oz 0% fat Greek yogurt
2 tsp green cardamom pods, seeds removed
100g/4oz golden caster sugar
8–10 saffron strands
1 tsp milk
1 tbsp shelled pistachios, slivered, to
   decorate
sliced ripe mango, to serve

1 Place a piece of muslin or thick kitchen paper in a large sieve set over a large bowl. Spoon the yogurt into the sieve, cover with another piece of muslin or 2 sheets of kitchen paper and set aside at room temperature for 25–30 minutes (to remove excess moisture).
2 Crush the cardamom seeds using a pestle and mortar – you will need 1 teaspoon ground cardamom. Lift off and discard the top layer of muslin or paper from the yogurt, then scrape the yogurt into a bowl and stir in the sugar.
3 Mix the saffron strands with the milk and add to the yogurt with the ground cardamom. Stir well for a few minutes. Divide among six small glasses and scatter over the pistachios. Serve at room temperature, with fresh mango slices on the side.

■ Per serving 133 kcalories, protein 12g, carbohydrate 23g, fat none, saturated fat none, fibre none, added sugar 17.5g, salt 0.21g

Easy chocolate drop cakes

These generous cupcakes will be a hit with kids and grown-ups alike and are ideal for a birthday party or other celebration.

■ **Takes 30 minutes** ■ **Makes 12 large or 24 small**

150ml carton natural yogurt
3 eggs, beaten
1 tsp vanilla extract
175g/6oz golden caster sugar
140g/5oz self-raising flour, minus 1 tbsp
1 tbsp cocoa powder
1 tsp baking powder
100g/4oz ground almonds
175g/6oz unsalted butter, melted
12 chocolate buttons (optional), to decorate

FOR THE CHOCOLATE FROSTING
100g/4oz dark chocolate
140g/5oz unsalted butter
140g/5oz icing sugar

1 Line a 12-hole muffin tin or two 12-hole bun tins with paper cases and heat the oven to 190C/170C fan/gas 5. Mix the yogurt, eggs and vanilla extract. Put the dry ingredients into a large bowl, with a pinch of salt, and make a well in the middle.
2 Add the yogurty mix and the melted butter, and quickly fold in using a spatula or metal spoon – don't overwork it. Spoon the mixture into the cases (they will be quite full) then bake for 18–20 minutes, if you're making the larger cakes; 12–15 minutes if you're making smaller ones, or until risen and springy to the touch. Cool for a few minutes in the tin, then lift the cakes on to a wire rack to cool completely.
3 Beat the frosting ingredients together until smooth, spread on to the cakes then top with a chocolate button, if using.

■ Per large cupcake (with button) 492 kcalories, protein 6g, carbohydrate 47g, fat 32g, saturated fat 17g, fibre 1g, sugar 38g, salt 0.32g

Strawberry vanilla shortcakes

Strawberries and cream is always a winning combination, but it is especially so on these decadent summer shortcakes. The bases are a little like scones, but lighter and crisper around the edges.

■ **Takes 30 minutes** ■ **Makes 8**

350g/12oz self-raising flour, plus extra for dusting
100g/4oz butter, cold and cubed
100g/4oz caster sugar
1 vanilla pod, seeds scraped and reserved
100ml/3½fl oz milk, warmed
1 egg, plus a little extra beaten egg to glaze
squeeze of fresh lemon juice

FOR THE TOPPING
227g carton clotted cream
strawberry jam
250g/9oz strawberries, thickly sliced

1 Heat the oven to 220C/200C fan/ gas 7. Lightly flour a baking sheet. Put the flour, butter, sugar, half the vanilla seeds and ¼ teaspoon of salt into a processor and pulse until fine. Tip into a large bowl. Beat the milk, egg and lemon juice together, tip into the dry mix and bring to a clumpy dough using a knife.
2 Lightly flour the work surface then shape the dough into a smoothish disc. Cut out eight rounds using a 7cm cutter (you'll need to pinch together the trimmings). Glaze the tops only with the beaten egg, lift on to the baking sheet and bake for 10–12 minutes or until risen and golden. Cool on a wire rack.
3 Beat the remaining vanilla seeds into the cream (it will go runny then get thicker again). Cut the very top off each shortcake and top with jam, the vanilla cream and a mound of strawberries.

■ Per shortcake 502 kcalories, protein 6g, carbohydrate 55g, fat 30g, saturated fat 18g, fibre 2g, sugar 22g, salt 0.82g

Crumbly cinnamon and chocolate squares

The subtle combination of chocolate and spices makes these blissful bites a heavenly treat.

■ **Takes 1 hour 10 minutes** ■ **Serves 15**

175g/6oz butter, at room temperature, cubed
200g/8oz golden caster sugar
175g/6oz plain flour
3 eggs
3 tbsp milk
1 tsp baking powder

FOR THE TOPPING
100g/4oz dark chocolate, roughly chopped
1 tsp ground cinnamon
100g/4oz light muscovado sugar
85g/3oz chopped mixed nuts

1 Heat the oven to 180C/160C fan/gas 4. Line the base of an 18 x 27cm cake tin with greaseproof paper. Put the cake ingredients into a large mixing bowl, then beat with an electric hand mixer until well blended and creamy.
2 Tip the mixture into the cake tin, spread evenly right into the corners, then scatter the chocolate on top. Mix the remaining topping ingredients and scatter over the top of the chocolate. Lightly press to compact the mixture, then bake for 40 minutes or until risen and firm to the touch. Cool in the tin before cutting into 15 squares.

■ Per square 294 kcalories, protein 4g, carbohydrate 35g, fat 16g, saturated fat 8g, fibre 1g, added sugar 25g, salt 0.39g

TOP: Easy chocolate drop cakes

BOTTOM LEFT: Strawberry vanilla shortcakes

BOTTOM RIGHT: Crumbly cinnamon and chocolate squares

TOP: Choc and nut caramel slice

BOTTOM LEFT: Clotted cream splits

BOTTOM RIGHT: Easter egg cupcakes

Choc and nut caramel slice

A dark-chocolate topping gives this classic tray bake a grown-up twist.

- **Takes 1 hour 20 minutes, plus chilling**
- **Serves 16**

175g/6oz plain flour
25g/1oz cornflour
50g/2oz golden caster sugar
85g/3oz whole blanched almonds, toasted and finely chopped
140g/5oz unsalted butter, cold and cut into cubes
seeds from 1 vanilla pod

FOR THE CARAMEL
225g/8oz golden caster sugar
142ml pot single cream
50g/2oz butter, cubed

FOR THE TOPPING
200g bar dark chocolate (70% cocoa solids)
85g/3oz butter

1 Heat the oven to 160C/140C fan/gas 3 and lightly butter a 20 x 23cm shallow baking tin. Sift the flours together, stir in the sugar, almonds and a pinch of salt. Rub in the butter and vanilla seeds to make fine crumbs. Press the mix into the tin. Put the tin in the freezer for 5 minutes. Bake for 35–40 minutes then allow to cool.
2 For the caramel, put the sugar and 100ml/3½fl oz water in a heavy-based pan, heat gently until the sugar dissolves, then turn up the heat until it turns a very dark amber. Stir in the cream in four additions until smooth. Stir in the butter and half a teaspoon salt. Pour over the shortbread and cool.
3 For the topping, melt the chocolate and butter together, then pour over the caramel and smooth with the back of a spoon. Chill until firm, for at least 30 minutes, before cutting into 16 slices.

- Per serving 358 kcalories, protein 4g, carbohydrate 34g, fat 24g, saturated fat 13g, fibre 2g, sugar 22g, salt 0.15g

Clotted cream splits

You'll have some clotted cream left over if you make only 12 cakes, but it's not hard to find a reason to finish off the pot!

- **Takes 30 minutes ■ Makes 12**

150ml pot natural yogurt
3 eggs, beaten
1 tsp vanilla extract
175g/6oz golden caster sugar
140g/5oz self-raising flour
1 tsp baking powder
100g/4oz ground almonds
175g/6oz unsalted butter, melted

TO SERVE
Jar raspberry jam
100g/4oz raspberries
550g pot clotted cream
icing sugar, to dust

1 Line a 12-hole muffin tin with paper cases and heat the oven to 190C/170C fan/gas 5. In a jug, mix the yogurt, eggs and vanilla extract. Put the dry ingredients into a large bowl with a pinch of salt and make a well in the middle.
2 Pour in the yogurty mix and melted butter, and quickly fold in with a spatula or metal spoon – don't overwork it. Spoon the mixture into the cases (they will be quite full) and bake for 18–20 minutes or until risen and springy to the touch. Cool for a few minutes, then lift the cakes on to a wire rack to cool completely.
3 Cut the tops off the cupcakes and set aside. Spoon a dollop of raspberry jam on to each one and top with a few raspberries and generously heaped teaspoons of clotted cream. Put the tops back on, then dust with icing sugar and serve.

- Per split 378 kcalories, protein 6g, carbohydrate 32g, fat 26g, saturated fat 13g, fibre 1g, sugar 23g, salt 0.33g

Easter egg cupcakes

Kids will love helping with these cute cupcakes. They're perfect for serving at Easter, but equally delicious at any time of the year.

- **Takes 40 minutes ■ Makes 24**

250g pack butter, softened, plus extra for greasing
175g/6oz golden caster sugar
5 eggs, beaten
250g/9oz self-raising flour, plus extra 2 tbsp for tossing
1 tsp baking powder
zest of 1 orange, plus 2 tbsp juice
200g/8oz glacé cherries, chopped
250g/9oz natural marzipan, coarsely grated (easiest if chilled beforehand)
½ tsp almond essence (optional)

TO DECORATE
100g/4oz icing sugar
chocolate mini eggs

1 Heat the oven to 180C/160C fan/gas 4 and butter and line two 12-hole bun tins with paper cases. Beat the butter and sugar until light and fluffy. Add the eggs, flour, baking powder, orange zest and juice and then beat well until creamy and even.
2 Toss the cherries in the extra flour and fold into the batter along with the grated marzipan and almond essence (if using). Spoon into the cases and bake for 20–25 minutes or until well risen and golden. Allow to cool.
3 Mix the icing sugar with just over 1 tablespoon of water to make a loose icing, spoon over the cupcakes, then fix a few chocolate mini eggs on top of each.

- Per cupcake 281 kcalories, protein 3.7g, carbohydrate 38.7g, fat 13.4g, saturated fat 6.1g, fibre 0.6g, sugar 30g, salt 0.41g

Blueberry lemon cake with coconut crumble topping

This sticky, crumbly bake is totally irresistible and makes a comforting pudding that comes straight from the tin.

■ **Takes 1 hour** ■ **Serves 16**

300g/10oz butter, softened
425g/15oz caster sugar
6 eggs
zest of 1 lemon
250g/9oz self-raising flour
300g/10oz blueberries
200g/8oz desiccated coconut
200g/8oz lemon curd

1 Heat the oven to 180C/160C fan/gas 4 and grease and line a 20 x 30cm cake tin. Beat 250g/9oz butter, 250g/9oz sugar, 4 eggs and all the zest until creamy. Fold in the flour and a third of the blueberries. Spoon the mixture into the tin. Sprinkle over another third of the blueberries. Bake for 20 minutes or until the surface is set.
2 For the topping, melt the rest of the butter, then stir in the coconut, remaining sugar and eggs until combined. Warm the lemon curd gently for a few minutes in a small pan until it is runny and pourable.
3 Scatter the remaining blueberries over the cake, drizzle with lemon curd then crumble over the coconut mixture. Bake for 20–25 minutes more or until the coconut is golden and the cake is cooked. Cool in the tin then cut into 16 squares.

■ Per square 446 kcalories, protein 5g, carbohydrate 50g, fat 27g, saturated fat 17g, fibre 43g, sugar 34g, salt 0.55g

Best-ever brownies

These brownies are just as they should be – intensely chocolatey and gooey in the middle and with a slight crust.

■ **Takes 40 minutes** ■ **Makes 16**

200g/8oz butter
200g/8oz dark chocolate
175g/6oz dark muscovado sugar
140g/5oz granulated or caster sugar
4 eggs
50g/2oz ground almonds
50g/2oz plain flour

1 Heat the oven to 180C/160C fan/gas 4, then grease and line a 20cm-square brownie tin. Heat the butter and chocolate in a pan until melted. Stir through the sugars.
2 Leave to cool for 5 minutes, then stir in the eggs until smooth. Mix in the almonds and flour then pour into the tin. Bake for 30–35 minutes or until just cooked through in the middle.

■ Per brownie 287 kcalories, protein 3.6g, carbohydrate 31.3g, fat 17.2g, saturated fat 9.1g, fibre 0.6g, sugar 28.7g, salt 0.25g

Apple pecan muffins

Although fruity, these lunchbox-friendly muffins aren't too sweet and are delicious eaten with a slice of cheese.

■ **Takes 30 minutes** ■ **Makes 12**

350g/12oz plain flour
25g/1oz butter
50g/2oz dark muscovado sugar, plus 1 tbsp for the topping
50g/2oz pecan nuts, chopped
2 tsp baking powder
½ tsp bicarbonate of soda
1 tsp ground cinnamon
3 eating apples (about 140g/5oz each), peeled and cored
284ml pot soured cream
1 egg, beaten
3 tbsp milk

1 Heat the oven to 200C/180C fan/gas 6. Line a 12-hole muffin tin with cases. To make the topping, rub 50g/2oz of the flour with the butter to make breadcrumbs. Stir through one tablespoon of sugar and the chopped pecans.
2 In a large bowl, sift together the remaining flour, baking powder, bicarbonate of soda and a pinch of salt. Stir in the sugar and cinnamon and set aside. Coarsely grate two apples, then beat together with the soured cream, egg and milk. Make a well in the dry ingredients and quickly fold through the wet ingredients.
3 Spoon the mixture into the muffin cases and sprinkle over the topping. Thinly slice the last apple and poke slices into the muffin tops. Bake for 20 minutes or until golden and a skewer inserted comes out clean.

■ Per muffin 226 kcalories, protein 5g, carbohydrate 32g, fat 9g, saturated fat 5g, fibre 2g, sugar 9g, salt 0.56g

Healthier oat cookies

Made with olive oil spread and plenty of oats to help keep down cholesterol levels, these oat cookies are a fantastic healthy treat for snacking adults and children alike.

■ **Takes 30 minutes** ■ **Makes 15**

100g/4oz olive oil spread
50g/2oz light muscovado sugar
2 tbsp clear honey
¼ tsp ground mixed spice
100g/4oz self-raising flour
100g/4oz porridge oats
50g/2oz raisins

1 Heat the oven to 170C/150C fan/gas 3½. Put the spread, sugar and honey into a heatproof bowl, then microwave on High for 1 minute until everything's just melted (or melt it all together in a small pan). Stir in the mixed spice, flour, oats and raisins, then mix together to combine.
2 Line two baking sheets with non-stick baking paper and spoon tablespoons of the mixture, spaced well apart, on to the prepared sheets. Flatten the tops slightly with a fork. Bake for 15 minutes or until golden brown and crisp on the base. Leave to cool, then store in an airtight container.

■ Per cookie 135 kcalories, protein 2g, carbohydrate 17g, fat 7g, saturated fat 1g, fibre 1g, sugar 7g, salt 0.07g

Squidgy muesli bars

Making your own cereal bars is easy and really satisfying – particularly as you know exactly what's in them.

■ **Takes 30 minutes** ■ **Makes 12**

175g/6oz light muscovado sugar
100g/4oz olive oil spread
50g/2oz clear honey
300g/10oz high-fibre muesli
50g/2oz dried mixed fruit, chopped
1 tbsp golden linseed or sesame seeds

1 Heat the oven to 180C/160C fan/gas 4. Grease and line an 18cm-square tin with non-stick baking parchment.
2 Put the sugar, olive oil spread and honey in a pan and heat until the spread has melted. Stir well then mix in the high-fibre muesli and the mixed fruit. Spoon into the prepared tin and flatten the top with the back of a spoon. Sprinkle over the linseed or sesame seeds and bake for 20 minutes or until golden brown. Leave to cool in the tin for at least 30 minutes, then cut into 12 bars.

■ Per bar 237 kcalories, protein 3g, carbohydrate 36g, fat 10g, saturated fat 2g, fibre 2g, sugar 23g, salt 0.05g

Coconut and chocolate macaroons

You'll be amazed how simple it is to make your own macaroons. Mini versions make delicious petits fours after dinner.

■ **Takes 40 minutes** ■ **Makes 12 or 24 mini**

1 egg white
200g/8oz caster sugar
4 tbsp plain flour
200g/8oz coarsely grated fresh coconut (about 1 coconut)
150g bar dark chocolate (70% cocoa solids), chopped

1 Heat the oven to 180C/160C fan/gas 4. In a clean bowl, whisk the egg white until stiff then gradually add the sugar, whisking continuously until thick and glossy. Sift in the flour and fold into the egg white with the coconut until completely combined.
2 Squash spoonfuls of the mixture on to a baking sheet lined with non-stick baking paper. (You may need to do this in two batches.) Bake for 15–18 minutes or until golden around the edges and just starting to brown on top. If you're making mini macaroons, check them after 10 minutes. Leave to cool. Transfer to a wire rack.
3 While the macaroons are cooling, melt the chocolate in a microwave or over a pan of simmering water and leave to cool slightly. Cover the smooth side of the macaroons with chocolate and leave to set in the fridge.

■ Per macaroon 206 kcalories, protein 2g, carbohydrate 30g, fat 10g, saturated fat 7g, fibre 2g, sugar 26g, salt 0.03g

Birthday biscuits

These are a twist on classic iced party rings, but the dough and icing would work just as well to make biscuits in other shapes, such as stars or hearts.

■ **Takes 40 minutes** ■ **Makes 24**

250g/9oz plain white flour
85g/3oz golden caster sugar
175g/6oz unsalted butter (at room temperature), cubed
2 tbsp lemon curd
250g/9oz white icing sugar, sifted
1 tbsp strawberry fruit spread (we used St Dalfour)

1 Heat the oven to 180C/160C fan/ gas 4. Whizz the flour, sugar and butter in a food processor to make crumbs. Pulse a little more to form a ball. Turn the dough out on to a sheet of lightly floured non-stick baking paper. Roll out to the thickness of two £1 coins. Stamp out 24 rounds using a 5cm fluted cutter and cut out the centres with the end of a piping nozzle. Lift the rounds on to baking sheets. Bake for 10 minutes until pale golden. Cool on a wire rack.
2 Mix the lemon curd with 2 tablespoons of boiling water until smooth. Sieve in 175g/6oz of the icing sugar and stir until smooth. Mix the jam with two teaspoons of boiling water and sieve in the remaining icing sugar.
3 Spoon lemon icing over the biscuits, then drizzle over the pink icing. Set for 20 minutes.

■ Per biscuit 149 kcalories, protein 1g, carbohydrate 24g, fat 6g, saturated fat 4g, fibre none, sugar 16g, salt 0.01g

Smiley raspberry cookies

Kids will just love these jammy biscuits – and they're simple enough that they can get involved in making them.

■ **Takes 35 minutes, plus chilling and decorating** ■ **Makes 14**

250g/9oz butter, softened
140g/5oz caster sugar
1 egg yolk
2 tsp vanilla extract
300g/10oz plain flour
1 tsp ground cinnamon

FOR THE FILLING AND TO DECORATE
6 tbsp raspberry jam
6 tbsp icing sugar
50g/2oz icing sugar, sifted

1 Beat the butter and sugar in a large bowl, then add the egg yolk and vanilla. Beat briefly to combine. Sift in the flour and cinnamon and stir well – use your hands to give it a good mix. Shape into two balls, wrap, then chill for 20–30 minutes.
2 Heat the oven to 180C/160C fan/gas 4. Roll out the dough balls on a floured surface, then stamp out 14 biscuits from each using a 8cm cutter. Transfer the biscuit shapes to lined baking sheets. Using a 5cm cutter, cut out the 'noses' from half the biscuits. Bake for 10–12 minutes until pale golden, then cool on a wire rack.
3 Mix the jam and icing sugar, and spoon a little on to each whole biscuit. Carefully sandwich the other biscuits on top. To decorate, mix a few drops of water with the icing sugar, then use to pipe on faces.

■ Per cookie 295 kcalories, protein 2g, carbohydrate 39g, fat 15g, saturated fat 10g, fibre 1g, sugar 22g, salt 0.29g

Ginger choc chip cookies

Make these with the kids for an hour of messy fun – and get some deliciously crumbly cookies to show for it.

■ **Takes 20 minutes, plus chilling** ■ **Makes 20 cookies**

200g/8oz butter, softened, plus extra for greasing
85g/3oz light muscovado sugar
250g/9oz self-raising flour
2 tbsp golden syrup
1 tsp vanilla extract
100g/4oz dark chocolate drops or dark chocolate, chopped
50g/2oz preserved ginger from a jar, or crystallized ginger, roughly chopped

1 Butter and line two large baking sheets with non-stick baking paper. Heat the oven to 200C/180C fan/gas 6. Beat together the sugar and butter until pale and creamy. Stir in the remaining ingredients until you have a soft dough. Roll the dough into walnut-sized pieces and space them out generously on the lined baking sheets. If you have time, leave the dough to chill in the fridge for 30 minutes at this point.
2 Bake the cookies for 12–15 minutes until lightly golden; they will still feel quite soft in the middle. Leave on baking sheets until firm, about 5 minutes, then transfer to a wire rack to cool completely.

■ Per cookie 169 kcalories, protein 1g, carbohydrate 20g, fat 10g, saturated fat 6g, fibre 1g, added sugar 11g, salt 0.28g

TOP: Birthday biscuits

BOTTOM LEFT: Smiley raspberry cookies

BOTTOM RIGHT: Ginger choc chip cookies

TOP: Bitter orange and poppy seed cake

BOTTOM LEFT: Classic Victoria sponge

BOTTOM RIGHT: Squidgy lemon–ginger cake

Bitter orange and poppy seed cake

An easy Middle-Eastern-style cake that uses a very British ingredient.

■ **Takes 1¼ hours** ■ **Serves 8**

3 tbsp good-quality thick-cut marmalade
150g pot natural bio yogurt
3 eggs
175g/6oz golden caster sugar
200g/8oz self-raising flour
½ tsp baking powder
175g/6oz butter, softened
zest of 1 orange
2 tsp poppy seeds, toasted

FOR THE STICKY TOPPING
juice of ½ orange
5 tbsp good-quality thick-cut marmalade

1 Heat the oven to 160C/140C fan/gas 3. Butter a 20 × 10cm loaf tin and line the base. Melt the marmalade in a pan, beat in the yogurt and let it cool.
2 Mix together the remaining cake ingredients until smooth. Quickly beat in the yogurt mix, then pour the batter into the tin. Leave it mounded in the centre to help it rise in the middle.
3 Bake for 1 hour or until golden and a skewer inserted in to the centre comes out clean. If the cake has taken on a lot of colour after 45 minutes, loosely cover it with baking paper.
4 Meanwhile, melt the orange juice and marmalade together. When the cake is ready, cool in the tin for 10 minutes, then turn out on to a wire rack. Once the cake is just warm, spoon over the glaze.

■ Per serving 422 kcalories, protein 6g, carbohydrate 54g, fat 21g, saturated fat 12g, fibre 1g, sugar 35g, salt 0.80g

Classic Victoria sponge

There's no secret to making the perfect sandwich cake when you use this brilliant all-in-one recipe.

■ **Takes 30 minutes** ■ **Serves 10**

200g/8oz caster sugar
200g/8oz butter, softened
4 eggs, beaten
200g/8oz self-raising flour
1 tsp baking powder
2 tbsp milk

FOR THE FILLING
100g/4oz butter, softened
140g/5oz icing sugar, sifted
drop of vanilla extract (optional)
340g jar good-quality strawberry jam
icing sugar, to decorate

1 Heat the oven to 190C/170C fan/gas 5. Butter and line two 20cm-sandwich tins. In a large bowl, beat all the cake ingredients together until you have a smooth, soft batter.
2 Divide the mixture between the tins, smooth the surface with a spatula or the back of a spoon, then bake for 25 minutes or until golden and the cake springs back when pressed. Turn out on to a wire rack and leave to cool completely.
3 To make the filling, beat the butter until creamy, then gradually beat in the icing sugar and vanilla extract, if using. Spread the buttercream over the top of one of the sponges, top with jam, then sandwich together with the second sponge. Dust the top with a little icing sugar before serving.

■ Per serving 558 kcalories, protein 5g, carbohydrate 76g, fat 28g, saturated fat 17g, fibre 0.6g, added sugar 57g, salt 0.9g

Squidgy lemon-ginger cake

This cake improves with keeping – if it lasts that long! It is much easier to grate root ginger from frozen, so store a chunk in a bag in the freezer until needed.

■ **Takes 2 hours** ■ **Serves 12**

200g/8oz butter, cubed
200g/8oz dates, stoned
300g/10oz dark muscovado sugar
2 eggs
50g/2oz fresh or frozen root ginger, grated
grated zest of 1 lemon
200g/8oz self-raising flour
1 Bramley apple (about 250g/9oz) peeled and chopped into pea-sized pieces

TO DECORATE
50g/2oz white chocolate
1 tbsp candied lemon peel, chopped
1 tbsp sugar 'coffee crystals'

1 Heat the oven to 160C/140C fan/gas 3. Butter and line a 20cm-round cake tin. Put the dates in a bowl and cover with boiling water. Melt the butter in a large pan, then stir in the sugar. Allow to cool slightly.
2 Drain the dates and chop them finely. Beat into the melted butter along with the eggs, ginger and lemon zest. Stir in the flour and apple. Spoon into the tin and put it on a baking sheet, then bake for 1¼ hours or until well risen. A skewer inserted into the cake should come out with a few moist crumbs sticking to it. Leave the cake to cool in the tin.
3 Break the chocolate into a heatproof bowl and melt over a pan of simmering water. Remove the cake from the tin. Trickle the chocolate over the cake, scatter with the candied lemon peel and coffee crystals, and leave to set before serving.

■ Per serving 376 kcalories, protein 4g, carbohydrate 57g, fat 16g, saturated fat 9g, fibre 2g, added sugar 30g, salt 0.53g

Cherry and almond cake

This is so simple to make and is a delicious almondy twist on a traditional cherry cake. It's perfect to serve at Easter.

■ **Takes 1 hour 50 minutes** ■ **Serves 12**

250g butter, softened, plus extra for greasing
175g/6oz golden caster sugar
5 eggs, beaten
250g/9oz self-raising flour, plus an extra
   2 tbsp
1 tsp baking powder
zest of 1 orange, plus 2 tbsp juice
200g/8oz glacé cherries, halved
250g/9oz natural marzipan, coarsely grated
   (easiest if chilled beforehand)
½ tsp almond essence (optional)

TO DECORATE
100g/4oz icing sugar, sifted
50g/2oz flaked almonds, toasted
12 natural glacé cherries
zest of 1 orange

1 Heat the oven to 160C/140C fan/gas 3 and butter and line a 20cm/round, loose-bottomed tin. Beat the butter and sugar until light and fluffy. Stir in the eggs, flour, baking powder, the zest and juice.
2 Toss the cherries in the extra 2 tablespoons flour and fold into the batter along with the marzipan and almond essence (if using). Spoon into the tin and bake for 1½ hours, until risen and a skewer inserted into the centre comes out clean. Leave to cool in the tin for 10 minutes, then turn out on to a rack to cool.
3 Mix the icing sugar with 1 tablespoon water to make a loose icing. Scatter the almonds over the top of the cake and position the 12 glacé cherries around the edge. Use a little icing to fix each in place. Drizzle over the remaining icing. Finish with a scattering of orange zest.

■ Per serving 515 kcalories, protein 7g, carbohydrate 69g, fat 25g, saturated fat 12g, fibre 2g, added sugar 53g, salt 0.76g

Cappuccino cake

If you've offered to bake a treat for a stall at a fair or for your local coffee morning, this version of a classic is just the thing.

■ **Takes 45 minutes** ■ **Serves 12**

250g butter, softened
250g/9oz light brown soft sugar, plus
   2–3 tbsp extra
300g/10oz self-raising flour
4 eggs, beaten
50g/2oz walnut halves, toasted
   and finely chopped – using a food
   processor is easiest
200ml/7fl oz very strong coffee (fresh
   or instant), cooled

FOR THE FROSTING
500g tub mascarpone
2 tbsp light brown soft sugar
cocoa powder or drinking chocolate,
   to decorate

1 Heat the oven to 180C/160C fan/gas 4. Butter and line the bottoms of two 20cm sandwich tins with greaseproof paper. Beat the butter and sugar together with electric beaters until pale. Add the flour and eggs and keep beating until evenly mixed. Fold in the walnuts and half of the coffee. Spoon into the prepared tins and bake for 25–30 minutes or until golden and well risen. Leave in their tins for 5 minutes before cooling on a wire rack.
2 Sweeten the rest of the coffee with the extra sugar and drizzle 4 tablespoons over the sponges. Leave to cool completely.
3 For the frosting, beat the mascarpone, sugar and remaining coffee until smooth. Use half of the frosting to sandwich the sponges together. Spread the rest over the top of the cake. Decorate with a dusting of cocoa powder.

■ Per serving 559 kcalories, protein 5g, carbohydrate 48g, fat 39g, saturated fat 23g, fibre 1g, added sugar 29g, salt 0.72g

Date, banana and rum loaf

This fruity, crumbly loaf has loads of flavour but no added fat or sugar – ideal if you're watching your waistline.

■ **Takes 1¼ hours** ■ **Serves 10**

250g pack stoned, ready-to-eat dates
2 small bananas or 1 large about 140g/5oz
   total
100g/4oz pecan nut halves (85g roughly
   chopped)
200g/8oz raisins
200g/8oz sultanas
100g/4oz fine polenta
2 tsp mixed spice
2 tsp baking powder
3 tbsp dark rum
2 egg whites
a few banana chips and 1 tsp sugar, to
   decorate

1 Heat the oven to 180C/160C fan/gas 4. Line a 900g loaf tin with non-stick baking paper, using a little oil to hold it in place. Put the dates into a small pan with 200ml/7fl oz boiling water and simmer for 5 minutes. Strain the date liquid into a jug and put the dates in a food processor. Add the banana and 100ml of the date liquid to the dates and whizz until smooth. Mix the chopped nuts, dried fruit, polenta, spice and baking powder in a bowl, then add the date purée and the rum, and mix well.
2 Whisk the egg whites to soft peaks and fold into the cake mix. Tip the mix into the tin (it will be quite full), then top with the remaining pecans and the banana chips and sugar, if using. Bake for 1 hour or until golden and crusty and a skewer inserted into the centre comes out clean. Cool completely before cutting into slices.

■ Per serving 310 kcalories, protein 5g, carbohydrate 57g, fat 8g, saturated fat 1g, fibre 3g, sugar 49g, salt 0.39g

TOP: Cherry and almond cake

BOTTOM LEFT: Cappuccino cake

BOTTOM RIGHT: Date, banana and rum loaf

TOP: Lemon blueberry cake

BOTTOM LEFT: Plum, almond and ricotta cake

BOTTOM RIGHT: White and dark chocolate cake

Lemon blueberry cake

Lemon drizzle cake is a teatime classic – adding blueberries and cooking it in a ring mould gives it that extra-special finish.

■ **Takes about 1 hour** ■ **Serves 8**

175g/6oz butter, softened, plus extra
    for greasing
300g/10oz sugar
4 eggs, lightly beaten
zest of 1 lemon
142ml pot soured cream
250g/9oz plain flour
2 tsp baking powder
150g punnet blueberries

FOR THE ICING
100g/4oz icing sugar
4 tbsp fresh lemon juice

1 Heat the oven to 180C/160C fan/gas 4. Beat the butter and sugar until soft and creamy. Beat in the eggs a little at a time, then add the lemon zest. Fold in the soured cream then the flour, baking powder and a pinch of salt. Carefully mix the blueberries into the batter.
2 Butter a deep, 23cm diameter ring tin (if ridged, it may be easier to use an oil spray to get in the corners). Spoon in the mixture then level the top. Bake for 45–55 minutes or until springy and a skewer inserted into the middle comes out clean. Leave to cool for 10 minutes. Turn out of the tin on to a wire rack set over a large plate or tray. Allow to cool.
3 For the icing, mix together the icing sugar and lemon juice, drizzle it over the cake with a spoon and allow to set.

■ Per serving 608 kcalories, protein 7g, carbohydrate 79g, fat 31g, saturated fat 18g, fibre 2g, sugar 55g, salt 0.84g

Plum, almond and ricotta cake

This irresistible cake has the lightness of a sponge but the richness of a cheesecake. The cake base can also be used for other fruit, such as peaches, nectarines or apricots.

■ **Takes 1 hour 50 minutes** ■ **Serves 10**

250g pot ricotta
140g/5oz butter, melted
4 eggs, beaten
225g/8oz golden caster sugar, plus 1 tbsp
    for the top
250g/9oz self-raising flour
200g pack ground almonds
4 tbsp plum or apricot jam
5 plums, quartered (we used yellow plums)
handful of flaked almonds, toasted
icing sugar, to dust

1 Heat the oven to 180C/160C fan/gas 4. In a bowl, beat the ricotta, butter, eggs and sugar together, then fold in the flour and ground almonds. Spoon half the batter into a greased and lined 23cm round cake tin. Evenly blob the jam over the middle, then cover with the remaining batter.
2 Arrange the plum quarters over the top. Sprinkle over the extra sugar, then bake for 1½ hours until risen and golden and the plums have shrivelled and caramelized. Leave the cake to cool slightly, then remove from the tin and leave to cool on a wire rack. Scatter with the flaked almonds, dust with icing sugar and serve cut in slices.

■ Per serving 518 kcalories, protein 12.5g, carbohydrate 53.8g, fat 29.5g, saturated fat 10.7g, fibre 2.8g, sugar 34.6g, salt 0.61g

White and dark chocolate cake

For big celebrations this cake is a must.

■ **Takes 1 hour, plus decorating** ■ **Serves 12**

75g/6oz butter, softened, plus extra
    for greasing
100g/4oz white chocolate (choose a brand
    with real vanilla flecks)
100g/4oz dark chocolate (70% cocoa solids)
3 eggs
100ml/3½fl oz whole or semi-skimmed milk
175g/6oz caster sugar
1 tsp baking powder
200g/8oz self-raising flour
2 tbsp very strong coffee (instant is fine)
1 tsp vanilla extract

FOR THE GANACHE AND TO DECORATE
284ml pot double cream
200g/8oz dark chocolate (70% cocoa solids),
    broken into pieces
50g/2oz white chocolate, melted
1 small bag white Maltesers

1 Heat the oven to 180C/160C fan/gas 4. Butter and line two 20cm sandwich tins.
2 For the cake, break the chocolates into two separate bowls. Melt over simmering water. Put everything else, except the coffee and vanilla, into a bowl and beat until creamy.
3 Divide the creamy mixture between two bowls, add the coffee and dark chocolate to one, and the vanilla and white chocolate to the other. Stir until mixed through then spoon into the tins. Level, then bake for 25 minutes or until risen and springy. Cool on a wire rack.
4 For the ganache, bring the cream to the boil. Pour over the dark chocolate and leave for 5 minutes. Stir until smooth, let it thicken and cool. Split the cakes horizontally across the middle, then layer up with the ganache.
5 To decorate, zigzag the white chocolate over the top of the cake, then finish with the Maltesers.

■ Per serving 565 kcalories, protein 7g, carbohydrate 51g, fat 39g, saturated fat 22g, fibre 1g, sugar 37g, salt 0.62g

Carrot cake loaf with vanilla frosting

A tasty family favourite with a zingy orange-juice twist.

■ Takes 1 hour 20 minutes ■ Serves 10

85g/3oz sultanas
juice of 1 orange
125ml/4fl oz sunflower oil, plus extra for
   greasing
85g/3oz wholemeal flour
85g/3oz self-raising flour
175g/6oz light brown soft sugar
1 tsp bicarbonate of soda
1 tsp ground cinnamon
1 tsp ground mixed spice
2 eggs, beaten
175g/6oz carrots, peeled and coarsely grated
   (about 2 large carrots)
50g/2oz walnut halves, roughly chopped,
   plus extra to decorate

FOR THE FROSTING
85g/3oz full-fat soft cheese
25g/1oz butter, softened
1 tsp vanilla extract
175g/6oz icing sugar, sifted

1 Soak the sultanas in the orange juice for 3–4 hours or overnight. Heat the oven to 180C/160C fan/gas 4. Grease and line a 900g loaf tin. Sift the flours, sugar, bicarbonate of soda, spices and half teaspoon salt into a large bowl. Pour in the oil and eggs, and mix well, then fold in the carrots, walnuts and the sultanas with their orange juice.
2 Spoon the mixture into the tin then bake for 1 hour. Cool briefly, then transfer to a wire rack.
3 Beat the soft cheese, butter, vanilla and icing sugar until smooth, and chill. When cool, split the cake in half, spread the bottom with half of the frosting. Replace the top, then swirl over the remaining frosting. Decorate with walnuts.

■ Per serving 422 kcalories, protein 5g, carbohydrate 57g, fat 21g, saturated fat 5g, fibre 2g, sugar 45g, salt 0.88g

Sticky lime and coconut drizzle loaf

If you like lemon drizzle, you'll love this easy loaf.

■ Takes 1 hour 5 minutes ■ Serves 10

100g/4oz butter, softened
175g/6oz self-raising flour
1 tsp baking powder
175g/6oz golden caster sugar
2 eggs
½ × 400ml can coconut milk
finely grated zest of 2 limes

FOR THE ICING AND TO DECORATE
½ × 400ml can coconut milk
200g/8oz golden caster sugar
finely grated zest of 1 lime, juice 3 limes

1 Heat the oven to 180C/160C fan/gas 4. Butter and line a 900g loaf tin with baking parchment. Beat all the cake ingredients together until combined. Tip into the tin and smooth the top. Bake for 40 minutes, until golden and firm to touch.
2 For the icing, tip the coconut milk and 150g/5½oz of the sugar into a pan. Boil for 5 minutes or until syrupy (so you can see the bottom of the pan when you stir). Stir in the lime juice. Set aside. Mix the remaining sugar and lime zest to a paste, then set aside.
3 Leave the cooked loaf in the tin while you pour over the icing a little at a time – wait for the cake to absorb it before adding more. Cool, then carefully remove from the tin, sprinkle with the lime sugar and slice.

■ Per serving 364 kcalories, protein 4g, carbohydrate 54g, fat 16g, saturated fat 11g, fibre 1g, sugar 41g, salt 0.62g

Raspberry layer cake

This light, creamy raspberry cake makes a sublimely sweet summer treat.

■ Takes 50 minutes, plus overnight chilling
■ Serves 8

200g/8oz butter, softened
200g/8oz caster sugar
4 eggs, beaten
200g/8oz self-raising flour
1 tsp baking powder
icing sugar, to decorate

FOR THE SYRUP
85g/3oz caster sugar
50ml/2fl oz almond liqueur

FOR THE FILLING
284ml pot double cream
250g tub mascarpone
3 tbsp caster sugar
150g punnet raspberries

1 Heat the oven to 190C/170C fan/gas 5. Butter and line two 20cm sandwich tins. In a bowl, beat together all the cake ingredients until smooth. Spoon equally into the tins, then bake for 25–30 minutes, until golden and springy when gently pressed. Turn the cakes out on to a wire rack.
2 For the syrup, heat the sugar, 2 tablespoons water and the liqueur together in a pan, until the sugar has dissolved. Cool a little. Use a large serrated knife to cut each cake in half. Brush the syrup all over the four pieces of cake.
3 For the filling, whip the cream until it forms soft peaks. Beat the mascarpone and sugar in a large bowl to loosen. Fold into the cream. Layer the fruit, cream and sponges, starting and finishing with a layer of sponge. Press down lightly on the finished layer cake, wrap it tightly in cling film and chill overnight. Dust with icing sugar before serving.

■ Per serving 819 kcalories, protein 8g, carbohydrate 68g, fat 58g, saturated fat 33g, fibre 2g, sugar 50g, salt 1.02g

TOP: Carrot cake loaf with vanilla frosting

BOTTOM LEFT: Sticky lime and coconut drizzle loaf

BOTTOM RIGHT: Raspberry layer cake

TOP: Orange and saffron
syrup cake

BOTTOM LEFT: Raspberry and
lemon polenta cake

BOTTOM RIGHT: Whole orange
and chocolate cake

Orange and saffron syrup cake

Citrus syrup makes this cake wonderfully moist and elevates it from a simple teatime bake to a delicious dinner-party dessert.

■ **Takes about 1 hour** ■ **Serves 8**

100g/4oz hazelnuts, skinned and ground
50g/2oz semolina or polenta
175g/6oz golden caster sugar
1½ tsp baking powder
2 large oranges
4 medium eggs
200ml/7fl oz light olive oil
generous pinch of saffron threads
85g/3oz icing sugar
Greek yogurt or crème fraîche and orange segments, to serve (optional)

1 Heat the oven to 180C/160C fan/gas 4. Oil the base of a 23cm ring tin. Put the ground hazelnuts in a frying pan and toast over a medium heat, stirring frequently until evenly browned. Cool, then mix with the semolina or polenta, caster sugar and baking powder.
2 Beat the zest of one orange with the eggs and oil, then fold into the semolina/polenta mix. Pour into the tin and bake for 30–40 minutes or until risen and firm to the touch.
3 While the cake is baking, pare the zest from the other orange and cut it into very thin shreds. Put into a pan with the juice of both oranges, the saffron and icing sugar. Bring to the boil, then simmer gently for 5 minutes.
4 Leave the cake to cool slightly then turn out on to a plate. While the cake is still warm, skewer it and spoon over the orange and saffron syrup. Serve with Greek yogurt or crème fraîche and orange segments, if you like.

■ Per serving 455 kcalories, protein 7g, carbohydrate 43g, fat 30g, saturated fat 4g, fibre 2g, added sugar 33g, salt 0.4g

Raspberry and lemon polenta cake

Give sponge an Italian twist with this easy-to-make polenta cake.

■ **Takes 50 minutes, plus defrosting** ■ **Serves 8**

225g/8oz very soft butter
225g/8oz caster sugar, plus 1 tbsp for dusting
½ tsp vanilla extract
zest of 1½ lemons
4 eggs, beaten
175g/6oz fine polenta
50g/2oz plain flour
1½ tsp baking powder
200g/8oz frozen raspberries, left frozen
icing sugar, for dusting

FOR THE FILLING
100g/4oz soft cheese (at room temperature)
1 tbsp icing sugar, plus extra to taste
zest of ½ lemon, plus a squeeze of juice
142ml carton double cream
100g/4oz frozen raspberries, defrosted

1 Heat the oven to 190C/170C fan/gas 5. Butter and line two 20cm sandwich tins. Beat the butter, caster sugar, vanilla and zest together until creamy. Beat in the eggs until pale and fluffy. Mix the dry ingredients, then fold into the batter.
2 Spoon half the batter into each tin and level the top. Scatter over the raspberries and poke them in gently. Sprinkle one of the sponges with the extra tablespoon of caster sugar. Bake for 30 minutes or until risen and golden. Cool in the tin for 10 minutes, then on a wire rack.
3 For the filling, beat the soft cheese with the icing sugar, zest and a little juice to loosen, if it needs it. Lightly whip the cream then fold into the cheese. Fold in the defrosted raspberries. Use the filling to sandwich the sponges together, placing the sugar-crusted one on top, and serve dusted with more icing sugar.

■ Per serving 608 kcalories, protein 8g, carbohydrate 58g, fat 40g, saturated fat 23g, fibre 2g, sugar 38g, salt 0.97g

Whole orange and chocolate cake

Whole orange, cooked until tender then added, skin and all, gives this chocolate cake a wonderful moistness and bitter citrus flavour. Serve warm with a scoop of ice cream.

■ **Takes 2½ hours** ■ **Serves 12**

175g/6oz butter, softened
1 small orange (about 200g/8oz)
100g/4oz self-raising flour
1 tsp baking powder
1 tsp ground cinnamon
1 tsp ground coriander
2 tbsp cocoa powder
100g/4oz ground almonds
175g/6oz light muscovado sugar
4 eggs, separated

1 Butter and line the base of a 23cm round tin. Put the orange in a pan and cover with water. Bring to the boil, then simmer, partly covered, for 1 hour. Drain and cool. Heat the oven to 180C/160C fan/gas 4.
2 Halve the orange, remove the pips, then chop (without peeling). Put in the food processor and work to a rough purée. Sift together the flour, baking powder, spices and cocoa in a bowl. Stir in the ground almonds.
3 Beat the butter and sugar in a separate bowl until light and fluffy. Beat in the egg yolks and the orange, then fold in the flour mix. Beat the egg whites until stiff, then fold gently into the cake mix in two batches. Pour into the prepared tin and bake for 40–45 minutes or until firm. Cool for 5 minutes in the tin, then turn out and cool on a wire rack.

■ Per serving 285 kcalories, protein 5g, carbohydrate 24g, fat 19g, saturated fat 9g, fibre 1g, sugar 16g, salt 0.52g

Strawberry and cinnamon torte

The perfect crumbly dessert for a Sunday lunch or dinner.

■ **Takes 1¼ hours** ■ **Serves 6–8**

175g/6oz butter, softened, plus extra
    for greasing
175g/6oz ground almonds
175g/6oz golden caster sugar
175g/6oz self-raising flour
1 tsp ground cinnamon
1 egg, plus 1 egg yolk
450g/1lb strawberries, hulled and sliced
icing sugar, for dusting
whipped double cream mixed with Greek
    yogurt, to serve

1 Heat the oven to 180C/160C fan/gas 4. Butter and line the base of a loose-bottomed 23cm cake tin. In a food processor, mix the ground almonds, butter, sugar, flour, cinnamon, egg and egg yolk until evenly mixed.
2 Tip half the mixture into the tin and smooth. Spread the strawberries on top. Top with the remaining cake mixture. Spread smooth.
3 Bake for 1 hour–1 hour 5 minutes. Check after 40 minutes – if the torte is getting too brown, cover loosely with foil. When cooked, the torte should be slightly risen and dark golden brown.
4 Cool slightly, then remove from the tin. Slide on to a plate and dust with icing sugar. Serve warm, in wedges, with spoonfuls of cream and Greek yogurt.

■ Per serving (8) 491 kcalories, protein 9g, carbohydrate 45g, fat 32g, saturated fat 13g, fibre 3g, added sugar 23g, salt 0.68g

Pineapple and almond upside-down cake

This scrumptious cake gives a serious nod to nostalgia – but tastes far better than you'll remember.

■ **Takes 1 hour** ■ **Serves 8**

85g/3oz butter
85g/3oz dark muscovado sugar
85g/3oz flaked toasted almonds
1 pineapple, peeled, cored and sliced, any
    juices reserved
100g/4oz natural glacé cherries

FOR THE BATTER
250g/9oz butter, softened
250g/9oz light muscovado sugar
4 eggs
200g/8oz plain flour
2 tsp baking powder
50g/2oz ground almonds
2 tbsp pineapple juice or rum

1 Heat the oven to 190C/170C fan/gas 5. Cream the butter and sugar, and liberally brush over the bottom and sides of a 23cm square tin. Scatter over the toasted almonds so that some stick to the sides and line the base with overlapping pineapple slices. Decorate with the cherries.
2 Tip all of the batter ingredients into a food processor and blitz until smooth. Pour the batter over the pineapple and bake for 50 minutes–1 hour until puffed up and golden. Leave the cake to relax for just a few minutes, then turn out, cut into squares and eat straight away with lashings of custard.

■ Per serving 781 kcalories, protein 11g, carbohydrate 82g, fat 48g, saturated fat 24g, fibre 3g, sugar 62g, salt 1.17g

Mango and passion fruit roulade

Whisked sponges are famously low in fat – especially if you use yogurt instead of cream as the filling. If you like, swap the fruit for whatever's in season.

■ **Takes 50 minutes, plus defrosting**
■ **Serves 10**

3 eggs
85g/3oz golden caster sugar, plus 1 tbsp
85g/3oz plain flour, sifted
1 tsp baking powder, sifted
1 tsp vanilla extract

FOR THE FILLING
1 tbsp golden caster sugar
flesh from 2 large ripe passion fruit
2 mangoes, peeled and cut into small chunks
250g pack frozen raspberries, defrosted
200g pot 2% fat Greek yogurt or very low-fat
    fromage frais

1 Heat the oven to 200C/180C fan/gas 6. Grease and line a 30x23cm/Swiss roll tin. Put the eggs and sugar into a large bowl and beat with an electric mixer until thick and light, about 5 minutes. Fold in the flour and baking powder, then the vanilla. Tip into the tin, level the mix, then bake for 12–15 minutes or until golden and just springy. Turn out on to another sheet of paper, dusted with 1 extra tablespoon of caster sugar. Roll the paper up inside the sponge, then cool completely.
2 Fold the sugar, passion-fruit pulp and one-third of the mango and raspberries into the yogurt. Unroll the sponge, discard the paper and spread with the filling, then roll up again. Serve with the rest of the fruit on the side.

■ Per serving 153 kcalories, protein 5g, carbohydrate 28g, fat 3g, saturated fat 1g, fibre 2g, sugar 21g, salt 0.26g

TOP: Strawberry and cinnamon torte

BOTTOM LEFT: Pineapple and almond upside-down cake

BOTTOM RIGHT: Mango and passion fruit roulade

TOP: Italian hazelnut cake

BOTTOM LEFT: Pear, hazelnut and chocolate cake

BOTTOM RIGHT: Prune and chocolate torte

Italian hazelnut cake

This cake is wonderfully light and nutty and is great served warm as a dessert or cut into thin slices for tea.

■ **Takes 1 hour 10–20 minutes** ■ **Serves 8**

200g bag blanched hazelnuts
5 eggs
175g/6oz caster sugar
100g/4oz butter, melted
1 tsp vanilla extract
icing sugar, for dusting

1 Heat the oven to 180C/160C fan/gas 4. Butter and line the base of a deep 20cm/round cake tin. Grind the hazelnuts in a food processor or blender until they are as fine as you can get them. If they seem damp, spread them out on a baking sheet to dry for half an hour or so, stirring occasionally.
2 Separate the eggs into two large bowls. Tip the sugar on to the yolks and use an electric beater for about 3 minutes or until the mixture leaves a trail on the surface when the whisk blades are lifted. Gradually whisk in the melted butter, then fold in the hazelnuts and vanilla.
3 Using clean blades, whisk the egg whites until stiff, then fold into the cake mixture in four equal batches. Pour into the tin and bake for 50–60 minutes or until firm but springy. Cool in the tin for 10 minutes, then turn out and leave to cool. Dust with icing sugar.

■ Per serving 394 kcalories, protein 9.7g, carbohydrate 54.3g, fat 17g, saturated fat 14g, fibre 4g, added sugar none, salt 1g

Pear, hazelnut and chocolate cake

If you have any leftovers, serve cold with mugs of tea. But it does only keep for a few days because it's so fruity.

■ **Takes 1½ hours** ■ **Serves 8**

175g/6oz butter, cut into small pieces, plus extra for greasing
100g/4oz blanched hazelnuts
140g/5oz self-raising flour
140g/5oz golden caster sugar
2 eggs, beaten
5 small ripe Conference pears
50g/2oz dark chocolate, chopped into small chunks
2 tbsp apricot jam
single cream, to serve

1 Heat the oven to 160C/140C fan/gas 3. Butter and line the base of a 20cm round cake tin. Grind the hazelnuts in a food processor until fairly fine. Mix in the flour. Add the butter and pulse until it forms crumbs. Tip in the sugar and eggs, and mix briefly.
2 Peel, core and chop two of the pears. Stir the pears and chocolate lightly into the cake mixture. Spoon the mixture into the prepared tin and smooth the top.
3 Peel, core and slice the remaining pears and scatter over the top of the cake. Press down lightly and bake for 50–60 minutes, until firm to the touch. Cool in the tin for 10 minutes, then turn out and cool on a wire rack. Warm the jam and brush over the top of the cake. Serve warm with cream.

■ Per serving 470 kcalories, protein 6g, carbohydrate 47g, fat 30g, saturated fat 14g, fibre 3g, added sugar 18g, salt 0.5g

Prune and chocolate torte

Rich with brandy-steeped prunes, this is a cake for real lovers of chocolate.

■ **Takes 1 hour 5 minutes, plus soaking**
■ **Serves 8**

250g/9oz no-soak prunes, halved
4 tbsp brandy
50g/2oz butter
25g/1oz cocoa powder
100g/4oz dark chocolate (at least 70% cocoa solids), broken into pieces
175g/6oz golden caster sugar
4 egg whites
85g/3oz plain flour
1 tsp ground cinnamon
lightly whipped cream or crème fraîche, to serve

1 Soak the prunes in brandy for about 30 minutes. Heat the oven to 190C/170C fan/gas 5. Butter a 23cm loose-bottomed cake tin. Put the cocoa, chocolate, butter and 140g/5oz of the sugar in a pan, add 100ml/3½fl oz hot water, and gently heat until smooth. Leave to cool slightly.
2 Whisk the egg whites to soft peaks, then gradually whisk in the remaining sugar. Sift the flour and cinnamon over and gently fold in with a metal spoon, until almost combined. Add the chocolate mixture and fold in until evenly combined.
3 Pour the mixture into the tin and arrange the prunes over the top. Sprinkle over any remaining brandy and bake for about 30 minutes until just firm. Serve with cream or crème fraîche.

■ Per serving 311 kcalories, protein 5g, carbohydrate 51g, fat 10g, saturated fat 6g, fibre 3g, added sugar 31g, salt 0.18g

Lemon mascarpone roulade

The Swiss roll gets a makeover with this delicious lemony filling. If using shop-bought rather than homemade lemon curd, add a little more fresh lemon juice for extra zest.

■ **Takes 45 minutes** ■ **Serves 6**

6 eggs
175g/6oz golden caster sugar, plus extra for dusting
175g/6oz self-raising flour
1 heaped tsp caraway seeds (optional)
grated zest of 1 lemon
50g/2oz butter, melted
icing sugar, to dust

FOR THE FILLING
juice of 1 lemon
300g/10oz lemon curd
250g tub mascarpone

1 Heat the oven to 200C/180C fan/gas 6. Line a 27 × 40cm Swiss roll tin with non-stick baking paper. Whisk the eggs and sugar together for 5 minutes, until light and fluffy. Fold in the flour, caraway seeds (if using) and lemon zest, then gradually fold in the butter. Tip the mix into the tin and bake for 12–15 minutes or until pale, but springy in the middle. Cool a little, then turn out on to a sheet of baking paper dusted with caster sugar, roll up and leave to cool.
2 While the sponge is cooling, mix the lemon juice and half the lemon curd with the mascarpone and set aside. When the sponge is completely cool, unroll it, discard the paper and spread with the mascarpone mix. Spread the remaining lemon curd over the top, then roll it up again. Dust with icing sugar to serve.

■ Per serving 708 kcalories, protein 12g, carbohydrate 90g, fat 36g, saturated fat 18g, fibre 1g, sugar 57g, salt 0.8g

Fruity choux buns with caramel sauce

The perfect decadent dinner-party dessert for a warm summer evening.

■ **Takes 40 minutes, plus cooling** ■ **Serves 6**

85g/3oz butter
100g/4oz plain flour, sifted
3 eggs, beaten

FOR THE CARAMEL SAUCE
50g/2oz butter
5 tbsp light muscavado sugar
142ml pot double cream

FOR THE FILLING
142 or 284ml pot double cream (depending on how creamy you like your choux buns)
1 tbsp icing sugar, sifted
3 tbsp dessert wine (sweet muscat works well)
2 ripe peaches, stoned and sliced
150g punnet blueberries

1 Put the butter and 200ml/7fl oz cold water into a pan and bring to a rolling boil. Take off the heat and quickly tip in the flour and a pinch of salt. Whisk the mixture to a smooth paste that leaves the sides of the pan. Cool on a plate.
2 Heat the oven to 200C/180C fan/gas 6 and line a baking sheet. Return the paste to the pan and beat in the eggs, little by little; stop when you have a shiny paste that drops from a spoon.
3 Spoon on to the sheet in six round blobs. Bake for 20–25 minutes or until dark golden. Make a hole in the base of each bun to let out the steam. Bake for 5 more minutes. Cool on a wire rack then cut each bun in half.
4 For the sauce, heat everything together for 5 minutes, stirring, until silky. Whip the cream, sugar and wine for the filling together. Spoon the cream and fruit into the buns. Drizzle over the sauce.

■ Per bun (142ml cream) 589 kcalories, protein 7g, carbohydrate 34g, fat 48g, saturated fat 27g, fibre 2g, sugar 21g, salt 0.75g

Choc and nut sundae cake

If you like ice cream sundaes, you're going to love this.

■ **Takes 45 minutes, plus cooling, freezing and defrosting** ■ **Serves 8**

85g/3oz butter, melted and cooled, plus extra for greasing
4 tbsp cocoa powder, plus 1 tsp, sifted
5 eggs
175g/6oz golden caster sugar
100g/4oz plain flour

FOR THE SAUCE
100g bar dark chocolate (70% cocoa solids)
50g/2oz butter
1 tbsp golden syrup
1 tbsp instant coffee granules
3 tbsp just-boiled water

FOR THE FILLING AND TO DECORATE
2 × 500ml tub good-quality vanilla ice cream, softened for 5 minutes
4 Cadbury's Flake bars, crumbled
100g/4oz toasted hazelnuts, roughly chopped

1 Heat the oven to 190C/170C fan/gas 5. Butter and line a 23cm springform cake tin, then butter the lining. Coat with the extra teaspoon of cocoa, tapping out the excess.
2 Whisk the eggs and sugar for 5 minutes until thick and pale. Fold in the butter, then the flour and cocoa. Bake for 20 minutes or until risen and springy. Cool briefly then transfer to a wire rack.
3 Melt all the sauce ingredients together, stir, then set aside.
4 Cut the cake in half. Scoop one tub of ice cream evenly on to the base and top with half the Flake and hazelnuts. Sit the second half of cake on top. Cover with remaining ice cream, chocolate and nuts. Serve with the drizzled sauce or freeze for up to 1 month. If frozen, transfer the cake to the fridge 1 hour before serving.

■ Per serving 708 kcalories, protein 13g, carbohydrate 67g, fat 45g, saturated fat 22g, fibre 3g, sugar 53g, salt 0.58g

TOP: Lemon mascarpone roulade

BOTTOM LEFT: Fruity choux buns with caramel sauce

BOTTOM RIGHT: Choc and nut sundae cake

TOP: Orange and white chocolate sponge

BOTTOM LEFT: Simple simnel cake

BOTTOM RIGHT: Lollipop cake

Orange and white chocolate sponge

This cake is a real crowd-pleaser – moist, chocolatey and indulgent!

■ **Takes 1 hour 10 minutes** ■ **Serves 10**

175g/6oz butter, softened, plus extra for greasing
175g/6oz golden caster sugar
zest of 4 oranges and juice of 1
4 eggs, separated
100g/4oz self-raising flour
1 tsp baking powder
100g/4oz ground almonds

FOR THE FILLING AND TOPPING
200g/7oz white chocolate
200ml pot crème fraîche
chocolate curls, to decorate (optional)

1 Heat the oven to 180C/160C fan/gas 4. Butter and line two 20cm sandwich tins. Beat the sugar, butter and orange zest until pale and fluffy, then beat in the egg yolks. Sift in the flour and baking powder, then fold in lightly. Fold in the almonds and the orange juice. Whisk the egg whites until they just hold their shape. Fold them into the batter in three lots, taking care not to overmix.
2 Divide the mix between the tins and bake for 30–35 minutes. Cool in the tins for 5 minutes, then cool completely on a wire rack.
3 For the filling and topping, melt the chocolate over a pan of barely simmering water, then leave to cool. Whip the crème fraîche until thick, then fold in the melted chocolate. Sandwich and top the cake with the icing and chill for at least 1 hour. Top with chocolate curls, if using.

■ Per serving 567 kcalories, protein 9g, carbohydrate 45g, fat 40g, saturated fat 21g, fibre 1g, sugar 37g, salt 0.7g

Simple simnel cake

This updated version of the Easter classic makes a great weekend cake.

■ **Takes 1 hour 20 minutes** ■ **Serves 10**

grated zest and juice of 1 orange
1 tbsp Cointreau
175g/6oz dried mixed fruit
50g/2oz whole glacé cherries
100g/4oz soft butter, diced
100g/4oz golden caster sugar
175g/6oz self-raising flour
2 eggs
1 tbsp milk
100g/4oz marzipan (rolled to the width and length of the tin)

FOR THE CARAMEL ALMONDS
100g/4oz caster sugar
50g/2oz whole blanched toasted almonds

FOR THE ICING
125g/4½oz icing sugar
zest of 1 orange
1–1½ tbsp fresh orange juice

1 Heat the oven to 160C/140C fan/gas 3. Mix the orange zest and juice, Cointreau, mixed fruit and cherries in a bowl. Grease and line a 900g loaf tin.
2 Put the butter, sugar, flour, eggs and milk in a bowl, and beat until smooth. Stir in the fruit and their juices. Spoon half the mixture into the tin, then cover with the marzipan. Top with the rest of the cake mix and smooth the top. Bake for 1 hour or until risen and firm to the touch. Cool.
3 To make the caramel almonds, gently heat the sugar in a non-stick pan until it becomes a golden, liquid caramel. Add the almonds. Pour on to a greased baking sheet to set.
4 Mix together the icing ingredients, then pour over the cake. Chop up the caramel, scatter it over the icing and allow to set.

■ Per serving 425 kcalories, protein 5.4g, carbohydrate 72.5g, fat 14.3g, saturated fat 6g, fibre 1.6g, sugar 59.2g, salt 0.40g

Lollipop cake

A stunning but simple idea for a birthday cake based on a basic sponge cake. Decorate with your choice of colourful lollipops and sweets.

■ **Takes 1½ hours** ■ **Serves 12–16**

300g/10oz butter, very well softened
300g/10oz golden caster sugar
6 medium eggs
200g/8oz self-raising flour
50g/2oz custard powder or cornflour
finely grated zest of 2 lemons or oranges

FOR THE FILLING AND TOPPING
about 6 tbsp thick lemon curd, plus extra for brushing
½ × 454g pack ready-to-roll icing
lollipops
candles and jelly sweets or Smarties

1 Heat the oven to 160C/140C fan/gas 3. Butter and line the bottom of a 20cm-round cake tin. Beat together all the cake ingredients in a large bowl until creamy. Spoon the mixture into the tin, then bake for about 1 hour or until risen and springy to the touch. Leave to cool briefly in the tin, then turn the cake out and cool on a wire rack. If the cake peaks a bit, slice off the top to level it.
2 Cut the cake in half and sandwich back together with the lemon curd. Brush the top of the cake with a little more lemon curd. Roll out the icing and cut into a 20cm round. Carefully place on top of the cake, smoothing it with your hands. Stick the lollipops into the icing at different levels, add the appropriate number of candles, then scatter on some jelly sweets or Smarties.

■ Per serving (16) 353 kcalories, protein 4g, carbohydrate 49g, fat 17g, saturated fat 10g, fibre none, added sugar 42g, salt 0.7g

Chunky mince pie slices

These appealing little slices make a lighter, really fruity alternative to mince pies.

■ **Takes 35 minutes** ■ **Makes 15**

300g/10oz mincemeat
25g/1oz pecan nuts, mix of broken and whole
25g/1oz pistachio nuts, halved lengthways
2 tbsp flaked almonds
25g/1oz dried cranberries
½ small apple, peeled cored and finely chopped
finely grated zest of 1 lemon, plus 2 tsp juice
375g ready-rolled puff pastry
1 rounded tbsp ground almonds
50g/2oz icing sugar

1 Heat the oven to 220C/200C fan/gas 7. Combine the mincemeat with the nuts, cranberries, apple and lemon zest.
2 Unroll the pastry on to a floured work surface. Slice off a strip across one end to leave a 23cm square of pastry. Cut out 15–30 star shapes from the strip, re-rolling the trimmings until it is all used up.
3 Lay the pastry square on a baking sheet and scatter over the ground almonds. Spread the mincemeat mixture over so that it comes right to the edge of the pastry. Lay the stars in lines across the mincemeat, slightly overlapping them to fit, if necessary, so that you can cut out 15 slices when baked.
4 Bake for 15 minutes or until the pastry is golden. Leave to cool. Mix the icing sugar with two teaspoons of lemon juice. Drizzle over the cool pastry then cut into 15 slices.

■ Per slice 204 kcalories, protein 3g, carbohydrate 27g, fat 10g, saturated fat 3g, fibre 1g, sugar 17g, salt 0.21g

Richly fruited hot cross buns

The ultimate sticky, spicy bun for teatime, and so much better than bought. To serve, simply split and butter them or toast until golden.

■ **Takes 50 minutes, plus rising time**
■ **Makes 12**

500g pack white bread mix
50g/2oz caster sugar
1 tbsp mixed spice
85g/3oz butter, melted
250ml/9fl oz milk, warmed
1 egg, beaten
250g bag mixed fruit (including peel)

TO DECORATE
100g/4oz plain flour, plus extra for dusting
2 tbsp golden syrup or honey, to glaze

1 Combine the bread mix, sugar and spice in a bowl, and make a well in the centre. Tip the butter, milk and egg into the well, and mix to a soft dough. Knead on a lightly floured surface for about 5 minutes or until smooth. Transfer to a lightly oiled bowl, cover with oiled cling film and leave until doubled in size.
2 Knead briefly then press out into a large rectangle. Sprinkle the fruit over, then roll the dough up around the fruit and knead until evenly dispersed. Split into 12 even-sized balls.
3 Transfer the buns to a large greased baking sheet, 2–3cm apart. Cover and leave until risen and pillowy.
4 Heat the oven to 200C/180C fan/gas 6. Whisk 6 tablespoons of water into the flour until smooth. Spoon the mixture into a freezer bag, snip off the end and 'pipe' across the buns. Bake for 15–20 minutes or until risen and golden. Cool for a few minutes, then lift on to a wire rack. Heat the syrup then brush over the warm buns.

■ Per bun 300 kcalories, protein 7g, carbohydrate 52g, fat 9g, saturated fat 4g, fibre 3g, added sugar 23g, salt 1.16g

Light and dark choc puds

Time the cooking carefully to get the insides nice and gooey.

■ **Takes 25 minutes** ■ **Serves 6**

100g/4oz butter, chopped
50g/2oz plain flour, plus extra for dusting
100g bar dark chocolate, broken into pieces
3 eggs
85g/3oz golden caster sugar
8–10 squares of milk chocolate
sea salt flakes (optional), for serving

1 Heat the oven to 200C/180C fan/gas 6. Butter and lightly flour six 150ml ramekins.
2 Melt the dark chocolate and butter in a bowl in the microwave for 2–3 minutes on Medium, stirring halfway through.
3 Whisk the eggs and sugar until the mixture leaves a trail on the top when the whisk blades are lifted. Stir in the flour, then the melted chocolate mix. Divide between the ramekins and push 1 or 2 squares of milk chocolate into the centre of each. Put on a baking sheet and bake for 12 minutes exactly.
4 Cool for 5 minutes, then turn out onto plates and sprinkle each with a pinch of sea salt, if you like. They are good eaten warm or at room temperature.

■ Per serving 396 kcalories, protein 7g, carbohydrate 34g, fat 27g, saturated fat 15g, fibre 1g, added sugar 24g, salt 0.39g

TOP: Chunky mince pie slices

BOTTOM LEFT: Richly fruited hot cross buns

BOTTOM RIGHT: Light and dark choc puds